A CONCISE
INTRODUCTION
TO PHILOSOPHY

A CONCISE INTRODUCTION TO PHILOSOPHY

Second Edition

WILLIAM H. HALVERSON
The Ohio State University

 Random House · New York

ISBN: 0–394–31667–3

Library of Congress Catalog Card Number: 72-172891

Manufactured in the United States of America
Composed by H. Wolff Book Mfg. Co. Printed and bound by
Halliday Lithograph Corp., West Hanover, Mass.

Design by Charlotte Staub

Second Edition

987654321

To Marolyn

Who will forgive me for stating publicly
that of all the students who have enrolled
in my classes, she is my all-time favorite.

PREFACE

The half decade that has passed since the publication of the first edition of *A Concise Introduction to Philosophy* has seen a significant upsurge of interest in questions relating to ethics and political philosophy. The war in southeast Asia, the demand for full economic and political equality by blacks and other minority groups, the disclosure of the extent to which our way of life is wasting our natural resources and despoiling our environment—these and other urgent problems have focused the concern of sensitive men and women once again on some very fundamental questions: What are the bases of right and wrong? What is intrinsically good? What is the basis of the authority of government? Can our opinions on matters such as these have the status of knowledge or not?

Nowhere is this new concern more evident than among today's college students. What began a few years ago as a rather meek quest for "relevance" has erupted into a strident demand that those responsible for the enterprise of education at least take seriously—if they cannot answer—the questions that are being so passionately asked. No doubt it is true that some of those who are voicing this demand have yet to learn that many of the questions they are asking do not have definitive answers; that, after all, is something they cannot be expected to know until they have struggled with these questions for a while. But they will not accept as legitimate or serious an education that does not afford them an opportunity to explore them as deeply as their interest demands.

This edition of *A Concise Introduction to Philosophy* attempts to take appropriate account of these concerns. Three new topics are included—Freedom and Authority, Man's Highest Good, and World Views—and numerous additions have been made throughout the book. The sequence of topics has also been changed in accordance with the suggestions of many users of the first edition.

The *dialogue form* that is used throughout this book calls for a few words of explanation. Each topic is introduced in an introductory chapter in which I attempt to clarify the problem that is to be discussed, define the principal alternatives, and introduce any technical terms that may be necessary for the discussion that is to follow. Each succeeding chapter on that topic is then written *from the point of view of a convinced advocate of the view in question.* Only in Part I (Chapters 1–5) and in the introductory chapters of each succeeding part do I write, so to speak, "in my own name." The remaining chapters should be read as if they had been written by many different authors.

What is gained by this somewhat unusual format is a combination of the principal advantages of an anthology and of a single-author text. Like an anthology, *A Concise Introduction to Philosophy* keeps the discussion in the first person. The various writers are not merely talking *about* something: they are advocating a point of view, trying to secure agreement. Also like an anthology, it is able to give a fair hearing to a variety of philosophical views: it does not bias the argument in favor of any one philosophical tendency or school. But *A Concise Introduction to Philosophy* is also like a single-author text in certain respects: it has the coherence and, most important, the terminological consistency that cannot be expected in a book that is the product of many different authors.

This edition of *A Concise Introduction to Philosophy* owes much to the helpful comments and suggestions of numerous users of the first edition. Very special thanks are due to Donald Walhout of Rockford College, whose assistance in the planning of this revision has been so generous as to almost warrant the title of co-author. Vere Chappell has also found time, in the midst of new duties as Chairman of the Department of Philosophy at the University of Massachusetts, to read and comment on the manuscript. My editor, Richard Kennedy, has been both helpful and patient throughout the time the manuscript has been in preparation. To him and to his capable staff I express my sincere thanks. Thanks are due also to Janet Robinson for typing the final manuscript.

Lastly, however, I must express once again my very great debt of gratitude to the students with whom I have had the privilege of "talking philosophy" over a period of several years. My own understanding of many philosophical issues has certainly been enhanced immeasurably by those discussions. Should some of my former students chance to read this book, they may be pleased to discover in the dialogues that follow many reflections of some heated discussions in which they themselves participated.

Columbus, Ohio   W. H. H.
January, 1972

CONTENTS

PART I

THE PHILOSOPHICAL ENTERPRISE

1

THE STUDY
OF PHILOSOPHY

Of all the elements that play a role in determining the affairs of men, none are so pervasive or so far-reaching in their influence as the ideas to which men subscribe. The idea, for example, that certain men have the authority to rule other men by "divine right" was an immensely powerful idea in the predemocratic era; the lives of countless numbers of people who accepted or were powerless to oppose this idea were molded to fit a society whose goals, social structure, and economic system were all based upon it. The ideas, on the other hand, that all men have by nature certain inalienable rights and that the right to govern derives from the consent of the governed have been equally influential in determining the course of events in the modern world.

Nations have been formed, empires built, wars fought, institutions created for the sake of ideas such as these—ideas that have fired the imaginations of men. Whatever else he is, man is clearly a creature who in large measure orders his life according to the ideas that he espouses.

Some ideas are obviously more influential than others. The idea that kings rule by divine right was clearly more influential in determining the shape of human life in the medieval world than the idea that the earth is flat; and both of these were more pervasive in their influence than the idea that prolonged exposure to the light of the moon is likely to have a detrimental effect on one's sanity (whence the term "lunatic").

The ideas that appear to have the greatest influence on human affairs are those that we may term the fundamental beliefs or convictions by which men attempt to order their lives. To some extent man,

like other organisms, acts on the basis of purely instinctual drives—
hunger, thirst, sex, etc. But much of what man does depends also
upon his beliefs, his convictions regarding what is worth doing, what
he ought to do, where he and his fellows fit into "the scheme of
things," and so on. The influential power of a belief depends, presumably, on the number of people who hold it and on the degree to which
it is believed to have practical implications for the ordering of human
affairs.

Philosophy is concerned precisely with the fundamental beliefs
through which men try to make sense of their lives and by which they
try to order their lives. Philosophy asks the enduring questions about
God and man and the world—questions that seem very important and
on which there appear to be no "final answers" on which all men can
agree. To study philosophy is to enter into the serious discussion of
such questions. To be a philosopher is to devote one's efforts to clarifying such questions and to searching for the bases of warranted beliefs.

The student who approaches his first course in philosophy has,
surely, some preliminary impression of "what philosophy is." He has
heard the term "philosophy" used many times—he has probably used
it himself—and he knows, perhaps, that such men as Plato, Aristotle,
Immanuel Kant, and Alfred North Whitehead are commonly called
"philosophers." What are these usual preliminary impressions? How
have they been formed?

Common Impressions

Many people understand the term "philosophy" to mean a general
theory about something, particularly a general theory about how to
approach some broad kind of undertaking. Thus, for example, it may
be said that "Edmund Muskie and Richard Nixon have some fundamental disagreements in *political philosophy*," or "public education
has recently had to come to terms with a radically different *educational philosophy*." A moment's reflection makes it evident that in
either of these cases we could substitute the term "theory" for the
term "philosophy" without changing the meaning of the statement.
Hence, it is clear that in these instances philosophy means, simply,
"theory." And since this is one of the most common ways in which
people who are not professional philosophers hear and use the term, it
is one of the strongest impressions that people have of philosophy.

It may be of some importance to note in this connection that "philosophy," when it is used in this way, always has a very practical
orientation: it is a theory about how to do something in a given area
of human concern. Indeed, the broader the area, the more appropriate
it seems to speak about activity in that area as being guided by some

"philosophy." We do not hesitate to talk about a man's "political philosophy" or his "educational philosophy"; it would seem very odd to talk about a man's theories regarding gardening or house painting as his "gardening philosophy" or his "house-painting philosophy."

Not too far removed from this impression of philosophy is the idea that philosophy means a general view of life, or a general theory about how we ought to go about the living of our lives. Here, too, "philosophy" is understood to have a very practical orientation—only the activity envisioned in this case is not restricted to this or that area, but includes the whole of life. A man can live for gain, or he can live to serve: it depends, we sometimes say, on his "philosophy of life." And a "philosophy of life" would presumably include views on such things as the nature of man and man's place in the universe, some convictions as to what things are worth living for, etc. When the term "philosophy" is used without a qualifying adjective (political, educational, economic), most people probably understand it to mean "philosophy of life."

It also seems to be a very common notion that philosophy has to do with matters that are very abstract and/or profound. People by and large are of the opinion that philosophers are very wise and learned men—though they may not have any very clear idea what it is that these men are so learned about, or how they acquired their peculiar wisdom. Some students are, therefore, a little anxious about their ability to master so forbidding a field when they approach their first course in philosophy.

Perhaps one reason for this impression regarding philosophy is that, as already noted, the term "philosophy" is often understood to mean "general theory." People do know in a general way what is meant by "political philosophy," or "philosophy of education," or "philosophy of life," but very few people have a specific and detailed knowledge in any of these areas. Indeed, it is almost axiomatic that a theory must be somewhat mystifying before we are willing to dignify it with the name of "philosophy"; hence we readily accept the view that someone who has worked out the details of a "philosophy" of something must be a man of superior wisdom. We can all easily understand how to paint a house or raise a garden; thus it seems ridiculous to call views on these things "philosophy." But a theory about how to organize an economic system, or about the purposes of education, or about the best way of life, is a different matter. Here the perspectives are so broad, the content so vast, the categories so obscure: this we call "philosophy."

Another possible reason for this impression is that we have often heard it said when someone makes a vague or general statement about something that he is "getting philosophical." It is not clear in such cases whether it is the broad generality of the statement or its vagueness that makes it "philosophical," but "philosophical" is what it is called. And so, many people have gotten the impression that, at best, philosophy is concerned with matters that are very profound, beyond the understanding of most men, or, at worst, that philosophy is simply vague and imprecise.

There is another fairly widespread impression regarding philosophy, namely that it is dangerous. Well-meaning people sometimes warn college students (in the words of St. Paul) to "see to it that no one makes a prey of you by philosophy and empty deceit" [1]—the inference being that all philosophy is nothing but "empty deceit" that will "make a prey" of the unwary. Not uncommonly, perhaps, philosophy is regarded as a threat to religious faith, to morality, and perhaps to citizenship; the conclusion is drawn that for this reason it ought to be avoided by anyone who values these things.

It is interesting to note that this impression regarding philosophy is very old, dating in fact from the earliest days of the Western philosophical tradition. The most notable example of the "bad press" from which philosophy has long suffered is, of course, the trial and conviction of Socrates on grounds of "impiety" and "corrupting the youth." Socrates, in making his defense to the Athenian court, is quite explicit about the fact that the court's opinion of him is prejudiced because of their negative opinion of philosophy. He tells the court:

> I have had many accusers complaining to you, and for a long time, for many years now, and with not a word of truth to say. . . . These . . . got hold of most of you while you were boys, and persuaded you, and accused me falsely. . . . These, gentlemen, who have broadcast this reputation, these are my dangerous accusers; for those who hear believe that anyone who is a student of that sort of lore must be an atheist as well.[2]

Whether or not this reputation is deserved—that is, whether or not philosophy really is dangerous, or potentially dangerous, to the generally accepted values of society—is a question that the student will have to decide for himself after he has acquired a sufficient acquaintance with philosophy to be entitled to an opinion. The point is indisputable, however, that philosophy is regarded by many people in this way, and one result is that students who register for their first course in philosophy often do so with the feeling that what they are about to study is mildly subversive.

Finally, it is not unusual to hear it suggested that philosophy is a waste of time. The indictment might read like this: "Scientists and technicians do things that help to provide the necessities and com-

---

1 Colossians, 2:8.

2 Plato, *Apology*, in W. H. D. Rouse (ed.), *Great Dialogues of Plato* (New York: New American Library, 1956), p. 424.

forts of life; doctors and dentists work to alleviate human suffering; athletes and musicians provide enjoyable entertainment—but what do philosophers do for their fellow men? They speculate and dream and talk nonsense and undermine the faith of men. Anybody who wants to amount to anything will do well to leave philosophy alone."

It cannot be denied that these impressions indicate a rather consistently negative attitude toward philosophy. In some respects, perhaps, these impressions derive from the actual character of the philosophical enterprise; in other respects, they show a total misunderstanding of that enterprise. The student will be able to assess their accuracy for himself as soon as he has developed some understanding of what the philosophical enterprise is about. For the present, it may be of some value to make a few generalizations about philosophy that relate to the popular views we have just discussed.

A Preliminary Characterization

It is just as well, when undertaking a study of philosophy, to be aware from the very outset that philosophy, as distinguished from many other fields of study, is "impractical" in the sense that a mastery of it is not primarily a means to some vocational goal. In this respect, the study of philosophy is similar to the study of literature; an appreciation of it is valuable in and of itself, and this is the justification for spending time on it. You can, of course, teach literature, just as you can teach philosophy; but this would be quite pointless if the study and appreciation of either were not worthwhile in itself.

It must be admitted that the values that have guided the thinking and behavior of our society in recent years have not been conducive to the flowering of philosophy, literature, or the arts. Our society tends to value what pays and to devalue what does not pay. We are, so to speak, consistently "commercial" in our values. Works of art, for example, are considered "art" if people are willing to buy them. Music is considered a "worthwhile" field of study if someone "has what it takes" to become a successful performer, composer, or teacher of music. An English major, if he is really talented, may eventually make a decent living as a novelist, a writer of short stories, or as a member of the editorial staff of a periodical; at the very least, he can become an English teacher. In any case, he is not in any great danger of being left unemployed.

What is missing in this very commercialized account, however, is any appreciation of the intrinsic and nonsaleable value of developing a genuine capacity for appreciation in these areas. If an acquaintance with, and an appreciation of, art or music or literature is not worthwhile in itself—if the cultivation of such an appreciation does not justify itself simply on the ground that it makes life richer and broader and more human—then the teaching or promotion of these things is wholly unjustified.

Because of the commercialization of values in our society, it is necessary to remind ourselves from time to time that there is a difference between education and job training. Education is concerned with the development of our capacities as a human being—our capacities for understanding, for appreciation, for interpersonal relationships, for creative participation in the ongoing common life of man. Job training is concerned with the preparation for some particular kind of employment. To forget this distinction, and to think only in terms of the latter, is to render irrelevant a considerable part of what is typically included in a baccalaureate program.

Philosophy, like literature and the arts, belongs essentially to what we have called education rather than job training. Unlike the others, however, it is almost impossible in the case of philosophy to make the mistake of regarding it, or rather the study of it, as preparation for a career. The major in philosophy is not, by virtue of his major, prepared to do any particular job (though he may, of course, go on to graduate school and become a professor of philosophy).

Why, then, should anyone study philosophy? Simply because, in ways that will shortly become apparent, it is an essential part of becoming a truly educated person. Do not approach the study of philosophy—or, for that matter, of history, music, literature, or art—with the expectation that in this study you will acquire some saleable knowledge or skill. Chances are that you will not. Approach it rather with the hope that it will enhance your understanding, broaden your horizons, increase your self-awareness and enrich your appreciation of the powers as well as the limits of the human mind: then you will not be disappointed.

The beginning student in philosophy would also do well to bear in mind from the outset that philosophy is by its very nature critical of the status quo, unwilling to accept as unquestionable even the most widely held beliefs. It was Socrates who said, "The unexamined life is not worth living." [3] Philosophy ever since has taken its cue from him. Therefore, do not be dismayed if you encounter views that seem preposterous—as you undoubtedly will. The beliefs that are called in question may indeed be true; the philosopher's point is simply that their truth ought not to be taken for granted.

We shall have more to say on this point in connection with our discussion of the critical side of the philosopher's task. For the present it is enough to note that the suspicion with which many people regard philosophy derives in large part from the fact that philosophers almost invariably stand in a critical, questioning relation to prevailing

---

[3] *Ibid.*, p. 445.

modes of thought. It is not strange that people regard with suspicion an enterprise whose main business often seems to be the raising of provocative questions.

Philosophy and Liberal Education

John Henry Newman once said:

> A University training is the great ordinary means to a great but ordinary end. . . . It is the education which gives a man a clear conscious view of his own opinions and judgments, a truth in developing them, and a force in urging them. It teaches him to see things as they are, to go right to the point, to disentangle a skein of thought, to detect what is sophistical, and to discard what is irrelevant. It prepares him to fill any post with credit, and to master any subject with facility.[4]

Those words were written in 1852. At the time they were written they summed up, beautifully and accurately, the ideal end product of liberal education: a man of broad learning and culture, a conscious inheritor of the cultural riches of the past, an expert in the exercise of reason, a master of the art of conversation, a gentleman. Such a man, said Newman, is "at home in any society." He has "the repose of a mind which lives in itself, while it lives in the world, and which has resources for its happiness at home when it cannot go abroad." [5] He is, in short, a liberally educated man.

Much has happened since 1852 to make the university a very different place from that described by Cardinal Newman. The educated man of Newman's ideal was a generalist; the university graduate of today is expected to be a specialist. Higher education, as Newman conceived it, was supposed to be available only to the privileged few; today it is regarded as the right of the many. The university, as Newman described it, was aloof from society, a sanctuary of the mind well removed from the cacophony of the market place; the university of today is a mirror of society, highly solicitous of its support and responsive to its needs. The university of Newman's day functioned chiefly as conservator of the old; the university of today places a far higher priority on the discovery of the new. The "university" whose idea Newman so eloquently proclaimed has all but disappeared; in its place has appeared what Clark Kerr has aptly called the "multiversity." [6]

---

[4] John Henry Newman, *The Idea of a University*, in Henry Tristram (ed.), *Newman's Idea of a Liberal Education* (New York: Barnes & Noble, 1952), pp. 104–105.

[5] *Ibid.*

[6] Clark Kerr, *The Uses of the University* (Cambridge, Mass.: Harvard University Press, 1963), Chapter 1.

For the student, the multiversity can be a very confusing place. The courses that he takes, for example, all seem to be "specialty" courses: one hour he has history, the next hour he has chemistry, then he has sociology, and so on through the day. But there are times when he must find himself asking, "Don't these various fields of study relate to each other in some way? Does education really consist in nothing more than the acquisition of information in all of these isolated compartments? Surely there must be *some* context in which I can comprehend these various bits of information as somehow hanging together —even as the universe, with all of its variety, is after all one single universe."

An important function of philosophy is to provide a context in which such integration can in fact be realized. The great questions of philosophical controversy—such as those we shall be discussing—are by no means the rather odd and special preoccupations of just one more group of specialists called "philosophers"; they are, on the contrary, questions that cut across the artificial barriers of our academic specialties and compel us to *relate* our little pockets of specialized knowledge (and opinion, and conjecture, and even feeling) in some coherent way. The study of philosophy should not be approached, therefore, as if it were just one more area of specialized knowledge to be placed beside all of the others. "Philosophy," said René Descartes, "is like a tree, of which metaphysics is the root, physics the trunk, and all the other sciences the branches that grow out of this trunk . . ." [7] The study of philosophy should be approached in the hope that it will provide a context within which to relate and integrate what is learned in the various specialized fields. To the extent that this hope is realized, the study of philosophy can yield one of the choicest fruits of a liberal education: the capacity "to see life steady and to see it whole."

STUDY QUESTIONS

1. Do you or do you not agree that the ideas to which men subscribe are uniquely influential in determining their behavior? Might it not rather be the case that most or all of our ideas are merely so many ways of rationalizing behavior that is the result of other causes?
2. What prior impressions about philosophy do you bring with you to this study? How have you gotten these impressions?
3. Write four or five sentences in which it seems natural to you to use the term "philosophy." In what sense or senses are you using the term?
4. How widespread, in your judgment, is the view that philosophy is "dangerous" and "a waste of time"? As far as you can judge, do the people who hold these views know enough about philosophy to be entitled to an opinion?
5. Do you think it is fair to say that our society is quite consistently

---

[7] René Descartes, *The Principles of Philosophy,* in *A Discourse on Method and Selected Writings,* John Veitch (tr.). (New York: Dutton, 1951), p. 174.

"commercial" in its values? With what sort of evidence could you either support or oppose such a statement?

6. Can you see any possible value in questioning beliefs that most people just take for granted? Would it not be better to leave such matters alone and to concentrate all our efforts on attempting to find solutions to the social, economic, and political problems that plague mankind today?

2

THE TWO SIDES OF
THE PHILOSOPHICAL TASK

When we pick up a book purporting to introduce a field of study with which we are more or less unfamiliar, we approach it with certain legitimate expectations. We expect that our study will give us some kind of overview of the field in question rather than a study in depth of some one aspect to the complete exclusion of others. We expect our study to expose us to some of the most representative thinking in the field to insure that our initial understanding is not distorted. And we expect that what we read in an introductory text will represent the consensus of scholars in the field. We do not wish to be subjected to novel or untried proposals: these can wait until we have achieved some perspective from which to evaluate them. What we need first is a distillation of the best knowledge available in the field, an intelligible account of what is considered the common ground by most practicing scholars in that field.

Unfortunately, it is not possible at the present time to state anything that might be called a consensus among philosophers as to what it is that constitutes the task of the philosopher. There is, in fact, substantial disagreement among men who call themselves philosophers as to just what it is that they are, or are supposed to be, doing. There are reasons for this uncertainty, and before we proceed to outline our own proposal for a definition of the philosopher's task, it may be helpful to look briefly at a few of these reasons.

Reasons for Uncertainty

One development that has played a role in the creation of the present crisis in philosophy is the progressive takeover by the special sciences of various areas of inquiry formerly belonging to philosophy. Aristotle, for example, included in his "philosophical" inquiries a large number of matters that are now customarily divided among biologists, physiologists, psychologists, zoologists, political scientists, literary critics, and so on. For Aristotle, "philosophy" was virtually a collective name for the quest for knowledge—in whatever area, by whatever means. But since the time of Aristotle, and particularly during the past three or four hundred years, the quest for knowledge has been carried on by a wide variety of specialists who have developed to an incredibly fine point the methods of investigation appropriate to this or that area of inquiry. What, then, remains for the philosopher to do? Philosophers —that is, men who occupy professorships in philosophy in colleges and universities—are not entirely agreed as to how this question should be answered. This disagreement is one reason for the current turmoil over the nature of the philosophical enterprise.

There is a second reason, closely related to the first. For some time after the advent of modern science, with its division of labor among the various special sciences, there was a widely held view among philosophers that the peculiar domain of the philosopher (as distinguished from the several sorts of natural scientists) was *metaphysics*. The relation of metaphysics to the special sciences was a matter of some dispute, but for a time everyone seemed happy with the arrangement whereby philosophers concentrated on metaphysics and scientists claimed the various kinds of merely "factual" inquiries as their own.

During the eighteenth century, however, questions were raised about the validity of the whole idea of metaphysical knowledge. David Hume and Immanuel Kant, in very different ways, both asked, in effect, "But does the emperor (in this case metaphysics) really have any clothes at all? Is there anything to the claims of philosophers, or are their speculations really empty?" Hume recommended consigning all such treatises to the flames. Kant, more gentle, only called on metaphysicians to suspend their labors until they had validated the methodology upon which they based their metaphysical assertions. In both cases, however, the enterprise that had become the central business of the philosopher was radically questioned, and it could only be a matter of time until philosophers would have to give some kind of answer to this challenge.

At length, after about a century or more, the strictures of Hume and Kant sank in. Here and there—in England, in Austria (the "Vienna Circle"), in America—some philosophers began to question the validity of the philosophical enterprise as it was being pursued by most of their contemporaries. Presently a loosely organized movement became discernible, the most obvious features of which were a common abandonment of metaphysics and a common affinity for the empirical methods of the natural sciences. This does not mean that these philosophers attempted to transform philosophy into an empirical enterprise—a quasi-science, so to speak. But their affinity for the empirical methods of the natural sciences was one of the prominent causes of their disenchantment with traditional metaphysics.

But what, then, remains for the philosopher to do? If the several natural sciences have taken over the empirical inquiries that were once a part of the philosophical enterprise, and if metaphysics is abandoned as unwarranted and/or empty speculation, does there remain anything for the philosopher to do? This question haunts present-day philosophers, and the many conflicting statements that are made about "what philosophy is" give some idea of how far the discussion remains from anything like a consensus.

There is quite general agreement among philosophers on one point, however: at least one part of the traditional philosophical enterprise remains an important responsibility of the philosopher, namely *logic*. Some philosophers are of the opinion that logical studies, broadly conceived, constitute the whole of philosophy; others believe there must be something more to philosophy, but are uncertain what that "something more" might be. And still others, of course, retain the belief that metaphysics is still possible, though it is no longer regarded as the "queen of the sciences."

The Nature of the Question

Perhaps we may take a small step toward the formulation of a defensible proposal if we clarify the nature of the question that we are asking when we ask, What is the proper task of the philosopher?

Let us note first that our question is not a *moral* question. We are not asking, What *ought* philosophers to be doing?—as if there were some prescribed task that they had been assigned to perform, in such a way that their nonperformance of it (or their failure to perform it to the best of their ability) would be blameworthy. There is, admittedly, a kind of common agreement about the sort of competence that a man should have if he claims to be a chemist, a physicist, a mathematician, or a philosopher, and it would certainly be misleading for a man to call himself any of these things if he were lacking in the appropriate competence. But it clearly is not the case that any person or agency or group has "assigned" this or that sort of inquiry to scholars of a given designation. It may be misleading for a man to call himself a philosopher if he does not, in fact, engage in a certain kind of enterprise, but it does not by any means follow that he is morally culpable because of this fact. Our question is not a moral question.

But neither is our question an arbitrary verbal one, a matter of simply assigning some useful meaning to the phrase, "the philosophical task." This is why it is not helpful to say, as has sometimes been said, that "Philosophy is what philosophers do." We could, of course, assign some random function to a group of men—basket weaving, for example—and say, "That is what we shall hereafter call 'philosophy.' The task of the philosopher is to weave baskets." But this would obviously be confusing. The question concerning the task of the philosopher is not answered by making an arbitrary assignment and calling it "philosophy." And the reason the question is not satisfactorily answered in this way is that we are not asking an arbitrary verbal question.

The question is, rather, a historical question. It might be rephrased like this: There is, as everyone knows, a tradition of intellectual inquiry—a discipline—that began in Greece in about the sixth century B.C. and that has included such men as Socrates, Plato, Aristotle, St. Augustine, St. Thomas Aquinas, Descartes, Kant, and many others. Is there some common enterprise in which all of these men were engaged by virtue of which they are all called philosophers? If so, what is that enterprise?

Our question is, however, a bit more complicated than this rephrasing might suggest. We have noted, for example, that Aristotle engaged in a number of inquiries that today belong to such specialized disciplines as biology, physics, political science, literary criticism, and so on. Furthermore, a number of men who regard themselves as philosophers today are convinced that what some philosophers in the past regarded as the unique task of the philosopher is an unperformable task. Taking account of these qualifications, we may rephrase our question thus: Is there not some task that (a) has traditionally been performed by men who have called themselves philosophers, (b) has not been taken over by any of the special sciences, and (c) is still performable? If such a task can be identified, it is that task that is most appropriately designated "the task of the philosopher."

The Critical Task

In the previous chapter mention was made of Socrates, the great Greek philosopher and martyr who lived and worked in Athens during the fifth century B.C. (469–399 B.C.). Socrates, as we learn in the *Apology,* was convicted by the Athenian court of "atheism" and "corrupting the youth" and was condemned to die. The death of Socrates is beautifully and movingly described by Plato in the concluding pages of the dialogue entitled *Phaedo.*

What was Socrates doing that led to his being haled into court on these charges? Evidently it was not his deliberate intention to promote impiety or to corrupt youth. What was his intention, then, and how did he go about pursuing it?

According to the *Apology*, which is considered to be a fairly accurate account of the historical Socrates, the facts are these. A friend of Socrates—Chairephon—inquired of the oracle at Delphi whether anyone was wiser than Socrates and received the reply that no one was. Hearing this, Socrates—who, as he says, knew in his conscience that he was *not* wise—proceeded to test the oracle's statement by interrogating some of his fellow-citizens who were generally regarded to be wise and learned men. Socrates comments as follows on his interrogation:

> I approached one of those who had the reputation of being wise for there, I thought, if anywhere, I should test the revelation and prove that the oracle was wrong. . . . But when I examined him, . . . and when I conversed with him, I thought this man *seemed* to be wise both to many others and especially to himself, but that he was not. . . . After that I tried another, one of those reputed to be wiser than that man, and I thought just the same; then he and many others took a dislike to me.[1]

Socrates took it to be his unique task to interrogate his fellow-citizens to see whether or not their opinions could stand up under close scrutiny. Wherever Socrates found people holding opinions, or making truth-claims, there he went to work. Does Meno claim to know whether or not virtue can be taught? "Meno," asks Socrates, "What is virtue? Do you really know what virtue is? And if you do not know what virtue is, how can you possibly know whether or not it can be taught?" Or does Euthyphro claim to know that his father is guilty of impiety? "Euthyphro," says Socrates, "I do not even know for sure what piety and impiety are. Could you instruct me in this?" The critical examination of opinions, the testing of truth-claims—that was the task in which Socrates was engaged.

This picture of Socrates going about questioning the men of Athens as to the soundness of their opinions symbolizes what we may call the *critical* side of the philosophical enterprise. We all take many things for granted, and we live and think and work on the basis of what we take for granted—on the basis, that is, of our assumptions. Very often, perhaps most of the time, we are scarcely aware of what our assumptions are. But the philosopher is tremendously interested in the assumptions that underlie various kinds of supposed knowledge. He wants to know what those assumptions are and

---

[1] Plato, *Apology*, in W. H. D. Rouse (ed.), *Great Dialogues of Plato* (New York: New American Library, 1956), p. 427.

whether or not they are reasonable. And so, like Socrates, he examines them.

Socrates, of course, went about his business in a very informal and very personal way. He queried individuals and examined their claims to knowledge, claims that usually did not stand up under close scrutiny. Since Socrates' time, however, the whole business of knowledge and learning has been more or less institutionalized—and so also has philosophy. This has had the effect of making philosophy a more formalized, but less personal, undertaking. The questions that the philosopher raises in this context are directed not so much at individuals as at fields of learning. The philosopher asks his questions not of the scientist, but about the truth-claims of science; not of the religious person, but about the truth-claims of religion; and so on. Philosophy is, so to speak, the "gadfly" in the curriculum of a modern college or university, just as Socrates attempted to be a gadfly to his fellow-citizens in ancient Athens.

The Constructive Task

Philosophers, however, do not engage in this critical task just to make a nuisance of themselves. Indeed, the central aim of philosophers has always been a positive one. What, then, is this positive aim, this constructive task of the philosopher?

The answer suggested by a careful scrutiny of the work of many generations of practicing philosophers is this: the positive goal of the philosopher is to construct a picture of the whole of reality, in which every element of man's knowledge and every aspect of man's experience will find its proper place. Philosophy, in short, is man's quest for the unity of knowledge: it consists in a perpetual struggle to create the concepts in which the universe can be conceived as a *uni*verse and not a *multi*verse. The history of philosophy is the history of this attempt. The problems of philosophy are the problems that arise when the attempt is made to grasp this total unity.

It will be granted that the theoretical goal of the natural sciences is to produce a description of the universe so complete that everything that occurs—every phenomenon from the behavior of the tiniest particle within the simplest atom to the most complex processes that we can observe in the most advanced organisms—can be understood as instances of regularities that we call "laws." Let us suppose, for the sake of argument, that this goal were to be reached: our "picture of the whole of reality" would still be incomplete. We would still want to ask questions such as the following: What are good and evil? What is their place in the universe whose physical workings we now understand so completely? Is this complete description of the universe that we have produced a description of the universe as it is, or is it—

wholly or in part—merely a description of the universe as we perceive it? Is beauty a quality in objects that we call beautiful, is it something "in the eye of the beholder," or is it something else? Does the physical universe exist as a self-subsistent entity, or is it dependent for its being on some reality beyond itself? Is the consciousness that we ourselves experience a merely physical phenomenon, or is it something else? Our awareness of suffering, of tragedy, of injustice, of good and evil, of beauty and ugliness, of meanness and nobility leaves us dissatisfied with a merely physical description of the universe: these, too, are part of the complete picture of reality. We cannot be content until the truths about these (and other) dimensions of our experience have also been understood and brought into some coherent relationship with what we know about the universe as a system of purely physical phenomena.

It cannot be denied that this attempt stands without rival as the most audacious enterprise in which the mind of man has ever engaged. Just reflect for a moment: Here is man, surrounded by the vastness of a universe in which he is only a tiny and perhaps insignificant part—and he wants to *understand* it, to conceive the whole thing in his mind, in such a way that no reality that confronts him, no event that occurs, no fact that he discovers, nothing that he experiences is beyond the categories of his understanding. Audacious indeed; but what are the alternatives?

One alternative would be to make no effort to understand anything at all. Perhaps, if he tried hard enough, man could learn to control his propensity to ask questions and could just gape at the world, responding to it only as might be necessary for the preservation of his species. Apparently other species of life do no more and survive rather well in the struggle for life.

In all seriousness, however, it does not appear likely that man ever could or would do this, even if it were desirable. It seems to be characteristic of man, as Aristotle said long ago, that he by nature desires to know.[2] Moreover, although a part of man's quest for knowledge appears to stem from a desire to control his environment, it has deeper roots as well. Man desires to know not solely in order that he may more effectively manipulate his environment, but simply and purely for the sake of knowing. The total abandonment of the quest for understanding is not a promising alternative to constructive philosophy.

Another alternative would be for man to be content with piecemeal knowledge—to establish what can be established in each of the special sciences and to make no attempt to discern the features of the "total picture" of which each of these fragments is presumably a part.

---

[2] Aristotle, *Metaphysics*, I, i, in Richard McKeon (ed.), *The Basic Works of Aristotle* (New York: Random House, 1941), p. 689.

This view is occasionally expressed in statements like, "It is better to know one thing well than to know a little bit about everything," or "It is better to be a good chemist than a poor philosopher."

But here, too, is a problem, and it is one that makes it impossible to hold such a view except in the half-jesting mood reflected above. For as we focus our attention on first one area, then another, we are sometimes driven to conclusions that appear to be in conflict with one another. One of the by-products of such "compartmentalized" thinking is what we may call "apparent incompatibles," and these a healthy mind does not easily accept. How, we insist on asking, do these apparently conflicting truths fit together? How, for example, can man be free in the sense that ethics seems to require if, as appears to be the case, the whole universe is subject without exception to causal law? If all knowledge comes to us through experience, and if experience yields only probability, how does it come about that in mathematics we are able to establish our conclusions with absolute certainty? These and other questions thrust themselves upon us, almost in spite of ourselves. It is out of such tension—tension among the various elements of our piecemeal knowledge—that much philosophical thinking arises. For to ask such questions is precisely to ask for the wider concept, the total picture, in which what is legitimate in each of these competing truth-claims can be given its due.

Philosophy, on its constructive side, is the systematic quest for the unity of human knowledge. Reality discloses itself to man in a wide variety of ways. The philosopher asks: How does it all fit together? How can I conceive of reality as a whole?

Many philosophers would grant that the quest for the unity of human knowledge was indeed the quest that motivated the great philosophers of the past. And it is apparent to everyone that this task has not been taken over by any of the special sciences. But many would say the task that has just been described is simply not performable; therefore it cannot be a part of the philosopher's present task.

How are we to understand such an objection? If, as we have already argued, the only alternatives to such a quest are either (a) to abandon altogether the quest for knowledge or (b) to be content with piecemeal knowledge, and if neither of these is a practicable course to follow, then it would appear that somebody must continue to pursue this task within the household of learning. Who should it be if not the philosopher? On what grounds, or for what reason, could a present-day philosopher forswear this task as being "unperformable" in the modern world?

The answer to the puzzle is something like this: those philosophers who decline to embrace the traditional philosophical quest for the unity of man's knowledge recognize that any proposals that they might make with respect to the total picture cannot exhibit either the precision or the empirical probability of a scientific hypothesis, and they are reluctant to commit themselves to any proposals that do not meet these qualifications. Their objection, in effect, is that the traditional philosophical task is not performable *with the same degree of precision* as are the several tasks of the special sciences. This is indisputably true, and its truth should be a warning to any philosopher to make his proposals with considerable caution if he nonetheless elects to pursue this quest. But if our previous reasoning was sound, this consideration ought not prevent pursuit of this quest with such precision as the nature of the inquiry will allow. Ours is indisputably an age of science, and we are all captivated by the precision and the power of the scientific method; but not all questions are scientific questions, and where other sorts of questions are asked, other sorts of answers must be expected and other methods must be employed in searching for them.

One thing, at least, seems clear: the quest for the total picture, the struggle to discern the unity that we instinctively believe must somehow lie behind the apparent inconsistencies of our little fragments of knowledge—in short, the constructive philosophical quest—will go on, with or without the cooperation of professional philosophers. The student who undertakes the study of philosophy because he finds himself involved in a similar quest will discover that he is in the company of the great philosophers from Plato to the present, and he may legitimately expect to find a new and exciting challenge as he considers the answers that philosophers have given to the profoundest questions that men have dared to ask.

STUDY QUESTIONS

1. What precisely do you understand to be the "critical" task of philosophy? What are some of the questions that a philosopher might ask in attempting to pursue this task?
2. Are you convinced that the *only* alternatives to "constructive philosophy" are: (a) giving up the quest for understanding altogether, or (b) settling for "piecemeal" knowledge? How might one go about trying to refute this claim?
3. Are you inclined to agree or to disagree with the following statement: "The constructive task of philosophy is a task that cannot be avoided: the only question is whether it is to be pursued carefully and systematically or informally and haphazardly"?

3

PHILOSOPHICAL PROBLEMS AND PHILOSOPHICAL SYSTEMS

The history of philosophy, we have observed, is the history of man's quest for a comprehensive picture of reality, in which every element of man's knowledge and every aspect of man's experience finds its proper place. The problems of philosophy, we suggested, are the problems that arise when one pursues this quest. But when is a problem a philosophical problem? How does an answer to a philosophical problem relate to this quest for the total picture? And how does all of this relate to the so-called "philosophical systems" about which we hear from time to time?

Although it may not always be convenient to do so, it is always possible to state a problem in the form of a question. It is seldom convenient to do so, say, in the case of an arithmetical problem. It is much easier (because shorter) to write $7 + 5 = ?$ than to ask, What is the sum of seven and five? But in the case of most philosophical problems, we do not have a precise symbol system in which to abbreviate our problems. The best that we can do is to state our problem in terms of a precise question. Let us ask, then, When is a question a philosophical question? that is When does a question express a philosophical problem?

Characteristics of a Philosophical Question

Consider the following questions: (a) At what temperature does pure water freeze, assuming sea-level barometric pressure? (b) What is the name of the capital of India? (c) Who held the office of President of the United States in 1797? (d) Is the atomic theory helpful in explaining the process of photosynthesis? (e) What is religion? (f) Is moral responsibility compatible with the determinism assumed in most scientific inquiries?

Of these six questions, the first three are obviously not philosophical questions. Anyone who is remotely familiar with how the labor of inquiry has been divided up among the several academic fields will readily recognize that question *a* belongs to physics, question *b* to geography, and question *c* to history. If we wanted an answer to any of these questions we would turn, respectively, to the physicist, the geographer, and the historian for our information.

Question *d* may puzzle us for a moment. Is it a question for the botanist to answer, or is it one for the physicist? We are not sure. But note this: we do recognize it to be a scientific question, our reason for hesitation being only that we are uncertain as to which of the sciences is competent to handle it. Such questions we shall call "intrascientific" questions; they arise because of the particular ways in which the several natural sciences have marked out the boundaries of their inquiries.

Questions *e* and *f* present some new features. First, there is evidently no existing science that is competent to handle either question. Consider, for example, question *e*. We could imagine a number of scientists having opinions about the answer to the question, What is religion? Sigmund Freud, for example, felt strongly enough about his opinion regarding this question to write a book about it. But it is not, strictly speaking, within the competence of a psychologist *as a psychologist* to answer this question. The same must be said about the sociologist, the anthropologist, and the archaeologist: each of these scientists, pursuing his own proper inquiries, may discover some important facts about religion (this is within his competence), and each may go on to form an opinion as to "what religion really is." But in forming such an opinion, the scientist is no longer speaking *as a scientist*—as a psychologist, a sociologist, an anthropologist, or whatever. All may indeed contribute something to the answer, but none is competent within the limits of his own academic specialty to answer the question. A moment's reflection will make it evident that the same holds true for question *f*.

This, it will be found, is one of the defining characteristics of philosophical questions. Philosophical questions are questions that do not fall within the competence of any of the special sciences, or even within the competence of any combination of the special sciences. Philosophical questions, in short, are neither straightforwardly scientific nor intrascientific: this is part of what we are saying when we call them philosophical questions.

A second feature of questions *e* and *f*, and a second defining characteristic of philosophical questions, is that we cannot readily imagine what sorts of evidence, if any, would be relevant to answering them.

There is something bewildering, something puzzling, about such questions. With respect to question *e*, for example, we suppose that some of the findings of psychologists, sociologists, archaeologists, anthropologists, and historians would be relevant. But which? And how would we go about gathering the relevant data? These are puzzling questions, and it is characteristic of philosophical questions that they puzzle us in just this way.

Third, philosophical questions are questions whose possible answers appear to have far-reaching consequences for our whole worldview. Philosophical questions have a kind of multiple relevance: any answer that is given has implications that touch many areas of human concern. If, for example, we decide with respect to question *f* that determinism is not compatible with moral freedom and that determinism is true, what are the consequences for our view of man's moral responsibility? for our understanding of the penal system? for the status of law? for the conduct of international diplomacy? for our estimate of our own conduct, and of the conduct of our fellow-men? It would be possible to go on and on finding areas of human concern to which any answer to this question is directly or indirectly relevant, and we could make the same point by using as an illustration any one of dozens of philosophical problems that have been discussed over the centuries. But let our single example suffice. A philosophical question is one any answer to which has profound and far-reaching consequences for a total world-view—consequences of which we may be only vaguely aware or even totally unaware when the problem is initially raised.

Another way of putting the same point would be to say that philosophical questions are questions that are *logically fundamental*: the answers that we give determine to some extent what questions we can reasonably ask at other (less fundamental) logical levels and determine also what sorts of answers we can reasonably give. If, for example, we hold (in reply to question *e*) that religion consists of illusory beliefs invented to enable men to cope with their fear of the unknown and of a group of practices based upon those beliefs, we can no longer reasonably ask the theological question, Is God omnipotent, or is His power, however great, limited in some way? Philosophical questions are questions about the most fundamental—logically fundamental—beliefs and assumptions that men hold. This is why the answers that we adopt, whatever those answers may be, have the far-reaching consequences of which we spoke earlier.

Finally, philosophical questions are typically questions of very broad generality. The philosophical question, Is man free in the sense required to render him morally responsible? is not a question about the freedom of this particular individual (such as a psychoanalyst might ask), or of this particular group of citizens (such as a political scientist might ask); it is a question about the freedom of man as such. In order to answer this question we do not study the case histories of individuals or the political fortunes of groups of people: rather, we attempt to analyze carefully the *concept* of freedom as it relates to the ascription of moral responsibility to man, and then we consider whether this quality or power (or whatever "freedom" turns out to be) is ascribable to man, and if so under what circumstances.

These characteristics of philosophical questions all derive from the fact that the overall goal of the philosophical quest is, as we have said, to achieve a picture of the whole, an all-inclusive concept of reality in which no truth fails to receive its proper due. Every philosophical problem is, in fact, an integral part of this broader project; it is only because (or perhaps insofar as) we are interested in the larger project that we find ourselves interested in the particular problems. Students of philosophy whose only impression of philosophy is that of a group of loosely related or unrelated problems would do well to explore the many relations among problems that become evident when they are viewed in the context of the broader philosophical task.

Types of Philosophical Questions

Any question exhibiting the above characteristics will be a philosophical question. During the long span of time in which Western philosophers have been discussing questions of this sort, however, philosophical inquiry has come to assume a fairly well-defined structure, as a result of which it is possible to speak of various "departments" of philosophical inquiry and, accordingly, of various "types" of philosophical questions. There is, of course, nothing final or definitive about this typology, but it is of value, nonetheless, as a system of points of reference when attempting to get a bearing in the field.

Many philosophical questions are what may be called "logical" questions. That is to say, they are questions that arise in that department of philosophical inquiry known as *logic.* It is not easy to define logic in a way that does justice to the wide range of problems with which logicians are concerned. A definition acceptable to most logicians would be: an inquiry concerning the principles whereby one may distinguish between correct and incorrect reasoning. Some representative problems of this type would be: What is the relation between words and things? What constitutes the "meaning" of a proposition? What does it mean to say of an argument that it is "valid"? How does one test the validity of an argument?

Some philosophical questions are what may be called "ontological" (or metaphysical) questions. These are questions that arise in that department of philosophical inquiry known as *ontology* (or *metaphysics*). Again, it is difficult to give a definition that would be acceptable to everyone concerned. Ontology has been defined as "[the science of] being *qua* being"[1] and as "[an investigation concerning] the character of everything that is insofar as it is."[2] It is assumed that simply to *be*—not to be a man or a house or a tree, but simply to *be*—a thing must have a certain "structure." Ontology is the attempt to ascertain what that structure is. Some philosophers, though they allow that the metaphysical proposals of the past are appropriate subjects of historical study, would maintain that it is not possible to pose an intelligible question of this type, much less to give an intelligible or, at any rate, a defensible answer. The student may wish to reserve judgment on this until he has had an opportunity to reflect on the questions raised in Parts IV, VI, IX and X of this text.

A third general type of philosophical question consists of a group of questions commonly called "epistemological." *Epistemology* is that department of philosophy in which the attempt is made to ascertain the nature and limits of human knowledge. Under what conditions may we properly be said to "know" so-and-so? Does all knowledge of the real world arise out of experience, or do we have some knowledge that is in some degree independent of experience? If all knowledge does arise out of experience, and if experience can only yield varying degrees of probability, how is it possible to achieve the absolute certainty that we do achieve in logic and in mathematics? These are only a few of the epistemological questions in which philosophers are interested.

A fourth type of philosophical question is technically called "axiological," although the terms "axiology" and "axiological" are not very commonly used among philosophers at the present time. Instead, philosophers speak of *theory of value* and of questions that arise in this context as questions concerning the nature of value. Some typical questions of this type would be: Are beauty and goodness qualities that are objectively present in things, or are they not? If so, how is their presence or absence ascertained? If not, are they simply sentiments in the mind of the person who judges that something is good or bad, beautiful or ugly? And if this is not the case, what *is* the status of beauty and goodness? That branch of axiology that is principally concerned with the nature of *nonmoral* values (particularly the values of special relevance for the arts) is called *aesthetics*. The branch of axiology that deals with the nature of (and fundamental principles governing) good and evil, right and wrong—*moral* values—is known as *ethics*, or *moral philosophy*.

It may be that all philosophical questions can be reduced to one of

---

[1] Aristotle, *Metaphysics,* IV, i, in Richard McKeon (ed.), *The Basic Works of Aristotle* (New York: Random House, 1941), p. 731.

[2] Paul Tillich, *Systematic Theology* (Chicago: University of Chicago Press, 1951), Vol. I, p. 163.

these four types. In philosophy of science, for example, philosophers typically ask logical and epistemological questions arising out of their reflections on the methods and theories of the various natural sciences. In philosophy of religion they commonly ask questions of all four types concerning the presuppositions and claims of religion; and so on. Be this as it may, it is at least the case that *most* philosophical questions (questions possessing the defining characteristics discussed above) belong to one of these four types; and at times it can be helpful to clarify a philosophical question by determining just what type of question is being asked.

Philosophical Systems

In view of the fact that the philosophical quest has been going on for a very long period of time, it is not surprising that by this time a considerable number of proposals have been made. To make such a proposal—to suggest that such-and-such are the key elements in the total picture of reality, in terms of which every element of reality can be understood—is to offer a philosophical "system." That is what a philosophical system is: a view of the whole which purports to do justice to every element of human knowledge and every aspect of human experience.

There is considerable hesitation among philosophers today to talk about philosophical systems, just as there is a certain reluctance to accept the quest for unity as we have described it as the central task of the philosophical enterprise. The day of system-building, in the view of many philosophers, is past; it came to an end when—within the memory of some philosophers still living—it was concluded that constructive metaphysics is an impossible undertaking, a building of castles in the air.

In actuality, however, we do not need to be convinced of the possibility of metaphysics in order to hold that philosophical systems are not only possible but necessary—any more than we need to hold to the possibility of constructive metaphysics in order to acknowledge that the proper business of philosophy is to seek the total view. The truth is that every human being (including philosophers who do not like systems) carries on his thinking within some kind of a philosophical system. To say that someone's philosophy constitutes a "system" is a perfectly innocuous statement: it is only to say that (a) his views on various matters (whatever matters he *has* views on) are logically consistent with each other and (b) they are logically interdependent. Not everyone, of course, is explicitly aware of the "system" with which he operates, and even fewer people are sufficiently confident of the superiority of their system to recommend its adoption by others. But an intelligent being with no philosophical system whatsoever is unthinkable.

To avoid being overwhelmed by the sheer number of philosophical systems encountered in the study of philosophy, it is helpful to think of philosophical systems as belonging to one or the other of two "families" of systems, that is, the naturalist family and the transcendentalist family. A philosophical system may be said to be "naturalistic" if it affirms that (a) there is only one order to reality, (b) this one order of reality consists entirely of objects and events occurring in space and time, and (c) this one order of reality is completely self-dependent and self-operating. A system may be said to be "transcendentalistic" if it asserts that (a) the world of space and time depends for its existence on a reality that transcends space and time, (b) reality is therefore *not* limited to objects and events occurring in space and time, and (c) explanations of even spatiotemporal phenomena may, therefore, take thought beyond the spatiotemporal world to the dimensions of reality that transcend it. As a matter of historical fact, the dialogue between proponents of these two great types of philosophical systems has provided much of the impetus for philosophical discussion all through the long and sometimes tortuous history of Western philosophy. Many philosophical controversies that would otherwise be trivial take on profound importance when viewed in the context of this dialogue.

All philosophical thinking is implicitly "systematic" in character. This is why philosophers defend so passionately their views on what sometimes appear to be relatively trivial matters. Because of the systematic character of all philosophical thinking, because of the multidimensional relevance of all philosophical questions, no philosophical question is trivial. Every philosophical problem is, so to speak, a test case: our whole world-view (the entire "system" in the context of which we attempt to understand the complex array of data coming before our consciousness) is at stake. The position we adopt with respect to a given philosophical problem inevitably limits the options available on other problems that we may encounter at a later time.

Would it not be advisable, then, simply to suspend judgment? Should we not refuse to commit ourselves on any point until its relevance to all the others is known? Ah, but we are forgetting: *as rational beings we have no alternative but to philosophize*. We can, of course, suspend judgment on some points some of the time, but not on all. At the very least, we must think and act *as if* we had decided about a vast number of things. The alternative of not philosophizing at all is not available to us. We can only decide whether we will do it carelessly and poorly, or deliberately and with care.

STUDY QUESTIONS

1. Review the characteristics of philosophical questions suggested in this chapter. Can you think of any questions—questions that may have puzzled you—that are "philosophical" according to these criteria? What are they?
2. Consider carefully the questions you have formulated in response to the previous question. Can you identify them as belonging to one or another of the four types (logical, ontological, epistemological, and theory of value) discussed in this chapter?
3. If it is true that "an intelligent being with no philosophical system whatsoever is unthinkable," then (presumably) every reader of this book has such a system. What are some of the elements of your "system"? What are some of the ways that your philosophical system is different from that of, say, an uneducated member of some primitive society, or an educated member of an advanced non-Western society?
4. As far as you understand these matters at present, does it seem to you that the philosophical system with which you operate is "naturalistic" or "transcendentalistic"? Does this strike you as being an important question? Why?

4

FIRST STEPS
IN PHILOSOPHY

Getting bearings in philosophy, like getting bearings in any new field, requires a bit of disciplined effort. The key is to employ a method of approach that is appropriate to the mastery of the field. The purpose of the present chapter is to suggest a method that will enable the beginning student to make maximum progress toward a mastery of philosophy.

The student should take encouragement from the fact that he has on many occasions, probably without knowing it, concerned himself with philosophical problems. Very often in the study of philosophy we find ourselves involved in a rigorous and systematic discussion of a problem encountered before, but not pursued for lack of direction. This is one of the great rewards of studying philosophy. The fact that everyone who comes to the point of studying it has already been introduced to philosophy in this informal way makes it much easier to "establish a beachhead" in the field than would otherwise be the case.

Alternative Approaches to Philosophy

There are basically two ways to approach the study of philosophy, and each has its peculiar advantages and disadvantages. One way to approach philosophy is through the history of philosophy. This approach has two unique advantages and two serious disadvantages. One advantage is that the student becomes acquainted, perhaps to some extent firsthand, with the thought of the greatest philosophical thinkers. He also comes to recognize the intimate relation that always obtains between the philosophical reflection of a given period and other elements of the culture of that day. The disadvantages of making a first approach to philosophy via the historical route are, however, extremely serious. It is very confusing to spend several weeks or months studying the history of something whose essential nature is not understood. What is the history of philosophy the history of? Second, there is a semantic problem that is not readily resolvable through a purely historical approach. Different philosophers, unfortunately, frequently use different terms to express the same idea. The student who studies their work without some prior systematic orientation is often bewildered by the sheer profusion of terms used to discuss ideas with which he is also unacquainted.

Many teachers of philosophy, therefore, prefer what may be called a *systematic* approach to philosophy. This approach has three distinct advantages over the historical approach. The first is that it greatly minimizes the semantic problem by providing an opportunity for the student to build up his philosophical vocabulary step by step in the context of philosophical discussions that, with reasonable effort, he is able to clearly understand. The second advantage is that it provides the novice in philosophy with a more familiar starting point, namely, problems and concerns that he has already encountered and that do not seem so strange and unfamiliar as would, for example, the theories of Thales and Heraclitus (two early Greek philosophers). Third, the systematic approach enables the student to identify with the philosophical enterprise and to participate in philosophical discussion far more readily than does the historical approach. To really understand a philosophical problem—almost any philosophical problem—is to see its relevance for many areas of concern that previously may not have seemed at all related.

These remarks are not meant in any way to disparage the study of the history of philosophy. The point is, rather, that as a first introduction to philosophy the systematic approach has a great deal to commend it. The study of the history of philosophy is considerably enriched if it is begun with the kind of prior understanding and equipment that the systematic approach is intended to provide. There is no substitute, however, for an actual encounter with the writings of the great philosophers. The student who does not go on to participate in this encounter is depriving himself of one of the most enriching experiences a liberal education has to offer.

The present book, in any case, uses the systematic approach. This means that we shall be considering, in succession, a number of philosophical problems, and for each of them we shall attempt to understand the possible ways of solving that problem. We shall, of course, refer from time to time to philosophers of the past and of the present who have addressed themselves in one way or another to the problems under discussion. But our purpose is not, except perhaps incidentally, to acquire historical information. Our purpose is to acquire a certain kind of understanding and thus to enter into the philosophical arena as participants rather than as mere spectators. The suggestions that follow are intended to help the student in focusing his efforts in such a way as to make maximum progress toward this kind of understanding.

Three Steps Toward Understanding

There are three distinct determinations to be made and understood with respect to any given philosophical problem. First, attempt to understand precisely *what the problem is.* Note well: *understanding a problem is not the same as memorizing some approved formulation of it.* There are undoubtedly some things that must be learned by rote, but there is very little in philosophy that can profitably be learned in this way. To understand a philosophical problem is to know what question you are asking, to know what sort of an assertion would count as an answer to the question. If you do not know this—if you cannot imagine anything that would qualify as a possible answer to your question —then you have not really asked a question: you have only made a little interrogative noise.

Most of us, unfortunately, are so much in the habit of deceiving ourselves (and others) about what we really understand and what we understand only in a general, hazy way, that it is necessary to apply some very strict self-discipline if we are to overcome this deception in our struggles with the philosophical problems that follow. The deception is rendered all the more difficult to get rid of by the fact that there is no sure method for determining when we are and when we are not guilty of it. The following may, however, be offered as a general rule: if you really understand something, it should be possible for you to vary the expression of it. If you cannot express an idea in more than one way, confident that in so doing you have retained the original meaning, then you have not understood that idea.

It is impossible to overemphasize the importance of insisting on *understanding* if you are to make any significant progress in philosophical learning. We can memorize facts and words, but meanings and relations must be understood; and philosophy is concerned with meanings and relations. I know the *meaning* of the question, Is New York City more populous than London? Thus, I can ask the same question in a variety of ways: Is the population of New York City greater than that of London? Do more people live in New York City than in London? Does New York City have a greater population than the capital of England? But I am not at all sure what people mean when they ask, What is the meaning of life? I cannot hope to make any progress in my reflections on this question until I understand precisely what is being asked; then, and only then, can I imagine what sort of assertion might count as a possible answer to the question. Then, too, I can rephrase the question in a number of ways—but not before. Until I can do this I am not, strictly speaking, asking a question: I am only uttering an interrogative sentence.

The second step toward the kind of understanding that we seek in philosophy is to determine precisely what are the possible ways of answering the question that has been raised. If the question being asked is really understood, this is not usually too difficult: a part of understanding a philosophical problem is knowing what sort of an assertion would count as an answer to it. It is possible, however, to have an accurate but limited understanding of a problem without being explicitly aware of *all* of the possible solutions. It is, therefore, of great value to make a conscious and determined effort in each case to ascertain *all* of the alternative ways of answering the question. Then, and only then, can we weigh the arguments for and against the various positions and perhaps make up our minds on the matter, confident that we have not simply neglected to consider some position that, if examined carefully, might commend itself more strongly than any of those under consideration.

Some philosophical problems allow as few as two possible alternative "positions." An example of such is the epistemological problem discussed in Part VII of this book. More commonly a problem will allow three or four possible solutions. Sometimes, however, it is not possible to state with certainty that such-and-such are the *only* possible positions to take with respect to a given problem. Examples of such problems will be found in Parts II and V. Even in such a case, however, it is extremely important to make the attempt to "define the alternatives," since in so doing we may discover why it is not possible to set a limit to the number of possible solutions. And we may, of course, be reasonably confident that we have considered all of the plausible alternatives, even though we have not surveyed all of those that may be logically possible.

If we demand precision in understanding the problem and precision and completeness in understanding what alternative positions are possible, we have in hand a powerful instrument for organizing subsequent philosophical inquiry. Consider: if I have understood a given problem P, and if I have determined that positions A, B, and C are the only possible positions to take with respect to it, then nothing that anyone can say with respect to P can be completely novel to me. If Plato, or Aristotle, or Kant, or Bertrand Russell, or anyone else addresses himself to this problem, he must do so in behalf of (or in opposition to) position A, or position B, or position C—no matter what terminology he may employ. Hence, I can attend carefully to his arguments and can enter into the discussion with a clear understanding of what the discussion is all about.

The third step toward philosophical understanding is a consideration of the arguments for and against the various alternative positions. Now to the making of arguments there is no end, and it is impossible to state with respect to any philosophical position that thus-and-so are *the* arguments for or against such a position. Practically all philosophical discussion consists in bringing forth arguments either (a) in favor of some position in an attempt to establish it or (b) in opposition to some position in an attempt to refute it. Step three toward philosophical understanding is never completed: it is the arena of philosophical discussion into which we are qualified to enter as soon as steps one and two have been mastered (with respect to any given problem).

Again, there is no great value in memorizing a list of "approved" philosophical arguments—for example, three or four arguments in favor of rationalism and three or four arguments in favor of empiricism (see Part VII). Rather, you should ask: What sorts of considerations would tend to support the rationalist thesis? What sorts of considerations would tend to refute it? What sorts of considerations would tend to support or to refute the empiricist thesis? Then you will be in a position to assess any arguments that you may encounter—and, perhaps, to devise a few of your own.

The Importance of Terminology

At each step along the route to philosophical understanding it is important to observe one cardinal rule: maximum care must be taken at all times to establish the exact meaning of terms, and terms once defined must be used in just those ways that are appropriate to their definitions.

For the purposes of ordinary discourse we can often get on well enough without demanding absolute precision in the language that we are using. We can, for example, discuss the weather, and even agree that it is a "nice day," without being too picayunish about just exactly what qualities a day must have before it qualifies as a "nice" day. Anyone who is inclined to question whether or not we do operate with relatively imprecise language in our everyday conversation might try giving precise definitions to such phrases as "a nice day," "a good ball game," "a boring speaker," or "a snap course."

For some purposes, however, it is important that language be used with as near-perfect precision as we can possibly give to it. For the purposes of mathematical computation, for example, it is obviously important that the symbols employed have precise meanings and that those meanings remain constant throughout the course of computation. The ideas of "force," "mass," "velocity," and many others have been given similarly precise meanings in physics; calculations involving these concepts would not be possible were it not for this precision.

In philosophy, unlike the natural sciences, it is seldom possible to define terms mathematically. What we must do, therefore, is to define them in nonmathematical terms and to make the definitions just as precise as nonmathematical language will allow. The technical and semitechnical language of philosophy has been developed precisely for the purpose of enabling philosophers to discuss what they wish with greater precision than would otherwise be possible. The serious student of philosophy will make every effort to master this terminology as he goes along, for, however esoteric it may sound at first, its real and valid function is to enable us to think and speak precisely about matters that in everyday language remain obscure and imprecise.

More than this, however, we must learn to be on the lookout for ambiguities in everyday language that, if not detected, may mislead and confuse. If, knowing that Socrates died in prison, we hear someone say, "Socrates was a freer man on the day he died than those who brought about his imprisonment," the chances are that we shall find the statement confusing. In one sense of "free," Socrates clearly was *not* as free as his accusers: they were free to go about the streets of Athens and to spend time with their families, and Socrates was not. What, then, does the speaker mean? Is he talking about some "inner state," which Socrates allegedly had on the day of his death in a greater degree ("freer") than his accusers? Or is the speaker suggesting that in dying Socrates is somehow "freed" from his body, and in this way becomes "freer" than his accusers—or what? Some careful thinking about the meaning of the term "free" is needed if we are to dispel the bewilderment that such a statement can create. And to think critically, carefully, analytically about the exact meanings of terms is to observe the rule stated above.

Being What We Are

Finally, it is of the utmost importance in philosophical study that we develop the habit of intellectual honesty in our consideration of each philosophical problem that we encounter. Very often in the study of philosophy we have the peculiar experience of discovering that we already have an opinion on the question under discussion—in spite of the fact that we have never consciously considered the question before and have certainly never given careful consideration to the arguments for or against that position. We have, as we say, simply "taken it for granted." It is easy to become embarrassed about the fact that we have opinions we have never examined, or did not even know we had, and to try to conceal this from those with whom we are discussing the issue in question. It is this concealment that we must work hard to avoid. If we are to make significant progress in philosophical study, it is precisely *our opinions* that must be put to the test. If we approach philosophy as a body of knowledge that can be kept at arm's length—something to be memorized and, after a time, largely forgotten—we shall miss the whole point. Philosophy is about us—our beliefs, our opinions. We progress in philosophical study only insofar as we clarify and either reinforce or alter the beliefs and opinions with which we begin.

STUDY QUESTIONS

1. What is the history of philosophy the history of? Why is the philosophical reflection of any given period intimately related to other elements of the culture of that day?
2. What is the difference between asking a question and merely uttering an interrogative sentence? Can you do one without doing the other?
3. Has your education thus far tended to obscure the difference between (a) understanding something, and (b) memorizing some "recommended" or "official" verbal formulation regarding the subject in question? What sorts of behavior by parents and teachers might tend to obscure this distinction? What steps might you take to overcome whatever unfortunate habits of this kind you may have developed?

5

ARGUMENTS

Philosophy, we have said, is a dialogue, a conversation in which varying points of view are expressed about the questions that force themselves upon us when we try to conceive of the whole of reality in such a way as to make due allowance for every element of human knowledge and every aspect of human experience. The vehicle of this dialogue is, of course, language; and the dialogue consists, for the most part, of *arguments* put forward in support of or in opposition to a position that we are attempting to support or oppose. In philosophical study it is of the utmost importance, therefore, that we pay very close attention to how language is being used and to the arguments on the basis of which we are being asked to accept certain conclusions.

Real Disputes and Verbal Disputes

Interesting philosophical questions are always controversial: they are questions to which there are at least two more or less plausible answers, both (or all) of which cannot be correct. Philosophical questions are the occasion for disputes among the proponents of opposing positions. When two parties appear to be in disagreement with each other, however—one assenting to a given statement and the other denying it—it still remains to be determined whether their dispute is *real* or merely *verbal*. In order to have a real dispute, it is necessary that the parties to the dispute be in genuine disagreement as to what is the case. If they are in agreement about the facts, but are simply using certain terms with different meanings, then their dispute is not real but verbal. A real dispute can be settled only by determining what really is the case. A verbal dispute can be resolved only by securing agreement as to the meanings of the terms that are being used in different senses by the disputants.

Suppose, for example, that two men are arguing about the question, Are all men created equal? *A* says, "All men are created equal. No one has a right to any special privileges by virtue of his race, religion, or social status. All men have an equal right to life, liberty, and the pursuit of happiness." *B* says, "I disagree with you: all men are not created equal. They differ in their physical and intellectual endowments by virtue of their differing heredity and in their privileges and opportunities by virtue of their birth into either wealth or poverty. To deny this is simply to blind oneself to the facts."

It is clear upon a moment's reflection that, although *A* and *B* are talking as if they were in genuine disagreement with each other, the dispute between them is merely verbal. *A* is arguing that all men have equal rights; *B* is arguing that they have unequal endowments and opportunities. What *A* is asserting, therefore, is not at all incompatible with what *B* is asserting, but this fact is obscured by the apparent incompatibility of the two statements, "All men are created equal" and "All men are not created equal."

Unfortunately, however, it is not always as easy as in this example to determine whether a given dispute is merely verbal or not. Language is an extremely complex phenomenon, and it is quite possible for intelligent and able men to debate long and hard over a question that, as they later discover, posed a merely verbal issue. Only if there is agreement on the meanings of the key terms employed in the discussion can it be determined whether or not there is genuine disagreement on a substantive issue.

It must be admitted that there is no method that can guarantee the detection of verbal disputes. There have been philosophers who have maintained that all philosophical questions are merely verbal in character, but in the judgment of most philosophers this does not seem very likely. It is undoubtedly true, however, that the discussion of many philosophical questions of substance is frequently obscured by issues that are merely verbal, and it is, therefore, a sound principle to be on the alert for such confusion-producing issues.

Fallacies

Let us suppose that we have satisfied ourselves that a problem we are considering is a substantive one—that what separates the disputants is not merely different ways of using certain terms, but a genuine disagreement as to what is the case. They may, then, enter into a serious discussion of the issue, and each party to the dispute will present arguments intended to persuade others to agree with his position.

An argument is a piece of rational discourse in which some propositions (the premises) are offered as grounds for assenting to some other proposition (the conclusion). If it is claimed that the premises offer conclusive evidence for the truth of the conclusion—if it is claimed that the conclusion follows necessarily from the stated premises—the argument is termed *deductive*. If it is claimed only that the premises offer some evidence in support of the conclusion—if it is allowed that the conclusion might be false even if the premises are true—the argument is termed *inductive*.

In the case of deductive arguments, if the conclusion does follow necessarily from the premises—if the truth of the premises does guarantee the truth of the conclusion—the argument is said to be *valid*. If this is not the case—if it is logically possible (in the case of a deductive argument) for the conclusion to be false even if the premises are true—the argument is said to be *invalid*.

That a given deductive argument is valid does not, of course, establish that the conclusion of that argument is true: it establishes only that the conclusion is true *if the premises are true*. If you agree that a given deductive argument is valid, you cannot reasonably accept the premises and reject the conclusion. You can reasonably point out, however, that the truth of the premises remains to be determined. The claim that an argument is *sound* involves the dual claim that it is valid and that its premises are true.

To say that an argument is invalid is to say that it is "logically incorrect" in one of several specifiable ways: it contains, as logicians say, a *fallacy*, a logical error. It may be incorrect as to its form, in which case it contains what is called a *formal* fallacy. Such fallacies are easily detected, however, and so are unlikely to confuse the discussion of an issue for very long. The troublesome fallacies are the *informal* fallacies—logical mistakes that occur in the course of reasoning and that cannot be detected by the purely mechanical methods that suffice for the detection of formal fallacies. It is customary among logicians to distinguish two general classes of informal fallacies: *fallacies of relevance* and *fallacies of ambiguity*.

A fallacy of relevance is committed whenever an argument is offered in which the premises are logically irrelevant to the conclusion. Suppose, for example, that someone argues for the existence of God on the grounds that "millions of people believe in the existence of God, and those millions of people cannot be mistaken." Now the fact that millions of people believe a proposition to be true is logically irrelevant to the truth of that proposition: millions of people were for many years mistaken, for example, in their belief that the earth was flat. But to some people this argument is psychologically persuasive—perhaps because they hesitate to set up their own private judgment against that of all those millions of people—and so they fail to notice that the belief of those millions is quite irrelevant to the truth of the proposition in question.

There is, as we have said, no certain method for detecting such fallacies. They deceive us by virtue of the fact that they are psychologically persuasive: they make us want to accept the conclusion, or they make us feel that somehow we ought to accept the conclusion, and thus they divert our attention from the fact that the grounds on which we are being asked to accept the conclusion are logically irrelevant. All that we can do if we suspect that we are being deceived in this way is to ask the question, Do these premises provide logical grounds for accepting the proposition in question? If we conclude that they do not, but still find the argument psychologically persuasive, the likelihood is that we are dealing with an argument containing a fallacy of relevance.[1]

A fallacy of ambiguity is a logical mistake that occurs as a result of the ambiguity of the language in which an argument is framed. Many words have a variety of meanings, and it sometimes occurs that in the course of an extended argument the same term will be used in more than one sense, whereas the logical persuasiveness of the argument presupposes that each term is used in the same sense throughout the argument. Sentences, too, or parts of sentences, can sometimes be construed in more than one way—depending, for example, on which terms are emphasized, or how one understands the grammatical construction of the sentence or phrase. If in the course of an argument the meaning of a term, a sentence, or a phrase undergoes a subtle shift of meaning, the argument may contain a fallacy of ambiguity.[2]

Suppose, for example, that someone asserts that no men have ever been morally responsible for any of their actions, and argues in support of this proposition on the grounds that (a) in order to be morally responsible one must be free, but (b) no one has ever been truly free, for all men are in some degree slaves of fear, passion, prejudice, ignorance, and a host of other weaknesses. We may sense, in considering this argument, that something is wrong with it, but it may not be immediately apparent that what is wrong with it is that it contains a fallacy of ambiguity. It uses the term "free" (a very tricky term, by the way) in two rather different senses. The first premise asserts that in order to be morally responsible one must be "free" in some unspecified sense; the second premise asserts that in fact no one has ever been "free" in the sense of being *free from*—wholly without—fear, passion, prejudice, etc. The argument, therefore, is fallacious, and the logical error by virtue of which it is fallacious is a fallacy of ambiguity.

There is, happily, a fairly reliable method for eliminating such fal-

---

[1] Several distinct types of such fallacies have been identified and given special names. A helpful discussion of the most common of these may be found in Irving M. Copi, *Introduction to Logic,* 3rd ed. (New York: Macmillan, 1968), pp. 53–69.

[2] See *ibid.,* pp. 73–82 for a discussion of several types of fallacies of ambiguity.

lacies. The method consists in substituting a more precise formulation for the term, phrase, or sentence suspected of being ambiguous. In the case of a term suspected of ambiguity, for example, one substitutes for the offending term a precise definition of that term (a definition, hopefully, that does not itself contain any ambiguous terms). If the argument does contain a fallacy of ambiguity, and if we have correctly identified the ambiguous term (or phrase, or sentence), the result of the reformulation should be a patently unconvincing argument. Note how this works out in the argument we considered a moment ago. We define "free" in the sense required by the second premise: "wholly without fear, passion, prejudice, ignorance, and other human weaknesses." Using this definition in both premises, the argument becomes:

> In order to be morally responsible one must be wholly without fear, passion, prejudice, etc.
> No one has ever been wholly without fear, passion, prejudice, etc.
>
> ---
>
> Therefore no one has ever been morally responsible.

Thus stated, the argument is highly unconvincing because the first premise no longer strikes us as plausible. Arguments containing fallacies of ambiguity deceive us by concealing implausible assertions under a façade of plausibility. A precise reformulation rips away the façade and enables us to judge each assertion on its own merits. The method of reformulation, if we are careful to avoid new ambiguities in the reformulation, is therefore an effective method for the detection and elimination of fallacy-producing ambiguities.

The Reductio Ad Absurdum *Argument*

There is one type of argument that appears with such frequency in philosophical discussion that it is advisable to become familiar with it as soon as possible. This is what is called the *reductio ad absurdum*. The *reductio ad absurdum* is a powerful form of argument for the purpose of refuting the position of an opponent. It consists in showing that the position attacked implies absurd consequences. Suppose that I wish to attack position A: if I can show that A implies X, Y, and Z, and that X, Y, and Z are absurd or contrary to fact, then I have shown that A is absurd; for from a true proposition you cannot validly deduce false consequences. This type of argument may also be used constructively in situations where there are only two possible positions on a given problem: if either A or B must be the case, and if A is shown (by a *reductio ad absurdum* argument) to be untenable, then B must be the case. If there is more than one alternative to the position, then separate arguments must, of course, be constructed against each of the alternative positions.

In attempting to assess such an argument, two questions must always be asked: Do the alleged consequences really follow from the position in question? Are they really absurd? If the answer to either of these questions is negative, the attempted *reductio* is not successful.

Learning by Doing

Thus far we have been talking *about* philosophy. Such talk has its place, namely, at the beginning of a book whose purpose it is to introduce philosophy to those previously unintroduced. But it is now time to stop talking *about* philosophy and to begin engaging in philosophical discussion. And here, philosophy being what it is, the student must be prepared to play his appropriate role.

"Philosophy being what it is"—what do we mean by this? We mean that philosophy is an activity in which we can learn to participate, not a body of information that we can commit to memory. As with any skill, there are some points of information that must be mastered. In learning to ski, for example, there is a certain amount of information that we have to learn with respect to where we should put our weight, what to do with the poles, how to use the edges of the skis, etc., if we are to learn to execute the various maneuvers that constitute "skiing." But the point of it all is to learn to do something, not simply to acquire some information. And this is true also for philosophy: the point in studying it is to learn to philosophize.

What this means for the student is this: he should approach the discussions that follow not simply as a spectator, but as a participant. The first chapter in each part will provide him with his "ticket" to the arena: a statement of the problem and a description of the alternatives. These must, of course, be very carefully studied and thoroughly understood. Beyond that, it is altogether a matter of arguments: each "position" is allowed to speak for itself, to marshal whatever arguments it can in support of its own position and in refutation of all others. Not all of the arguments used are good ones, obviously, since for most philosophical problems there is room for only one "correct" position, and the arguments that allegedly "prove" some other position must, therefore, be unsound. But which position is "correct" in each case? And which arguments are unsound? Those, obviously, are questions that no one can answer with finality. Within the living dialogue that is philosophy there is room for differences of opinion on these matters. Indeed, it is these differences of opinion—differences that must occur when honest men seek answers to questions that have long puzzled the greatest minds—that keep the dialogue alive.

And now, to the dialogue itself.

STUDY QUESTIONS

1. Consider the questions that follow. In each case decide whether you think differing answers to the question would represent a *real* dispute or a *verbal* dispute:
   a. If a clap of thunder occurs in a place where no one is around to hear it, was there or was there not a sound in that place?
   b. A cow is at position X. A dog goes in a complete circle around position X, but the cow turns in such a way that she is always facing the dog. Does the dog go around the cow or doesn't he?
   c. Does Telstar go around the earth? Is it stationary?
   d. Is *Gone With The Wind* one of the ten greatest movies of all time?
   e. Is a Buick a better car than a Chrysler?
   f. Are some people naturally brighter than others?
   g. Are some teachers better teachers than others?
   h. Do men sometimes act freely, or is their behavior always the result of antecedent causes over which they have no control?
2. Write definitions for the following terms: argument, inductive, deductive, valid, invalid, sound, fallacy, formal fallacy, informal fallacy, fallacy of relevance, fallacy of ambiguity, *non sequitur.*
3. True or False:
   a. All arguments are either inductive or deductive.
   b. All arguments are either valid or invalid.
   c. If an argument is valid, it is sound.
   d. If an argument is sound, it is valid.
   e. If the conclusion of an argument is true, its premises must be true.
   f. If the premises of a sound argument are true, the conclusion must be true.
   g. If an argument contains a fallacy, its conclusion must be false.
   h. If an argument contains no fallacies, its conclusion must be true.
   i. If the conclusion of an argument is true, it is a sound argument.
   j. If an argument is sound, it contains no fallacies.
4. Give an example of a *reductio ad absurdum* argument (not necessarily relating to a philosophical question). On the basis of what has been said about this type of argument in the present chapter, what uses do you anticipate will be made of arguments of this sort in the discussions that follow?

FOR FURTHER READING [1]

Ayer, A. J. *Philosophy and Language*. New York: Oxford University Press, 1960.

Hahn, Lewis E. "Philosophy as Comprehensive Vision," *Philosophy and Phenomenological Research*, XXII (1961), 1–25.

Jaspers, Karl. *Way to Wisdom,* tr. by Ralph Manheim. New Haven: Yale University Press, 1951 (paperbound). See especially Chapters 1–3.

Krikorian, Yervant H. (ed.), *Naturalism and the Human Spirit*. New York: Columbia University Press, 1944. See especially Chapter 15, "The Nature of Naturalism," by John Herman Randall, Jr.

Loewenberg, Jacob. *Reason and the Nature of Things*. La Salle, Ill.: Open Court, 1959.

Merleau-Ponty, Maurice. *In Praise of Philosophy*, tr. by John Wild and James M. Edie. Evanston, Ill.: Northwestern University Press, 1963. See especially Pages 33–64.

Nagel, Ernest. *Logic Without Metaphysics*. New York: Free Press, 1956. See Part I, Chapter 1, "Naturalism Reconsidered."

Newell, R. W. *The Concept of Philosophy*. London: Methuen, 1967.

Passmore, John. *Philosophical Reasoning*. London: Gerald Duckworth, 1969 (paperbound). An examination of some common forms of philosophical argument.

Plato, *Apology*. Many editions. Plato's moving account of Socrates' defense —of himself and of philosophy—before the Athenian court.

Russell, Bertrand. *The Problems of Philosophy*. New York: Oxford University Press, 1959. See especially Chapter 15, "The Value of Philosophy."

Ryle, Gilbert. "Systematically Misleading Expressions," in Antony Flew (ed.). *Essays on Logic and Language*, First Series. New York: Philosophical Library, 1951.

Sheldon, W. H. "Critique of Naturalism," *The Journal of Philosophy*, 42 (1945), 253–270.

Smart, J. J. C. *Philosophy and Scientific Realism*. New York: Humanities Press, 1963. See especially Chapter 1, "The Province of Philosophy."

Supek, Ivan. "The Task of Philosophy Today," *Philosophy and Phenomenological Research*, 24 (1963), 117–124.

Waismann, Friedrich. "How I See Philosophy," in H. D. Lewis (ed.). *Contemporary British Philosophy*, Third Series. New York: Macmillan, 1956.

White, Morton. *Toward Reunion in Philosophy*. Cambridge, Mass.: Harvard University Press, 1956.

---

[1] Dates given are usually for the most recent edition available, which sometimes differs from date of original publication. If books cited are available in paperbound editions, this is indicated. Books published abroad but distributed here are listed with the distributor.

PART II

FREEDOM
AND AUTHORITY

6

SOCIETY AND THE INDIVIDUAL

As John Donne said, no man is an island. We are born into a world that has been shaped and molded by those who lived before us, and we live our entire lives surrounded by other human beings whose individual and collective wishes impinge upon us in innumerable ways. During our formative years we are surrounded by people—parents, teachers, other adults—who make every effort to mold *us* as well, to make us fit into the society into which we have been born. We are taught to speak its language, adopt its customs, espouse its values—so that they become our language, our customs, our values. We are all members of human society; we cannot, even by the most bizarre efforts imaginable, totally depart from its influence. As in childhood, so in adulthood, society surrounds us with a variety of *authorities* whose commands we are expected to obey.

The Concept of Authority

What does it mean to say of someone that he is an "authority"? Evidently it can mean either of two things: (a) it might mean that he possesses specialized knowledge in some particular area, that he is an "expert" on some subject; or (b) it might mean that he has the right to control (to some extent) the behavior of others.

There is no mystery about the concept of authority in the first sense. One becomes an authority in this sense by learning more about some subject than most other people. Such an authority does, indeed, claim that other people ought in general to believe what he says when he speaks on the subject on which he claims to be an authority, but only because he happens to have investigated the field more thoroughly than most men and hence is in a position to speak about the relevant facts on the basis of a first-hand knowledge that they do not possess. Theoretically, anyone can become an authority on any subject he chooses—provided only that he pursues his inquiries to the point where his knowledge of that subject greatly surpasses that of most of his contemporaries.

But what does it mean to be an authority in the sense of "the right to control (to some extent) the behavior of others"? This definition does not take us very far because it defines one puzzling word, "authority," in terms of another equally puzzling word, "right." It is no better than if we had said, "authority (in the second sense) means the *authority* to control (to some extent) the behavior of others." Clearly, that is not very helpful.

Let us consider a hypothetical case in which we would be inclined to say that someone is an authority in the second sense. Consider, for example, a judge in a court of law. The judge, when he is exercising his office rather than acting as a private citizen, can do certain things that the generality of men cannot do: he can issue commands with the expectation that they will be obeyed ("Silence in the court!" "Proceed with the examination!" etc.); he can invoke force to compel obedience to his commands; he can make decisions (or, in some cases, participate in making decisions) about the guilt or innocence of persons charged with unlawful conduct; and he can impose penalties upon those who are judged to be guilty. He exercises his authority as a judge precisely insofar as he does these things that a private citizen could not do. In saying that he has the authority to do these things we are saying—what? That he has the right (that word again) and the power to control the behavior of others.

Suppose that in place of a judge on the bench we imagine these same prerogatives being exercised by the acknowledged leader of a small gang of thieves. An acquaintance of one of the gang members is suspected of tipping off the police about the gang's latest job, in which two members of the gang got caught. He is "brought to trial" before the gang, and the leader does the very things the judge was said to do when he was exercising his authority. He issues commands with the expectation that they will be obeyed ("Lefty, stand up!"); he invokes force to compel obedience to his commands ("Shorty, give Lefty's arm a twist and see if you can't make him a little more cooperative"); he decides that Lefty is "guilty"; and he imposes a penalty that will be enforced ("be permanently out of town in one hour or you'll end up in the river"). We would not, in such a case, say that the gang leader was exercising "authority." Why not? Because, although he had the power, he did not have the right to act as he did.

We are in a dilemma. It appears that we can distinguish between a judge in a court of law (who is an authority in the required sense) and a gang leader who behaves in a judge-like way (but is not an authority) only by saying that the judge has the power *and the right* to act as he does, whereas the gang leader has only the power. What, then, is a "right"?

Let us try this: a right is an opportunity to act (or to refrain from acting) in some specified way, which opportunity is guaranteed by law or by the general consent of the community. What distinguishes the situation of the judge from the situation of the gang leader who acts in a judge-like way is that the judge's exercise of power, unlike the gang leader's, is sanctioned by the will of the community as expressed in the laws defining those powers. The judge is an authority by virtue of the fact that he exercises *legitimate* (according to law) power, whereas the gang leader's power has no such sanction.

If we accept this definition of "right," our definition of "authority" begins to make some sense. An "authority" is one who has the right (as defined above) to control (to some extent) the behavior of others and the power to enforce that control. Right + Power = Authority *whenever the right in question is the right to control the behavior of others.* To be an authority is to have such a right and the power to enforce it. To exercise authority is to act according to that right, that is, to constrain others to act in certain ways that may or may not be to their liking—invoking force, if necessary, to implement one's will.

The exercise of authority involves, therefore, a limitation upon the freedom of the individual who is subject to that authority. If a police officer on traffic duty has the authority to tell me when I may and when I may not proceed through an intersection, or how fast I may drive, then my freedom to proceed through the intersection when *I* want to, or to drive at a speed faster than he will allow me to drive, is being curtailed. Where there is authority, there also is a limitation upon the freedom of those subject to that authority.

The Authority of Society

Every society exercises some degree of authority over its citizens. It does this by passing laws that all citizens are expected to obey and by imposing penalties upon those who do not obey those laws. The paradigm examples of "authorities" are, indeed, those who are charged with the responsibility of enforcing the law, trying those accused of breaking the law, and punishing those adjudged guilty.

The philosophical question to which we shall be addressing ourselves in this section is this: On what grounds, if at all, does society have the authority to restrict the freedom of the individual to do as he pleases? Society, we have said, exercises authority over its citizens. What is the source of this authority? What, if any, is the justification for society's exercise of authority over its citizens?

It will be readily acknowledged, I suppose, that this question has considerable relevance for the contemporary political situation in the United States and, indeed, throughout the world. Self-proclaimed "revolutionary" groups have arisen in various places, claiming that they are subject to no law except revolutionary law, no authority except revolutionary authority. Planes are hijacked, property is destroyed, men are executed in the name of this or that revolutionary cause—and those who perform these acts contemptuously dismiss existing law, the police, the courts, and the will of society as an oppressive rule that has no legitimate authority over them.

The question has, however, been discussed by philosophers for many centuries. Plato deals with it in *The Republic*, and Aristotle in the *Politics*. It is, in some ways, the central question in political philosophy. Let us look briefly at the principal ways in which it has been answered.

It is possible to argue, first, that the laws of society have the force of law because (or insofar as) they are sanctioned by natural law. This view is called, therefore, the *natural law* theory. According to this theory, there are certain fundamental principles of right and justice that human reason can discern merely by attending carefully to the propositions asserting those principles. Such a principle is expressed, for example, in the proposition, "The needless destruction of human life is evil." This proposition, according to the theory, cannot be proved, nor does it need to be: any right-thinking person will, upon reflection, acknowledge its truth. Laws prohibiting murder, then, are derived from this principle. Society's right to restrict the freedom of its citizens (for example, to prohibit the taking of another human life) is based on its perception of what is right, that is, on its perception of what is prescribed or prohibited by eternal and immutable natural laws.

A second alternative is what is called the *social contract* theory. According to this theory each citizen of the state, by virtue of accepting the benefits of an ordered society, is giving his tacit consent to the government that maintains that order. Each citizen is, so to speak, agreeing with every other citizen to accept certain limitations on his own freedom in order to secure the greater security that is thereby made possible. This view was initially advocated by such theorists as Thomas Hobbes (1588–1679), John Locke (1632–1704), and Jean Jacques Rousseau (1712–1788), and was strongly influential in the thinking of the framers of the American Constitution.

Thirdly, one can defend the legitimacy of certain restrictions on the freedom of individuals in society according to the theory of *social utilitarianism*. According to this theory, the natural function of government is to promote the general well-being of its citizenry, to secure the greatest happiness for the greatest number. The justification for restricting by law the freedom of each individual to do as he pleases is that such restriction will tend to promote the general welfare. It is a corollary of this view that any restriction of freedom that cannot be shown to actually promote the general welfare is unjustified.

A fourth alternative is to assert that there is no justification for society's restriction of the freedom of its individual members, that is, *theoretical anarchism*. To the question, By what authority does society restrict the freedom of the individual to do as he pleases? theoretical anarchism replies: Society has no such authority; it does so nonetheless because it has the *power* to do so and because it perceives a practical necessity to do so. What society calls "authority" is, however, merely superior power—whether it be wielded in the name of monarchy, or oligarchy, or even majoritarian democracy. Civil authority is always merely de facto, never de jure.

These, then, are the principal ways in which the question as to the justification of society's restriction of individual freedom may be answered. Let us now consider in some detail the arguments that may be urged in support of each.

STUDY QUESTIONS

1. What are the two senses of "authority" distinguished in this chapter? Are you satisfied with the definition of authority offered on p. 49? If not, how would you improve on it?
2. Is a philosophy instructor an authority, and if so, in what sense?
3. What exactly is the question about authority that is posed in this chapter? List all of the ways of answering this question that seem to you to have at least some measure of plausibility.
4. Do you think it is the case that any right-thinking person will, upon reflection, agree that "the needless destruction of human life is evil"? What apparent relevance does your answer have for the question at issue?
5. What is your present opinion regarding the question posed in this chapter?

7

THE NATURAL
LAW THEORY

The question before us is, What is the justification for society's exercise of authority over its citizens? I shall argue that this authority is justified insofar as the laws through which society exercises its authority are derived from natural law. I shall, in short, defend the natural law theory.[1]

The Theory

The natural law theory involves the following claims: (a) there are some basic and unchanging principles of right and justice that ought to govern the affairs of men, (b) these principles can be known by man, and (c) laws have the force and authority of law insofar as they are derivable from these principles.

No one has, to my knowledge, ever attempted to codify all of the basic principles of right and justice which together make up the natural law, but it is not at all difficult to produce numerous examples. The preceding chapter gave one example: The needless destruction of human life is evil. Many such principles are stated in the Universal Declaration of Human Rights adopted by the General Assembly of the United Nations, such as "All human beings are born free and equal in dignity and rights" (Article 1), "Everyone has the right to life, liberty and security of person" (Article 3), and "Everyone has the right to own property alone as well as in association with others" (Article 17 [1]). Additional examples could easily be given, but let these suffice.

Two things should be noted about these principles. First, they are

---

[1] The reader is reminded that the "I" of this and of subsequent chapters is in each case a hypothetical advocate of the view in question. See the Preface.

fundamental in the sense that they apply to all men at all times, in all places, in all circumstances. Any society that did not attempt to embody these principles in its laws would be regarded by all decent men as degenerate and inhuman. Second, these principles are not capable of being *proved*. If anyone is so base as to assert that some people are entitled to greater dignity than others (contra Article 1), or that there is nothing wrong with arbitrarily depriving some people of their life or liberty (contra Article 3), there is no way in the world that you can prove him wrong. If he professes not to believe such a principle the best that you can hope for is that he will consider it more carefully and by so doing come to see that it is true.

Unprovable though these principles are, however, they can be known by man because they are *self-evident*. They are, so to speak, laws that nature has inscribed upon the heart of man. We *know* that every man has a right to life, liberty, and security of person—whether he be an American, a Russian, an Indian, or some other nationality, and whether or not that right is actually guaranteed by the laws of the country in which he happens to live. "We hold these truths to be self-evident," said the authors of the American Declaration of Independence; the advocates of the natural law theory take this to be the status of all of the fundamental principles of right and justice.

In saying, then, that laws have the force and authority of law insofar as they are derivable from these principles I am saying, quite simply, that laws are valid and worthy of obedience insofar as they embody these principles. As St. Thomas Aquinas said, "Every human law has just so much of the nature of law as it is derived from the law of nature. But if in any point it departs from the law of nature, it is no longer a law but a perversion of law." [2] The basic principles of right and justice contained in the natural law are principles to which all men ought to be subject. The "oughtness" of the laws of any society derives from this source. Government is, so to speak, nature's surrogate in ordering the affairs of men according to nature's laws.

In asserting that valid laws are derivable from natural law I do not mean to be asserting that every particular valid law can be rigorously deduced from natural law by a series of valid syllogisms. The principle that every person has a right to security of his person, for example, justifies in general the limiting of the speed of automobiles in populated areas, but you cannot strictly conclude from this (and other relevant propositions) that the maximum allowable speed on Third Avenue between Apple Street and Cherry Boulevard should be exactly twenty-five miles per hour. Whoever is responsible for establishing speed limits has to exercise judgment in a matter such as this; he

---

[2] St. Thomas Aquinas, *Summa Theologica*, I–II, Ques. 95, Art. 2, in Anton C. Pegis (ed.), *Basic Writings of St. Thomas Aquinas* (New York: Random House, 1945), Vol. II, p. 784.

might reasonably settle on any of several speeds as the one that shall be regarded as the "legal limit." Such a law, nonetheless, "embodies the principles" of natural law and is therefore a valid law.

This, then, is the natural law theory with respect to the justification of society's curtailment of the freedom of the individual citizen. Let us turn now to a consideration of the principal arguments that may be given in support of this theory.

Just and Unjust Laws

Consider, in the first place, that if there were no natural law it would follow that there would be no criterion for distinguishing between just laws and unjust laws. As Plato said, "What is to be the standard of just and unjust is the point at issue." [3] Were it not for the natural law written in the heart of man, men would be without any moral basis for opposing tyranny. Legislators could enact laws to further their own interests and those of their friends, and the hapless citizens whose interests were violated by these laws would have no recourse to any higher tribunal. They could not appeal to the conscience of mankind, but would be powerless victims whose only hope for redress must lie in overthrowing those in power.

But in fact we *do* distinguish between just and unjust laws. We recognize, for example, that the federal Fugitive Slave Law of 1793, which allowed slave "owners" to capture and retrieve slaves who had sought freedom in another state, was a profoundly unjust law. It was unjust because it violated the basic principle that every human being has a right to his personal freedom, that compulsory servitude—slavery—is morally wrong. The Fugitive Slave Law, even though it was for many years the law of the land, did not have the force of law because it was inconsistent with the natural law and was therefore repugnant to the moral sense of good men everywhere. Were it not for our common awareness of such a "higher law" we could not make such a judgment.

We recognize, then, that laws subjecting men to arbitrary arrest, or arbitrary seizure of their property, or unnecessary limitations on their freedom are unjust laws. They are unjust whether or not they are consistent with the constitution (if there is one) of the country in which they hold sway and notwithstanding the fact that they may have the majority or even unanimous approval of the lawmaking agency or of the population of that country. On what principle do we pronounce them unjust? On the principle that they are inconsistent with the unwritten natural law that binds the consciences of all men everywhere.

---

[3] Plato, *Laws*, IV, in *The Dialogues of Plato*, B. Jowett (tr.) (New York: Random House, 1937), Vol. II, p. 485.

The Treatment of Aliens

A second argument that may be adduced in support of the natural law theory is that aliens are held to be punishable if they break a just law of a country other than their own even though the lawmaking agency of that country has no legal mandate to control their behavior. The British Parliament, for example, has no power to make laws governing the behavior of anyone except citizens of Great Britain. Yet we freely grant that an American citizen who commits, say, theft or murder in Great Britain is rightly punished for his crime according to British law. It is as if nature had assigned to each sovereign state the task of enforcing the natural law on all men who happen in the course of their lives to come within the geographical borders of this or that state. It is, in the last analysis, the conscience of mankind that renders a verdict when a judge or a jury decides a case. Were it not for the universal applicability of the natural law, men would leave the reign of law whenever they left the country whose laws they are, as citizens, legally bound to obey.

Moral Legislation

The natural law theory is supported by yet another line of reasoning. Many laws that are in force in most of the civilized nations of the world can be justified only by an appeal to natural law. Consider, for example, the practice of homosexuality. It cannot be reasonably argued that homosexual acts between consenting adults are in any way harmful to the community. It therefore is not necessary for the community to protect itself by prohibiting such acts. Yet such acts are commonly prohibited by law. On what grounds? On the grounds that such acts are wrong, immoral, contrary to what the consciences of most men perceive as being good and right—contrary, that is, to natural law.

Consider another example. Suppose that some individual, contrary to the practice of all civilized people, chose to go about in public (weather permitting) without any clothes. Such a person would most certainly be arrested for indecent exposure and either jailed or committed to a mental institution. On what grounds? On the grounds that such behavior is contrary to what civilized men regard as being decent and right. Take away natural law and you must take away much of the moral legislation that governs the everyday life of all of us.

Our Knowledge of Natural Law

In appealing to natural law as the ultimate source of the authority of the actual laws under which men live I do not mean to be implying that our knowledge of natural law is either complete or infallible. The training of the conscience of mankind is clearly a long and laborious process. I would be the first to admit that we undoubtedly have a long way to go before we shall have arrived at the point where we can plausibly claim that we have fully comprehended the content of the natural law. Our knowledge of the natural law, like our knowledge of the laws governing the physical universe, is incomplete and subject to error. But in neither case is our partial ignorance a reasonable excuse for ignoring or denying that portion of the whole that we clearly understand. Our legislators must legislate according to their understanding of what is good and right, just as our engineers must design our transportation and communication systems on the basis of their present understanding of the relevant physical and chemical laws.

A legislator, then, is not free to enact as law just anything that might happen to suit his fancy or his private interest. In a constitutional democracy he is, of course, bound by the constitution. But even in a country where there is no constitution defining the limits of a legislator's authority, a legislator is bound by the authority of an unalterable natural law to which all men are subject. When he is considering a piece of proposed legislation he must continually ask, Is this right? Is it just? Does it protect the inalienable rights of our citizens? Does it promote the common good? And to answer these questions he must look not to the constitution, for that is at best an incomplete summary of the basic principles of right and justice, but to the natural law itself. The law that he enacts will have the force of law and will be binding upon the behavior of the citizens only on the condition that it is grounded in the principles of natural law. To the extent that this is achieved the law will commend itself to good men everywhere.

The Need for Written Law

But why, it might be asked, is written law even necessary if, as you say, the natural law is known to all? I would answer as follows: Written law is necessary for two reasons. It is necessary, first, because although the natural law is *knowable* by all men, it is not equally *known* to all because not all men have the interest or the patience or the time to attend to it. The patient consideration of the dictates of natural law, the conceptualization of the truly good society, requires a concentrated effort for which few men have either the leisure or the sustained interest. Written law is necessary, therefore, in order that men may nonetheless be taught to live according to the precepts of the natural law.

Written law is necessary, secondly, in order to counterbalance the tendency of each individual to make an exception in his own case whenever the requirements of natural law come into conflict with his own self-interest. It is one thing to acknowledge what justice requires in a certain situation; it is quite another thing to be willing to do what justice requires when it happens not to be consistent with what I perceive to be my own self-interest. I may agree, for example, that citizens ought to pay taxes in proportion to their ability, but I may selfishly desire that an exception be made in my own case because I would rather use that money to purchase something for myself. The written law, therefore, not only prescribes in detail how much a person in my circumstances must pay, but it prescribes penalties for nonpayment that are sufficiently severe so that it becomes in my self-interest to do what the law requires. The natural law tells me, in general, what I ought to do; the written law, through its system of penalties, makes reasonably sure that I will do what the natural law requires.

In a world of perfectly reasonable and perfectly good men, no written law would be required. In such a world all men would know the natural law and would willingly do what it requires. But we must deal with the world as it is, and in this world we have to accept the fact that men are neither perfectly reasonable nor perfectly good. Hence there is a need for written law notwithstanding the fact that the natural law is knowable by all.

STUDY QUESTIONS

1. List the three propositions that Natural Law Theorist (NLT) says constitute the theory he is attempting to defend. Restate them in such a way as to demonstrate that you understand them.
2. Judging by the examples given in this chapter, what do you take to be the defining characteristics of a "natural law"? Can you produce additional examples that fit the definition?
3. "Were it not for the natural law written in the heart of man, men would be without any moral basis for opposing tyranny." Attack or defend this statement.
4. What arguments does NLT use to support his theory? What is your opinion as to the soundness of each?
5. Objection: If the natural law is "written on the hearts" of all men, there should be no need for written law. What is NLT's answer to this?

8

THE SOCIAL CONTRACT

It seems to me that Natural Law Theorist (hereafter NLT) has not provided a satisfactory answer to the question with which we are dealing—the question, What is the justification for society's exercise of authority over its citizens? NLT's answer is that the laws through which society exercises this authority have the force of law insofar as they embody the principles of natural law, and that government is a kind of "surrogate for nature" in enforcing these laws. This view is then supported by a series of arguments, and NLT concludes by explaining why (according to his view) written law is necessary in spite of the fact that the natural law is theoretically knowable by all.

I say that this is not a satisfactory answer, and I want to prepare the way for what I am convinced is a better answer by showing what is wrong with NLT's position. I shall then go on to expound what I believe to be the correct solution to this problem, namely, the social contract theory.

Critique of the Natural Law Theory

The crux of the difficulty with the natural law theory is this: even if it be granted that there is a natural law knowable by all men and that the mandates of written law derive their authority from natural law, the question as to why some individuals should have the right to enforce compliance with the law upon some other individuals remains unanswered. NLT, so far as I can see, has provided no answer to this objection. From the fact that some particular written law embodies the relevant principles of natural law he simply assumes that whoever enforces that law upon his fellow men has the right to do so. But this surely will not do. The question is not, Ought all men to obey the natural law? The question is, By what right does any group of men have the authority to compel other men to act or refrain from acting in some particular way? Let it be granted that you and I and all men ought to obey the natural law. Whence comes the authority of policemen and judges and juries to compel us to such obedience? Why is it not rather the case that each of us is responsible for his own behavior?

Consider, for example, the matter of penalties. They are necessary, NLT tells us, in order to counterbalance the tendency of man to act in his own self-interest even when he knows that such action is contrary to the requirements of natural law. I agree. But where does the legislator get the right to impose such penalties? They are invented by the legislator on the assumption that he has the right to force compliance with the law. Whence comes this right? NLT has no answer.

It is interesting to note that NLT's arguments in support of his position are really only arguments in support of the proposition that there is a natural law. NLT is guilty of a *non sequitur*. From the arguments put forward by him it does indeed follow that there is a natural law, but it does not follow that anyone in particular has the right to enforce that law upon his fellow men. The fundamental question with which we are dealing remains to be answered.

The State of Nature

Let us imagine, now, a state of affairs in which no man or group of men has assumed or been delegated the authority to enforce the natural law upon his fellow men. Each individual man, then, is responsible for his own behavior according to the natural law as he understands it. If he breaks the natural law, he is answerable only to his own conscience—with one important exception: if his behavior results or threatens to result in injury to the person or property of some other man, that man has a right to defend himself and to demand reparation from the offender. Each man, in this state of affairs, is judge and jury in any case in which his own interest is involved, and each man must seek to enforce justice as best he can when he finds it necessary to render a judgment. Let us call this the state of nature, since it is the state in which nature places man pending some action on the part of man himself to create a different state of affairs.

What would it be like to live in this state of nature? It must be apparent in the first place that in such a state no man could be really secure, for he could never be certain that someone stronger than himself, or some combination of men whose combined power is stronger than his own, would not endanger his life and property. If there is law (natural law) but no one to enforce the law, then the situation is almost as bad as if there were no law at all. Every man, in the state of nature, is potentially at war with every other man, and life is likely to be (as Hobbes once said) "nasty, brutish, and short."

Second, men living in the state of nature could not fail to observe that justice is rarely achieved, for self-interest will cause men always to favor their own side of the matter whenever they find it necessary to resolve a dispute. If I am judge and jury in any case in which my interest is involved, I am most assuredly going to make sure (if I can) that I get at least what is coming to me, and perhaps a little more. Since my opponent will be just as careful to watch out for his private interest, we shall in all probability end up fighting, and the decision will favor not the one having the greater justice but the one who is able to muster a superior force.

The question facing mankind in the state of nature, then, is this: How shall we put an end to this war of all against all? How shall we obtain a state of affairs in which there may be security of person and where our disputes may be resolved not by force but according to the canons of justice?

The Social Contract

Government is mankind's solution to the problems inherent in the state of nature. It is as if the men of a certain region came together and agreed to delegate to some of their number the right to articulate and enforce the law—in exchange for the greater security and the increase in justice that would thereby result. Each individual in the state of nature has the right to enforce the natural law (as best he can) in any case in which his own interest is involved. It is that right that he gives over to the government when he contracts with his fellows to put an end to the state of nature. Every legitimate government is, at root, founded on such a social contract.

In saying that all government derives its authority from a certain authority originally held by individual men I am not, of course, suggesting that as a matter of historical fact all existing governments came about in just this way. We are discussing political philosophy, not governmental history. I am saying that the theoretical basis for the authority of government lies in the will of the governed to avoid the insecurity and injustice of the state of nature. Whether as a matter of historical fact such a state ever existed is not at issue, nor is it relevant to our discussion.

Every individual who accepts the benefits of government—the protection of its laws, the greater security that results from government under law—gives his tacit consent to the social contract upon which that government rests. When someone is born into a situation in which people live under law (as all of us are), then his allegiance to the government (that is, his consent to the social contract) is simply taken for granted unless he declares otherwise. If he emigrates to a foreign country he must formally swear allegiance to this new land: he must, so to speak, explicitly affirm that he wishes to become a party to the social contract that binds together the people whom he is adopting as his countrymen.

Supporting Arguments

The first argument that I would put forward in support of this theory is that it provides an inherently plausible account of why some men (those who govern) have the authority to enforce the law upon other men (those who are governed). The social contract theory, unlike the natural law theory, does not side-step the central issue in this dispute. To the question, What is the justification for society's exercise of authority over its citizens? the social contract theory replies: This authority is derived from the antecedent right of each individual to enforce the natural law in defense of his own interests. The social contract is the theoretical precondition of the authority of society, through its legally constituted government, to enforce the law equally upon all.

I would argue, secondly, that this theory is consistent with the widely-held view that the right to govern derives from the consent of the governed. The Universal Declaration of Human Rights explicitly states, as a matter of fact, that "The will of the people shall be the basis of the authority of government" and that "this will shall be expressed in periodic and genuine elections which shall be by universal and equal suffrage and shall be held by secret vote or by equivalent free voting procedures" (Article 21 [3]). Through the voting process the people are reaffirming the contract by which they are constituted a body politic and are deciding who shall exercise the authority they have delegated to the holders of various offices.

Third, the social contract theory is consistent with the general view that the responsibility of government is to resolve internal disputes, to protect from external danger, and to promote the common good. It is consistent with the views of most civilized men regarding both the *scope* and the *limits* of the authority of government.

What is the scope of government's authority according to the social contract theory? Answer: all the problems inherent in the state of nature. It must, therefore, resolve disputes between men. This it does by (a) developing a body of law clarifying the rights and duties of each individual (the legislative function), (b) enforcing those laws (the executive function), and (c) adjudicating cases in which some individual is alleged to have broken one of those laws (the judicial function). It must, further, promote the realization of true justice.

This it does by passing and enforcing laws designed to assist the poor, the weak, and the helpless to achieve a decent life in a world in which they would otherwise be overwhelmed by those stronger and more richly blessed than they.

There are, however, definite limits to the authority of government. It has only such power as has been delegated to it in order to put an end to the perpetual conflict and injustice of the state of nature. The right to enforce the natural law is given over to government by the social contract; all other rights that are man's natural heritage remain in full force and may not be abrogated by government. Hence government cannot legitimately subject him to arbitrary arrest, invade his privacy, confiscate his property, or do any of a long series of things that would constitute a breaking rather than an enforcement of the natural law.

We should not minimize the risk involved in handing over to a group of designated individuals the authority originally vested by nature in each individual. Government—any government—is a desperate solution to a desperate problem, and the risk involved is enormous. History is replete with horrible examples of men who have used the power of government for their own selfish gain and who have squandered the lives and properties of their helpless subjects in the process. Unjust laws have been decreed, senseless and immoral wars have been fought, police powers have been exercised beyond all reasonable measure, and justice has been perverted in a thousand ways. Yet men cling to the necessity for government under law and seek a world in which "liberty and justice for all" shall become a reality. Why? Because they cannot tolerate a return to the certain injustice of the state of nature. The social contract is the bargain men must make with one another if they are to live together in a world where the interests of each man are in potential conflict with those of all his fellows. Man's quest for a form of government that will make this a good bargain—his agonizing search for a government that will fulfill his longing for security and justice without itself becoming tyrannical —is one of the most poignant stories to be read in the pages of human history.

STUDY QUESTIONS

1. What is Social Contract Theorist's (SCT) main objection to the natural law theory? Is he right on this point?
2. What exactly does SCT mean by "the state of nature"? Does he seem to you to be describing an actual state of affairs that existed at some time in the past, or is the state of nature merely a logical construct?
3. What arguments does SCT use to support his theory? Do you find his arguments convincing?
4. "The social contract is the bargain men must make with one another

if they are to live together in a world where the interests of each man are in potential conflict with those of all his fellows." Does this imply that one might at some point conclude that it was a bad bargain, and revoke the contract? If so, under what circumstances?

9

SOCIAL
UTILITARIANISM

Strictly speaking, the authors of the two preceding chapters have given but one answer to the question, What is the justification for society's exercise of authority over its citizens? That answer, precisely stated, is (a) the function of government, as the agent of society, is to enforce the "natural law" and (b) the authority to do this derives from a "social contract" by which the antecedent right of each individual to enforce the natural law, whenever his own interests are at stake, is given over to the governing body. Natural Law Theorist (NLT) devotes his efforts to demonstrating that there is in fact such a thing as "natural law," which is a logical precondition of the theory; Social Contract Theorist (SCT), building further on this foundation, argues in support of the "social contract" part of the theory. I think that this theory is wrong on all major points, and I am therefore compelled to attack the main theses of both NLT and SCT.

No Natural Law

Let us consider first the assertion that there is a natural law. This, in my opinion, is nothing but a holdover from the ancient view that there is "in the mind of God" a kind of plan for the government of His creation, an "eternal law" that is "natural" insofar as it is knowable by human reason unaided by divine revelation. St. Thomas Aquinas, whom NLT quotes with approbation, defines natural law in precisely this way. St. Thomas writes:

> The whole community of the universe is governed by the divine reason. Therefore the very notion of the government of things in God, the ruler of the universe, has the nature of a law. And since the

divine reason's conception of things . . . is eternal, . . . this kind of law must be called eternal. . . .[1]

The rational creature . . . has a share of the eternal reason, whereby it has a natural inclination to its proper act and end; and this participation of the eternal law in the rational creature is called the natural law . . . It is therefore evident that the natural law is nothing else than the rational creature's participation of the eternal law.[2]

That the natural law theory is an offspring of a theological view of ancient origin is not, of course, an argument against its validity. I would argue, however, that the theory loses much of its plausibility when divorced from that context. The natural affinity of natural law theory is not with the social contract theorists of the seventeenth and eighteenth centuries, but with the divine right theorists of an earlier day. It is understandable that NLT, as a son of the twentieth century, does not endorse the divine right theory. It is even understandable that SCT, in an attempt to salvage the remnants of the medieval view, would appeal to a mythical "social contract" to fill the void left by the collapse of the view that the authority to rule is derived by appointment from the antecedent authority of God. But let us leave these historical considerations and consider the arguments by which NLT attempts to convince us that there is in fact a natural law.

NLT has argued, in the first place, that if there were no natural law there would be no criterion for distinguishing between just and unjust laws. His argument is, then, an attempted *reductio ad absurdum* of the view that there is no natural law. My answer to this is that the alleged consequence does not follow. All that is required for men to distinguish between just and unjust laws is some common agreement as to what is to count as just. The opinions of men as to what is just and what is unjust are, in fact, constantly changing. To say that the current opinions regarding justice and injustice constitute a kind of reading of an immutable "natural law" is superfluous. "Just" is a word we use to describe laws that are to our liking, "unjust" a word to describe laws we do not like. The appeal to "natural law" in support of the view that a given law is just or unjust is nothing more than an attempt to invoke the pale shadow of a vanished deity to support an opinion that we hold on other grounds.

NLT's argument about the punishment of aliens, which was originally put forward by Locke,[3] is a puzzling one, and I am not at all clear as to how the argument supports his position. In any case, I

---

[1] St. Thomas Aquinas, *Summa Theologica*, I–II, Ques. 91, Art. 1, in Anton C. Pegis (ed.), *Basic Writings of St. Thomas Aquinas* (New York: Random House, 1945), Vol. II, p. 748.

[2] *Ibid.*, Ques. 91, Art. 2, p. 750.

[3] John Locke, in Peter Laslett (ed.), *Two Treatises of Government*, 2d ed. (Cambridge, England: Cambridge University Press, 1967), pp. 290–291.

think he is simply mistaken in asserting that the legislative body in a given country has authority to legislate only with respect to the citizens of that country. A legislature's authority has, I should say, both a geographical and a citizen domain: it covers the relevant behavior of all people within a given geographical area (regardless of their citizenship) and the relevant behavior of its citizens (whether they are at home or abroad). We have yet to say how it comes by this authority, but the fact that legislatures and other governmental agencies do exercise such authority does not seem to me to support the natural law theory in any way.

NLT's third argument—that without natural law a good deal of "moral legislation" would be found to be without justification—is correct as a simple assertion, but the assertion does not in fact support the natural law theory: it rather supports the view that many laws now on the books have no justification and ought to be repealed. In short, I accept the consequence of this attempted *reductio,* but I deny that it is absurd. Laws of this type, in my opinion, are unjustified attempts to meddle in the private affairs of individuals. They are all in the same category as the notorious "blue laws" of Colonial New England, which forbade Sunday indulgence not only in drinking and dancing but even in honest work. The view that there is a theoretical justification for governmental authority does not necessarily commit one to the defense of everything that governments do and have done under the guise of legitimate authority. NLT, in my opinion, is not sufficiently sensitive to the need for defining definite limits to the authority of government over the lives of individual citizens.

There is, moreover, a decisive consideration that may be urged against the idea of natural law, namely, that there are no criteria for determining when an assertion is or is not a "part" of the natural law. NLT concludes from this that the natural law is known directly; I conclude that it is not known at all, for the very good reason that it does not exist. To decide whether a piece of proposed legislation ought to be enacted the legislator must look not to some mysterious natural law written, presumably, in heaven, but to the probable consequences of that legislation. I shall return to this point later in this essay.

No Social Contract

The idea of a social contract is no less a fiction than that of natural law. Indeed, SCT seems almost to recognize this when he tells us that he is not suggesting that "as a matter of historical fact" actual governments were created in just this way. What SCT seems to be arguing, then, is that the idea of a social contract is a *useful* fiction: it is a vivid way of stating what he considers to be the correct theory as to the origin of the authority of government. I do not wish to quarrel with his use of the concept of a "social contract" merely as a literary device—my quarrel is with the theory itself.

What the social contract theory comes down to, once isolated from the twin fictions of an imaginary "state of nature" terminated by an imaginary "social contract," is the idea that individuals have an antecedent natural right to enforce the natural law whenever their own interests are at stake and the idea that they voluntarily hand this right over to the government they create in order to secure certain benefits —greater security, justice, etc.

This theory is wrong, first of all, because it presupposes the existence of natural law, which is either nonexistent or unknowable (and probably both). It is wrong, secondly, because it presupposes the existence of "rights" prior to the enactment of any law, which is a contradiction in terms. SCT would, I think, accept the definition of a "right" given in Chapter 6: "an opportunity to act (or to refrain from acting) in some specified way, which opportunity is guaranteed by law or by the general consent of the community." He thinks he can talk about "natural rights" because he thinks the opportunities pertaining to those rights are guaranteed by natural law. But without natural law there are no natural rights, hence there is nothing for the individual to hand over to the government that he creates. Rights are created by the enactment of law, which presupposes the existence of a lawmaking agency that, according to the social contract theory, comes into being only as a result of the social contract. Without natural law, the social contract theory falls to the ground.

An Alternative Proposal

In dealing with the question of the justification of the authority of society to limit the freedom of individual citizens it is important that we be very clear about precisely what question we are asking. The question with which we are dealing is not (as my opponents appear to have assumed) equivalent to the questions, Who originally had the authority that we now see being exercised by government? How did government get this authority from those who originally held it? The authority of government, insofar as it can be justified, is justified not by its *origin* but by its *ends*. Government is a creature of society, a social institution. Like any social institution it is good insofar as it accomplishes the purposes for which it was created.

Why do men create governments? Chiefly, in my opinion, for purposes of self-protection. What every man desires is an opportunity to live his own life, to do as he pleases, without interference from anyone else—in short, to be perfectly free. The trouble is that in a world where everyone is free to do as he pleases, to pursue his own self-interest without regard for the interests of anyone else, everyone would be involved in perpetual conflict with everyone else. We need government, therefore, to protect ourselves against our fellows. In order to secure a situation in which all of us—the weak as well as the strong—shall have an opportunity to live our lives without the constant fear of attack by our fellows we need a system of rules by which each of us accepts certain restraints upon our actions on the condition that everyone else accepts those same restraints. It is the business of government to make those rules and to enforce them in such a way that it becomes in the self-interest of everyone to obey them. The exercise of governmental authority is justified insofar as it protects each individual member of society from the evils that might be inflicted on him by his fellows were they not restrained by law.

Two important corollaries of this theory should be noted. The first corollary is this: the scope of government's authority is limited to those areas in which unregulated behavior is likely to do harm to someone else. Government has no business meddling in the private affairs of men, or restraining them in any way, except as this is necessary to protect the rest of society from some probable harm. If a man wishes to drive sixty miles an hour through a heavily populated area, government has a right to restrain him; if he wishes to wear his hair at shoulder length, that is his own private business—however much the majority may disapprove.

The second corollary is this: no particular type of government is a priori better than any other type. In one situation it may be the case that a monarchical type is best; in another it may be that a democracy is best; and in yet another it may be that a military dictatorship is most effective. The "best" type in each case is defined as the type that is most effective in accomplishing the purpose for which government exists, that is, the protection of the members of society from the harm that would result if everyone were permitted to do as he pleases.

Supporting Arguments

In support of this position, which I shall call *social utilitarianism,* I would argue first that it justifies the exercise of governmental authority in the only way that any social institution can be justified, namely, by reference to its consequences. How do we judge whether an educational system is good? Clearly, we judge it by its consequences: we observe the quality of its graduates. How do we judge the practice of medicine? By the consequences: we observe the degree of success physicians have in restoring to health those who are ill. So with government: its "justification" lies in its consequences, in the degree to which every citizen is able to pursue his own interests insofar as those interests do not impose harm on others.

I would suggest, secondly, that this defense of the authority of government is exactly consistent with the way in which individual pieces of proposed legislation are justified by their supporters. It is absurd to suggest that legislators "look to the natural law" in trying to decide whether a given piece of proposed legislation ought to be enacted. Legislators should not waste their time gazing into the empty lawbook of nature—nor do they. They should, and do, attempt to assess the probable consequences of the law they are proposing to enact. All argument about the wisdom or unwisdom of a proposed law is concerned with its probable consequences. And that is exactly what we should expect given the account of the authority of government I am here proposing.

Lastly, the utilitarian account of the authority of government provides a usable criterion for determining when government is and when it is not exercising its authority in a defensible way. When the intent of legislation is to eliminate some actual or potential evil, the exercise of governmental authority is justified. When, however, the intent of legislation is to impose on an unwilling minority the private tastes or wishes of the majority, or even of the lawmakers themselves, the exercise of the power of government has no justification whatsoever. Insofar as the behavior of a man, however unconventional or unusual it may be, imposes no harm on others, government has no legitimate reason to interfere. The "rights" of the individual, properly understood, mean just this: the presumed freedom of every man to do as he pleases insofar as his actions do not inflict harm on others. Government preserves such rights not by passing laws, but by refraining from passing laws in areas where it has no legitimate authority.

STUDY QUESTIONS

1. "All that is required for men to distinguish between just and unjust laws is some common agreement as to what is to count as just." Is this correct? Defend your answer.
2. Why, according to Social Utilitarian (SU), is it a contradiction in terms to assert that men have rights prior to the enactment of any law?
3. What does SU say is the scope of the authority of government? Do you agree?
4. What arguments does SU offer in support of his theory about the authority of government? Do you find these arguments convincing?

10

THEORETICAL ANARCHISM

I want to distinguish the position that I represent—theoretical anarchism—from two other positions with which it is easily confused. First, theoretical anarchism should not be confused with *militant anarchism*. Militant anarchism is not so much a theory as a political posture: to be a militant anarchist is to be committed to the overthrow of existing government without regard to the practical consequences and with no intention of supporting some new government that might be established in its place. A militant anarchist may admit, for example, that in the absence of all government there would be widespread chaos, but he would say, "Nonetheless, I prefer that situation to the present one in which all of these bureaucrats presume to tell me what I can and cannot do. I am willing to live in the midst of chaos in order to be truly free." That is not the position I represent.

Second, theoretical anarchism should be distinguished from what I shall call *naïve anarchism,* that is, the view that society would in fact be better off if there were no established governmental authority. Naïve anarchism holds that in the absence of governmental authority chaos would not result, but on the contrary there would be a greater realization of both freedom and order than there is under any form of government. Naïve anarchism holds an extremely optimistic view of man, for it holds that in a society without governmental authority men would in fact limit their own desires in such a way that they would not be in perpetual conflict with one another. I do not share this optimistic view of man, and as a consequence I cannot accept this theory.

Theoretical anarchism, which I do hold, is simply the view that there is no theoretical justification for the authority of government. To the question, What is the justification for society's exercise of authority over its citizens? theoretical anarchism replies: There is none. Society may exercise such authority as a matter of practical necessity, but it has no theoretical right to do so. This is the position that I shall now attempt to establish.

I cannot, of course, be expected to bring forward affirmative arguments in support of my position. Theoretical anarchism is not a theory about the justification of the authority of government: it is rather the dilemma in which you find yourself when you discover that none of the theories really answer the question. The only arguments available in support of theoretical anarchism are the arguments demonstrating the inadequacy of all attempts to justify governmental authority.

Social Utilitarianism

I am almost inclined to argue that Social Utilitarian (SU) is on my side in this dispute, since he does not in fact offer a theoretical justification for governmental authority. What he offers instead is a *practical* justification: governmental authority is desirable, he tells us, because it is a necessary means to the desirable end of protecting society from the evils that would result if everyone were free to do as he pleases. And since it seems clear to anyone except a naïve anarchist that society would be in even more serious trouble than it is were it not for the restraining hand of government, SU appears to win an easy victory without even entering into the intellectual puzzles that seem to me to be so insoluble.

Let me say forthrightly that in my opinion SU has not offered a wrong answer to the question with which we are dealing: he has simply offered an answer to a different question. The question to which NLT and SCT addressed themselves—the question to which I wish I could find an answer but cannot—is this: *By what right* do some men (governors, legislators, policemen, judges, etc.) exercise coercive authority over the rest of society? I know as well as SU that certain goods are achieved through the agency of governmental authority. Indeed, NLT and SCT are equally clear about this. But the question still remains: Where does government get the authority to do what needs to be done in order to secure these goods? How is authority constituted in a world in which nature appears originally to have made us political equals? To this question SU gives us no answer at all.

The Social Contract Theory

The social contract theory at least has the merit of being an honest theoretical effort to solve the theoretical problem with which we are dealing. In many ways it is a very attractive theory. Indeed, I think the theory can be stated in a more persuasive form than SCT has stated it and in a way, moreover, that completely escapes SU's criticisms of the theory as stated by SCT. I want to present this restatement, because I think it offers the best hope we have of finding a solution to this vexing problem. I shall then state my own reasons for rejecting the theory even in this purified form, as a consequence of which I find myself compelled to be an "agnostic" in political philosophy—a theoretical anarchist.

The form of the social contract theory that I have in mind is this: Quite apart from any theory about natural law, which SU quite rightly criticizes, it seems evident that in the absence of any civil authority each individual would have no choice but to defend himself against the possible aggressive behavior of his fellow men. We could imagine, then, a group of men in this "natural condition" getting together and saying, "Let's put an end to all this fighting among ourselves. Let's draw up some rules—we'll call them 'laws'—and let's appoint somebody to make sure that we all behave the way the laws say we should." This, I am saying, would be a kind of social contract—without the cumbersome doctrine of natural law that renders the whole theory suspect. Each subsequent individual, as in SCT's account, tacitly enters into the contract by accepting the benefits that are secured by government. No natural law, no natural rights, nothing but a "deal" made by a group of human beings who mutually agree to stop making war so that they can get on with other, more interesting, pursuits. Doesn't this give us the justification we have been seeking? Unfortunately, no. Let me explain why.

First, it assumes the explicit assent of each and every individual who is to be subject to the authority thus created—an impossible condition to realize in actuality. If some individual says, "I choose not to enter into the contract; I prefer to do as I please and defend myself as necessary," he is precisely the individual who would be singled out (if he does what he says) for punishment under the law. If the whole human population consisted of only ten men, it would require the consent of all ten to establish the state. If one dissents, the question remains: *By what right* do the other nine presume to coerce him against his will? A cynical answer suggests itself: not by right but by power.

There is a second difficulty. Suppose that, after a time, one of the original parties to the agreement decides that it was a bad bargain and announces that he is pulling out. What is to prevent him from doing this? Must we say that his original decision to enter into the contract is irrevocable? That is not convincing. If he entered into the contract on grounds of self-interest, then on those same grounds he should be able to terminate it. But this means, in actuality, that any individual who considers that his self-interest would be best served by breaking the law should be free to do so—and by so doing to terminate his participation in the social contract—in which case the civil authorities would cease to have any right to take action against him. You see the dilemma: the social contract establishes the authority of government *except when it is really needed.* In precisely the cases where it would like to exercise legitimate authority, all it has is naked power.

Then there is the problem of the second and subsequent generations, who *ex hypothesi* were not original parties to the contract but are, so to speak, born into it by virtue of being descendants of the original covenanters. Their theoretical case is even stronger than that of the founding father who decides he wants to terminate the contract since they have never explicitly assented to the bargain and cannot with any degree of plausibility be said to have made an "irrevocable" commitment. By what right does the government established by their parents presume to govern them? Why should they obey a government in whose founding they had no part and to whose authority they have never explicitly assented?

The social contract theory justifies the authority of government only insofar as the governed consent to that authority. Those among the governed who do not consent to that authority are, so far as the theory is concerned, merely the victims of superior power. It may be prudent for them to do what the law requires, but the *right* of government to restrict their freedom has in no way been established.

The Power of Government

The truth of the matter seems to me to be this. Wherever the human species has appeared, some men have succeeded in gaining the power to compel obedience, to rule. Their wishes have been the law, their decisions the decrees of justice, their arms the means of enforcing obedience. They have been obeyed not because they had any right to be, but simply because they had the power to compel it. What men call "the duty of obedience" to one who exercises "legitimate authority" is nothing but the habit of bowing to the superior power of one who has assumed the role of ruler. The ruler may, in time, be compelled to share his power with some other powerful individuals (resulting in an oligarchy), or even with the people themselves (producing some form of democracy); yet the power of government, by whomever it is exercised, remains what it was in the beginning: naked power. The difference between a judge and the leader of a band of thieves is just this: the judge has more constituents.

I do not conclude from this that government is in general a bad thing, or that society would be better off in the absence of government. I think those theorists are right who say that in the absence of government the aggressive and acquisitive tendencies of men would create a situation of danger and chaos—a "state of nature" as SCT calls it—in which none of us would willingly choose to live. Even bad government is better than no government at all. The practical challenge, as I see it, is to achieve the security and order that we expect our civil authority to provide without creating a monster that seeks to dominate every aspect of our lives. Having said this, however, I do not pretend that I have solved the theoretical problem of the rationale for the authority of government. That problem, in my opinion, has no solution. The authority of government has no higher sanction than the will of some to impose upon all some particular kind of order. If we accede to such authority, as most of us do, it is not because we think its claim to legitimacy has been established. It is simply because as a practical matter we acknowledge the need for civil authority in a society that consists of people like us.

STUDY QUESTIONS

1. Theoretical Anarchist (TA) distinguishes three types of anarchism. Are the distinctions clear? Is it logically possible to be both a theoretical anarchist and a militant anarchist? both a theoretical anarchist and a naïve anarchist? Explain.
2. "SU has not offered a wrong answer to the question with which we are dealing: he has simply offered an answer to a different question." Is this correct?
3. How does TA's formulation of the social contract theory differ from that contained in Chapter 8?
4. Summarize TA's objections to the social contract theory. Do they seem to you to be convincing? Can you defend the theory against these objections?

FOR FURTHER READING

Aquinas, St. Thomas. *Summa Theologica* II–I, Questions 90–97. See Pegis, Anton C. (ed.), *Basic Writings of St. Thomas Aquinas*. New York: Random House, 1945, pp. 742–805. (The opening chapters of St. Thomas' famous Treatise on Law.)

Aristotle. *Politics.* Many editions. See especially Book VII.

Barry, Brian. *Political Argument.* New York: Humanities Press, 1965.

Bosanquet, Bernard. *Philosophical Theory of the State.* London: Macmillan, 1920.

Crocker, L. G. *Rousseau's Social Contract.* Cleveland: Cleveland Press of Case Western Reserve University, 1968.

d'Entreves, A. P. *Natural Law.* London: Hutchinson, 1951.

Fuller, Lon L. *The Morality of Law.* New Haven: Yale University Press, 1964. Deals with the status of law and its relation to moral rules.

Gierke, Otto. *Natural Law and the Theory of Society.* New York: Cambridge University Press, 1934.

Gilson, Etienne. *Medieval Universalism and Its Present Value.* New York: Sheed and Ward, 1937.

Gough, J. W. *The Social Contract,* 2nd ed. Oxford: Clarendon Press, 1957.

Hart, H. L. A. *The Concept of Law.* New York: Oxford University Press, 1961.

———. *Law, Liberty and Morality.* New York: Random House, 1963. Three lectures regarding "the proper scope of criminal law."

Hobbes, Thomas. *Leviathan.* Many editions. Originally published in 1651. See especially Part One, Chapters 13–15.

Hutchins, Robert M. *et al. Natural Law and Modern Society.* Cleveland: World, 1963.

Locke, John. *Two Treatises of Government.* Many editions.

McPherson, Thomas. *Political Obligation.* London: Routledge and Kegan Paul, 1967. Reviews and criticizes several theories as to the basis for civil authority.

Maritain, Jacques. *The Rights of Man and Natural Law.* New York: Scribner, 1945.

Mill, John Stuart. *On Liberty.* Many editions. Originally published in 1859. See especially Chapters 1 and 2.

Montesquieu, Charles de. *Spirit of the Laws,* tr. by Thomas Nugent. New York: Hafner Publishing Co., 1949.

Negley, Glenn. *Political Authority and Moral Judgment.* Durham, N.C.: Duke University Press, 1965. Critique of several theories regarding the basis of civil authority.

Popper, Karl R. *The Open Society and Its Enemies.* Princeton: Princeton University Press, 1950.

Rousseau, Jean-Jacques. *The Social Contract.* Many editions. Originally published in 1762.

Russell, Bertrand. *Authority and the Individual.* New York: Simon and Schuster, 1949.

Wild, John. *Plato's Modern Enemies and the Theory of Natural Law.* Chicago: University of Chicago Press, 1953.

PART III

MAN'S HIGHEST GOOD

11

THE STRUCTURE
OF ETHICAL THINKING

Whatever may be the form of government under which a man lives, and whatever may be his views regarding the justification of the authority of government, he cannot but be aware of the fact that much of his behavior and the behavior of his fellows is constantly being appraised in moral terms. Some behavior is appraised positively: an act is said to be good, or noble, or generous, or right. And some behavior is appraised negatively: an act is said to be evil, or vile, or selfish, or wrong. Indeed, not only acts but men themselves are sometimes judged in moral terms: this man is said to be good, kind, humane, virtuous; that man is said to be evil, bestial, inhumane, corrupt. Just as man cannot escape involvement in a political community, so also he cannot escape involvement in a moral community. His life and behavior are enveloped by what we may call "the moral sphere."

The Moral Sphere

What are the marks of that peculiar kind of behavior or activity that we regard as being appropriately subject to moral appraisal? What are the defining characteristics of the moral sphere?

It is apparent that we appraise only *human* behavior in this way. Nothing that ever happened on the moon (so far as we know) was subject to moral appraisal until man stepped upon it—but had one of our moon-walkers done something to harm his fellow astronaut (for example, had he unplugged his life support system), that act would have been denounced as evil, as morally wrong. Again, we do not apply terms of moral appraisal to the behavior of animals or insects. We do not criticize the mating practices of antelopes, or the predatory habits of leopards, or the "slave" systems of ants or bees. Only human beings and their behavior are called good or bad, right or wrong, virtuous or vicious.

It is not all human behavior, however, that we appraise in this way. It is only human behavior in situations involving *choice* that we regard as appropriately subject to moral judgments. We assume, when we ascribe praise or blame to a piece of human behavior, that other alternatives were available to the person whose behavior is being judged. We neither praise nor blame a man for doing something if we believe that, under the circumstances, it was the only thing he could do.

However, not even all human behavior in situations involving choice belongs to the moral sphere. Under ordinary circumstances, for example, it seems clear that my decision to have juice and cereal for breakfast rather than eggs and toast has no moral significance. (Of course, we can imagine a set of unusual circumstances in which this choice would have moral significance—if, for example, I and another person were both on the verge of starvation, a single serving of each was available, and he was seriously allergic to eggs whereas I was not.) The third defining characteristic of the moral sphere is, then, that some *moral rule or principle* is relevant to the behavior in question: there is something that a human being in that situation ought or ought not to do, some choice that he ought or ought not to make, simply by virtue of the fact that he is a human being in those particular circumstances. It would be morally wrong for me to contribute knowingly to the demise of my allergic friend by eating the cereal that could sustain his life when another alternative is available to me. Why? Because I have a moral obligation to preserve human life when I have the opportunity to do so. The generalized version of this idea— that one ought to preserve human life when one has the opportunity— is an example of a moral rule or principle.

Normative Ethics

All of us, then, act in ways that are or may be subject to moral appraisal, and all of us make moral judgments about the behavior of others.

In clear-cut cases we make these judgments without difficulty: we praise the courageous act of a man who risks his life to prevent a homicide, or of a mother who rushes into flames to rescue a child. In such cases we judge almost instinctively, as if there were no reasoning involved.

In other cases, however, our moral judgments are more problematic. Is "mercy killing" ever morally defensible, and if so under what circumstances? Is conscientious objection morally superior to being a soldier? Are some wars morally defensible and others not? Was it or was it not morally right for the United States to drop atomic bombs on Hiroshima and Nagasaki? In such cases we tend to be less certain about our answers, and we often disagree with one another in the answers we give. And when we disagree, we try to resolve our disagreement by appealing to relevant general principles of right and wrong and by showing that the position we hold is consistent with those principles.

Normative ethics is an attempt to answer the question, What sorts of things really are right and wrong, and why? The aim of the ethical theorist is to introduce order and consistency into our ethical beliefs and to relate them, if possible, to some universal principle or principles from which they supposedly derive their validity as rules for the guidance of our behavior. If I ought to help old Mrs. Jones cross a busy intersection when I see her standing there, it must be because there is some rule or principle that prescribes what I ought to do and in terms of which I am appropriately praised or blamed for what I do or fail to do. And if I also ought to attempt to rescue a child who is drowning, the same reasoning applies. The ethical theorist asks, What is it that these two cases, and hundreds of others that might be mentioned, have in common? Is there not some general principle that governs these and all other cases of moral obligation? To ask, and attempt to answer, such questions is to engage in the peculiar sort of inquiry called normative ethics; to exhibit a set of ethical beliefs as a coherent system deducible from one or more general principles is to construct an ethical system.

Two Types of Ethical Thought

The efforts of philosophers to introduce order and consistency into our thinking about the moral sphere have resulted in two general types of ethical systems.

The first type may be termed *teleological*. The moral value of any act, according to this type of theory, consists in the tendency it has (or is intended to have) to produce a good or bad result. Some things are intrinsically good, and other things are good or bad depending on their tendency to promote or to hinder that which is intrinsically good. If health is considered intrinsically good, for example, then the praiseworthy character of certain acts (giving food to the hungry, medical care to the ill, etc.) and the blameworthy character of other acts (knowingly selling or serving contaminated food) can be understood in terms of their relation to this good. Everything that is morally praiseworthy, according to this type of theory, is so because of its tendency to realize that which is intrinsically good: the intrinsically good is the end or goal (*telos*) at which all behavior having moral value is aimed. We shall return to a further consideration of this type of ethical system shortly.

Not all ethical theorists are convinced, however, that the whole of the moral sphere can be understood in terms of the relation of various acts to whatever may be said to be intrinsically good. Some acts, say these theorists, are obligatory in themselves—quite apart from any tendency they may have to produce an intrinsically good result. It may be argued, for example, that a person has the moral obligation under virtually any set of conceivable circumstances to tell the truth or to keep a promise, whether or not he believes that by so doing he will promote the realization of the intrinsically good. Some acts are "morally right" in and of themselves; they are not right merely by virtue of their tendency to realize some other good. Ethical systems that attempt to understand the moral sphere along these lines are variously termed *formalist* or *deontological* theories.

The Summum Bonum

Among philosophers who have attempted to understand the moral sphere in teleological terms, a much-discussed question has been: What is man's *summum bonum*—man's highest good? Some of man's "goods" are obviously good solely because of their instrumental value. Medicine, for example, is good only because of its value in producing health. Very well, let us then consider health. Why is it good? If we say that health is good because it is a precondition to being able to engage in enjoyable activity, then it, too, is an instrumental good (though it may also be an intrinsic good). Well then, why is enjoyable activity good? Is it instrumentally good in that it contributes to the realization of some higher good? If so, where does this process come to an end? What is man's "highest" good? What is the one good that (a) is worthy of being desired in and of itself; (b) is not instrumentally good; and (c) is the cause of the goodness of other things insofar as they contribute to its realization?

Note that our question is an "open-ended" question. It is logically possible to answer this question in an infinite number of ways, though few of the answers would be likely to appear plausible. Let us look briefly at some of the answers that have appeared sufficiently plausible to win the support of at least some philosophers.

Some Possible Answers

It can be plausibly argued that *pleasure* is man's highest good, indeed that it is the only thing that is good in and of itself. This view is called *hedonism* (from the Greek *hedone*, meaning "pleasure"). One of its earliest and best-known advocates was the Greek philosopher Epicurus (341–270 B.C.), who wrote:

> We recognize pleasure as the first good innate in us, and from pleasure we begin every act of choice and avoidance, and to pleasure we return again, using the feeling as the standard by which we judge the good.[1]

Some critics of hedonism contend that such a view treats man as if he were a lower animal, a merely sensuous being. The truth is, they say, that man's uniqueness consists in the fact that he is a rational being. *Man's* highest good, therefore, is not pleasure—which may indeed be the highest good of a pig or a dog—but *activity according to reason.* This view we shall call *rational eudemonism* (from the Greek *eudaimonia,* meaning "happiness"). It was first advocated by Aristotle (384–322 B.C.), the great Greek philosopher and tutor of Alexander the Great.

Some ethical theorists who have addressed themselves to this problem have concluded that there is no one thing that is man's highest good, but that several things are worthy of being desired for their own sakes. Man's highest good, therefore, consists in realizing as many of these intrinsic goods as he can. This view, also advocated by a number of philosophers, we shall call *ethical pluralism.*

It has been argued, finally, that all of the foregoing views presuppose that man is a merely temporal being. But this, say some philosophers, is not the case: man has a destiny that transcends this world; his highest good consists not in any temporal attainment but in *eternal blessedness.* This view, which has no generally accepted technical name, has been advocated by many philosopher-theologians including St. Augustine (A.D. 354–430) and St. Thomas Aquinas (A.D. 1225–1274).

Although these four are the answers that have been given most frequently to the question we are now considering, it is obvious that they by no means exhaust the possibilities. We shall, however, limit our consideration to these four, beginning with a consideration of some of the arguments that may be adduced in support of hedonism.

STUDY QUESTIONS

1. What are suggested in this chapter as the defining characteristics of the moral sphere? Do you agree with this definition? Can you think of an example of human behavior that you would regard as being appropriately subject to praise or blame that does not fall within the moral sphere as so defined? Can you think of any example of behavior

---

[1] Epicurus, "Letter to Menoeceus," in Whitney J. Oates (ed.), *The Stoic and Epicurean Philosophers* (New York: Random House, 1940), pp. 31–32.

that fits this definition, but which you would exclude from the moral sphere?
2. What is normative ethics?
3. What precisely is the difference between teleological ethics and deontological (or formalist) ethics?
4. Precisely what are you asking when you ask the question, What is man's highest good? Rephrase the question in a way that you think exhibits more clearly the point of the question.
5. Can you think of any plausible answers to the question "What is man's highest good?" in addition to those suggested in this chapter?

12

THE CASE
FOR HEDONISM

The advocates of hedonism have always had to contend with the very peculiar problem that their critics have rather consistently exhibited a kind of perverse determination to misunderstand and misrepresent what they are trying to say. The reason for this, I suppose, is that there is a simple-minded line of reasoning that seems to lead from the assertion, "Pleasure is man's highest good," to the assertion, "The highest rule of morality is: enjoy yourself!" Since it seems obvious to everyone (including hedonists) that the injunction to enjoy oneself is not a very promising starting-point for ethics, it is lightly concluded that the fundamental axiom of hedonism—that pleasure is man's highest good—is mistaken.

In order to rid our consideration of hedonism of this spurious reasoning, I propose that we begin our deliberation at a somewhat different point. Let us suppose that you and I are engaged by a very wealthy man to look after the raising of his children. His instructions to us are as follows: "The care of my children is entirely in your hands. You are to spare no effort and no expense to assist them in every possible way to achieve the very best life of which they are capable. Everything that would be for their good you are to provide; everything that would be for their evil you are, so far as possible, to omit from their experience. I leave it to you to judge what would truly be for their good and what would not."

Now, we have some very important decisions to make. We must decide what really is good—indeed, what really is best—for our charges. On what principle shall we decide? I say on the pleasure principle and would like to persuade you to agree with me.

The Pleasure Principle

When I assert that pleasure is man's highest good I am *not* asserting that sensuous gratification is man's highest good. Man is not a pig. Man's highest good consists in the optimum realization of the pleasures of which *man* is capable. Man is capable, to be sure, of pleasures of sensation, and such pleasure is most certainly to be preferred to pain. But man is capable also of what may be termed the "higher" pleasures. He is capable, for example, of experiencing intellectual pleasure, by virtue of which knowledge is a great human good. He is capable of experiencing pleasures of feeling and imagination, by virtue of which he perceives poetry, music, painting, and the other products of the visual and performing arts as goods. He is capable of experiencing pleasure in the very act of serving a human need, by virtue of which the moral sentiments acquire for him an intrinsic value all their own. Man's highest good is *human* pleasure. What is pleasurable for man, and therefore good for man, is different from what would be pleasurable for a creature with more limited capacities.

Pleasure is an experience, a state of being, that occurs whenever an awakened desire is satisfied. There is pleasure in eating food when you are hungry and in drinking a glass of cold water when you are thirsty. There is pleasure also in beholding a beautiful sunset when inspired by a love of beauty and in mastering a theorem when stimulated by a hunger for knowledge. Any good thing that you or I can do for any other human being will be, must be, a contribution to his pleasurable experience. To say that an act of such and such a kind is morally good or right is to say that it is the sort of act that on the whole tends to enhance human pleasure.

You see, then, how very far we hedonists are from asserting that the first principle of ethics is, "Enjoy yourself!" Such a principle cannot be derived from anything I have said and is in fact as repugnant to me (as a moral principle) as to any other ethical theorist. Two questions need to be clearly distinguished. The first question is, What is man's highest good? I have replied that pleasure (as defined above) is man's highest good. A second and very different question is, About whose good ought I, as a moral agent, to be concerned? To this second question I would reply that I ought to be concerned about the good (the pleasure) of all men, myself included. To be concerned exclusively about my own good (my own pleasure) would be sheer selfishness and would be deserving of moral disapproval. To be as concerned about the good (the pleasure) of others as about my own is the essence of morality and is summed up in the admonitions, "Do unto others as you would that others do unto you" and "Love your neighbor as yourself."

Supporting Arguments

The assertion that pleasure is man's highest good is not capable of strict and conclusive proof. It can, however, be supported by two probable arguments.

To say that something is man's highest good is to say that it is worthy of being desired for its own sake, that it is intrinsically desirable. That pleasure is intrinsically desirable is rendered highly probable, it seems to me, by the fact that it is universally desired. You demonstrate that something is visible by showing that people actually see it. You demonstrate that something is audible by showing that people actually hear it. In like manner, I would suggest, the desirability of pleasure is evident from the fact that people actually desire it.

This argument is weakened not at all by examples that may be brought forward of individuals who have freely subjected themselves to experiences that they fully expected to be more or less painful. Consider, for example, a father who permits one of his kidneys to be transplanted into the body of his daughter, whose kidneys had been removed because of disease. Does this man thereby demonstrate that he prefers pain to pleasure? Surely not. He demonstrates only that he is willing to suffer pain himself in order that his child may have an opportunity to experience the pleasures of a normal life. His pain is chosen not for its own sake, but for the sake of the pleasure he might give to someone he loves. Every instance of pain freely accepted of which I can think can be understood in the same way: as a means to the enhancement of some human pleasure that is valued for its own sake.

Second, the assertion that pleasure is man's highest good is broadly supported by the fact that it renders intelligible, "makes sense of," the moral rules and principles by which most men agree we ought to try to live. Why is it morally wrong to steal? Because human pleasure is enhanced when men respect each other's property rights. Why is it morally wrong to lie? Because life proceeds more serenely, more happily, when men can be counted on to tell the truth. Why is it virtuous to feed the hungry, to visit the sick, to comfort the bereaved, to aid the destitute? Because in doing these things we are assuaging human pain and enhancing human pleasure. Hedonism, then, only makes explicit the principle that has unconsciously guided the conscience of mankind through the thousands of years in which the moral code by which most civilized men live has been developing. The explicit assertion of this principle makes possible the further development of the moral code as society moves rapidly into a new era in which the rules of the past may prove to be insufficient to guide us in facing new problems.

Qualities of Pleasure

Let us now return to the point where we began: the task of providing for the children of our wealthy employer "everything that would be for their good" and shielding them from "everything that would be for their evil." How shall we proceed? What pleasures shall we teach them to enjoy? What pains shall we seek to eliminate from their experience?

We shall, of course, provide adequately for their physical needs: food, shelter, clothing, and the like. We shall let them feel the warmth of the sun on a summer day and the refreshing coolness of a stream when they are old enough to swim. We shall employ the best medical knowledge available to protect them from disease and to heal them when sick.

But clearly, if we are to provide "everything that would be for their good" we must do much more than this. We must awaken in them the higher faculties, the uniquely human desires, in order that they may experience the sublimer pleasures that man alone, so far as we know, is capable of enjoying. Therefore, we shall attempt to awaken their thirst for knowledge, to make them curious about themselves, their world, and their fellows. Then we can guide them toward the discovery of answers to the questions they are asking in order that they may experience the incomparable pleasure of learning.

We shall also attempt to awaken in our young charges a love for beauty, in order that they may experience the sublime pleasures of art, music, sculpture, and nature itself. We shall expose them to mountains and oceans and sunsets, to the paintings of the masters, to the mighty symphonies of Beethoven and the exquisite music of Mozart, to architectural creations of exceptional beauty, to opera, cinema, and dance. We shall cultivate in them a taste for beauty in shape and form and movement, an aesthetic sense that will provide them with immeasurable pleasure throughout life.

We shall, finally, attempt to awaken in them a moral sense, a natural preference for good and an abhorrence of evil. We shall teach them to desire the pleasure of all men, indeed of all sentient creatures, and shall attempt to inculcate in them that natural kindness and generosity of spirit that is the essence of virtue. We shall not, certainly, seek to make of them either ascetics or grim moralists, but we shall teach them to value the pleasurable experience of every creature, and especially of every human being; and we shall teach them when the occasion demands it to forego some pleasure themselves in order that some greater or rarer pleasure may be experienced by others.

"That all sounds very lovely," someone may say, "but let me ask a very practical question. If pleasure is man's highest good, why not maximize the *quantity* of pleasure for your young charges and stop worrying about the *quality*? If money were man's highest good, it would make no difference whether he got it in fives, tens, or hundreds; only the total quantity would be relevant. Why not with pleasure?"

To this question I would reply as follows: no man would be willing to exchange his higher faculties—his capacity to experience intellectual and aesthetic and moral pleasure—for any quantity whatsoever of merely sensual pleasure. Promise a man every variety of sensual pleasure, in any quantity imaginable, on the condition that he cease to be a man and become a lower animal, and he will refuse it. Why? Because in fact men do value some pleasures above others and are on occasion willing to endure a fair amount of physical discomfort for the sake of securing some of the higher pleasures. All pleasure, *qua* pleasure, is good and worthy of being desired; but in the judgment of those who have experienced a wide spectrum of pleasures (and they alone are competent to judge), some forms of pleasure are more valuable, more worthy of being desired, than others.

Our problem as tutors, then, is not merely to maximize the quantity of pleasure for our charges, but to orchestrate the variety of pleasures in such a way as to guide them toward a truly satisfying life. This, admittedly, is no easy task, for there is danger of imbalance in many directions. We do not want them to become sensualists, or esthetes, or arid intellectualists, or rigid moralists: we want them to become well-rounded men, sensitively balancing the various forms of pleasure in their own experience and seeking to further a similar balance in the lives of others.

Let me conclude by underscoring the point with which I began: the greatest problem that we hedonists have to face is that our position is so often misrepresented in such a way as to make it into something that no man with any sense of human dignity would espouse. This is usually done by defining pleasure in purely sensual terms and then suggesting that each individual should be concerned only about *his own* pleasure (so defined). But this, I repeat, is a gross parody of hedonism. Hedonism is indeed the view that pleasure is the greatest human good. But hedonists affirm that what is pleasurable for man is different from what is pleasurable for a lower animal, for man is capable of enjoying a rich variety of pleasures. If moral virtue consists in desiring what is good for all men and doing what will tend to achieve it, then from a hedonist's point of view a moral agent must desire and work for human pleasure in all its various forms.

STUDY QUESTIONS

1. What exactly is pleasure? Write your own definition, then compare this with the definition in a dictionary.

2. "Any good thing that you or I can do for any other human being will be, must be, a contribution to his pleasurable experience." Do you agree? If you do agree, does that settle the issue for you—that is, does it follow that pleasure is man's highest good?

3. "The assertion that pleasure is man's highest good is not capable of strict and conclusive proof." Do you agree? In general, how would you go about trying to support the claim that X (pleasure, or what-have-you) is man's highest good?

4. Objection: If pleasure is man's highest good, then the more pleasure there is the more good there is regardless of the *quality* of pleasure involved. Do you agree?

13

A LIFE
OF REASON

I want to begin my contribution to this discussion by reintroducing the beautiful word, *eudemonia,* from Chapter 11. It is usually translated "happiness," but it means much more: literally, "having a good spirit"; connotatively, good fortune, fulfillment, a rich destiny. Eudemonia is that for which a man would exchange all that he has. It is the pearl of great price, the goal and desire of every human being.

It is a mere tautology to say that man's highest good is to achieve eudemonia. The question is, In what does man's eudemonia consist? Hedonist tells us that man's eudemonia consists in the experience of pleasure. I think he is mistaken in this assertion, and I shall attempt to show why he is mistaken.

Critique of Hedonism

Let us look first at Hedonist's reasoning. The intrinsic desirability of pleasure is evident, he says, from the fact that it is universally desired. For just as something is visible by virtue of the fact that people actually see it, and audible by virtue of the fact that people actually hear it, so a thing is desirable by virtue of the fact that people desire it. Ergo, he concludes, pleasure is desirable.

This reasoning is altogether specious; indeed, it is nothing more than a play on words. To say that something is visible or audible is to say that it is *capable* of being seen or heard. To say that something is desirable, on the other hand, is to say that it is *worthy* of being desired. "Desirable" is like "despicable" and "lovable," not like "visible" and "audible." That people desire something does not at all tend to show that it is truly desirable, that is, worthy of being desired. It only shows that it is desired.

I must also take issue with Hedonist's attempt to square his assertion that pleasure is man's highest good with the idea that some forms of pleasure are more desirable than others by virtue of their higher quality. On the premise that pleasure is man's highest good, what can "higher quality" possibly mean? It can only mean, it seems to me, "more pleasurable": it can be of a higher quality only in the way that a ten-dollar bill is of a higher quality (if you want to put it that way) than a one-dollar bill. And if a man is criticized for neglecting his intellectual and aesthetic and moral development for the sake of being a pure sensualist he could, on Hedonist's premise, convincingly defend himself by arguing that he finds sensual pleasure more pleasurable than the others. I know that Hedonist does not want to say this, indeed that his theory about "qualities of pleasure" is intended precisely to avoid this conclusion. My point is that he cannot have it both ways. If pleasure is man's highest good, then one pleasure can be "higher" than another only by virtue of being more pleasurable. If various forms of pleasure differ as to quality, then they must differ by virtue of some component other than pleasure itself and it must not be the case that pleasure is man's highest good.

That Hedonist's argument contains some specious reasoning does not, of course, prove that he is mistaken in his assertion that pleasure is man's highest good. Good theories are sometimes supported with bad reasons, and when this happens we must be wise enough to look beyond those bad reasons and consider the theory on its own merits. Let us now do this with Hedonist's theory. Let us forget the faulty reasoning with which he has attempted to support his theory and consider directly the question, Is pleasure man's highest good? I shall, of course, argue that it is not.

Consider, first, the following situation. Imagine a man enjoying throughout a long life in a very high degree all of the pleasures that Hedonist has described—sensual pleasures, intellectual pleasures, aesthetic pleasures, pleasures of every conceivable kind. According to Hedonist's theory, then, he would be a living example of a man who has achieved man's highest good and should wish for nothing more. But let us suppose something more about this man. Though he possesses an abundance of pleasure at every moment, he does not possess memory, and so he cannot remember that he has experienced pleasure in the past. Moreover, though he is experiencing immense pleasure moment by moment, he is not conscious of experiencing pleasure, nor is he able to anticipate that he will experience pleasure in the future. This man, in short, though by our hypothesis he experiences an abundance of pleasure, lacks those faculties by which he could be *conscious* that he was experiencing pleasure. Would we really say that he was realizing man's highest good? We would not—but if pleasure is man's highest good we clearly should.

"Well," Hedonist may say to us, "you are just nit-picking. Any reasonable man must know that when I say that pleasure is man's highest good I mean that the *consciousness* of pleasure is man's highest good. Certainly I don't mean to assert that pleasure, apart from the consciousness of it, is good." Very well, let us accept this revision of Hedonist's theory. It still does not stand up under close scrutiny.

This time let us imagine a man who has been put to sleep with an anesthetic, and all necessary arrangements have been made to take care of normal bodily processes—supplying food and water, getting rid of bodily wastes, etc. Now, medical science being at a very advanced stage, his brain is artificially stimulated in such a way that he has the *consciousness* of experiencing in a very high degree all of the pleasures that Hedonist describes as constituting man's highest good. He experiences every imaginable form of sensual pleasure, every form of aesthetic pleasure known to man, and the highest reaches of intellectual ecstasy. And let this experience of sheer ecstasy, unadulterated by any consciousness of pain, go on and on and on—let it continue forever. Would we say that this man is an example of someone who was realizing man's highest good? We would not. Yet, if the consciousness of pleasure were man's highest good, we should assent to this.

Or consider this: If pleasure, or the consciousness of pleasure, were man's highest good, then the best of all possible worlds for man would be one in which half the people on earth were sadists and the other half masochists. There would, certainly, be a great deal of pleasure in such a world—much more, presumably, than there is now—but I for one would not call it a better world. Yet, if I were to accept the thesis that pleasure is man's highest good I would be obliged to applaud such a world.

Hedonism, then, is not an acceptable theory about what it is that constitutes man's highest good, man's eudemonia. Let me present an alternative view.

Rational Eudemonism

Suppose that we were discussing the highest good of a fish rather than a man. In what does the eudemonia of a fish consist? It is apparent that it consists in the state of affairs that would enable the fish to do those things that nature has equipped it to do. If you begin to enumerate the various things that a fish is equipped by nature to do, you will surely arrive at the activity of swimming as one in which the fish is somehow expressing its uniqueness as a fish. In order to identify the highest good of any species of living thing you have first to identify what it is about that species that is unique. For the highest good of any creature is that activity or state of affairs in which it is, so to speak, fulfilling its unique destiny, realizing its purpose for being.

What, then, is unique about man? His capacity for growth and reproduction he shares with all other living things, plants as well as animals. His capacity to experience sensation (sight, hearing, touch, taste, smell) and to move about (locomotion) he shares with all the animals. That which is unique in man is not to be found in these areas. Man differs from every other species of living thing by virtue of his reason. Man alone is able to seek and to know truth—though admittedly he often falls into error in his quest for truth. This capacity to exercise reason, then, to seek understanding, knowledge, science, wisdom, is man's unique endowment.

Man's *highest* good, then, must consist in the exercise of his highest faculty. He has, to be sure, many lesser goods—food, companionship, pleasurable sensations, and the like. But man's highest good, that in which his eudemonia essentially consists, is the right exercise of his rational faculty. Man is most fully man when he is engaged in inquiry and learning.

It is the function of man's reason, however, not only to seek and to know the truth but also to instruct him regarding what is good and right. Man is exercising his rational faculty not only when he is seeking or contemplating truth, but also when he is acting according to what reason tells him is good and right.

Thus we arrive at the view that man's highest good consists in *activity according to reason.* Man is most fully man when he is acting according to reason, either in the quest for truth or in practical activity according to what reason tells him is good and right.

I freely admit that this high goal of always acting according to reason is rarely achieved by man. For there is in man, as every serious student of the human psyche from Plato to Sigmund Freud has told us, a powerful irrational element that seeks expression in those very actions that we have said are supposed to be controlled by reason. Indeed, the sharp difference between Hedonist's position and my own is vividly illustrated at this point; for Hedonist is bound to say that insofar as the expression of libido is pleasurable it is good, whereas I affirm that insofar as it leads to behavior that is not in accordance with reason it is bad. Man progresses toward his highest good not by following the path of least resistance (which hedonism would appear to counsel him to do), but by striving—sometimes heroically—to bring his various drives and appetites under the control of a disciplined reason. This may not always be maximally pleasurable, for there is undoubtedly pleasure in the fulfillment of an awakened desire and disappointment in its denial, but it is the way to eudemonia.

We noted a few moments ago that the view that there are various qualities of pleasure, and that the "higher" pleasures are to be preferred to the "lower" pleasures, is not consistent with the basic thesis of hedonism that pleasure constitutes man's highest good. I would now suggest that the concept of "qualities of pleasure," which does appear to be valid, can best be understood in conjunction with the theory I am here defending. What does it mean to say that one sort of pleasure is higher than another? It means, I would suggest, that there is more of reason in it. A child's delight in playing in the snow is surely as innocent as any pleasure imaginable, but it is of a lower order of pleasures because there is little of reason in it. The pleasure of a student of physics in finally mastering relativity theory is of a higher order of pleasures because there is much of reason in it. The scale according to which we rank pleasures as being higher or lower is the scale of reason.

Let it not be thought that in affirming that activity according to reason is man's highest good I am denying that pleasure is a good. On the contrary, I hold that pleasure is a very high-level good, and that it is worthy of being desired insofar as it does not detract from the pursuit of the highest good, which is activity according to reason. We should aim, it seems to me, at being rational men, at realizing in practice the goal of activity according to reason; it will then follow, as a natural concomitant of such a life, that we will experience such pleasures as are good for man.

STUDY QUESTIONS

1. What is Eudemonist's objection to Hedonist's claim that the fact that pleasure is universally desired shows that it is desirable? Who is right on this point?
2. "If various forms of pleasure differ as to quality, then they must differ by virtue of some component other than pleasure itself and it must not be the case that pleasure is man's highest good." Do you agree?
3. Eudemonist presents two *reductio ad absurdum* arguments to show that pleasure is not man's highest good. Do they succeed? How might Hedonist defend himself?
4. How does Eudemonist support his claim that man's highest good consists in activity according to reason? Do you find his argument at all convincing?

14

ETHICAL PLURALISM

Discussions about the *summum bonum* often seem to me to confuse several questions that we need to clearly distinguish if we are to avoid utter confusion. I propose to preface what I have to say on the subject of man's highest good by distinguishing the several questions that are sometimes discussed almost interchangeably and by indicating which of these questions I mean to be answering in the remainder of this essay.

Four Questions

In asking, What is man's highest good? it is possible, first, to be asking for a description of the best conceivable state of affairs for man. We might, in attempting to answer such a question, let our imaginations run rampant and describe, for example, a world in which the temperature at ground level is always 72° Fahrenheit, where no illness or suffering of any kind ever occurs, where men do not grow old and die but remain youthful forever, and so on. Such a description might even be of some practical value as defining a remote ideal toward which our efforts in the real world might fruitfully be directed, but it would not be a description of "man's highest good" in the sense in which I shall be discussing it.

Second, this question could be construed to mean, What is the best possible state of affairs for man, the laws of nature being what they are? To answer this question we would have to describe a kind of ideal society, in which all the remediable ills of society as we know it are somehow cured. Plato tried to do this in the *Republic*, and Thomas More in *Utopia*; but this is not the question I shall be discussing.

A third possible meaning of the question concerning man's highest good is this: Of the various good things that men may for various reasons desire, which are worthy of being desired for their own sakes? Some things, as was pointed out in Chapter 11, are desired because of their instrumental value in achieving something else (instrumental goods); other things are desired for their own sakes (intrinsic goods). What, then, are the intrinsic goods for man? What things are worthy of being desired by man for their own sakes? I shall be addressing myself to this question shortly.

There is yet a fourth way in which the question about man's highest good may be construed, however, and that is this: Of the various things that are worthy of being desired for their own sakes, which one thing is *most* worthy of being desired? It is possible to suppose that there is a multiplicity of things that are intrinsically good, but to hold that some one of them is so much better than the others that it should be desired even at the cost of losing the other, and lesser, intrinsic goods. I shall have something to say on this point also in what follows.

Which of these four questions have Hedonist and Rational Eudemonist been discussing? I would suggest that Hedonist has addressed himself to question three and Rational Eudemonist to question four. Hedonist, with question three in mind, has argued that pleasure alone is intrinsically good and worthy of being desired for its own sake and that whatever else is good for man is good only insofar as it is productive of human pleasure. Rational Eudemonist, on the other hand, has conceded that pleasure is *a* good, perhaps even an intrinsic good, but has argued that another intrinsic good—activity according to reason—is the *highest* intrinsic good for man, that is, the intrinsic good most worthy of being desired.

In order to defend my position against both Hedonist and Rational Eudemonist, therefore, I am obliged to address myself to both question three and question four. Against Hedonist I shall argue, first, that pleasure is only one of several intrinsic goods for man; and against Rational Eudemonist I shall argue that man's highest good consists not in the maximum realization of some one intrinsic good to the virtual or at least possible exclusion of all others, but rather in the maximization of all.

A Word About Method

It is notoriously difficult to argue for or against any theory about what things are intrinsically good and worthy of being desired as ends in themselves. Hedonist frankly admits that he cannot provide a "strict and conclusive proof" of his position; Rational Eudemonist does not even try. The method that seems to me to be most appropriate to the subject at hand is what I shall call the method of *imaginative isolation*. Let us suppose that we are trying to decide whether x is intrinsically good. We then imagine a universe in which x is absent, and one in which x is present, and we ask: Does the presence of x in the second case provide any reason for preferring the second universe over the first? If the answer is affirmative, x may be presumed to be intrinsically good; if the answer is negative, we conclude that x is not intrinsically good.

Pleasure

If we now apply this method to the case of pleasure, we shall not be surprised to discover that pleasure is indeed an intrinsic good. For let us imagine a universe in which sentient beings are always in pain, and another identical in all respects except that sentient beings consistently experience pleasure rather than pain: we say without hesitation that the second universe is to be preferred to the first. In saying this we are acknowledging that pleasure is intrinsically good.

It does not seem to be the case, however, that all pleasure is intrinsically good. For let us suppose that some great tragedy occurs—the 1970 hurricane that devastated East Pakistan, for example—and let us suppose that someone contemplates this awful tragedy *with pleasure*. Surely, we would say, a universe in which men felt sorrow in the face of tragedy would be a better world than this because this pleasure is *not* good. Or, again, suppose that someone experiences pleasure in doing some reprehensible act: a universe that lacked such pleasure, we want to say, is to be preferred over one that contains it.

These exceptional cases raise a very difficult question: If we assent to the proposition that on the whole pleasure is good and worthy of being desired, precisely why do we object to its occurrence in these cases? The answer would appear to be that it is not to the pleasure as such that we object, but to pleasure-caused-by-something-intrinsically-bad. All other things being equal, we prefer a universe where sentient beings experience pleasure to one in which they experience neither pleasure nor pain; but we should prefer the latter universe to one in which some sentient beings experience pleasure in contemplating the suffering or death of others.

The result of our analysis appears to be, then, that pleasure is good except in those cases in which it is caused by something that is intrinsically bad.

Knowledge

I would suggest, secondly, that by the same method we shall get the result that *knowledge* is intrinsically good. For imagine a universe in which there is a definite quota of pleasure but no knowledge, and another in which there is an exactly equal quantity of pleasure but, in addition, widespread knowledge of the laws of nature and of human society: it seems clear that we should without hesitation choose the latter. And note that we do not (as Hedonist might argue) value the knowledge because of the pleasure it gives, for according to our hypothesis the amount of pleasure in the two cases is exactly equal. It is clear, therefore, that we value the knowledge for its own sake.

Are there exceptions in the case of knowledge, as we discovered there were in the case of pleasure? It would seem that there are. Most of us would feel obliged to conceal from a young child, for example, information that we feel would be hurtful or acutely embarrassing to him —that his mother had abandoned him, or that his father was a famous criminal. Eventually, we realize, the child should know even these painful truths, but while he is young and possibly capable of severe emotional damage we might feel obliged to "protect" him from this knowledge. Again, in the case of a person of any age who is very ill, we can easily imagine information that we would be inclined to conceal from him on the grounds that sharing it with him would (we think) only aggravate his condition, or add mental torture to the pain he is already suffering.

The generalization to which we are entitled on the basis of these considerations is that knowledge is good except in those cases in which its occurrence would lead to consequences sufficiently bad to outweigh the good that would accrue were the individual in question to acquire some particular piece of knowledge. Perhaps we could even say that knowledge is always good; but there are cases in which this good cannot be realized without simultaneously realizing an evil of such magnitude that it is a poor bargain.

Moral Virtue

I do not wish to become involved at this point in a hair-splitting discussion about the exact definition of moral virtue, but I cannot avoid mentioning it if my list of intrinsic goods is to be at all complete. By moral virtue, then, I mean what I think is just the common and accepted meaning of this phrase, namely, those qualities of character that predispose someone to do his duty, to act kindly toward his fellow men, and in general to behave in ways that he considers good and right.

Now it seems clear to me that such qualities of character and the actions in which they are expressed are intrinsically good. Again we apply our method of imaginative isolation: consider a world that contains a definite quantity of pleasure and knowledge but no moral virtue, and consider another universe containing exactly the same amount of pleasure and knowledge but moral virtue as well. We would, I think, unhesitatingly choose the latter; and if we would, it is clear that we regard moral virtue as something that is good in itself apart from its consequences—though it is probably true that in actuality we prize it also for its consequences. Moreover, it seems to me that in this case the conclusion holds without exception: I can think of no case in which we would be inclined to say that it would be better for virtue not to exist because of its allegedly bad consequences.

Other Intrinsic Goods

Are there other things that, by a further application of the method of imaginative isolation, might be identified as intrinsic goods? I find it difficult to answer this question with any degree of confidence. Other candidates suggest themselves: justice, creativity, optimism, even life itself. But some of these, I think, are reducible to some combination of the intrinsic goods we have already identified, and others appear to be merely instrumental goods. In any case, I am not willing to say flat out that pleasure, knowledge, and virtue are the only intrinsic goods for man, but I am unable at this time to extend the list any further myself. If by the careful application of the method of imaginative isolation other intrinsic goods can be identified, then so be it: it does not affect my argument in the least.

Man's Highest Good

Is some one of these intrinsic goods more worthy of being desired than others? Many philosophers would answer this question in the affirmative. Hedonist, for example, elevates pleasure to the highest level and treats all other goods merely as means to the production of pleasure. Rational Eudemonist, by elevating activity according to reason to the highest rank, ends up with a definite order of preference: knowledge, then virtue, then pleasure. We have not heard in this debate from anyone who holds that virtue is man's highest good, but we are reminded of the words of Socrates at the end of the *Apology*:

> When my sons are grown up, I would ask you, O my friends, to punish them; and I would have you trouble them, as I have troubled you, if they seem to care about riches, or anything, more than about virtue. . . .[1]

Now it seems to me plainly foolish, if pleasure, knowledge, and virtue are all intrinsic goods, to elevate any one of them to the position of the *summum bonum* to the possible exclusion of the others. These three are related not as superordinates and subordinates, but as co-equal goods worthy of being desired by all men. Man's eudemonia consists not in being a mere pleasure-seeker, nor in being an arid

---

[1] Plato, *Apology*, in *The Dialogues of Plato*, B. Jowett (tr.) (New York: Random House, 1937), Vol. I, p. 423.

intellectual, nor in being a grim moralist: his eudemonia consists in being a man. Insofar as he is intellect, his eudemonia consists in the acquisition of knowledge; insofar as he is will, in the cultivation of virtue; insofar as he is feeling, in the experience of pleasure. Man's *summum bonum* is to realize so far as possible every intrinsic good, in such balance and proportion as his natural endowments and his circumstances may permit.

STUDY QUESTIONS

1. What are the "four questions" that Pluralist attempts to distinguish on pp. 96–97? Is he right in saying that: "Hedonist has addressed himself to question three, and Rational Eudemonist to question four"?
2. What is "the method of imaginative isolation"? How is it supposed to be useful in the discussion of the present issue?
3. List the things that Pluralist identifies as intrinsic goods. Do you agree that these are intrinsic goods? Would you add anything else to this list?
4. What is Pluralist's final answer to the question: What is man's highest good? Do you agree with him?

15

ETERNAL HAPPINESS

I enter this debate as a modern advocate of a view that has a long and distinguished history. In the Greco-Roman world it vied successfully with several of the theories set forth in preceding chapters, and it was for many years the universally accepted opinion regarding man's highest good. In recent years, however, this view has been abandoned by many people in favor of one or another of the alternative theories. I remain convinced, however, that this is the correct view and propose to present it as convincingly as I am able.

Some Generalizations

Let me begin by making some generalizations that seem to be warranted on the basis of the foregoing discussion. First, all parties to the debate appear to be agreed that man's highest good consists in the fulfillment of man's deepest longings and desires. Man is, so to speak, an "unfinished" creature. He longs for completeness, for fulfillment, for the satisfaction of his desires. The assertion that pleasure, or knowledge, or virtue, or all of these together, constitutes man's highest good really means that in realizing this man's deepest needs will be satisfied, that he will experience completeness. If pleasure, or knowledge, or virtue, or whatever else may be proposed, does not achieve this, then what is being proposed is not in truth man's *highest* good but merely, at best, some lesser good.

It follows, therefore, that any view about the *summum bonum* presupposes some judgment about man's deepest needs, some judgment about what it would take to render man truly complete. If you really believe that all that man lacks in order to be truly complete is a goodly quantity of pleasurable experiences of various sorts, then (and only then) are you justified in adopting hedonism; and so on for any other proposal that may be put forward.

I would ask you to note, further, that each of the previous writers has evidently assumed that man's deepest longings and desires are capable of fulfillment in this life. It is assumed that pleasure, knowledge, and virtue—singly or in combination—are states of being that are attainable in a high degree by many people simply as a result of putting forth an adequate amount of effort. Circumstances may, indeed, prevent their realization in the degree that we might desire, but in theory at least they are assumed to be attainable in this life.

An Alternative View

I am convinced that if we consider seriously the true need and longing of man—if we look deeply into the restless, searching heart of man—we cannot be content with a view that identifies man's highest good as something attainable in this life. With St. Augustine, therefore, I must affirm that "life eternal is the supreme good, death eternal the supreme evil," [1] and that "We must neither come short of this nor go beyond it: the one is dangerous, the other impossible." [2] My task in the remainder of this essay is to elucidate and defend this view.

Let us begin by considering very carefully that deep and restless longing of man the satisfaction of which would constitute his highest good, his true eudemonia.

As an intellectual being, man has an insatiable desire to know the truth. This is evident not only from our own experience, for each of us takes great delight in achieving some new understanding, but also from observation: we observe that there are many men who spend their entire adult lives in pure research, with little or no thought being given to any possible practical consequences of their hard-won knowledge. As Aristotle remarked, "All men by nature desire to know" [3]; this desire to know is not satisfied by any quantity of learning that may be achieved in this life.

As a moral being, there is also in man a desire to live rightly, to do what is good and just and to refrain from doing wrong. But this desire, however great may be the measure of its achievement by the noble few, is never fully satisfied in this life. Selfish desires, the lusts

---

[1] St. Augustine, *The City of God*, XIX, iv, Marcus Dods (tr.) (New York: Modern Library, 1950), p. 676.

[2] St. Augustine, *The Morals of the Catholic Church*, Chap. VIII, in Whitney J. Oates (ed.), *Basic Writings of St. Augustine* (New York: Random House, 1948), Vol. I, p. 325.

[3] Aristotle, *Metaphysics*, I, i, in Richard McKeon (ed.), *The Basic Works of Aristotle* (New York: Random House, 1941), p. 689.

of the body, ignorance and frailty conspire to prevent us from achieving that moral perfection to which we aspire. That perfection, if it is to be achieved at all, must await another life.

There are, further, certain goods that we all desire as members of human society, as citizens. We desire honor and appreciation for the good that we have done, we desire to be well known among our fellows, and we desire such riches as may enable us to be comfortable and secure as we face an uncertain future. Our desire for such honor, fame, and wealth, regardless of the magnitude of its realization, is never fully satisfied in this life.

There is also in us, as Hedonist has emphasized, a desire to experience pleasure; indeed, so intense is this desire in some of us that we sometimes run about from pleasure to pleasure as if we believed that our restless hearts really could be quieted if only we could experience a sufficient quantity and variety of pleasures. But from every such venture, however great the momentary ecstasy, we return to the world of reality to find that the void still remains, the restless heart is still restless, the spirit still unsatisfied.

There is in us, finally, as Spinoza has beautifully put it, a desire to "persevere in our being . . . [through] indefinite time." [4] We do not want our life to come to an end, and we demonstrate this by taking all sorts of measures to protect ourselves from danger and to guard our health. Yet we know that this earthly life will eventually come to an end, and so in this life our desire to "persevere in our being" will finally be thwarted.

There is, to be sure, a kind of earthly happiness that consists in such satisfaction of these several longings as we are able to secure in this life. But over all the wanderings and searchings of this life, over our pathetic and halting efforts to make of this life the paradise that seems forever to elude our grasp, stand those haunting words of St. Augustine in the opening chapter of *The Confessions:* "Thou hast formed us for Thyself, and our hearts are restless till they find rest in Thee." [5] Man's highest good, man's true eudemonia, does not consist in anything that he can achieve in this life: it consists in that life of eternal blessedness that God desires to give to all His children.

What do we mean by a life of eternal blessedness? We mean, first, a life in which our desire for knowledge is fully satisfied, in which all that we are capable of knowing is known completely and without error. We mean, secondly, a life in which our quest for virtue reaches its goal, a life in which our characters at last reach the perfection that forever eludes us in our present life. We mean, thirdly, a life in which

---

4 Benedict de Spinoza, *Ethics*, Sec. Part, Prop. VI and VIII, in John Wild (ed.), *Spinoza Selections* (New York: Scribner, 1930), pp. 215, 216.

5 St. Augustine, *The Confessions*, I, i, in Oates (ed.), *op. cit.*, p. 3.

our desire for honor, fame, and wealth is fulfilled insofar as it is good for us and extinguished insofar as it is not, a life in which we shall experience the "glory and wealth" of which the psalmist speaks (Psalms 111:3). We mean a life in which we shall experience pleasure of such purity and such permanence as we never dreamed of in this life, a blessedness that is not only for a moment but forever. And we mean, finally, a life in which we no longer labor under the depressing knowledge that sooner or later it will come to an end, but one in which we have the blessed certainty that it will continue forever. Such a life, I say, and nothing less than this, would constitute the true happiness, the eudemonia, the fulfillment, of a being whose needs and longings are what we know our own to be.

A Choice

If we grant that man really does have the needs and longings that I have enumerated and that his highest good does not consist in anything attainable in this life, then there are three alternatives among which we must choose. We may assert, first, that eternal happiness is a real possibility for man, in which case we should spare no effort to attain such a life. Or, second, we may conclude (as many evidently have) that eternal life is not possible for man and that there is no possibility of ever being truly and completely happy. The practical alternatives, if we accept this position, are (a) to attempt to stifle our desires since they cannot be satisfied (this is Stoicism), or (b) to sullenly accept some limited set of attainable goods as the best we can hope for. It is no accident, I think, that the prevailing ethic of our time is a strange mixture of Stoicism and a very superficial hedonism.

Given these three alternatives, in any case, I do not hesitate to adopt the first and to assert that eternal happiness is a real possibility for man. I want in the remainder of this essay to offer some persuasive reasons in support of this view.

Supporting Arguments

I am impressed, first, by the fact that for every natural appetite there is a corresponding way by which that appetite is naturally satisfied. For the appetite of hunger there is food, for thirst there is drink, for sexual desire there is intercourse, for loneliness there is human companionship, and so on. Now it is inconceivable to me that nature should have endowed man with a set of appetites—those deep needs and longings of which we spoke earlier—if there were no way for them to be satisfied. It would be a cruel trick if man's hunger for eternity should turn out to be the one hunger for which there is no satisfaction

—for this is the deepest hunger of all. Thus it seems probable that a state of eternal blessedness, in which this longing would be fully satisfied, is a real possibility for man.

I would call your attention next to the "over-endowment" of man if this life is the only life for which he was intended. The evolutionary process has in general equipped each organism with just those qualities that it needs to survive in the struggle for life. Man, however, is a remarkable exception. His capacity for abstract knowledge, his moral aspirations, his love of beauty, his spiritual ideals, go far beyond what is needed to secure his mere survival in the struggle for life. These endowments mark him off as a creature destined for higher things—destined, indeed, for a life of eternal blessedness.

I appeal, thirdly, to what I shall call the "presentiment of immortality" in the souls of virtually all men, ourselves included. The great spiritual leaders of mankind—Socrates and Plato and Kant, Buddha and Jesus and Mohammed, St. Augustine and St. Thomas Aquinas and countless others—have spoken unashamedly of this sense of immortality; their words express the hopes and feelings of the great majority of men. It is not unreasonable to hold that the sentiments expressed with such unanimity by those whom we revere as the greatest and the holiest of men express a genuine insight into the true destiny of the human spirit.

There is even some straightforward empirical evidence in favor of human immortality as the result of research that has been done in the area of parapsychology. Numerous cases are on record of persons who have apparently conversed with deceased loved ones or acquaintances and in the course of these conversations have secured information they could have secured in no other way. The number of qualified researchers working in this area is unfortunately very small, because parapsychology does indeed regard as possible some things that are very unpalatable to the typical contemporary scientific mind. The evidence in support of the theory that the soul survives the death of the body is growing, however, and this theory is of course an essential part of the view that eternal happiness is a real possibility for man.

One further argument in support of human immortality may be suggested for those who approach this question with a prior belief in God. If God exists, and if (as theism asserts) He loves His creation, then it is not unreasonable to assume that He desires and will provide for the preservation and happiness of man, the crown of His creation. If we are in doubt about the existence of God, then we have to resolve that question before we can decide on the merit of the present argument. If we believe in the existence of God, then a belief in human immortality seems more plausible than disbelief.

I acknowledge, however, that these arguments do not by any means conclusively prove my case. The evidence is inconclusive: we cannot know with certainty that we shall survive death, and we cannot know with certainty that we shall not. We must, therefore, as Blaise Pascal said, wager one way or the other. And so I would suggest, finally, that it makes supremely good sense to wager on the possibility of an eternal life in which our every need and longing shall be fully satisfied. This makes sense, I say, because it gives to this present life a quality, a meaning, and a perspective that make it a much richer adventure than it otherwise would be. We may never succeed in making this world a paradise, but we need the concept of paradise in order that the ideal of the perfect life may ever be before us and in order that we may endure with tranquility the sorrows and disappointments that beset us as we make our way through life. If in wagering on a future life we should turn out to be mistaken, we shall still be the gainers by virtue of the richness lent to this life by the hope of another; if we are right, we shall experience in reality that eternal happiness that constitutes man's true eudemonia.

STUDY QUESTIONS

1. What exactly is the proposal of this chapter concerning man's highest good? To which of Pluralist's four questions does this theory appear to be addressed?
2. "If it be granted that man really does have the needs and longings that I have enumerated, . . . then one is left with three alternatives from which one must make a choice." Do you agree? Do you agree with the if-clause? What are the "three alternatives"? Are there others?
3. What arguments are offered in support of the view that "eternal happiness is a real possibility for man"? Do you find these arguments at all persuasive?
4. "It makes supremely good sense to wager on the possibility of an eternal life in which our every need and longing shall be fully satisfied." Does it?

Aquinas, St. Thomas. *Summa Contra Gentiles*. Many editions. See Book III, Chapters 25–37, 48, and 60–63.

Aristotle. *Nicomachean Ethics*. Many editions. See Book I.

Augustine, St. *The City of God*. Many editions. Book XIX deals with the question of the *summum bonum*.

————. *The Morals of the Catholic Church*. Many editions. See Chapters I–XIV.

Bentham, Jeremy. *An Introduction to the Principles of Morals and Legislation*. Several editions. See especially Chapters 1, 2, 4, and 10. Of interest especially because of its description of the "hedonistic calculus."

Broad, C. D. *Five Types of Ethical Theory*. New York: Humanities Press, 1956.

DeWitt, N. W. *Epicurus and His Philosophy*. Minneapolis: University of Minnesota Press, 1954.

Epicurus. *Extant Writings* (Letter to Herodotus, Letter to Pythocles, Letter to Menoeceus, Principal Doctrines, Fragments, Diogenes Laertius' "Life of Epicurus"), in Whitney J. Oates, *The Stoic and Epicurean Philosophers*. New York: Random House, 1940, pp. 3–64.

Ewing, Alfred C. *The Definition of Good*. New York: Macmillan, 1947.

Gosling, J. C. B. *Pleasure and Desire: The Case for Hedonism Reviewed*. Oxford: Clarendon Press, 1969.

Lucretius. *On the Nature of Things*. Many editions. See Books III and IV. A well-known statement of the hedonistic view by an ancient admirer of Epicurus.

MacKinnon, D. M. *A Study of Ethical Theory*. London: A. and C. Black, 1957.

Mill, John Stuart. *Utilitarianism*. Many editions. A classic statement of the hedonistic theory.

Moore, G. E. *Principia Ethica*. Cambridge, Eng.: Cambridge University Press, 1903. Chapter III is a detailed critique of hedonism; Chapter VI is a statement of the pluralistic view.

Plato. *Philebus*. Many editions. Difficult reading, but of great interest for its critique of hedonism and its advocacy of a pluralistic view.

Ross, W. D. *Foundations of Ethics*. Oxford: Oxford University Press, 1939.

————. *The Right and the Good*. Oxford: Clarendon Press, 1930. See Chapter Five for a carefully reasoned statement of the pluralistic view.

Stocks, J. L. *Aristotle's Definition of the Human Good*. Oxford: Basil Blackwell, 1919.

Tsanoff, Radoslav A. *The Moral Ideals of Our Civilization*. New York: Dutton, 1942.

PART IV

THE
LANGUAGE
OF MORALS

16

THE CENTRAL PROBLEM
OF METAETHICS

The problem to which we now turn has attracted a great deal of discussion among philosophers during recent years. It was first formulated with clarity by G. E. Moore in his celebrated book *Principia Ethica*.[1] Every philosopher since, who has ventured to write on ethical matters, has felt obliged to address himself to the problem so effectively raised by Moore. Unfortunately, a large number of alternative solutions have been proposed to Moore's problem and we shall have to proceed carefully in our study if we are to avoid confusion as to what the problem is about.

Let us begin by making a few distinctions to give us direction in the somewhat rare atmosphere of what is called "metaethics." We shall then be in a position to understand the problem formulated by Moore and to see some of the alternative solutions.

It will be recalled from our earlier discussion of the structure of ethical thinking (Chapter 11) that the moral sphere consists of that peculiar kind of behavior or activity that we regard as being appropriately subject to moral appraisal and that the defining characteristics of such behavior are that (a) it is the behavior of human beings, (b) it is behavior involving a choice among available alternatives, and (c) some moral rule or principle is relevant to the behavior in question. It will be further recalled that normative ethics is the attempt to determine what sorts of things really are right and wrong and why. The goal of the normative ethicist is to set forth a body of views regarding what really is right and wrong and to support these views with reasoned argument in such a way that his readers will be led to agree

---

[1] G. E. Moore, *Principia Ethica* (Cambridge, England: Cambridge University Press, 1959. Originally published, 1903.)

with him and, hopefully, to behave in ways that are consistent with those views.

It is possible, however, to think about ethical beliefs and, more particularly, the language in which they are expressed in quite a different way. It is possible to ask *logical* questions about moral discourse (the moral appraisals that men make in actual concrete situations) and about ethical discourse (the general principles of right and wrong, good and evil, etc., that are formulated in normative ethics). Such questions and the proposed answers to them constitute what is called *metaethics*. In metaethics we do not ask questions of the sort, Is it always a moral duty to keep a promise? That is a question for normative ethics. Rather, we ask questions of the sort, Does the statement "Promise-keeping is good" logically entail that it is always a moral duty to keep a promise? Does the statement "X is my duty" logically entail that I ought to do X? The metaethicist is a logician who is inquiring into the logical structure of moral and ethical discourse. The questions he asks, and the answers he gives, are directed toward an elucidation of that logical structure.

The distinction between morality, ethics, and metaethics might be likened to the distinction between physical phenomena, natural science, and philosophy of science; or religion, theology, and philosophy of religion. In each instance we have (a) a sphere of actual processes or occurrences (physical, moral, religious), (b) a system of beliefs relevant to them (natural science, ethics, theology), and (c) an inquiry concerning the logical status of those beliefs and the character of the reasoning by which they are supposedly established (philosophy of science, metaethics, and philosophy of religion). Throughout this section we shall be operating at this third level, and the object of our interest will be the statements that people make either at the level of concrete "lived" morality or at the level of systematic normative ethics.

The Problem About Moral Predicates

It is evident that at the level of actual everyday experience we frequently say things like "He ought not to have done that," "That was a terrible thing to do," "She is an awfully good person," and the like. It is also evident that at the more reflective level of normative ethics we say things like "We ought to promote human happiness as much as we can," "The infliction of needless pain is evil," and "Do unto others as you would have others do unto you." Let us call sentences of this type "moral sentences"; and let us call the appraisal words that occur in such sentences—good, bad, right, wrong, praiseworthy, blameworthy, etc.—"moral predicates." (It should be noted that not all moral sentences are of the simple subject-predicate type. Such things as advice, commands, and even expressions of feeling—"How I wish you wouldn't do that!"—may be properly classified as moral sentences under certain circumstances. But these distinctions need not concern us here.)

The metaethical problem with which we shall be concerned may be stated as follows: How are we using language when we say of something *in a moral sense* that it is good or bad, right or wrong? What is the logical status of sentences employing moral predicates? What is the meaning of a moral predicate and how do such predicates function in sentences expressing moral appraisal? In order to understand more clearly the point of the question, let us look at some of the ways in which it can be answered. The options are distressingly numerous.

The Options

Reflection upon the various ways that language is used leads to the conclusion that all language appears to serve four principal functions: to request information (the interrogative function), to convey information (the informative function), to direct behavior (the directive function), and to express feeling (the expressive, or emotive, function). If this analysis is correct, then it is evident that moral discourse must also be reducible to one or more of these functions, or types of discourse.

It seems evident that moral discourse does not serve an interrogative function; consequently, we may dismiss this at once. Perhaps, then, moral discourse is a species of informative language. Many metaethicists are agreed that it is. But what information does it give? Here opinions vary, and among philosophers who hold that moral discourse is a species of informative language we may distinguish at least four different answers to our question.

Some philosophers hold that to apply a moral predicate to the appraisal of something is to assert the presence or the absence of a certain empirical quality, or certain empirical qualities, in the thing being appraised. It may be said, for example, that to call an act "praiseworthy" or "good" is to say that it is productive of pleasure; the question whether or not an act is productive of pleasure is obviously an empirical question. Or it may be said that to call a certain form of conduct "good" is to say that it is characteristic of those beings who have proceeded the farthest or the highest along the evolutionary path; this assertion, if spelled out in some detail, is also capable of being determined empirically. We shall call this view (which is developed in Chapter 17) *naturalistic objectivism:* "naturalistic" because it affirms that moral predicates denote the presence or absence of some natural (empirically ascertainable) qualities, "objectivism" because such qualities are asserted to be in, or absent from, the object being judged.

Other philosophers hold, however, that moral discourse is informative in the sense that it asserts the presence or absence of some *non*-natural quality in the thing being appraised. This was the view of G. E. Moore, who said:

> If I am asked, What is good? my answer is that good is good, and that is the end of the matter. Or if I am asked, How is good to be defined? my answer is that it cannot be defined, and that is all I have to say about it. . . . My point is that "good" is a simple notion, just as "yellow" is a simple notion; that, just as you cannot, by any manner of means, explain to anyone who does not already know it, what yellow is, so you cannot explain what good is.[2]

This position, which is developed in Chapter 18, is variously called *nonnaturalistic objectivism* or, more commonly, *intuitionism*. The reasons for calling it the former are evident when one compares it with its "naturalistic" counterpart. The reason for calling it "intuition-ism" is that since the quality in question is, according to the theory, nonnatural, it is not subject to empirical investigation and must, accordingly, be "intuited," that is, rationally discerned. (The term "intuition," as used by philosophers, does not mean what it means in the everyday expression, "a woman's intuition." It means, rather, direct apprehension, or rational discernment: it denotes the act by which, according to rationalists, the intellect directly grasps some truths.)

It may be, however, that moral discourse is informative in a different way. It may be that "moral judgments," as they are called by some philosophers, convey information not about the object or the act being judged, but about the likes or dislikes of (a) the person making the judgment or (b) some group of people for whom he speaks. Such views are called *subjectivist* views, and depending on whether it is (a) the speaker's likes or dislikes or (b) the likes or dislikes of some group for which he speaks, you have, respectively, *private subjectivism* (Chapter 19) and *societal subjectivism* (Chapter 20). A statement such as "Honesty is good," according to these views, means either "I am in favor of honesty" (private subjectivism) or "We are in favor of honesty" (societal subjectivism). Moral sentences, according to these views, say nothing at all about what appears to be the "object" of the judgment: they say something, rather, about the likes or dislikes of some subject or subjects.

It may be, however, that moral sentences are not informative at all, but serve instead to express the feelings of the speaker. This view is known as *emotivism* and is similar to, though not the same as, private

---

[2] *Ibid.*, pp. 6–7.

subjectivism. According to the private subjectivist view, "Honesty is good" means "I approve of honesty": it is an informative statement about the feelings of the speaker. According to the emotivist view, "Honesty is good" is interpreted to mean, roughly, "Hurray for honesty!": it is not a report about the feelings of the speaker, but rather an expression of those feelings. This view is discussed in Chapter 21.

Or it may be that the function of ethical sentences is neither to convey information nor to express feeling, but to direct behavior. Perhaps ethical discourse is a species of *directive* language—"veiled commands," as they are sometimes called. Perhaps every moral utterance, even the most general moral principle imaginable, is an elliptical expression the real purpose of which is to say, "Act in such and such a way." This view, which is favored by a number of philosophers at the present time, is called *imperativism* and is discussed in Chapter 22.

There is no certainty whatsoever that the six views just distinguished constitute all of the possible ways of answering the question about the nature of moral discourse. First, it is not possible to state with certainty that the four "functions" of language from which our analysis began are the only functions that an exhaustive study of language might reveal. Should some other function be identified, it is possible that a case could be made for the view that ethical discourse is a species of that function of language. Second, it could be maintained that ethical discourse serves several functions simultaneously and therefore is not correctly accounted for by any one of these positions (see Chapter 23). With such a *multifunctionalist* view the possibilities become endless: with so many variables, dozens of possibilities have to be considered in attempting to analyze a single sentence—and different combinations have to be supposed to apply to other sentences.

The diagram of ethical discourse on p. 116 may be helpful in distinguishing the six single views that we have just defined. The sentences that appear in parentheses indicate the "translations" that would be proposed by each view to exhibit the supposed real meaning of the sentence "Honesty is good."

Even though the alternatives listed are not mutually exclusive, it does seem worth the effort to see what kind of case can be made for each; since, if we are to construe moral and ethical discourse as involving some combination or combinations of these functions, it is first necessary that we clearly understand the "pure types." While we cannot claim to be absolutely sure that the four functions of language we distinguished constitute an exhaustive list, we may be reasonably confident that it is; and we may, accordingly, be reasonably confident that moral sentences are correctly construed either in one of the six ways defined or in some combination or combinations of these ways.

We may observe, finally, that this problem is by no means a purely

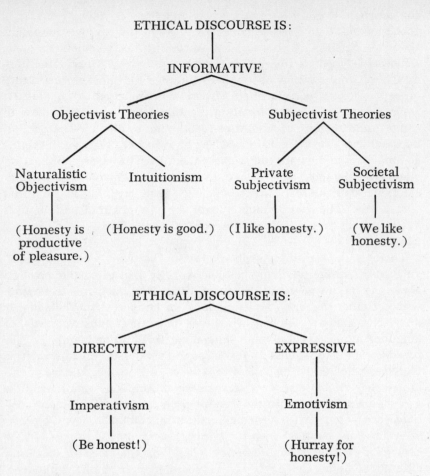

technical problem in which only philosophers have an interest, although discussion of it along these lines has been confined largely to
professional philosophers. We sometimes hear it said, for example,
that moral principles are "just a matter of opinion," and this clearly
seems to be a metaethical view. Discussions about the "objectivity" or
the "subjectivity" of moral principles are also discussions of this problem. To say that minority groups have a "valid claim" to equal civil
rights and that laws preventing them from obtaining such rights are
"unjust" is to make certain assumptions about the status of moral
principles and about the logic of the sentences in which they are expressed. Any decision we make on this matter will inevitably affect
the way we think about the ethical issues about which our society is so
deeply concerned at the present time. In this sense, the problem about
ethical language, though seemingly far removed from the concrete
realities of life, is actually an intensely practical philosophical problem.

STUDY QUESTIONS

1. Define "morality," "normative ethics," and "metaethics." To which of these does each of the following belong?
   a. The opinion that racial segregation is wrong.
   b. The lynching of a suspected rapist.
   c. The theory that moral goodness consists of the tendency to enhance human happiness.
   d. If your enemy hungers, feed him.
   e. He governs best who governs least.
   f. To say that something is good is to say nothing more than that you like it.
   g. Nothing is good or bad but thinking makes it so.
   h. The cardinal rule of all ethics is this: so act that you could will that the maxim according to which you act should become a universal law.
2. What do you understand to be "the central problem of metaethics"? Does this seem to you an important problem? What bearing, if any, does it have on such matters as the civil rights controversy or the struggle between East and West?
3. What do subjectivist theories regarding the meaning of moral sentences have in common with objectivist theories? What is it that distinguishes them? What is the difference between naturalistic objectivism and intuitionism? between private and societal subjectivism? between private subjectivism and emotivism?
4. Why is it impossible to conclude with certainty that one has surveyed all of the possible answers to the question posed in this chapter?

17

NATURALISTIC OBJECTIVISM

Ethical naturalism, or naturalistic objectivism, is the view that moral sentences—both those employed in everyday moral judgments and those employed by writers on normative ethics—are reports about the presence or absence of certain natural qualities in the person, act, or state of affairs that the sentence in question is about. Moral sentences, in this view, are translatable without loss of meaning into sentences that do not employ any of the so-called "moral predicates" (good, bad, right, wrong, etc.). It is this view that I shall elaborate and defend.

Since different definitions of the key moral predicates are compatible with the central features of naturalistic objectivism, let me begin by indicating what all of us hold in common and what is the point upon which some of us within this general category hold conflicting views. I shall then go on to state the particular version of naturalistic objectivism that I hold to be correct and why.

It may be helpful to say a word at this point about the status of naturalistic objectivism—or, for that matter, of any metaethical theory. I should like to make it clear that we who hold this theory are not offering an arbitrary verbal definition of key ethical terms, nor are we making a recommendation as to how people generally *ought* to use these terms. Our claim is that people *do* use these terms, and the sentences in which they occur, in certain ways—even if, as philosophers, they believe in some other metaethical theory, or if, as plain men, they believe in no metaethical theory at all. The structure of language, we hold, allows only certain ways in which a sentence can have meaning; naturalistic objectivism is a theory about which of these ways correctly describes the particular kind of meaning that moral sentences have.

Naturalistic objectivists hold that (a) to say that something is good or bad, right or wrong, is to say that it has, or does not have, certain empirically ascertainable qualities. This implies at least two other things about moral sentences that all naturalistic objectivists hold in common, namely: (b) moral sentences are, like all informative sentences, true or false and (c) questions about the truth or falsity of such sentences are resolvable by straightforward empirical means. These three points constitute the defining characteristics of the naturalistic objectivist view; it is incumbent on anyone who holds this position to show that moral sentences do in fact exhibit these features.

There should not be any disagreement as to the method by which this matter must be resolved. Since a metaethical theory is a view about what is actually meant by moral sentences, we must have recourse at all times to the actual judgments that people make: the theory must conform to actual usage. To ask for the meaning of "good" (when used in a moral sense) is to ask for a definition that is adequate to the extension of the term as it is actually employed by plain men and ethical theorists when they frame what we call "moral judgments." If we lose sight of this—if we depart from actual usage —we shall not be able to avoid getting lost in a never-never world of arbitrary definitions that will not contribute in any way to the task at hand.

Naturalistic objectivists are agreed, as I have said, that (a) moral sentences are informative sentences asserting the presence or absence of certain qualities in the object being judged, (b) moral sentences are true or false, and (c) their truth or falsity is ascertainable by straightforward empirical means. Where, then, do we disagree among ourselves? We disagree as to *which* qualities it is whose presence or absence is being asserted when something is judged to be good or bad, right or wrong. I shall not take time, however, to survey the various proposals that have been made by naturalistic objectivists on this point, but shall proceed directly to an exposition and defense of my own view. If I can succeed in presenting a convincing case, then it will follow that naturalistic objectivists who disagree with me on this point, as well as metaethicists who hold fundamentally different views about the logic of moral discourse, are mistaken.

The Meanings of "Good"

If any one term may be said to be of central importance among the moral predicates, that term is "good" (in the moral sense). But this term, unfortunately, has so many meanings that we shall have to analyze it very carefully in order to see its central significance in ethical thinking.

The most important moral sense of "good" is the sense in which it is the antithesis of "evil." All of the other moral predicates are definable in relation to good and evil, as I shall shortly attempt to show. But first, we must distinguish some other senses of "good," in order that in what follows we shall not be confused by them.

There is a completely *non*moral sense of "good" in which that word means the opposite of "poor." We speak, for example, about good knives and poor knives, about good novels and poor novels, about good runners and poor runners; by "good" and "poor" in such cases we mean, apparently, "conforming to (good), or failing to conform to (poor), the criteria appropriate to the assessment of such things." A good knife is one that cuts well (etc.), a good novel is one that makes for enjoyable reading (etc.), and a good runner is one who runs swiftly; a poor knife, or novel, or runner is one that does not meet these criteria. "Good" in this sense is not a moral predicate at all and must not be confused with "good" in its centrally important moral sense as the opposite of "evil."

There is still another sense of "good," however, in which it is the opposite of neither "poor" nor "evil," but of "bad"; and in this sense it usually is a moral predicate. (Not always, however: we talk about good and bad pitches in baseball, good and bad shots in basketball, and we clearly do not in such cases intend to make a moral judgment.) I shall speak of "good" in this sense as the *secondary* sense of "good" and of "good" when it stands opposed to "evil" as the *primary* sense of good. My reasons for so doing will soon become apparent. There are three sorts of things that we call good (or bad) in this secondary sense: men, certain mental acts of men (thoughts, intentions, desires, purposes), and overt acts of men. I am unable to think of anything else that we would call good or bad in this clearly moral sense except in a metaphorical way.

The relation between "good" in this secondary sense and "good" in the primary sense is as follows: to say that something is good in the secondary sense is to say that it promotes, or tends to promote, what is good in the primary sense. "Good" as opposed to "evil" means "*intrinsically* good"; "good" as opposed to "bad" means "*instrumentally* good." This is the reason for calling the latter a secondary, or derivative, sense of good.

All of the other moral predicates can be defined in relation to "good" in the primary sense. My "duty," for example, is to do what, all things considered, I ought to do—"duty" and "what I ought to do" are synonymous expressions; and what I ought to do is the act that, among all the things I might do, will have the greatest tendency to promote what is good in the primary sense. Any act that tends to promote what is intrinsically good is to that extent *right*; any act that tends to hinder the achievement of what is intrinsically good, or to promote what is intrinsically evil, is to that extent *wrong*. An act that has no tendency to promote either good or evil is *morally indifferent*. It is evident, therefore, that "good" in the primary sense of "intrinsically good" is the key concept in our ethical thinking.

The Primary Meaning of "Good"

The crucial question that we must ask in metaethics, therefore, is: What is the meaning of good in the primary sense? To this question the correct answer, as I conceive it, is "maximally conducive to human happiness." This is what we mean by calling something "good" in the primary sense; everything else that depends on the disposition and choices of men is good or bad, right or wrong, praiseworthy or blameworthy, insofar as it tends to promote or to hinder the achievement of human happiness.

Perhaps the best way to exhibit the truth of what I am stating is to consider a hypothetical case in which two people are disagreeing as to whether or not a certain proposed course of action is "good" or "right." Let us suppose that the argument concerns the right or wrong of using tear gas to quell a riot. A thinks it would be wrong to use it; B thinks it would be wrong *not* to do so. So far, then, A and B are in disagreement about whether the proposed act is good or bad in the *secondary* sense defined above.

How, then, might either party attempt to support his view? The best way would be to indicate the probable results of the proposed action. A might argue, "If tear gas is used, the rioters will retaliate by using fire-arms, and the situation will be even worse than it is now. So far, all we have to worry about is a small riot; the course you are proposing could turn it into a civil war." B might argue, "I think you are mistaken. Tear gas has been thoroughly proven as an effective means of controlling riots, and it should be used immediately. The longer this situation is allowed to remain out of control, the greater is the danger of its turning into a civil war—the very thing you fear. I say tear gas should be used without delay."

What is worthy of note in this dispute is that both parties are agreed that the "right" course of action is the one that will have the greatest tendency to promote human happiness—or, what comes to the same thing, to prevent human suffering. If A were to become convinced that the result of using tear gas would be as B says, he would on his own premises have to concede that the proposed action is indeed right; and if B were to become convinced that the result would be as A described it, he would have to concede to A. The argument of both assumes that what is right or wrong in the case in question can only be decided by attempting to calculate the human consequences.

The same point can be reinforced in another way. Suppose that a third party, C, enters the dispute. "I agree with B," says C. "I think tear gas should be used—although I agree with A that it will probably lead to civil war. Nonetheless, even though it will cause suffering for many people, I think it is the right thing to do." *A* and *B*, surely, would be equally astonished by such a statement. They could only ask, "What on earth does *C mean* by 'good'?" Obviously, *C* does not mean by "good" what most people mean by it; for most people, when they use this term, mean "that state of affairs, among the options available to us, in which the maximum of human happiness and the minimum of human suffering are achieved." If this meaning is not assumed, the whole context in which the dispute was carried on is destroyed, and the dispute itself becomes unintelligible.

Let us consider a second example. Most people would agree, I think, that the excessive drinking of alcoholic beverages is morally wrong—though if there are some who disagree, it makes no difference to the argument. In any case, those who do hold that the excessive drinking of alcoholic beverages is morally wrong do so because of certain well-known consequences: it is injurious to one's health; it can (and often does) become a causal factor in the occurrence of auto accidents; it can deprive a family of many of the conveniences and even the necessities of life (because of its cost); it poisons human relationships by changing people who are normally pleasant and kind into people who are belligerent and cantankerous; and so on. If the excessive drinking of alcoholic beverages did not have these consequences (as the drinking of water in any quantity does not), we should not regard it as wrong, and "drunkenness" would not be a term of moral disapprobation. But it does have, or tend to have, these consequences; hence, it is widely regarded as wrong. But these consequences, it is evident, are all descriptions of some adverse effect that the act or habit in question has, or tends to have, on human happiness. Thus it seems clear that it is human happiness that is regarded as intrinsically good, and that everything else is regarded as being good or bad insofar as it tends to promote or to hinder that end.

One could continue to give examples indefinitely, but it hardly seems necessary or worth the effort. Consider any example that you wish, and you will discover that anything that people commonly assess in moral categories—people, their thoughts, dispositions, intentions, or acts—lends itself to such appraisal solely by virtue of its assumed tendency to promote or to hinder human happiness. If we could know (a) what state of affairs would achieve the absolute maximum of human happiness together with a minimum of human suffering, and (b) what acts would have the maximum tendency to promote that state of affairs, we should have no difficulty in deciding in any particular case what is the right thing to do. The moral dilemmas that we face are due not to our ignorance of what "good" means, but of what to do in order to achieve that ideal state of affairs in which the maximum of human happiness and the minimum of human suffering are realized.

When I say that a moral judgment consists in the assertion that some empirically ascertainable qualities are or are not present in the thing being judged, I do not mean that these qualities are precisely ascertainable in the way that, say, the presence or absence of sodium chloride in a solution is precisely ascertainable. I do mean, however, that there is nothing over and above the empirical facts to which we must attend in order to decide whether the judgment in question is true or false. The problematic character of many moral judgments is due not to the supposed fact that "goodness" consists in some odd nonempirical quality, but to the fact that such judgments often involve suppositions—even conjectures and guesses—about the probable results of this or that action that we cannot make with certainty with our present knowledge. But it is a mistake to look beyond or behind the empirical facts for some nonempirical quality to remove the uncertainty from our judgments: the uncertainty will remain and must remain until we are able to calculate much more precisely the human consequences of alternative courses of action.

The chief reason that this account is not as obvious to most people as might be expected (in view of the fact that they handle the language of moral appraisal without difficulty almost every day of their adult lives) is that most of us are taught moral principles in a way that does not clearly exhibit their relation to human happiness. We are taught as children that certain sorts of things (like slapping or biting other children, or taking things that belong to them, or telling lies) are "naughty," and certain other sorts of things (like paying compliments, helping people in need, or visiting the sick) are "nice." If we pause to reflect on the many rules we have learned in this way, we may be puzzled and tempted to look for some odd quality that gives these rules their "obligatory" character. What we fail to understand if we think in this way, however, is that the rules have been formulated precisely because they specify some of the most common ways in which human happiness can be enhanced and human unhappiness minimized. To see moral principles in this light is to rid them of the purely arbitrary character they sometimes seem to have and to exhibit them as legitimate rules of behavior for anyone who desires to know and to do what is morally right.

I said earlier that anyone who holds the naturalistic objectivist view must be prepared to show that moral sentences are capable of being true or false and that their truth or falsity is ascertainable by empirical means. Let us now consider these features as they apply to what might be thought the most difficult case for a naturalistic objectivist to account for: one in which some particular person—Joe Doakes, say—is said to be (in the moral sense) "a good person" or "a good man."

Is there any evidence that would count against the statement, "Joe Doakes is a good man"? Yes. If we were to learn that Joe is a heavy drinker, or that he commonly mistreats his wife and children, or that he is habitually careless in his work, or that he does not get along well with most people, we would be inclined to regard the statement as false. To say that Joe Doakes is a good man is to say that he commonly acts in certain sorts of ways, and the ways we have in mind are not compatible with the ways just described. The difference between these two kinds of behavior—what makes one type of behavior "good" and the other "bad"—is precisely the tendency of each to promote or to hinder human happiness.

But the means by which it can be determined which of these ways is descriptive of Joe's behavior are clearly empirical. We must watch him to see how he behaves and listen to what other people say about his behavior. On that basis we make up our minds. If Joe is like most of us, it is quite certain that he is neither unambigously good nor unambiguously bad: sometimes he acts in ways that promote human happiness and sometimes in ways that decrease it. It is the facts about a man's actual behavior that determine whether and to what extent he is truly described as "good" or "bad," and these facts are ascertainable only by the empirical method of watching to see how he behaves. Ergo, moral sentences are true or false and confirmable or disconfirmable by empirical means.

STUDY QUESTIONS

1. True or false: A number of mutually incompatible theories belonging to *normative ethics* could be correctly described as "naturalistic objectivist" theories. Why?
2. What does Naturalistic Objectivist (NO) say is "the method by which this matter must be resolved"? Is he right? How do you determine what method is appropriate? Is it implicit in the question that is being asked, or is it determined in some other way? Can you think of any reason why any of the other parties to the dispute might object to this method?
3. Do you think NO is on the right track in distinguishing three meanings of "good"? Suppose that he is right: does this in any way substantiate his main thesis? Does he claim that it does?
4. Is NO right in saying that the statement, "Joe Doakes is a good man," can be refuted by empirical facts? How does this argument affect NO's case?
5. Summarize NO's arguments in support of his position. Can you think of any arguments against it?

18

INTUITIONISM

There are two kinds of hedonists: those who affirm that "good" just *means* "pleasurable" or "conducive to happiness" and those who maintain that whatever "good" means, pleasure (or happiness) is the only thing to which it applies. We might call these positions, respectively, "analytic hedonism" and "synthetic hedonism," since according to the one view the statement "Happiness is good" is an analytic statement and according to the other view it is a synthetic one.[1] Both forms of hedonism, I am convinced, are mistaken; but hedonism in its analytic form is by far the more seriously in error of the two. And Naturalistic Objectivist, unfortunately, is an analytic hedonist.

I may say at the outset that very much of what Naturalistic Objectivist has said appears to me to be both true and valuable. He is quite right, for example, in distinguishing three meanings of "good" (the nonmoral sense and the instrumental and intrinsic senses of moral goodness). He is right also in his contention that most (though not all, in my view) other moral predicates can be defined in relation to the very important concept of intrinsic goodness. But the crucial question for metaethics, as he himself says, is: What is the meaning of "intrinsically good"? And on this question I think he is profoundly mistaken.

The "Open-Question" Test

There is a simple test, which I shall call the "open-question" test, by which we can easily assess the accuracy of any proposed definition. Let us call a word for which some definition is being proposed the *definiendum* and the definition that is proposed the *definiens*. If we

---

[1] See the glossary for further clarification of the terms *analytic* and *synthetic*. See also the discussion on pp. 246–247.

ask a question of the form, Are all (definiens) really (definiendum)? it is evident that if our definition is accurate we shall not be putting a significant (or open) question; and if our definition is not accurate, we shall. Suppose, for example, that I define "bachelor" as (a) an unmarried male and as (b) an unmarried adult male human being. If I apply the test, it is clear that in the one case I do, and in the other case I do not, have an open question. If I ask, Are all unmarried males bachelors? I have an open (significant) question to which the correct answer is "No"; for preadult human males and nonhuman males of any age are unmarried males who are not bachelors. But if I ask, Are all unmarried adult male human beings really bachelors? it is equally evident that I am not asking an open, or significant, question; for the briefest reflection makes it clear that the definiens is what I mean when I use the term "bachelor."

If, now, we apply the test to Naturalistic Objectivist's proposed definition of "intrinsically good," it is evident at once that this definition will not do. For the question, Are all instances of human pleasure, or happiness, really good? is an open question, to which it is highly unlikely that an affirmative answer would be correct. Consider a few examples. Is it plausible to maintain that the enjoyment that a young boy might get out of torturing a frog (or some other sentient creature), or the happiness that a sadist might get out of tormenting another human being (even if his happiness should exceed his victim's suffering), or the perverted pleasure of a masochist who allegedly enjoys being punished are good? Clearly not. If we judge human happiness to be good, the reason is not that goodness simply *means* human happiness, but that we discern that the quality we denote by the term "good" is present in most (but not all) instances of human happiness. It is this insight that we express in our synthetic judgment, "Human happiness, by and large, is good."

There are, as Naturalistic Objectivist has pointed out, a number of rival theories of the naturalistic objectivist type, and space obviously does not permit us to list them and apply our test to each of them in turn. It may fairly be said, however, that the hedonistic version of this theory is by far the most plausible. Since it fails to pass the open-question test, we may be reasonably confident that any other theory of this type will also fail.

Refutation of Hedonism

The inadequacy of hedonism can be demonstrated apart from the open-question test. The test, it is to be noted, only shows the incorrectness of analytic hedonism; the arguments that I shall now put forward demonstrate the inadequacy of hedonism in both its analytic and synthetic forms. Although our discussion will require a brief venture into the domain of normative ethics, the digression is necessary in order to present more clearly what I consider to be the correct metaethical theory.

The incorrectness of hedonism is evident, first, from the fact that there are a number of things other than pleasurable states of mind that we regard as being intrinsically good. W. D. Ross has shown, for example, that (a) virtuous disposition and action, (b) the apportionment of pleasure and pain to the virtuous and vicious respectively, and (c) knowledge and right opinion are *intrinsic goods* and that they cannot be reduced to pleasurable states of mind or to acts tending to increase the sum of human happiness.[2] A universe in which these things obtain—quite apart from any consideration of the balance of human happiness that they may or may not produce—is intrinsically better than a universe in which these things do not obtain. We have only to contemplate the two states of affairs, assuming the quantity of human happiness to be equal in the two cases, to see that this is so.

The same conclusion may, however, be established in another way. There are some instances of human pleasure that, if we suppose them to occur, reduce the total quantity of goodness in the universe. Suppose, for example, that a person, *A,* suffers great misfortune; and suppose that another person, *B,* who has long been jealous of *A* because of *A*'s earlier good fortune, contemplates *A*'s misfortune *with pleasure.* There can be no doubt in this case that the quantity of pleasure in the universe is greater than it would be if *B* did not react in this way to *A*'s misfortune; but it is equally clear that *B*'s responding in this way is not a good, but an evil. Indeed, it would be better if there were *less* pleasure in the universe: there would be more good in the universe if *B* were sorrowful instead of happy. It seems obvious, therefore, that goodness is not simply identical with pleasure and that not all instances of human pleasure are good.

The inadequacy of hedonism can also be exhibited by the following *reductio ad absurdum* argument.[3] If human happiness were the only thing that is intrinsically good, and if the amount of good in the universe depended entirely on the amount of human happiness, then a universe in which there is but one individual who is moderately happy *forever* would be intrinsically better than one in which a finite number of individuals is happy in whatever degree for any finite length of time. But we obviously do not think this to be the case. Even if we were persuaded that some one person could be rendered moderately happy forever (thus producing an infinite quantity of happiness and, therefore, goodness in the universe), we would not, if it were necessary, approve of the annihilation of all other human beings in

---

[2] W. D. Ross, *The Right and the Good* (Oxford: Clarendon, 1930), Chap. V.
[3] See Chapter 5 for an explanation of the *reductio ad absurdum* form of argument.

order to achieve this, although, according to our hypothesis, their happiness is of a merely finite quantity and therefore inferior to that of our hypothetical eternal individual. Since we ought to draw this conclusion according to hedonistic theory, it is evident that the hedonistic theory is false.

The Indefinability of "Good"

We have been speaking—without any misgivings about the meaningfulness of what we have been saying—about a variety of things (states of mind, acts, states of affairs in the universe, etc.) that we would or would not call good. We have said that, contrary to the claim of ethical hedonists, we do not mean "pleasure" or "human happiness" when we call something good (analytic hedonism), nor is it only pleasure or human happiness that we regard as being good (synthetic hedonism). What, then, do we mean when we call something good? The correct answer to this question is, I think, the one given by Moore: we mean good, and nothing else. "Everything is what it is, and not another thing." [4] We can, indeed, find other words to denote the quality that we commonly denote by the word "good": we can use the German word *gut,* or the French *bon,* or even the English phrase "worthy of being valued in and of itself"; but that which we denote in these various ways is a simple, indefinable, nonnatural quality whose presence in a person, act, or state of affairs is what makes us call it good.

"Good" is indefinable because it is a simple concept. In order to define a concept, it is necessary that that concept be complex, that it be composed of simpler concepts. One can define "daffodil," for example, as "a yellow flower of the genus *Narcissus*" because these various elements—being yellow, being a flower, and being of the genus *Narcissus*—are all constituent parts of the complex concept of a daffodil. Of these constituent elements, "flower" and "genus *Narcissus*" can also be defined. But, as Moore pointed out, "yellow" cannot be defined (except, of course, ostensively) because it is a simple concept. All definitions must ultimately be built up out of such concepts, for the process of defining concepts by pointing to the elements of which they are composed cannot go on indefinitely: at length we must come to those elements that, like "good" and "yellow," are simple, and therefore indefinable.

"Good," like "yellow," is a simple and indefinable concept. But the quality that it denotes, unlike the quality denoted by the term "yellow," is not a natural quality. By this I mean, simply, that the good-

---

[4] Bishop Butler, quoted by G. E. Moore on the title page of *Principia Ethica* (Cambridge, England: Cambridge University Press, 1959. Originally published 1903).

ness of a person, act, or state of affairs is not something that can be perceived by the senses; it must be *rationally discerned,* or *intuited,* if it is to be apprehended at all. That this is, in fact, how we apprehend the goodness of things will become evident if we reflect on a few examples.

Let us consider again the illustration of the man who contemplates with pleasure the misfortune of another human being. There is no question here of the probable effects of B's malice: we can very well imagine that A is already dead, or that B expires shortly after entertaining his unkind thoughts about A's misfortune, and still we would judge that B's malice was evil. But how do we know this? Certainly it is in virtue of the supposed facts that we render our judgment; but our judgment that "B's pleasure in A's misfortune is evil" is not simply a confused way of reporting that B did entertain feelings of pleasure in contemplating A's misfortune. It is a judgment about the *moral significance* of those facts. And this judgment rests not on the perception of some additional natural qualities or some supposed tendency of B's act (of contemplation), but on our direct intuition of the evilness of the act itself.

Consider a second example. A person, X, has borrowed a sum of money from a wealthy friend, Y, and has promised to repay him on a certain date. The date arrives and X, being a man who keeps his word, repays the loan. This, although hardly an instance of moral heroism, is, I presume, an act on which we should without hesitation pronounce a favorable judgment. Since it is an instance of promise-keeping, and promise-keeping is something that we regard as a moral duty under normal circumstances, the act in question is judged to be good. But note: no calculation of the probable consequences of alternative possible courses of action is involved in this judgment. Indeed, it is highly likely that the same sum of money given to a poor family would produce more human happiness than it would if returned to the bank account of Y. But the calculation of consequences is not relevant in this case: X has contracted a duty in making a promise to Y and that duty takes precedence over all but the most unusual of circumstances. We judge, therefore, that X's act of returning the money on the date promised is good.

What are we saying, then, when we say, "this act is good," and on what basis? Clearly we are not saying that X's act is the one that, of all the alternatives available to him, has the greatest tendency to increase the sum of human happiness. Indeed, we can be quite sure this is not the case. We are saying, simply, that X's act, as an instance of promise-keeping, is good, and that is all we are saying. Our basis for saying this is not that we perceive some empirical facts in addition to those that make us call this act an instance of promise-keeping, but simply that we apprehend such an act as being good.

There is, I realize, a widespread tendency among philosophers to-day to reject intuition, or direct rational insight, as a mode of acquiring knowledge and to insist that the only knowledge available to us must come by empirical means. This bias against rational insight explains, I think, the great flurry of activity that has recently been in evidence in the empiricist camp to find some way to account for our knowledge of ethical truths and our ability to make valid moral judgments, without admitting these as instances of rational, or nonempirical, insight. But the effort is doomed to failure. Even our judgment that human happiness is, on the whole, good, is a synthetic judgment that we could not make apart from our direct apprehension that the quality of goodness is in fact present in most (but not all) instances of human happiness. It is this apprehension, and this alone, that allows us to distinguish between those many instances of human happiness that are good and those few that are not. What is apprehended, in such cases, is "not another thing" but *goodness itself*.

If this view is correct, any attempt to define "good" in terms of some natural quality or combination of natural qualities is mistaken: it consists in the mistake of confusing the nonnatural quality designated by the term "good" with something else that it is not. I propose, following Moore, to call this particular kind of mistake the "naturalistic fallacy." It is a fallacy because it is an error in logic, and it is naturalistic because it is the specific error of confusing a natural quality with a nonnatural quality. It is this fallacy, which exists regardless of the set of natural qualities proposed as a definition of "good," that is effectively exposed by the open-question test. Many writers on ethics, as Moore has shown, have been guilty of it.

A Word About Moral Duty

Earlier I stated that I am not in complete agreement with Naturalistic Objectivist's suggestion that all of the other moral predicates can be defined in relation to the centrally important concept "good." I want, in conclusion, to indicate why I am inclined to disagree with him on this point.

My chief misgivings on this score concern the concept of "moral duty." I do not think it is correct to say, as Naturalistic Objectivist does, that someone's moral duty is always to do the act that, of all the alternatives available, will produce the greatest total increase of good in the world. I think some acts have an obligatory character quite apart from their supposed consequences. But, I want first to make a preliminary observation about moral duty that may be of some help in clearing up this rather elusive concept.

It is important to distinguish between (a) objective duty and (b) apparent duty. This distinction is necessary in order to make intelligible the very commonplace fact that it is possible for a person to be mistaken about what is his moral duty in a certain situation. "I believe it is my duty to do thus and so" is an intelligible statement, and its intelligibility rests on the assumption that what I believe to be my duty may be different from what really is my duty.

It is certainly evident that we cannot possibly know which of the many things that we might do at any moment will in fact produce the greatest increase of good in the world; so if this is what Naturalistic Objectivist means, his view would entail that we never know what our duty is. And this, I think, is absurd. We must, then, interpret him to mean that we ought always do that act which *we believe* will produce the greatest increase of good in the world—in other words, we must construe his remark as applying not to our objective duty, but to our apparent duty. Even if we construe his remark in this way, however, his view does not stand up; for what I believe to be my duty on many occasions is not at all the act that I believe is likely to produce the greatest increase of good in the world, all things considered. Neither objective duty nor apparent duty, therefore, seems to be definable in relation to "good."

The "obligatory" or "dutiful" character of certain sorts of acts is a quality of those acts that must be rationally discerned in the same way that the goodness of certain states of affairs must be rationally discerned. There are, as Ross has pointed out,[5] various kinds of duties —duties of fidelity (telling the truth, keeping promises), duties of reparation (making amends for wrongful acts), duties of gratitude (expressing thanks for favors done by others), duties of justice (assisting the needy), duties of beneficence (relieving suffering), and so on. No doubt we sometimes err in thinking something to be our duty when it is not, just as we sometimes err in judging some state of affairs to be good when it is not; for our knowledge of moral truths is not infallible. But our knowledge of moral truths, insofar as we have such knowledge, is nonempirical; the qualities that we judge when we make a moral judgment—both the goodness of good things and the obligatoriness of acts that are our duty—are nonempirical, or nonnatural, qualities.

STUDY QUESTIONS

1. What is the "open-question" test? Can you think of any examples in which the test fails to prove what Intuitionist says it proves?
2. What distinction does Intuitionist make between "analytic hedonism" and "synthetic hedonism"? What is the relationship between hedonism of these two types and naturalistic objectivism? How does Intuitionist attempt to refute hedonism of both types?

---

[5] Ross, *op. cit.*, Chap. II.

3. Would it be logically consistent for a person to be both (a) an intuitionist, and (b) a synthetic hedonist? Explain.

4. Consider very carefully Intuitionist's examples of moral judgments. Does he convince you that they *cannot* be construed in the way that Naturalistic Objectivist would have us construe them? Does he convince you that they should be construed in the way he proposes? Try his proposal with a few examples of your own.

5. Would it be logically possible for Intuitionist to agree with Naturalistic Objectivist's analysis of "moral duty"? How does Intuitionist analyze "moral duty"?

19

PRIVATE SUBJECTIVISM

Neither of the two preceding theories constitutes a truly adequate and satisfactory account of the logic of moral discourse. Each of them, it seems to me, explains some of the facts about the language of morals and each leaves certain facts unexplained. Let us try to separate the truth from the error in the foregoing accounts and go on from there to develop a theory about the logic of moral discourse that is adequate to all the relevant facts.

Naturalistic Objectivist has argued that (a) "good" has three distinguishable meanings: namely, a primary moral meaning (good-evil), a secondary moral meaning (good-bad), and a nonmoral meaning (good-poor); (b) the most important concept for understanding the logic of moral discourse is "good" in its primary moral sense; (c) all other moral predicates are definable in terms of this concept; (d) the meaning of "good" in this primary sense is "providing a maximum of human happiness"; (e) moral judgments are, therefore, true or false; and (f) their truth or falsity is ascertainable by straightforward empirical means. Of these six propositions, Intuitionist has agreed, either explicitly or by implication, with propositions (a), (b), and (e) and has disagreed with the other three. He has argued, on the contrary, that (g) "duty," at least, is not definable in terms of "good" in the primary sense; (h) "good" in the primary sense is indefinable since it denotes a simple nonnatural quality, and (i) the truth or falsity of moral sentences is ascertainable by non-empirical means (intuition).

Of these nine propositions I think we can, without further ado, simply accept propositions (a), (b), (e), and (f). My reasons for holding propositions (e) and (f) to be true are, however, quite different from those given by Naturalistic Objectivist, as will shortly be apparent. I do think that moral sentences consist in the assertion (in a rather misleading way) of some very commonplace facts. I am, therefore, bound to hold that the two propositions in question are true. I have no wish to enter into the side argument between Naturalistic Objectivist and Intuitionist as to whether or not "duty" is definable in terms of "good" in the primary sense; so I shall refrain from expressing myself on propositions (c) and (g). I am inclined to doubt whether our moral concepts are as neatly organized into a coherent system as Naturalistic Objectivist has suggested; but I am even more certain that what we know when we know that something is our duty is not what Intuitionist says we know, nor do we know it in the way he says we do (proposition f). But this is, in any case, a trifling side issue, and I do not wish to commit myself to a definite position on it.

There are, then, three propositions among the nine that have been enunciated by my two predecessors—propositions (d), (h), and (i)—with which I definitely disagree. I propose to indicate briefly my reasons for rejecting each of them.

Let us consider first proposition (i)—the claim, put forward by Intuitionist, that the truth or falsity of moral sentences is ascertainable by nonempirical means. I disagree with this claim for two reasons. First, I hold that all of our knowledge of synthetic truths arises out of experience: I am, in short, an empiricist. If there were some other convincing examples of synthetic truths that are known a priori—"intuited," as Intuitionist says—then we might, of course, entertain the possibility that the truth of moral sentences is also known in this way. But it has been amply demonstrated by many philosophers that the most plausible examples of such truths can be easily accounted for in a way that is consistent with empiricism.[1] Since this is the case, it seems unlikely that moral truths are an exception to the rule. Second, even if the correctness of the general thesis of empiricism be disallowed, it cannot be plausibly argued that moral truths are examples of synthetic truths that are known a priori. These truths do not exhibit the qualities of necessity and universality—or of self-evidence—that are alleged to be the hallmarks of a priori knowledge. There is, admittedly, a certain oddness about moral sentences; but this oddness, as we shall see, is due to something quite different from the alleged fact that they are truths that are directly "intuited" as Intuitionist claims.

As for proposition (h), it is sufficient to point out that if proposition (i) is rejected, proposition (h) must be rejected as well—or else we must draw the conclusion that we are in complete ignorance with respect to moral truths. I think that in most cases we do know that what

---

[1] See Chapter 32 for a fuller explanation of empiricism.

we are asserting is the case, when we say that something is "good" or
"right," though we are seldom explicitly aware of exactly what it is
that we are asserting when we express ourselves in this way. I, therefore, conclude that the theory that "good" denotes a simple nonnatural
quality is incorrect.

Naturalistic Objectivist's thesis—that "good" means "providing for
a maximum of human happiness"—is inadequate in a number of
ways. Intuitionist has pointed out, for example, that our judgment
that a state of affairs is good, or that an act is right, does not vary
exactly with the quantity of human happiness supposed to be present;
and I think that in this he is right. But the inadequacy of the theory
can also be shown in another way. There is no valid argument by
which we can, from premises containing no moral predicates, deduce
a sentence that does contain a moral predicate. If Naturalistic Objectivist's thesis were correct, we ought to be able to argue as follows:

State X is a state of the universe in which there would be substan-
tially more human happiness than there is at present.

Act W is, of all the things I might do, the act that would be maximally conducive to the achievement of state X.

I *ought* to do act W.

Now it is apparent, I am saying, that we cannot validly argue in this
way. The "ought" that appears in the conclusion is not deducible from
the merely descriptive statements that constitute the premises of the
argument, whereas according to Naturalistic Objectivist's thesis it
should be. Moreover, insofar as we do feel that the conclusion is
somehow appropriate to (even though not deducible from) those
premises, it is because of another unexpressed premise—that one
ought, on the whole, to do things that are conducive to human happiness.

It seems to me, therefore, that the attempts of both Naturalistic
Objectivist and Intuitionist to describe the peculiar logical structure
of moral discourse must be regarded as failures. Moral predicates do
not refer to either observable or unobservable qualities in the objects
of which they seem to be descriptive. Hence, the conclusion is inescapable that moral predicates are not property-referring words at all,
and moral sentences are not informative in the sense of conveying
some information about the object that is said to be good or bad, right
or wrong. It remains to be seen, however, whether such sentences are
not informative in another sense.

The Case for Subjectivism

An important fact about moral utterances, for which objectivist theories give no account whatsoever, is that they are always expressive of some attitude, either positive or negative, on the part of the person making the judgment. Some moral predicates, like "good," "right," "praiseworthy," and "virtuous," are expressive of what we may call a "pro-attitude"; others, like "evil," "bad," "wrong," "blameworthy," and "vicious," are expressive of an "anti-attitude." This fact about moral predicates, and the sentences in which they are employed, is a valuable clue to the logical structure of the language of morals, for it suggests that what we are saying when we call something good or bad, right or wrong, is that we have, or tend to have, a favorable or unfavorable attitude toward it. The real meaning of the statement, "The infliction of needless pain is evil," is: "I disapprove of the infliction of needless pain." Moral sentences, in short, are not informative of the qualities of the apparent object of the judgment: they are informative of the attitude of the person rendering the judgment.

My point may be illustrated by considering the somewhat parallel case of food preferences. A says, "Rutabagas are good," B says, "I disagree: rutabagas are not good at all." On the surface of it, it looks as if A and B are engaged in a disagreement about rutabagas: do they, or do they not, possess the quality of "tasting good"? (And whether they do or not, is "good taste" a natural, or a nonnatural, quality?) It is evident upon reflection, however, that A and B are not really disagreeing about any empirical or nonempirical qualities of rutabagas at all. What A means by "Rutabagas are good" is "I, A, like rutabagas," and what B means by "Rutabagas are not good" is "I, B, do not like rutabagas." A and B have, then, different *attitudes* toward the taste of rutabagas, and their respective statements about the goodness or nongoodness of rutabagas are simply misleading ways of reporting their private tastes.

Moral sentences, I am suggesting, are misleading in exactly this way. Like statements about tastes, they look as if they are informative statements about the object that is said to be good or bad, right or wrong; but they are in fact informative only of the feelings, or attitudes, of the person making the statement. "Helping someone in need is praiseworthy" is like "Rutabagas are good," not like "Daffodils are yellow"; but the misleading character of moral sentences is less obvious than is that of sentences about food tastes.

There is one common, and at first sight quite plausible, objection to this view with which it will be convenient to deal at this point. The objection is this: it is apparent that people do argue about ethical matters, whereas on the theory here proposed it would seem that there is nothing to argue about. If you like rutabagas and I do not, there is no point in discussing the matter: the most we can do is recognize that our tastes differ at this point, and that is the end of it. But people do argue about ethical matters, and they even cite empirical evidence in support of their views. How, then, can this be accounted for in the subjectivist theory?

The answer is that (a) by and large people do tend to approve and disapprove of the same "ends" and (b) they disagree, when they do, about the most effective means of achieving those ends. Naturalistic Objectivist's example about the two men who disagreed about whether it would be right or wrong to use tear gas in a certain situation is a case in point. The two men, it will be recalled, did not disagree in what we may call their basic moral attitude: they both favored a restoration of order and regarded with disfavor the occurrence of a civil war. Their disagreement was only about the likely results of using the tear gas; because they held different opinions on this point, they held different attitudes toward the proposed action. Since empirical evidence is relevant to assessing the probable consequences of this or that course of action, the citing of evidence is appropriate in such circumstances.

As a general rule, significant disagreement on ethical matters is possible only if, and insofar as, the disputants tend to hold the same basic attitudes toward the same actual or imagined states of affairs. If they reach agreement about the facts but still persist in holding conflicting attitudes, there remains nothing that can be settled by rational argument: all that either can do, if he is not content to leave the other's attitude as it is, is to resort to name-calling or some other form of nonrational persuasion.

"But surely," it may be objected, "people do disagree in their basic moral attitudes and even try to persuade others to agree with them." Granted. People seem to feel more strongly about their moral attitudes than they do about their food preferences (we do not talk, for example, about our "culinary convictions"), and few people appear willing simply to accept differences at this point and let it go at that. But the methods by which anyone can persuade anyone else to change his basic moral attitudes are not those of rational argument but only the methods of nonrational persuasion: name-calling, intimidation, threats, and so on. This is probably why our language has words like "prude," "moral ignoramus," and the like.

Does this view lead to pessimistic conclusions about the possibility of achieving enough ethical agreement among men to make harmonious life possible? Not at all. To so conclude would be equivalent to a restaurateur's concluding that, since people's tastes differ, he might as well give up trying to develop a menu that will win the general approval of his customers. Fortunately, people by and large tend to approve and disapprove of the same sorts of things: that is why there is little disagreement with statements like "The infliction of needless pain is evil," or "It is good to help others who are in need." It is not the alleged objectivity of moral judgments, but the substantial similarity of our basic moral attitudes, that renders possible a reasonably harmonious society.

The Truth and Falsity of Ethical Statements

I have already stated that I agree with Naturalistic Objectivist's assertions that ethical statements are capable of being true or false and that their truth or falsity is ascertainable by empirical means. I want now to indicate why and in what sense I hold these assertions to be true.

Since ethical statements are assertions about the speaker's attitudes, such statements are always either true or false: they are true if the speaker really has the attitude that he claims to have and false if he does not. Moreover, the means by which we determine whether a person has the attitude he claims to have are straightforwardly empirical: introspection in the case of ourselves and observation in the case of others.

It seems to be possible, incidentally, for a person to be mistaken about his own attitudes and thus to make false ethical statements without any intent to deceive. At times a person can affirm general principles learned earlier in life, which may have been truly descriptive of his attitudes at that time, without realizing that his present attitude (as judged by his behavior) is no longer what it formerly was. A person who has been taught that all drinking of alcoholic beverages is wrong, for example, may continue to say this on occasion even if he engages in moderate drinking himself and has no objection to others doing the same. There is, so far as I can see, no logical inconsistency in this; it is just that the general principle learned earlier in life is no longer truly descriptive of this person's present attitude.

Moral Attitudes and Objectively Descriptive Inferences

There is a sense, however, in which moral utterances are implicitly descriptive of the objects that are asserted to be good or bad, right or wrong. It is true, as Naturalistic Objectivist says, that if someone is said to be "a good man," we should be very surprised to learn that he is a poor husband and father, difficult to get along with, careless in his work, and so on; and this gives some credence to the view that the statement "Joe Doakes is a good man" is an assertion to the effect that Joe Doakes has certain qualities and does not have others.

That the assertion "Joe Doakes is a good man" is not as straightforwardly descriptive as this example makes it appear to be, however, is apparent from the fact that what we would regard as its "objective descriptive content" would vary considerably depending on whether we understood the statement to have been uttered by (a) the president of the local temperance union, (b) a fundamentalist minister, (c) oneself, or (d) the head of the Mafia. There are some "objective descriptive implications" in each case, but their precise character varies depending on the speaker. How can this be?

The correct solution to the puzzle, I would suggest, is as follows. What is sometimes called the descriptive content of a moral utterance is a result of an inference that we make from (a) what we know or suppose about the basic moral attitudes of the speaker in conjunction with (b) the particular statement that he makes to the effect that so-and-so is good. We know, for example, that Mr. X, the head of the Mafia, generally approves of men who can rob a bank without getting caught, who always share their loot with the rest of the mob, and so on. If, then, Mr. X says "Joe Doakes is a good man," we infer that Joe Doakes is not a psalm-singing philanthropist but a man who exhibits the sorts of qualities that Mr. X is in the habit of commending. If we knew nothing about the attitudes of the speaker, we should be very much in doubt about what kind of a man Joe Doakes is even though he is said to be a "good" man.

If, when we hear someone described as a "good" or "virtuous" person, we are not usually in doubt about what sort of person he is, it is not because "good" or "virtuous" directly mean such-and-such a combination of qualities, but because people by and large tend to favor certain sorts of qualities and behavior in their fellow men. It is this fact that lends whatever plausibility there is to the naturalistic objectivist theory, and it leads us, mistakenly, to conclude that the primary meaning of moral utterances is their objective descriptive meaning. The variability of this descriptive meaning depending on the basic moral attitudes of the speaker makes it evident that this descriptive content is inferential rather than direct, and it is precisely the subjective theory of the primary meaning of moral utterances that enables us to account for this undeniable variation. I take this, therefore, as a most powerful confirmation of the correctness of the view here proposed.

STUDY QUESTIONS

1. What are the "three propositions" enunciated by one or the other of the two preceding writers with which Private Subjectivist (PS) feels obliged to take issue? With whom are you inclined to agree on each of these points? Why?
2. Is PS right in saying: "There is no valid argument by which one can, from premises containing no moral predicates, deduce a conclusion

that does contain a moral predicate"? If he is right, is this fact damaging to naturalistic objectivism? Explain.

3. What exactly is PS's own view about the meaning of moral sentences? Do the examples he gives especially lend themselves to this kind of interpretation? Can you think of any examples that he might find it difficult to interpret in this way?

4. In what sense does private subjectivism maintain that ethical statements are capable of being true or false? How according to this view can the statement, "The infliction of needless pain is evil" be contradicted?

5. What does PS mean by the statement that the "descriptive content" of ethical statements is inferential rather than direct? Do you think he is right?

20

SOCIETAL
SUBJECTIVISM

There can be little doubt that the view of moral judgments presented in the preceding chapter represents a decided advance over the two objectivist theories introduced earlier. It seems clear that pro-attitudes and anti-attitudes are involved in an important way in the meaning of moral judgments. Any theory that fails to take account of this fact must be regarded as inadequate.

Some things about Private Subjectivist's proposal, however, strike me as being very strange. I shall point out what I consider to be certain oddities in his theory—features that demonstrate beyond a reasonable doubt that it is not the whole and correct answer to our problem. I shall then suggest a slight emendation by means of which the difficulties inherent in the private subjectivist view can be overcome.

Some Oddities of Private Subjectivism

If we were to adopt the private subjectivist theory, we should have to conclude that moral judgments are never false except in the very unusual instance in which the person making the judgment has made some mistake in assessing his own attitude; and this seems very strange. Let us suppose that two people, A and B, are discussing the rightness or wrongness of r. A says, "r is right," B says "r is wrong." It would hardly be appropriate for A to say in this situation, "But B, you don't really disapprove of r, you do it all the time!" Even if A confronted B with evidence in support of the fact that he regularly had a pro-attitude toward r, this still would not make B withdraw his statement. We could imagine him replying, "I didn't say I *disapproved* of r, I said that r is *wrong*—notwithstanding the fact that I, reprobate that

I am, approve of it." And in speaking this way, *B* would not be talking nonsense.

This brings me to my second point. According to private subjectivism, it would be nonsensical (because self-contradictory) to say, "I approve of some things that are wrong," or "I disapprove of some things that are right." The self-contradiction is plain: "I approve of some things that are wrong" means, according to this theory, "I approve of some things that I do not approve of." But certainly it is not self-contradictory to speak of approving of some things that are wrong. A theory that requires us to banish such statements to the realm of nonsense is somehow mistaken.

There is another type of statement that has a perfectly legitimate use in ordinary discourse that becomes nonsensical according to the private subjectivist view. Consider the statement, "We ought never do anything that we believe to be wrong, even if we want to." Surely this is a statement that would be very natural in certain contexts—in a treatise on normative ethics, for example—and we should have no difficulty in understanding it or, probably, assenting to it. But according to the private subjectivist view this becomes a nonsensical statement because it means "I disapprove of people doing things that they disapprove of, even when they approve of them." Now the purpose of a metaethical theory is not to reform moral discourse, but to explain it. Since we do have a use for statements such as this and since private subjectivism does not allow that use, the theory surely needs some improvement.

Further, if the private subjectivist theory is correct, then it follows that treatises on normative ethics tell us nothing except the private likes and dislikes of their authors. This idea, to say the least, is a very strange one. No doubt the great ethicists of our culture—Aristotle, St. Thomas Aquinas, Immanuel Kant, and many more—did have their private likes and dislikes on moral questions, just as they presumably had their own peculiar tastes in food; but surely it is not because of a purely biographical interest that we read Aristotle's *Nicomachean Ethics*, St. Thomas Aquinas' *Summa Theologica*, or Kant's *Critique of Practical Reason*. We read them because we expect these men to help us understand, among other things, what we ought to approve of, what really is right or wrong, good or evil; and we should not be interested in such questions, or even be able to ask them, if these terms expressed nothing but the speaker's private likes and dislikes. On this score the private subjectivist theory appears to be inadequate.

Finally, it seems that part of the persuasiveness of Private Subjectivist's account results from a confusion of which he evidently is not aware and of which many of his readers may not be aware. I suspect that the most persuasive feature of private subjectivism for many people is its apparent capacity to account for shifts in the "objective-descriptive content" of ethical statements depending on who makes the statement. We infer certain things about the apparent object of the judgment, says Private Subjectivist, on the basis of what we know about the general likes and dislikes of the person making the judgment. What Private Subjectivist fails to note, however, is that when the statement "Joe Doakes is a good man" is made by, say, the head of the Mafia, it is no longer a moral judgment: it is a judgment employing "good" in a *non*moral sense such as we find in the sentence, "A Buick is a good automobile." When the head of the Mafia says that Joe Doakes is a "good man," he certainly does not mean that Joe is a paragon of virtue: he means that Joe is a good gangster—he does well the things the speaker expects a gangster to do. How, then, do we distinguish between the moral and the nonmoral uses of good? Actually, we distinguish without difficulty: we recognize immediately, once our attention is called to it, that the statement of the number-one man in the Mafia that Joe Doakes is a "good man" is not a moral judgment, whereas the same statement made by you or me normally would be a moral judgment. Private subjectivism fails to recognize this difference and is unable to account for it. Hence, we must look further for a metaethical theory that is adequate to all the relevant facts.

An Alternative to Private Subjectivism

The theory I should like to offer as an alternative to the one just weighed and found wanting is a theory known as *societal subjectivism*. Moral judgments, according to this view, are reports about pro-attitudes and anti-attitudes (as they are according to the private subjectivist theory); but the attitudes that they purport to describe are not necessarily or exclusively those of the person making the judgment, but rather those of some group with which he identifies. Basic moral attitudes, in short, are never simply the private attitudes of this or that individual. They are always the common attitudes of some community of which the individual is a part. Indeed, it is precisely the generality of such attitudes—their nonprivate character, in other words—that gives them the force of moral principles. Let us see how the features of moral discourse that have proved to be so perplexing for the private subjectivist theory can be understood if we construe moral sentences in the way I am proposing.

What sort of meaning can be allowed for the statements "I approve of some things that are wrong" and "I disapprove of some things that are right"? Both of these, as we have seen, are meaningless if we interpret them according to the private subjectivist theory. According to my view, however, they are perfectly intelligible statements. "I approve of some things that are wrong" means "I approve of some things that are not generally approved of by people whose opinions I ordinarily respect"; and "I disapprove of some things that are right" means "I disapprove of some things that are generally approved of by people whose opinions I ordinarily respect." As soon as we recognize that the approval or disapproval expressed in a moral judgment is not necessarily or exclusively that of the speaker, but of some "community" with which he identifies, the apparent self-contradiction of such statements disappears.

There is a certain deliberate vagueness in the expression "generally approved of by people whose opinions I ordinarily respect," and it is in order to discuss it at this point. There is considerable variation from one individual to another with respect to the "community" with which he identifies and consequently with respect to the opinions he takes into account when making his moral judgments. In every culture—especially in a self-consciously pluralistic culture such as our own—there are various subcultures that in many cases are the "communities" of which their members feel themselves to be a part. No one is just an American, or a Russian, or a Swede. A given American, for example, may be at one and the same time (a) an American, (b) a Catholic, (c) a Democrat, (d) a college professor, and (e) a member of the Society for the Prevention of Cruelty to Animals. Each of these "communities" may, on different occasions, be the one to which he has reference when he calls something right or wrong, good or evil. Which community is relevant in a given case depends on what sorts of basic attitudes are typical of each. For our hypothetical American it might vary depending on whether the topic under discussion were (a) the freedom of the press, (b) birth control, (c) the proper role of the federal government, (d) plagiarism, or (e) slaughterhouse procedures. It is to allow for this varying reference of moral judgments that I have used the phrase "generally approved of by people whose opinions I ordinarily respect," it being understood that *whose* opinions a man respects varies greatly from one individual to another and even from one occasion to another (depending on what is being considered). "Morally neutral" would then mean "an object of neither pro-attitudes nor anti-attitudes in any of the communities whose opinions I tend to respect."

All of the moral predicates are, I think, correctly construed as purported descriptions of the basic attitudes—positive or negative—of whatever community or communities the speaker has reference to in making his judgments. "Ought," however, is not a predicate, and it is not definable in terms of them. It too is descriptive, however, not of the attitudes, but of the *expectations* of the community with respect to its members. To say "I ought to do so-and-so" is to say "It is expected of me by those whose good will I cherish, that I do so-and-so." The meaning of the sentence "We ought never to do what we believe to be wrong, even if we want to" is, therefore, rather complex: it means, "It is expected of a person, by those whose good will he cherishes, that he refrain from doing the things they generally disapprove of, even if his personal inclination is to do them." This interpretation expresses exactly what we would understand a person to mean if he were to make the statement in question.

The societal subjectivist theory also enables us to understand how a person can make a false moral judgment apart from the rather unusual circumstance in which he might be mistaken about his own attitude. His own attitude is scarcely relevant to the truth or falsity of the moral judgment. According to societal subjectivism, a moral judgment is true if the people in the community to which the speaker has reference have the attitude that he is attributing to them, false if they do not. It is not at all unusual or puzzling that a person should occasionally be mistaken about the pro- and anti-attitudes of the members of his community with respect to some matter that he may never have had an opportunity to discuss with them—especially since most people are simultaneously members of several communities. Thus, at this point too the societal subjectivist theory appears to solve a puzzle that the private subjectivist theory left unsolved.

What, finally, is the content of treatises on normative ethics? Why are these works not the mere expression of the private likes and dislikes of the author, as private subjectivism would have them be? The answer is: an ethical treatise is an attempt by one member of a community to assist the other members of that community to clarify their moral attitudes, to eliminate any inconsistencies that may be present (to render them "coherent"), and to adopt certain additional attitudes that may be shown to be consistent with the attitudes already held. Indeed, a very daring and original ethical thinker may do even more: he may recommend adopting attitudes different from those currently held—in which case he will be regarded by the community either as a great teacher or as an eccentric, depending on whether or not his recommendations are accepted.

This brings us to the final difficulty that we noted in connection with the private subjectivist theory: the fact that no basis could be given for the difference we instinctively sense between moral and nonmoral meanings of "good." The question is, How do we know that the statement, "Joe Doakes is a good man," when spoken by the head of the Mafia, is not a moral judgment, whereas the same statement when spoken by someone else may be? I think the answer is as follows. The subculture to which the head of the Mafia has reference in calling Joe Doakes "a good man" is not a "community" in any meaningful sense of that word. It is only a group of men whose common bond is a parasitic relation to a community. If the head of the Mafia were to call Joe a good man in the *moral* sense of "good," he would have to have reference to the basic attitudes of the community—that is, to law-abiding society. Of course, this would be tantamount to saying that Joe is quite unfit for service in the Mafia. Were he to call Joe a good man in the moral sense of "good," therefore, we could only construe it as an expression of his disapproval of Joe. ("Buy off Joe Doakes? Forget it. He's a *good* man, unfortunately.") However, if he says "Joe Doakes is a good man" in an approving way ("You need somebody to help you on that Jones job? Take Joe. He's a good man."), we know immediately that what he is expressing is not a moral judgment at all, but simply what we may call "goodness of function." (Compare: "You need another car for the Jones job? Take mine. It's a good car.")

Concluding Unphilosophical Postscript

It should be apparent that the view presented here not only solves the difficulties noted in the private subjectivist view, but also retains everything that is most persuasive in that view. For example, the variability of the objective-descriptive content of a moral judgment depending on who happens to utter it—a fact that is absolutely fatal to any objectivist theory—is easily explicable in terms of the different communities to which a given speaker may have reference (or, as we said before, the same speaker on different occasions or with respect to different topics). No doubt the approval- and disapproval-habits of people tend on the whole to coincide with those of the communities with which they identify. Therefore, from our knowledge of a person's general attitudes we can often infer directly the descriptive statements implied in his judgment that something is good or bad (in the moral sense). The fact remains that we can distinguish between a person's private attitudes and his moral convictions, and our theory provides a basis for this distinction whereas the private subjectivist theory does not.

There is one further feature of moral judgments, which none of the previous writers has mentioned, that is rather important. The discussion of it will require us to venture briefly into the realm of social psychology, however, and here I can only offer my comments as a layman's surmise—a "concluding unphilosophical postscript" to what I have already said.

The feature of moral judgments to which I refer is what might be called their "constraining" or "obligatory" character. Moral principles sincerely held seem to make a claim, to demand (but not force) obedience. Discussion of moral issues, accordingly, always seems to be a matter of unique importance: we are concerned about them "in the center of our being," so to speak.

The explanation of this fact, I would suggest, is as follows. As social beings our acceptance by the communities with which we identify is deeply important to us. Consequently, our conformity to the expectations of the community and our identity with the community by way of sharing its basic moral attitudes are also very important to us. We do not exist as isolated individuals, but as men in community with other men. The attitudes and expectations of the community thus impinge upon us, constrain us, and make demands on us: it is this that gives us our sense of duty and obligation and our attitudes concerning right and wrong, good and evil, virtue and vice. Morality is a social phenomenon and we are social beings; therefore, moral questions, problems, and principles strike us as being among the most important matters with which we can be concerned.

STUDY QUESTIONS

1. List the objections that Societal Subjectivist (SS) raises with respect to private subjectivism. Are these serious difficulties for the private-subjectivist view? Can you think of any way to defend private subjectivism against these objections?
2. What does SS offer as an alternative to private subjectivism? To what extent does this involve disagreement with Private Subjectivist's position?
3. What analysis does SS offer of the sentences that he earlier cited as being "nonsensical" if interpreted according to the private-subjectivist theory? Are you satisfied with this analysis? Can you think of any moral sentences that Societal Subjectivist might have difficulty in construing in a way consistent with his theory?
4. Do we know that the statement "Joe Doakes is a good man," spoken (in an approving way) by the head of the Mafia, is not a moral judgment? How? (If you are not satisfied with SS's account, devise one of your own.)

21

EMOTIVISM

The number of metaethical theories to which we have been introduced is already so large that I almost feel compelled to apologize for
offering yet another alternative. Surely, there must be something very
odd about moral sentences if they are capable of being construed,
with at least some degree of plausibility in each case, in so many
different ways. Have any of the theories thus far discussed succeeded
in pinpointing the precise character of this oddness—have they succeeded in explaining the unique character of moral sentences? I do
not think that they have. The unique feature of moral sentences—
what gives them their distinctive "flavor"—is something that has been
ignored completely by the first three writers and only briefly hinted at
by the fourth.

In order to isolate this feature, however, it is first necessary to notice some of the *non*ethical language forms that commonly or even
regularly accompany ethical language. Once these have been accounted for, we have to ask: What is the character, or meaning, of
what remains? It will then be this remainder, or residue of meaning,
that constitutes the unique feature of ethical language.

The Nonethical Elements of Ethical Language

It cannot be denied that moral sentences are often obliquely descriptive of the object or act or state of affairs that is the apparent object of
the "judgment." If a man states, "You ought to stop drinking so
much," or "It is wrong for you to drink as much as you do," it is apparent that part of what he is saying is "You are currently drinking to
excess." The latter constitutes a straightforward empirical assertion
that might be either true or false. This is evident from the fact that
the person to whom such a statement was made might defend himself

by saying, "What do you mean? I haven't had a drink for six months!" The moral judgment, then, obliquely asserts that something is the case, that some state of affairs obtains; but it is not this empirical content that gives to moral utterances their unique character.

Further, moral utterances frequently contain not only oblique assertions of some alleged matters of fact, but also oblique predictions that a certain act or course of events will lead to such-and-such consequences. The man who says to his son, "Tom, you ought not to drive so fast," is not only asserting that Tom does in fact drive at excessive speeds: he is also predicting, in a rather vague and imprecise way, that if Tom continues to drive this way, he may become involved in an accident and thus be the cause of serious injury (or worse) either to himself or to others. This is why it is at least to the point, if not altogether convincing, for Tom to reply, "Don't worry, Dad, I may be a fast driver, but I'm always careful. Nobody is going to get hurt."

Because of these two characteristics of ethical language, ethical disagreements can be discussed up to a certain point. Two people who express varying "judgments" of right or wrong may disagree about some matters of fact (as in the first example), or they may disagree about the probable consequences of a certain act or pattern of behavior (as in the second example). These are obviously empirical questions that can only be settled (if at all) by trying to find out what the facts are and what are the probable consequences of the act or pattern in question. Questions of the latter sort are particularly difficult to settle; but the loosely "predictive" element in ethical sentences explains the appropriateness of, for example, bringing into a discussion of the rightness or wrongness of speeding information about the number of accidents caused each year by speeding, the number of people injured or killed in such accidents, and so on.

Moral sentences, however, do not consist only, or even primarily, in factual assertions and loose predictions. The statement, "You ought not to drive so fast" is not reducible to the conjunction of the two sentences, "You commonly drive at speeds that are excessive" and "If you continue to do so, you are apt to become involved in an accident." There is something more involved in this moral sentence, something expressed in the moral word "ought." What, then, is this additional element?

Another Look at Subjectivism

The most plausible suggestions that have been made thus far as to what it is that constitutes this additional element are those made by the two subjectivist writers. According to Private Subjectivist, affirmative moral "judgments" are statements to the effect that someone has feelings of approval toward the person, act, or state of affairs in question and negative moral "judgments" are statements to the effect that someone has feelings of disapproval. Quite apart from the difficulties that Societal Subjectivist has noted in this theory, however, it is obvious that this is not correct. Consider, once again, the sentence "You ought not to drive so fast." If we now add the private subjectivist account of "ought" to our earlier analysis of this sentence, we get the following: "You commonly drive at speeds that are excessive and if you continue to do so you are apt to become involved in an accident; moreover, I have feelings of disapproval toward your so doing." Quite obviously, this is not what we mean when we say "You ought not to drive so fast." On this ground alone, therefore, the private subjectivist theory is shown to be inadequate.

Societal subjectivism fares no better. According to this view, the meaning of the above sentence is "You commonly drive at speeds that are excessive and if you continue to do so you are apt to become involved in an accident; moreover, your mother and I, and many others whose opinions you normally respect, have feelings of disapproval toward your so doing." This, too, does not express what we mean by the moral sentence, "You ought not to drive so fast."

The Case for Emotivism

The proposal I should like to make is this: the specifically moral character of moral sentences consists not in the assertion that the speaker, or some group to which he has reference, has certain feelings, but in a nondescriptive expression of those feelings. Moral words, insofar as they have a distinctively moral flavor, are not descriptive either of the object being "judged" or of anybody's feelings: they are not descriptive at all. Grammatically, they have the status of an interjection. "You ought not to drive so fast" means, roughly, "You commonly drive at excessive speeds: for shame!"

Not all moral sentences, however, can be reduced to (a) a factual assertion ("You commonly drive at excessive speeds") plus (b) an expression of approval or disapproval ("for shame!"). A sentence like "Driving at excessive speeds is wrong," for example, has no factual meaning; its only meaning is emotive. It is as if someone said "driving at excessive speeds!" in a "raised-eyebrows" tone of voice, thus indicating his disapproval of the behavior in question. General moral sentences are, therefore, neither true nor false. Someone who says "Driving at excessive speeds is wrong" cannot be contradicted because he is not making an assertion; anyone who appeared to be disagreeing with him would only be expressing a contrary attitude.

It has already been pointed out that our moral words can, without exception, be classified according to whether the attitude that they express is positive (pro-) or negative (anti-). Within these two general categories, however, the moral words that appear in each can be loosely arranged on a scale according to the degree of feeling that they commonly are used to express. To say that something is "reprehensible," for example, is to express a far stronger negative feeling toward it than to say that it is "not very nice." To say that something is a "moral duty" is to express stronger positive feelings toward it than to say simply that it is "good." The point can be illustrated by the following diagram (where the direction of the arrow indicates decreasing feeling):

Pro-attitudes	Anti-attitudes
moral duty	reprehensible
virtuous (virtue)	vicious (vice)
ought to be done	ought not to be done
ought to be desired	evil
good	bad
worthy	naughty
nice	not nice

Emotivism and Private Subjectivism

Many people have great difficulty understanding the difference between emotivism and the private subjectivist view. The difference can be stated as follows: according to the private subjectivist theory, moral sentences are informative sentences; according to my view, they are not. Or the difference can be expressed in this way: according to the private subjectivist view, moral sentences are always either true or false; according to my view, they are not. According to the private subjectivist view, the statement "Driving at excessive speeds is wrong" can be contradicted by the statement "You do not really disapprove of fast driving." According to my view the utterance cannot be contradicted because it makes no assertion.

The difference between private subjectivism and emotivism is not over the point whether a person who utters a moral sentence has the feelings in question or not: both views assume that he normally does. The question is: Does the meaning of a moral sentence consist in an assertion by the speaker that he has such-and-such feelings, or is a moral sentence a nonreportive expression of those feelings? Private Subjectivist says the former; I say the latter. The difference is subtle, but important.

All of the facts about moral discourse to which the previous writers have called attention are easily explicable in terms of emotivism—and any metaethical theory must finally be judged primarily on the basis of its explanatory power. There are, however, three additional considerations that particularly favor the emotivist theory.

First, the theory is consistent with what we know about how people learn to use the language of morals. Children learn the meanings of moral words by hearing them in certain contexts. "Bad," "wicked," "naughty," etc., they learn to associate with frowns, spankings, cross voices and other nonverbal expressions of disapproval; "good," "nice," and "worthy," etc., they learn to associate with smiles, rewards, and other nonverbal expressions of approval. When they come to use these words themselves, they use them as a verbal expression of the attitudes they have learned to associate with them, precisely as would be expected. What else could they be supposed to mean by words learned in this way?

Second, the emotive theory is consistent with the purpose for which we normally utter moral sentences. That purpose is to influence other people's behavior—to create in them an inclination to act in certain ways and not to act in certain other ways. There can be little doubt that moral utterances do tend to influence us in just this way. The sentence, "So-and-so is morally wrong," spoken by someone whose opinions we normally respect, has a tendency to evince a negative attitude toward "so-and-so" corresponding to that of the speaker. Thus it seems very plausible to say that the meaning of a moral sentence is the feeling that it expresses, and because it has this meaning it is suitable for the purpose of influencing behavior. This is exactly what the emotive theory affirms.

Third, the emotive theory provides a convincing account of the nature of ethical disagreement. We can conceive of two sorts of ethical disagreement: (a) where the disputants share a broad range of common attitudes but have conflicting attitudes toward some particular act or state of affairs and (b) where the disputants have fundamentally conflicting attitudes toward a very large proportion of those things in which they both have an interest. It will be convenient to deal separately with these two types of cases.

Naturalistic Objectivist's example of the two men who disagreed as to whether it would be right or wrong to use tear gas to deal with a certain situation would be an example of the first type. Note how the discussion of the issue proceeds. Each of the disputants cites such evidence and advances such considerations as he thinks will be effective in *changing the attitude* of the other. One may talk about the probability of igniting a civil war, of the death and destruction that would ensue, and so on; the other may talk about the danger to life and property of the rioting itself and of the importance of putting an end to it by whatever means are available. But note well: the argument would be over as soon as one or the other of the disputants changed his attitude toward the action in question, *whether or not they had reached agreement on all of the facts*. This shows that it is conflict in attitude—not disagreement about the facts—that is central in a dispute of this kind. The reason it is worthwhile to talk about facts at all is that since the disputants share a common pattern of basic attitudes, it is reasonable to expect that if they were in agreement about the facts, they would (or probably would) adopt the same attitude toward those facts.

If the disputants in a case of ethical disagreement are people whose basic moral attitudes are fundamentally different, the situation is radically altered. In such a case, specific moral issues are hardly worth discussing. If there is to be any discussion at all, it must be directed toward finding some common basic attitudes and trying to enlarge this common ground as much as possible. Failing this, discussion of particular issues is futile. However much the disputants may agree regarding the empirical facts, they remain in unresolvable ethical disagreement so long as they hold conflicting basic attitudes; and agreement on particular moral questions under such circumstances is all but impossible to obtain.

To summarize: conflict in attitude is fundamental to ethical disagreement in two ways. First, it determines what empirical evidence is relevant to the dispute—what presumably will have some tendency to alter the attitude of one or the other of the disputants. Second, it is fundamental in the sense that it is only when agreement in attitude has been reached that the dispute is settled—regardless of whether or not the disputants have reached agreement concerning the facts. The emotive theory of the meaning of moral discourse, therefore, enables us to understand, in a way that we otherwise could not, the nature of ethical disagreement; and this provides additional confirmation of the correctness of the theory.

Normative Ethics

One implication of emotivism that some people will undoubtedly think strange is that there can be no such thing as scientific normative ethics. If the theory is correct, then the questions with which writers on normative ethics have traditionally been concerned—questions of the sort, "What things really are right and wrong, and why?" —are not meaningful. What, then, remains of normative ethics?

A man who writes a treatise on normative ethics may do many things that are interesting and valuable. He may, for example, do the work of an historian and provide us with interesting information about the moral attitudes of some of the well-known theorists of the past (Plato, Aristotle, Kant, etc.). He may do the work of a psychologist and help us to understand why we tend to feel approval or disapproval toward certain sorts of things. He may do the work of a metaethical theorist and help us to understand some of the peculiarities of the logical behavior of our moral terms. But insofar as he addresses himself to the questions with which writers on normative ethics have traditionally been concerned, his remarks can only be construed as personal exhortations designed to induce us to adopt certain attitudes that, for whatever reasons, he wishes his readers to adopt. His recommendations, however noble, have no objective validity whatsoever, for a sentence affirming that something is good or bad, right or wrong, praiseworthy or blameworthy is not an assertion at all. It is a verbal expression of the attitude of the speaker, the purpose of which is to encourage us to adopt a similar attitude.

There seems no doubt, therefore, that normative ethics, as it has been traditionally conceived, is based on a mistake—the mistake of assuming that (a) moral sentences are descriptive sentences capable of being true or false, and (b) reasons can be given to support the view that certain of them are true and certain others false. The truth of the matter is, to paraphrase Shakespeare, that "nothing is right or wrong but *feeling* makes it so." The job of explaining *why* we feel positively toward some things and negatively toward others is one that is best left to the psychologist.

STUDY QUESTIONS

1. What "nonethical" elements does Emotivist claim to find in ethical language? Is he right in asserting that these elements are frequently present? What justification is there for calling them "nonethical" elements?
2. What exactly is Emotivist's proposal regarding the meaning of moral sentences? How does it differ from the private subjectivist view?
3. Review Societal Subjectivist's objections to private subjectivism. Do they apply with equal force to Emotivism, or do they not?
4. Emotivist claims that "all of the facts about moral discourse to which the previous writers have called attention are easily explicable in terms of [the emotivist theory]." Is this the case? Can you recall any facts to which earlier writers have called attention that might prove difficult for Emotivist to explain?
5. What additional considerations does Emotivist offer in support of his theory? Do you find them convincing? Do they lend equal support to any of the other theories?

22

IMPERATIVISM

There is a tendency, both among plain men and among philosophers, to depreciate any uses of language other than the informative. This is most unfortunate, for it creates a desire to translate any sort of discourse that we value highly into informative language—to exhibit it as a species of the sort of discourse that we value most. It is difficult to believe that this tendency has not been at work in at least some of the discussion on the present problem.

One important fact about ethical discourse that seems to have been overlooked by all of the previous writers is that we all know how to *use* this type of discourse without too much difficulty. This fact should give us pause. If the status of ethical discourse is as mystifying as all this discussion would seem to indicate, how is it that all of us—even children—can use it with such apparent ease? It seems likely that if we look carefully at the way in which children learn to use this kind of discourse, and the purposes for which they and we employ it (ridding our minds of any bias in favor of informative discourse), we shall discover that moral talk is not nearly so mystifying as we have thus far been led to believe.

Before we do that, however, we shall have to consider emotivism. My quarrel with emotivism, as may have been surmised, is not that it fails to exhibit moral talk as a species of informative discourse, but rather that it interprets it in a way that is inconsistent with the general purpose for which we commonly employ such discourse. That moral utterances are frequently delivered with feeling no one will deny; but that the primary function of those utterances is simply to give vent to those feelings ought to be denied by anyone who knows how to use this sort of discourse.

Defects of Emotivism

I do not wish to dwell at great length on the defects of the emotivist theory. The theory has been widely and soundly criticized since it was first put forward some thirty years ago, and many of its early supporters have abandoned it in recent years. I do want, however, to mention just three or four of the most serious objections that have been raised against the theory.

The theory does not do justice to the seriousness with which moral sentences are commonly uttered. Questions calling for moral appraisal and decision are frequently matters of great moment: the fates of men and nations are sometimes at stake. To say that the sentence "War is evil" means "Boo for war" or that the sentence "Bravery is good" means "Hurray for bravery" is absurd. No doubt we frequently take ourselves too seriously, but we surely are not guilty of this when we say that our moral appraisals of war, of bravery, or of thousands of other things that we appraise in this way are serious and important matters. The "boo-hurray" theory offends us because it makes light of serious matters. For this reason alone it deserves to be rejected.

Moreover, a number of odd and distressing consequences follow if we assume this theory to be true. It would follow, for example, that we could never be in error in making a moral "judgment," and from this it would follow, in turn, that neither blame nor remorse is ever appropriate. Moreover, according to this theory, there could never be a rational basis for an ethical appraisal or decision. And most distressing of all, it would follow that ethical disputes cannot be resolved by rational means: if men or nations cannot agree on some matter of importance, there is nothing to do but to fight it out until the strongest one—man or nation—wins.

The issue resolves itself, really, to this: Are moral utterances rational, or are they not? The unanimous answer of our whole Western ethical tradition, from Plato and Aristotle to Kant, John Stuart Mill, Moore, and Ross, is that they are; the reply of the emotivists is that they are not. This is no trifling matter. If ethics can be rational, then moral progress—the gradual improvement of our moral principles by reflection and criticism—is possible; if not, such progress is not possible. Indeed, the very notion of "progress" becomes, in this theory, incomprehensible. Anyone concerned about the future of civilization would do well to ponder these consequences.

The best answer to emotivism, however, is not destructive criticism but a better theory—that of imperativism.

Some Features of Directive Language

Rational beings employ language for a variety of purposes, only one of which is to convey information. Because so much of our use of language does consist in this informative function, however, conventional logic has dwelt almost entirely on the logical behavior of language so employed. But the directive function of language—the use of language to guide behavior—is an equally rational function.

The difference between these two kinds of language might be understood in terms of the different kinds of questions to which each type might appropriately be conceived as an answer. We use language informatively (to convey information) only in instances where we presuppose a question of the form, What are the facts? or What is the case? We use language in its directive function only in instances where we presuppose a question of the form, What shall I do? To a question of the latter form, any statement of fact would be inappropriate; to a question of the former type, a moral appraisal would be equally inappropriate.

There are many different instances in which the function of the language used is quite evidently "directive." Consider the following list: a typical verbal communication from a sergeant to his platoon; a recipe; assembly instructions for a child's toy that is delivered unassembled; instructions from ground control to a team of astronauts; a teacher's remarks in preparation for an examination; a parent's word to a small child who is dallying after bedtime. All of these, and dozens of others, are instances of language being used directively—to guide behavior.

Language used directively, just like language used informatively, envisages a fairly specific state of affairs. "Johnny, go to bed" (directive), like "Johnny is going to bed" (informative), envisages Johnny's going to bed in the very near future. Both utterances are about Johnny's going to bed, but what is said about Johnny's going to bed is different in the two cases. The directive sentence is addressed to Johnny, and it might be translated, "Johnny's going to bed: do it!" The informative sentence is addressed to anybody who cares to listen, and it might be translated, "Johnny's going to bed: it is occurring."

Language intended to serve a directive function is typically addressed to the person or persons whose behavior is to be guided. Some directives are intended for some one specific individual ("Johnny, go to bed!"). Others are intended for whomever may be in a position to benefit from them ("Tear on dotted line"). Some appear to be addressed to everyone, that is, they are intended to be universally applicable ("Do not take for yourself what belongs to another"). We shall return to this shortly.

The directive function, like the informative, is *sui generis:* neither can be reduced to, or derived from, the other. A given sentence may, of course, serve both functions ("Bring me the book that is lying on the dresser"), but the functions themselves may, nonetheless, be distinguished.

We cannot determine the intended function of a sentence simply by identifying its mood. Function depends on the intentions of the speaker, whereas mood does not. The sentence in parentheses in the preceding paragraph, for example, is in the imperative mood, but it is bifunctional. "Johnny, go to bed" and "Johnny, it is past your bedtime" may both serve a directive function, but the two sentences differ in mood.

Ethical Discourse as a Species of Directive Language

Let us return to ethical discourse and see how the foregoing reflections on the nature of directive language may help us to understand this very common type of talk.

The vast majority of moral sentences are in the indicative mood. This may be one of the reasons why most of the earlier efforts to ascertain the status of moral sentences proceeded on the assumption that they must be understood as some subvariety of informative language. It is not at all inconsistent with this fact to suggest that the function of moral sentences is to guide behavior—is, in short, directive.

Consider, first, the way in which children learn to use moral concepts. A typical instance is the following: Johnny accompanies his mother to the grocery store, and seeing some tasty-looking candy within reach, he decides to help himself. Mother says, "No, Johnny, you must put that back. It is *wrong* to take something that belongs to someone else without paying for it." Three elements of this situation should be noted: (a) the moral sentence is uttered in a situation involving choice—a situation like many Johnny may be expected to encounter in the future where he must choose among alternative ways of behaving; (b) the evident function of the moral utterance is to serve as a principle for the guidance of conduct—a rule that may help Johnny decide how to act in future situations of this type; and (c) the moral principle thus enunciated is universal in scope—it applies not only to Johnny, but to everyone. It is chiefly this third characteristic that identifies it as a moral principle rather than a merely conventional rule.

Note also the situations in which we commonly employ moral talk: the same three features, it will be found, are always present. Moral principles, we might say, play a role among men analogous to the role of instinct in the behavior of animals. They serve as rules of conduct, guiding us in the multifarious choices that we are constantly called upon to make. Because moral principles are universal in scope, it is always in a way appropriate to state them, even when we are alone. The fact that moral judgments are sometimes spoken in solitude (for example, "How noble!" or "How reprehensible!" uttered while reading something) in no way invalidates the claim that the primary and normal function of such utterances is to guide behavior.

It may be thought that what I am urging as the primary function of ethical discourse is identical with Emotivist's suggestion that the purpose for which we normally utter moral sentences is to influence other people's behavior—to create in them an inclination to act in certain ways and not to act in certain other ways. This, however, is not the case. Uttering a moral principle is a wholly rational procedure: it is an attempt to supply an answer to the question, What shall I do in situations of such-and-such a kind? In Emotivist's view, uttering a moral sentence is an attempt to persuade or coerce someone to do something: it is a particularly prevalent kind of propaganda. I do not think moral talk is a kind of verbal club. I think it is an appropriate form of discourse for rational beings who share a common concern about how they ought to act. Just as in informative discourse there is a difference between *informing* and *convincing*, so in directive discourse there is a difference between *directing* and *coercing*. The difference is subtle but important.

We may observe, in conclusion, that it is absolutely impossible for men to live without principles of this kind—that a human being without an ethic is an impossibility. This is true for several reasons. First, our knowledge of the probable consequences of acting in this or that way is severely limited. We need general rules of conduct, embodying the accumulated wisdom of preceding generations, to guide our behavior in those situations in which we do not know how to calculate the likely consequences of various alternatives. Second, however extensive our knowledge of probable consequences may be, we require principles that will provide reasons for preferring one set of consequences over another. This would be true even if we were omniscient, knowing in precise detail what would be the short- and long-range consequences of each alternative before us. Finally, without such principles we should not be able to accumulate practical wisdom or to pass that wisdom on to our children. All learning, it must be remembered, involves generalization; it is only via generalizations that we escape the irrationality of sheer individuality. Moral principles are to the practical life what general truths are to the intellectual—they are the generalizations that relate the particulars of experience, thus casting them into an intelligible pattern.

There is no danger that men will cease to have ethical principles as a consequence of this or that inadequate metaethical theory, however widely such a theory may come to be held. There is danger, however, that widespread bewilderment about the meaning of moral utterances may lead to a weakening of their directive power, and thus to a chaotic situation in which the groping for new principles goes on without the benefit of the foundation of the old. It is necessary and important that these principles change, else men should not be able to adjust to the constantly changing conditions in which they live. But if change is to be healthy, it must be orderly—a creation of the new by way of a modification of, and addition to, the old. This cannot occur if old principles are simply ignored or if they altogether lose their directive power. Hence, it is a matter of more than casual importance that their status be understood and their role duly respected.

STUDY QUESTIONS

1. What exactly do you understand to be the imperativist theory about the meaning of moral sentences?
2. Summarize Imperativist's criticisms of the emotivist theory. Do these seem to be sound criticisms? How might Emotivist defend himself against these objections?
3. Summarize the "features of directive language" discussed by Imperativist. Do these features in fact distinguish directive language from informative language, as Imperativist apparently believes?
4. What arguments does Imperativist offer in support of his central thesis regarding the meaning of moral sentences? Do you find his arguments persuasive?
5. How does Imperativist's theory differ from Emotivist's suggestion that the *purpose* for which we normally utter moral sentences is "to influence other people's behavior"?
6. For what reasons, according to Imperativist, do we need moral principles? Is it possible to agree with him on this without accepting his main thesis?

23

MULTIFUNCTIONALISM

The discussion of the status of moral judgments is in need of summation. What would be most helpful at this point, I think, is a summary of the main facts about moral judgments that have emerged from the foregoing discussions. Each writer has emphasized certain facts and has offered a theory tailor-made to fit those facts. None thus far, however, has offered a theory that satisfactorily explains all of the relevant facts. The reason, I shall suggest, is that moral sentences serve a variety of functions, any one of which may predominate in a given instance. As a result, a number of "unifunctional" theories can be made more or less plausible since an advocate of such a theory can always find some examples in support of his theory. But, as we have seen, critics of each theory can with equal ease find examples that do not favor the theory in question and that cannot be plausibly explained by it.

Some Facts About Moral Judgments

A few logical and phenomenological observations have been made that are, as far as I can judge, completely neutral with respect to the competing theories. The neutral facts are: (a) moral judgments are applicable only to human behavior; (b) moral judgments are applicable to human behavior only in situations involving choice; (c) some terms that often function as moral predicates (e.g., "good," "right," and "ought") also function on occasion as nonmoral predicates; and (d) a distinction may be drawn between "instrumental" and "intrinsic" moral goodness: some things are said to be good (instrumentally) because they contribute to the coming-into-being of something else that is said to be good in itself (intrinsically good). These seem to be incontrovertible and completely unexceptionable facts about moral judgments, and I should suppose that all parties to the dispute about the status of moral judgments could accept them without in any way jeopardizing their respective positions.

Next we note a group of facts about moral judgments that tend to favor objectivist theories: (e) a consideration of the probable consequences of an act is usually relevant to the judgment that the act in question is good or bad, right or wrong; (f) empirical facts are frequently relevant to our judgment that a given act or state of affairs is good or bad, right or wrong; and (g) a moral judgment to the effect that so-and-so is a "good" or a "bad" man, or that such-and-such an act was a "virtuous" or a "vicious" one, does ordinarily convey some information, however imprecise, about the man or act in question. These, I am saying, are facts about moral judgments, facts that any theory about the status of moral judgments must somehow take into consideration.

There are also some facts about moral judgments that tend to favor subjectivist views: (h) moral judgments are normally associated with certain attitudes on the part of the person making the judgment—pro-attitudes with affirmative moral judgments and anti-attitudes with negative moral judgments; (i) people tend to have rather strong feelings about matters on which they render moral judgments—these matters commonly strike them as being important, serious, of great moment; and (j) the attitudes and expectations of the human community or communities with which someone identifies are evidently related in some way to the moral judgments that he makes.

In view of what has been said, one further fact may be noted: (k) children learn to associate the language of morals not only with certain sorts of conduct, but also with certain sorts of empirical facts and with attitudes of approval and disapproval. This being the case, it is easy to see that the defenders of various theories can appeal to the way in which children learn to use ethical discourse in support of their view, provided only that they emphasize those features of the learning process that tend to support their theory. (It is not my intention to suggest that this is done deviously, but only that the advocates of this or that theory tend to find in this learning process what they are looking for, and to overlook everything else.)

It seems evident that unifunctional theories of the objectivist type get established because of a one-sided emphasis on items (e), (f), and (g) in the above list and those of the subjectivist type because of an equally one-sided emphasis on items (h), (i), and (j). A rationalist who focuses his attention on the objectivist-favoring facts will probably advocate an intuitionist theory; an empiricist will more likely find himself adopting the naturalistic objectivist view. Both, however, will be guilty of overlooking, or of downgrading, the facts that are less favorable to objectivist theories. So also with theories of the subjectivist type (among which, for our present purposes, we may include the emotivist theory). A philosopher who fastens his attention on the feelings and/or attitudes of the individual making the moral judgment and who deemphasizes everything else will tend to favor either private subjectivism or emotivism. A philosopher who gives more weight to the way in which the attitudes and expectations of the community impinge on moral judgments will advocate a societal subjectivist theory. All, however, will be guilty of forgetting, or underemphasizing, those facts to which objectivists commonly point in support of *their* theories.

Imperativism is also a unifunctional theory, one that appeals particularly to the fact that the way in which we learn moral principles makes it inevitable that we associate them with conduct. This is, of course, true—but so are many other things that imperativism, unfortunately, leaves out of account. Thus imperativism is unable to account for moral judgments rendered with respect to people and/or events in the past. It is not at all plausible to say that the sentence "Judas ought not to have betrayed Jesus" really means "Judas, don't do it!" Similarly, imperativism would make a command to do something wrong self-contradictory: "Murder is wrong, but you must murder *A*" would mean, in this view, "Do not murder anyone, ever— but do murder *A*"; plainly, a self-contradictory command. Thus imperativism fares no better than the other unifunctional theories as an account of the whole meaning of the language of morals.

Therefore, there appears to be only one way out of the dilemma, and that is to say that moral talk serves a variety of functions, any one of which may be primary at any given time. The language of morals is not a solo instrument: it is an ensemble; at some times one instrument has the lead, at other times another. There is, after all, no good reason to suppose that all moral talk must be reducible to sentences of some one logical type: it may well be that to attempt to do so is to impose an artificial simplicity on moral talk that is not to be found in that talk itself. The failure of the various unifunctional theories that have been proposed strongly suggests that this is so. Let us see if we cannot make a more convincing case for a multifunctional theory.

The Moral Judge and the Moral Judgment

It is important to bear in mind, when talking about the meaning of language, that the meaning of any piece of discourse depends on what the speaker intends it to mean. Moral judgments are not autonomous entities, whose meaning is independent of the intentions of the persons making those judgments: they are the attempts of men—moral judges—to say something. What is it that people are trying to say when they utter sentences like "Joe Doakes is a good man," or "The infliction of needless pain is evil"?

Once we put the question this way, it becomes apparent that there are many things that people might want to say when they utter such sentences. What they are primarily intending to say in any given instance can only be determined by paying very close attention to the total context in which the sentence is uttered. Among the relevant contextual factors that have to be considered in each case are such things as the general pattern of likes and dislikes of the person making the judgment; the features usually possessed by people, acts, or states of affairs that this person is in the habit of commending; the nonverbal indications of feeling (facial expressions, vocal inflections) that attend his utterance; the person or persons to whom the judgment is addressed; and so on. In actual conversation we do normally note these things, and so we usually have little difficulty in "getting the meaning" of the person making the judgment. It is only when we abstract from the concrete situation in which a judgment is made and try to theorize about the judgments themselves that we encounter difficulty.

It is surely apparent (to use Imperativist's example) that a mother who says to her son, "It is wrong to take things that belong to other people without paying for them," is attempting to convey to him a rule of conduct. She is saying, in effect, "Do not ever just help yourself to other people's things." Moreover, she and her son both know perfectly well that that is what she means. She may also mean, of course, that she disapproves of what is called stealing, but that is a very subordinate part of her meaning in this instance. It is examples like this that give credence to the imperativist theory.

It is equally apparent, however, that the enunciation of a general principle of conduct would not be the primary purpose of a man who says, "Albert Schweitzer was a great and good man; his death was a great loss to good men everywhere." Such a sentence, uttered by almost anyone, would mean primarily that (a) Albert Schweitzer possessed in a high degree the qualities that we commonly commend in other men (humanity, compassion, unselfishness, etc.) and (b) the speaker thoroughly approves of people who possess these qualities. In this case the judgment is almost completely informative in character —informative with respect to the character of Albert Schweitzer and informative of the attitude of the speaker. The directive function, insofar as it is present at all, is quite subordinate to these other kinds of meaning.

Consider a third example. A man is reading his evening newspaper and comes upon the story of a hold-up in which an aged grocery store proprietor and his wife have been mercilessly killed. "How terrible!" he exclaims. "Whoever did this should be put away for life!" In this case it is clear that the moral judgment is primarily an expression and/or assertion of feeling—feeling so strong that it seems wholly inadequate to describe it simply as an anti-attitude. There is little or nothing in the way of "objective-descriptive content" in such an utterance, and nothing at all in the way of enunciating a rule for the guidance of future conduct. Moral judgments can (and to some extent usually do) express feeling, and in certain sorts of situations this function of moral utterances may overshadow or exclude all others.

It is quite impossible—and, fortunately, quite unnecessary—to lay down rules to determine when one function is predominating in ethical discourse and when another. We can say with a reasonable degree of assurance that when we have the moral instruction of children in mind, it is the directive function that predominates, but even this generalization is probably subject to exceptions. I return, however, to a point made earlier: in actual practice, we usually have little difficulty in understanding what it is that people are trying to say when they employ the familiar locutions of moral talk. Were it not for the fact that the whole discussion of this problem was undertaken on the mistaken assumption that all moral sentences must serve some one single function, the diverse meanings of such sentences would not have remained for so long unrecognized.

I would note, finally, that in order to adopt the multifunctionalist position it is not necessary to hold that *all* of the types of meaning moral discourse is sometimes said to have actually occur. We may, for example, rule out intuitionism on epistemological grounds[1] and still qualify as a multifunctionalist, provided only that we hold that the meaning implicit in moral discourse is not all explicable in terms of any one unifunctional theory. It is evident from the fact that so many theories can be defended with at least some degree of plausibility that the logic of moral discourse must be exceedingly complex. I am convinced that no unifunctional theory can do full justice to this complexity.

STUDY QUESTIONS

1. Can you think of any "facts about moral judgments" that Multifunctionalist has omitted from his summary? Are any of those he does list controversial—that is, likely to be denied by advocates of certain metaethical theories?
2. What objections does Multifunctionalist raise against imperativism? Are they sound? Defend imperativism against these objections as best you can.

---

[1] Private Subjectivist does this, for example. See p. 134.

3. Is it true that "the meaning of any piece of discourse depends on what the speaker intends it to mean"? If so, what relevance does this have for the present controversy?

4. Multifunctionalist offers several examples in support of his theory regarding the status of moral sentences. Could these same examples be interpreted in a way consistent with any of the theories discussed earlier? Which? Which, if any, might have difficulty with these examples?

Aiken, H. D. *Reason and Conduct: New Bearings in Moral Philosophy*. New York: Knopf, 1962.

Ayer, A. J. *Language, Truth and Logic*, 2nd ed. New York: Dover Publications, 1946 (paperbound), chap. VI.

Baier, Kurt. *The Moral Point of View*, Abridged ed. New York: Random House, 1965 (paperbound).

Blanshard, Brand. *Reason and Goodness*. New York: Macmillan, 1961.

Brandt, R. B. "The Emotive Theory of Ethics," *The Philosophical Review*, 59 (1950), 305–318.

————. *Ethical Theory*. Englewood Cliffs, N. J.: Prentice-Hall, 1959, chaps. 7–11.

————. "The Status of Empirical Assertion Theories in Ethics," *Mind*, 61 (1952), 458–479.

Edel, Abraham. *Science and the Structure of Ethics*. Chicago: University of Chicago Press, 1961 (paperbound).

Edwards, Paul. *The Logic of Moral Discourse*. New York: Free Press, 1955 (paperbound) chaps. VII–IX.

Ewing, A. C. *Second Thoughts in Moral Philosophy*. New York: Macmillan, 1959, chaps. I and II.

Falk, W. D. *"Goading and Guiding,"* *Mind*, 62 (1953), 145–171.

Frankena, W. K. "Moral Philosophy at Mid-century," *The Philosophical Review*, 60 (1951), 44–55.

Gewirth, Alan. "Meanings and Criteria in Ethics," *Philosophy*, 38 (1963), 329–345.

Hancock, Roger. "The Refutation of Naturalism in Moore and Hare," *The Journal of Philosophy*, 57 (1960), 326–334.

Hare, R. M. *Freedom and Reason*. New York: Oxford University Press, 1963 (paperbound).

————. *The Language of Morals*. New York: Oxford University Press, 1964 (paperbound).

Harsanyi, J. C. "Ethics in Terms of Hypothetical Imperatives," *Mind*, 67 (1958), 305–316.

Hudson, W. *Ethical Intuitionism*. New York: Macmillan, 1967. A short historical study of the intuitionist theory.

Kerner, George C. "Approvals, Reasons and Moral Argument," *Mind*, 71 (1962), 474–486.

————. *The Revolution in Ethical Theory*. Oxford: Clarendon Press, 1966.

Mill, John Stuart. *Utilitarianism*. Indianapolis, Ind.: Liberal Arts Press, 1960 (paperbound).

Moore, G. E. *Principia Ethica*. New York: Cambridge University Press, 1959 (paperbound), chaps. I–III.

Nowell-Smith, P. H. *Ethics*. Baltimore, Md.: Penguin Books, 1954.

Perry, R. B. *General Theory of Value*. Cambridge, Mass.: Harvard University Press, 1926.

Prichard, H. A. *Moral Obligation*. New York: Oxford University Press, 1949, chaps. 1, 2, and 5.

Prior, A. N. *Logic and the Basis of Ethics*. New York: Oxford University Press, 1949.

Raphael, D. Daiches. *Moral Judgment*. New York: Hillary House, 1955, chaps. IV, VII, and VIII.

————. *The Moral Sense*. New York: Oxford University Press, 1947.

Ross, W. D. *Foundations of Ethics*. New York: Oxford University Press, 1939, chaps. II, III and XI.

————. *The Right and the Good*. New York: Oxford University Press, 1930, chap. II.

Sidgwick, Henry. *The Methods of Ethics*, 7th ed., rev. by Constance Jones. Chicago: University of Chicago Press, 1962, chaps. III, VIII, and IX.

Singer, M. G. *Generalization in Ethics*. New York: Knopf, 1961.

Stevenson, C. L. *Ethics and Language*. New Haven: Yale University Press, 1960 (paperbound), chaps. I, II, IV, V, and VI.

Stroll, A. *The Emotive Theory of Ethics*. Berkeley and Los Angeles: University of California Press, 1954.

Taylor, Paul W. *Normative Discourse*. Englewood Cliffs, N. J.: Prentice-Hall, 1961.

Toulmin, S. E. *The Place of Reason in Ethics*. Cambridge, Eng.: Cambridge University Press, 1960 (paperbound).

Urmson, J. O. *The Emotive Theory of Ethics*. London: Hutchison's University Library, 1968.

Warnock, G. J. *Contemporary Moral Philosophy*. New York: St. Martin's Press, 1967. See also a critical review of Warnock's book by R. M. Hare in *Mind* lxxvii, 307 (July 1968), 436–440.

Wellman, Carl. *The Language of Ethics*. Cambridge, Mass.: Harvard University Press, 1961.

PART V

FREEDOM
AND DETERMINISM

24

THE PROBLEM OF FREEDOM AND DETERMINISM

We turn now to one of the most frequently discussed and most vexing problems in philosophy: the problem of determinism and free will. It is a problem in which almost everyone is interested—the scientist, the theologian, and the ethicist, as well as the philosopher and the man in the street. More than likely, you have encountered the problem in some form or other many times before. Let us begin, then, with an attempt to understand exactly what the problem is.

The Problem

Like many philosophical problems, the free-will problem arises because of an apparent conflict between beliefs based on two different groups of facts. On the one hand, certain facts of moral experience convince most of us that we are morally responsible. For example, we praise and blame one another on the basis of observed behavior. Moreover, we accept praise and blame from others (and occasionally from ourselves) for our own acts. We say things like, "I ought not to have done that," "What he did was shameful," and so on. We can summarize this by saying that we believe ourselves to be morally responsible, and we treat others as if they were morally responsible. And it seems very natural to say that if we are morally responsible, then we must be free: moral responsibility seems to presuppose moral freedom. This is one side of the picture.

But there are other facts that seem to support the view called universal determinism—the theory that every event in the universe is an inevitable consequence of antecedent causes. It seems self-evident to many people, for example, that "every event has a cause." Every scientific inquiry presupposes that the phenomena under investigation are governed by some laws and that these laws are capable of being discovered and stated with mathematical precision. We all act, as a matter of fact, as if the universe is orderly: we expect pure water always to freeze at 32° Fahrenheit at sea-level barometric pressure; we expect the laws of aerodynamics to remain constant when we take a plane trip; and so on. Moreover, an immense and steadily growing quantity of scientific evidence appears to bear out the hypothesis that this is an orderly universe, that every event has a cause, that everything that occurs is an inevitable consequence of antecedent causes. Thus, we are also readily persuaded that the deterministic hypothesis is correct.

However, if we try to affirm both these views, we encounter a serious problem. How can we be free in the way required to render us morally responsible if every event in the universe (including our decisions and our actions) is an inevitable consequence of antecedent causes? Does this not imply that we are not the real agent of our acts, and is not our belief that we are morally responsible mistaken? Or, if we are indeed morally responsible and free in the sense required to render us morally responsible, how can every event be an inevitable consequence of antecedent causes? Do moral responsibility and freedom contradict the mass of evidence supporting our belief in the orderliness and regularity of the universe?

It is apparent that a very important part of our thinking with respect to this question must be concerned with the nature of "moral freedom." So far we have spoken of moral freedom simply as that freedom (whatever its nature) that is a condition of moral responsibility. But a very important question is: What is the nature of the freedom that is a condition of moral responsibility? Is it consistent with universal determinism or is it not? If it is, then it should be possible to show that the apparent conflict between universal determinism and moral responsibility is only apparent—and the problem would be solved.

Precisely stated, therefore, the problem of freedom and determinism is this: Is the freedom that is a condition of moral responsibility compatible with universal determinism or not; if not, which is the case?

Three Alternatives

This question about freedom and determinism is capable of being answered in three different ways. One answer is: (a) the freedom that is a condition of moral responsibility is not compatible with universal determinism and (b) universal determinism is the case; therefore (c) man is not free in the sense required to render him morally responsible. This position is commonly called *hard determinism*. It has been maintained by a large number of eminent thinkers and is more plausible than it appears when stated in summary form as it is here.

A second answer is: (a) the freedom that is a condition of moral responsibility is not compatible with universal determinism and (b) man has this freedom; therefore (c) universal determinism is not the case. This position is commonly called *libertarianism*. It also can claim a large number of eminent defenders and is probably the view of most people prior to systematic reflection on the problem.

The third possibility is: (a) the freedom that is a condition of moral responsibility is compatible with universal determinism, and so (b) man may be morally responsible even if determinism is true. This view is commonly called *soft determinism*. It has been supported by such well-known philosophers as David Hume and John Stuart Mill and is probably the dominant view among British and American philosophers at the present time.

It should be noted that a soft determinist is no less a determinist than a hard determinist: both hold that universal determinism is true, that is, that every event in the universe is an inevitable consequence of antecedent causes. The difference between them is only in the consequences that they draw from this view. A hard determinist, because he believes that the freedom that is a condition of moral responsibility is not compatible with universal determinism, draws the "hard" conclusion that man is not morally responsible. A soft determinist, because he sees no incompatibility between universal determinism and moral freedom, draws the "soft" conclusion that man may be morally responsible even though universal determinism is true. This is a point that people who are only casually acquainted with the freedom-determinism problem often fail to understand.

Terminology

Before considering the grounds upon which any one of these positions is maintained, it is advisable to clarify some of the technical terminology that enters frequently into discussions of this problem.

Let us consider first the terms "determinism" and "indeterminism." *Determinism* (or *universal determinism*, as we have called it above) is a theory about the universe—the theory, namely, that every event in the universe is an inevitable consequence of antecedent causes. According to this theory, the state of the universe at any given moment in time determines in every detail what it will be like at any future moment. An omniscient scientist, if he existed, could (according to this theory) predict with perfect accuracy each and every detail of the future—precisely when each leaf would fall, when each organism would come into being, every detail of its life, the exact moment of its death, and so on. That we cannot in fact make such predictions now, say determinists, is due only to our ignorance of the relevant laws. If we only knew the relevant laws—as we do in the case of the motions of the planets—such prediction would be relatively simple.

Indeterminism is simply the denial of determinism. Like determinism, therefore, it is a theory about the universe—the theory, namely, that the universe is so constituted that some events occur that are not the inevitable (and therefore theoretically predictable) consequences of antecedent causes. Some events, according to the indeterminist, are uncaused, spontaneous, original. This does not mean, of course, that the universe as conceived by the indeterminist is utterly chaotic. An indeterminist readily admits that there are vast areas of the universe in which events are not only theoretically predictable, but actually predictable. His position is simply that however wide the domain of causal law may be, it is not universal: some events are not subject to it. These events are not inevitable, and our hypothetical omniscient scientist could not have predicted them despite his exhaustive knowledge of the universe.

We may also observe at this point that either determinism or indeterminism must be true: there is no third possibility. Determinism is the theory that every event in the universe is the inevitable consequence of antecedent causes; indeterminism is the denial of this. Since determinism either is or is not true, and since indeterminism is identical with the view that determinism is not true, it is evident that either determinism or indeterminism must be the case. A great deal of confusion in the literature relating to this problem might have been avoided if this simple point had been clear to everyone who has written on it.

Two other terms that should be clearly understood at the outset are "behaviorism" and the "free-will theory." These, unlike determinism and indeterminism, are theories about man rather than theories about the universe.

Behaviorism may be defined as the view that man is so constituted that the whole of his behavior—his every wish, thought, decision and act—is the inevitable consequence of antecedent causes. Behaviorism, then, is determinism as it applies to man. Man, according to this view, is not in any degree the original cause of his own actions; his decisions and his choices are only links in a complex chain of causes whose ultimate origins lie outside himself.

The *free-will theory*, stated negatively, is simply the denial of behaviorism (just as indeterminism is simply the denial of determinism). Positively stated, the free-will theory may be defined as the view that man is so constituted that he is in some degree the original cause of his own actions. According to this theory, it is impossible in principle to predict every detail of a man's behavior since some of the causes of his future behavior are not now present to be taken into account in making the prediction. Similarly, if we try to trace the chain of causes backward from a given act, it is impossible in principle to press the inquiry to a set of antecedent conditions lying outside the agent to which the act can be reduced as to a sufficient cause. However strong the influence of antecedent conditions may be, they are not sufficient to produce the act according to this view.

We shall have occasion in a later chapter to note in some detail the difficulties surrounding this notion of "free will." For the present, however, the student will do well to concentrate his attention on what the theory denies rather than what it affirms. He may justly expect of Libertarian (who is committed to affirming the free-will theory) that he will give a positive account of this theory in the course of stating and supporting his position.

The logical relations that obtain among these four theories may be summarized as follows:

1. If determinism is true, then
   a) indeterminism is false
   b) the free-will theory is false
   c) behaviorism is true
2. If determinism is false, then
   a) indeterminism is true
   b) the truth or falsity of behaviorism is unknown
   c) the truth or falsity of the free-will theory is unknown
3. If indeterminism is true, then
   a) determinism is false
   b) the truth or falsity of behaviorism is unknown
   c) the truth or falsity of the free-will theory is unknown
4. If indeterminism is false, then
   a) determinism is true
   b) behaviorism is true
   c) the free-will theory is false
5. If behaviorism is true, then
   a) the free-will theory is false
   b) the truth or falsity of determinism is unknown
   c) the truth or falsity of indeterminism is unknown
6. If behaviorism is false, then
   a) the free-will theory is true
   b) indeterminism is true
   c) determinism is false
7. If the free-will theory is true, then
   a) behaviorism is false
   b) indeterminism is true
   c) determinism is false
8. If the free-will theory is false, then

a) behaviorism is true

b) the truth or falsity of determinism is unknown

c) the truth or falsity of indeterminism is unknown

Two other more or less technical terms sometimes encountered in discussions of this problem are "fatalism" and "predestination." We shall not have occasion to use them in the debate that follows, but it seems advisable to discuss them briefly in order to forestall any confusion that might result from leaving them undefined.

Fatalism may be defined as the view that (a) determinism is true, therefore (b) whatever is going to happen is going to happen, no matter what anyone does. Fatalism implies what might be called a "what-the-hell" attitude toward life. It makes no sense, according to fatalism, to try to bring about some good result because whether or not that good result is going to occur depends solely on whether or not the desired result is "fated" (determined) to occur. For the same reason, obviously, it makes no sense according to fatalism to take any steps to prevent some undesirable event from occurring. A fatalist would say, "I'll go when my time comes—and until then, no matter what I do, I'm safe; when that time comes, nothing can save me." Fatalism, then, is not so much a theory as an attitude toward life. Insofar as it is a theory, however, it is clearly mistaken in asserting that on the premise that determinism is true it follows that whatever will be will be *no matter what you or I or anyone else may do.* What determinism implies is that what you or I or someone else may do can be very influential (as intermediate causes) in determining what is going to happen, but that our behavior, whatever it may be, is of course itself determined by antecedent causes. Much more could be said on this topic, but perhaps these few remarks are sufficient to show that fatalism is not a particularly useful concept in attempting to understand the free-will/determinism problem.

An equally unhelpful concept for our purposes is the concept of "predestination." This is a theological concept, and in Christian theology at least it has a very precise meaning: it is the view that God determines absolutely, without regard to any quality or condition in man, who shall be saved (or who shall be saved and who shall not be saved—which comes to the same thing). Predestination has to do only with God's alleged decision as to who is to be saved and who is to be damned, nothing else. Its only relevance to the free-will/determinism controversy is that it denies that man is in any sense free to decide what his eternal destiny will be. Since we have no need for this concept in the following discussion, there is no need to say any more about it.

It is crucially important for the discussion that follows, however, that the four concepts discussed earlier—determinism, indeterminism, behaviorism, and the free-will theory—be clearly and thoroughly understood. They will bear occasional review as we proceed with the debate.

STUDY QUESTIONS

1. State in two or three different ways what you understand to be the freedom-determinism problem.
2. How might this problem arise for each of the following: a physicist? a psychologist? a sociologist? a theologian? a juror?
3. Is it true that this problem is capable of being answered in just three ways? If so, explain why; if not, describe the additional alternatives.
4. Define carefully each of the following: hard determinism, soft determinism, universal determinism, indeterminism, libertarianism, behaviorism, free-will theory.
5. X says, "I do not believe in either determinism or indeterminism: I believe in *self*-determinism." Criticize this statement.

25

THE CASE FOR
HARD DETERMINISM

It is my purpose to persuade the reader that of the three alternative answers that can be given to the question posed in the preceding chapter, hard determinism is the most plausible. I shall begin by pointing out exactly what, as a hard determinist, I am obliged to defend. I shall then go on to support this position with what seem to be the strongest arguments available.

What Hard Determinism Is

Hard determinism is the view that (a) the freedom that is a condition of moral responsibility is not compatible with universal determinism and (b) universal determinism is the case; therefore, (c) man is not free in the sense required to render him morally responsible. I hold, that is to say, a certain view of what would have to be the case if man were to be morally responsible; I hold that this condition of moral responsibility is not compatible with universal determinism; and I hold that universal determinism is true. I conclude, therefore, that man is not in fact morally responsible. This conclusion—the assertion that man is not in fact morally responsible—follows inevitably from my two premises.

What Constitutes Moral Freedom?

It is first advisable to distinguish two different meanings that are often conveyed by the single word "freedom." One common meaning of the term is "the opportunity to do what you want to do." In this sense, we have the freedom to do whatever we are not hindered from doing by external constraints or natural limitations. Thus I am "free" at this moment to write or not to write, to remain sitting at my desk or to get up and leave it, to open my office door or to leave it closed. I am not "free" to help myself to all of the money in the vault of the nearest bank (because of external constraints) or to jump thirty feet into the air (because of natural limitations). Let us call this kind of freedom the "circumstantial freedom of self-realization." [1]

It is apparent that freedom in this sense varies greatly, depending on abilities and circumstances. The strong are "free" to do some things that the weak are not; the rich are "free" to do some things that the poor are not; the average citizen is "free" to do some things that the prison inmate is not "free" to do; etc. Circumstantial freedom of self-realization, the opportunity to do what we want to do, is a matter of degree.

Some writers, however, speak of man's freedom as a power of the self to enact any one of a number of genuinely open alternatives. This is what libertarians ascribe to man when they credit him with having a "free will." Let us call freedom in this sense the "natural freedom of self-determination."

It should be noted that freedom in this sense does not admit of degrees. Either man has it, or he does not. If he has it, he has it at all times—whether he is rich or poor, strong or weak, in prison or out of prison.

I assume that everyone will allow that freedom in the first sense—the circumstantial freedom of self-realization—is a necessary condition of moral responsibility. We do not hold people responsible for not doing something if we are satisfied that they wanted to do it but were not able to. This much is agreed to by everyone who is a party to the freedom-determinism dispute.

It is my view, however, that while the circumstantial freedom of self-realization is indeed a *necessary* condition of moral responsibility, it is not a *sufficient* condition. If man is to be regarded as morally responsible, it is also necessary to ascribe to him the natural freedom of self-determination. The libertarians are right, therefore, in affirming that this freedom—or "free will" as they like to call it—is a necessary condition of moral responsibility; but they are wrong in affirming that man has it.

The question is a very difficult one, and we must be careful not to get lost in a forest of abstractions and arbitrary definitions. To reiterate, our question is: In what sense must man be free if he is to be regarded as morally responsible? Or, more simply: What constitutes

---

[1] The terminology is borrowed from Mortimer J. Adler, *et al., The Idea of Freedom* (New York: Doubleday, 1958). This study constitutes the definitive analysis of the concept of freedom, and it is highly desirable that its terminological recommendations be adopted by all participants in the dispute over determinism and free will.

moral freedom? It would be easy to arbitrarily define moral responsibility in such a way that the circumstantial freedom of self-realization
would be a sufficient condition of its possibility. But we are not at
liberty to define moral responsibility in any way that happens to fit our
fancy: what we really mean by moral responsibility is implicit in the
ways in which we ascribe praise and blame and in the ways in which
we regard men as deserving reward and punishment.

In order to decide, therefore, whether or not the natural freedom of
self-determination is a condition of moral responsibility, we have only
to scrutinize carefully the sorts of judgments of praise and blame that
we make. Then we may ask ourselves: Would we or would we not
alter our judgment if we were persuaded that the agent of the act was
not "free" in the sense of possessing the natural freedom of self-
determination? I am confident that anyone who reflects carefully on a
few hypothetical cases of this kind will find that we would alter our
judgment in such a case, thereby demonstrating that our judgments
of praise and blame do presuppose that man is free in the sense of
possessing the natural freedom of self-determination.

Let us consider a hypothetical example. Two boys—Tom and
George—are apprehended attempting the armed robbery of a supermarket. Subsequent questioning reveals that the idea of robbing the
supermarket was first suggested by Tom, but that the detailed planning of the robbery was done in cooperation and that the two participated equally in the attempted holdup. Therefore, both are guilty of
committing a felony, and they are presumably deserving of equal punishment before the law.

If we were given no more information than this, I suppose the
moral judgment that most of us would pronounce on the matter would
be quite parallel to the legal judgment. Tom and George, we would
say, are equally blameworthy for planning and attempting to execute
this act. Indeed, if there is any difference at all in the blame attaching
to the two boys, the greater blame must be Tom's since it was he who
first suggested the idea. Nonetheless, we would say, both are highly
blameworthy and deserve the punishment that they will now presumably receive at the hands of the law.

But suppose that we acquire some additional information about the
two boys. Suppose we learn that Tom was raised in a family of habitual criminals and from earliest childhood had been taught that armed
robbery was a feat of heroism rather than a blameworthy act. Suppose
that George, on the other hand, was the product of a very different
kind of home: his father was the governor, his mother a leader in
civic affairs, and his elder brother a congressman. All the opportunities of a fine home and a good education were his, while Tom had
none of these.

Would we now alter our previous moral evaluation of the acts of these two boys? I am certain that we would—and in some readily predictable ways. We would say that George, having had the advantages of his upbringing, is much more deserving of blame than Tom. We would say that Tom, owing to the untoward circumstances in which he was raised, is almost more to be pitied than to be blamed. Whatever the status of these two before the law, we would maintain that so far as their moral guilt is concerned, they are not deserving of equal blame—for of him to whom much is given we expect much, and of him to whom little is given we expect less.

But what is the principle according to which we alter our judgment of moral guilt? Why do we judge Tom less harshly than George? Clearly it is because we partly attribute Tom's act to causes lying outside himself—to the environment in which he was raised—whereas we attribute George's act to his own perverse choice. In other words, *we do not hold a man responsible for any act insofar as we believe that act to be the consequence of causes lying outside himself.* Anyone who is willing to consider a number of hypothetical cases of moral judgment objectively will readily agree that this is an important principle on which our everyday moral judgments are formulated.

In order for a man to be morally responsible, then, he must be in some degree the original cause of his act. He is morally responsible for his act only if, and insofar as, he is the original cause. Moral freedom—the freedom that is a condition of moral responsibility— includes the natural freedom of self-determination. Without this— without "free will," as the libertarians say—there is no moral responsibility.

The Case for Determinism

Unfortunately, it is impossible for man to have the natural freedom of self-determination, although he would have to have it in order to be morally responsible. It is impossible because this is a deterministic universe. To complete my case, I shall set forth a number of arguments whose conclusions make it necessary for everyone who considers the matter carefully to adopt the determinist hypothesis.

First, every instance of regularity that is discovered in nature is evidence for the hypothesis that all macroscopic phenomena are reducible to the regular operations of natural laws. The quantity of evidence now available from the many special sciences is so great as to make the contrary hypothesis exceedingly improbable.

The era of modern science began when men ceased asking for the *purposes* of natural phenomena and asked instead for their *causes*. To the question, What is the purpose of the revolution of the heavenly bodies? all sorts of fanciful answers are possible, and no answer can ever be demonstrated to be the right one. But to the questions, What *uniformities* are exhibited in the motions of the heavenly bodies? or What are the *causes* of celestial phenomena? clear and mathematically precise answers can be given on the basis of data available to anyone who cares to concern himself with the question.

For a long time it was assumed that "lawlike regularity" applied only to the realm of inanimate matter and that human behavior, at least, was exempt from the reign of such laws. Severe doubt was cast on this view by the research of Charles Darwin, however. A short time later research into human behavior was undertaken by Sigmund Freud and others on the supposition that it, like any other phenomenon, is governed by laws that may be discovered by painstaking inquiry. This supposition has been progressively verified by the research of Freud's successors. As B. F. Skinner says, "We cannot apply the methods of science to a subject matter that moves about capriciously." [2] Every advance in descriptive psychology, every discovery that is made with respect to the laws governing human behavior, adds to the steadily and rapidly growing accumulation of evidence in support of the view that human behavior, too, is thoroughly subject to the vast network of causes that govern all phenomena.

Should anyone be disposed to quarrel with what has just been said, let him reflect for a moment on what it would be like for a scientist to abandon the determinist hypothesis. Given the determinist hypothesis, a scientist can ask about a given phenomenon he has chosen to investigate, What are its causes? What are the uniformities, the laws, exemplified in this phenomenon? Should he abandon the determinist hypothesis, he could not ask such questions. He would have to ask instead, Does this phenomenon have any causes—or is this perhaps one of those things that occur haphazardly, one of those things that do not have any regular causes? And this, I submit, is absurd. It would cut the nerve of the whole scientific enterprise, which has made its advances on precisely the opposite supposition.

In a less rigorous but perhaps equally important way, we all make a similar supposition whenever we have occasion to predict the behavior of other human beings. We know, for example, that if we want to avoid an argument we had better stay off the subject of politics whenever Uncle George is around. How do we know this? We know it because, in a rough and ready way, we know some of the "laws," the "regularities," that govern Uncle George's behavior. Consider any person that you know reasonably well: is it not true that you could, with a high degree of accuracy, predict how he would act in a wide variety of situations? To acknowledge this is to acknowledge that his behavior exhibits certain uniformities, uniformities that differ only in the degree to which they are known from the uniformities exhibited in the

---

[2] B. F. Skinner, *Science and Human Behavior* (New York: Macmillan, 1953), p. 6.

motions of planets, the interactions of chemicals, and the migration of birds.

That human behavior is not exempt from causal laws becomes evident when we reflect on the experience of "choosing among alternatives." Here, if anywhere, we would expect the "natural freedom of self-determination," which libertarians defend, to be evident. But it is not. Consider: we never choose without a motive. Just as motives are determined by desires, so choice is determined by motive: we always choose that alternative for which we find the strongest motive. But what constitutes the strongest motive for any given individual depends on his personal likes and dislikes, which are, in turn, the consequences of his heredity and environment. Thus, the "chain of causes" leading to an act stretches back indefinitely; "decision" is not an original cause, but merely one link in the chain.

I have dwelt at length on this matter of human behavior because it is, so to speak, the last outpost of indeterminism. If it is conceded that human behavior is as completely subject in principle to causal explanation as are other phenomena, then so far as I can see there will remain no further objection to adopting the determinist hypothesis. Thanks to the efforts of psychologists and sociologists, we have already come far in the direction of adopting a behaviorist view. We now speak without hesitation of "the causes of crime," "the conditions that create antisocial attitudes," and the like. We still have, admittedly, much to learn about the laws that govern human behavior. But it is not unreasonable to hope, with Skinner, that:

> Eventually a science of the nervous system based upon direct observation rather than inference will describe the neural states and events which immediately precede instances of behavior. We shall know the precise neurological conditions which immediately precede, say, the response, "No, thank you." These events in turn will be found to be preceded by other neurological events, and these in turn by others. This series will lead us back to events outside the nervous system and, eventually, outside the organism.[3]

It may be conceded that the foregoing considerations do not conclusively demonstrate the truth of the determinist hypothesis. Like any hypothesis, it does not admit of conclusive demonstration. What these considerations do suggest, however, is that it is more reasonable to affirm the determinist hypothesis than it is to affirm its only alternative—indeterminism. And this is the conclusion that I have been attempting to reinforce.

I want to deal briefly with one objection that is frequently raised against the determinist position. It is sometimes stated that the principle of indeterminacy, which was first formulated by the German

---

[3] *Ibid.*, p. 28.

physicist W. K. Heisenberg and which is now an accepted part of modern physical theory, demonstrates that determinism is not the case and lends empirical support to the libertarian position. Now I will concede that it is just barely possible that there is a real indeterminacy in the behavior of subatomic particles, although it seems to me most improbable that this is the case. The principle of indeterminacy is best understood, I think, as a limitation in our knowledge of subatomic events rather than a real hiatus in the network of mutually interacting events of which the universe is composed. Suppose, however, that I should turn out to be mistaken on this point. Suppose it is the case that there is a real indeterminacy at the subatomic level. What are the consequences? It is true, of course, that I would then be compelled to concede that in this one class of cases there does indeed seem to be some real indeterminacy in the universe, and so to that extent determinism is incorrect. But note this: such an admission would have no tendency whatever to establish the libertarian view that *man's* decision or actions are undetermined. Hard determinism is, to be sure, in considerable part an inference drawn from the belief that determinism is true, and to this extent hard determinists would (if Heisenberg's principle does in fact point to a real indeterminacy) have to modify their position. But the consequences for ethics are the same whether one is a determinist or merely a behaviorist, and the Heisenberg principle does nothing to undermine the behaviorist view. Thus the objection, while it is not exactly irrelevant to the issue we are discussing, falls far short of suggesting anything that could be of any help to the defenders of moral responsibility.

Consequences for Ethics

The conclusions to which I am driven on the basis of the foregoing considerations are, I confess, somewhat disturbing. Since moral responsibility presupposes the natural freedom of self-determination (free will), since this freedom is not compatible with universal determinism, and since universal determinism appears to be the case, we cannot avoid the conclusion—contrary to what most people certainly believe—that man is not morally responsible. And this inference, in turn, carries with it consequences such as the following:

1. No human act, however "noble" or "base," is ever worthy of either praise or blame. John F. Kennedy's heroism and dedication were as much a product of his heredity and environment as Lee Harvey Oswald's hatred and perversion were a product of his.

2. Punishment (or "retributive justice" as it is sometimes called) cannot be defended on the ground that a person who acts in a certain way is "guilty" and, therefore, "deserving of punishment." It makes no sense to talk about a criminal "paying his debt to

society." Like everybody else, the criminal has acted in the only way possible for him (given his heredity and environment) and therefore has incurred no such debt.

3. If we are to continue to praise and blame or reward and punish people on the basis of their behavior, it can only be on the ground that such things will tend to influence their behavior in certain desirable ways.

These, I admit, are "hard" conclusions. As a private citizen I will even admit that I do not like them and that I in fact continue to make judgments of praise and blame just like anyone else. But as a philosopher I know that such judgments, and indeed all moral behavior, have no rational justification. Our beliefs about moral responsibility and what we now know about the structure of the universe (and about man in particular) are in hopeless and irremediable contradiction. As a philosopher I have felt obliged to point out this contradiction notwithstanding the unpalatable consequences for ethical theory.

STUDY QUESTIONS

1. What precisely is the difference between "the circumstantial freedom of self-realization" and "the natural freedom of self-determination"? In what sense, according to Hard Determinist, must man be free if he is to be morally responsible? Do you think he is right about this?
2. What is the point of Hard Determinist's insistence that in the discussion of this question one must constantly refer to the "facts concerning the actual ways in which we handle the categories of moral responsibility"? Does this seem to be at all important?
3. Does Hard Determinist's example bear out his claim that we do not hold a person responsible for an act insofar as we believe that act to be the consequence of causes lying outside himself? Suggest three or four additional examples that either confirm or disconfirm this principle.
4. What arguments does Hard Determinist offer in support of the truth of the determinist hypothesis? Does this evidence seem to be conclusive? Can you think of any additional arguments in support of this hypothesis that Hard Determinist has failed to mention?
5. Do the "disturbing consequences" that Hard Determinist itemizes at the end of his essay really follow from his view, as he says? Are there other similar consequences that Hard Determinist has neglected to mention?

26

THE CASE FOR
SOFT DETERMINISM

It must certainly be acknowledged that Hard Determinist has made a very good case for the view that determinism is true and that this excludes the possibility of the freedom without which man cannot be morally responsible. His arguments in support of the determinist hypothesis are particularly cogent, and I am delighted to simply accept everything he has to say on that score as a part of the case that I propose to build in defense of *soft determinism*.

Before I do this, however, I should like to say that I do not particularly care for the name "soft determinism" that has come into common use as a description of my position. There are two reasons for my dislike of this title. The first is that it was invented by William James, a noted libertarian, who coined it precisely for the purpose of disparaging it. Just listen to James' words:

> Nowadays, we have a *soft* determinism which abhors harsh words, and, repudiating fatality, necessity, and even predetermination, says that its real name is freedom; for freedom is only necessity understood, and bondage to the highest is identical with true freedom.[1]

In other words, James used this title pejoratively; and if, to avoid confusion, I allow my position to be called "soft determinism," I insist that these pejorative connotations be laid aside and that my position be considered simply on its merits. If I reject Hard Determinist's conclusions with respect to ethics, it is not because I am "soft" but because I think his conclusions are unwarranted.

---

[1] William James, "The Dilemma of Determinism," in *The Will to Believe and Other Essays in Popular Philosophy, and Human Immortality* (New York: Dover, 1956), p. 149.

The second reason for my displeasure with the name "soft determinism" is that it has led to a great deal of confusion as to what my position really is. I am no less firm in my adherence to determinism than is Hard Determinist. I hold, with him, that the universe is so constituted that absolutely everything that occurs—including actions by human beings—is an inevitable consequence of antecedent causes. Both Hard Determinist and I are what may be called "strict determinists." The difference between us is not that he is more consistent in his determinism than I, but that he draws certain consequences from his determinism (with respect to ethics) that are in my view unwarranted. I propose now to show where Hard Determinist makes his mistake and how it is, therefore, possible to maintain a consistent determinism without drawing the dire ethical consequences that he insists must be drawn.

Moral Freedom

The crucial question that must be asked about this vexing problem is, *In what sense* must man be "free" if he is to be morally responsible? Hard Determinist has argued that he must be free in a contra-causal sense, that is, that he must possess a natural freedom of self-determination. It is at this point that he is mistaken, and it is because of this mistake that he feels obliged to deny that man is morally responsible. My view, on the contrary, is that the circumstantial freedom of self-realization—the opportunity to do what you please—is a necessary *and sufficient* condition of moral responsibility. I think that a careful consideration of the ways in which we actually ascribe praise and blame will demonstrate that this view is the correct one.

Let us suppose that Hard Determinist were right in his contention that man could be morally free only if this were not a deterministic universe, that man could be morally responsible for an act only if that act were not the inevitable consequence of antecedent causes. What then? We would be in the position of saying that a man is responsible for an act if and only if that act is uncaused. But to say that something is uncaused is to say that it is a "chance" event, a mere random occurrence. Apart from the difficulty of even conceiving of such a thing, it is absurd to maintain that a man could be morally responsible only if his actions, or some of his actions (those for which he would be held responsible), occurred "by chance." This is not what we have in mind when we say "So-and-so is morally responsible for doing *r*."

What, then, do we have in mind? Simply, I submit, that the agent had the opportunity—the circumstantial freedom—to do a number of things, and that he did what he did because he wanted to. We do ask, when applying appraisal concepts, whether the agent could have done otherwise had he so desired; we do not ask whether he could have desired to do otherwise. The reason we do not ask the latter is simply that it is not relevant to our judgment as to the praiseworthiness or blameworthiness of his actions.

Let us consider a hypothetical example. Johnny has been instructed always to come directly home from school, and his mother has learned (through repeated observation of Johnny's arrival time) that when he does he normally arrives home no later than 3:15 P.M. On a few occasions, however, Johnny has arrived home at a slightly later time, but on each of these occasions his mother has determined that "he could not have done otherwise": he had to stay after school, the extreme cold made it necessary for him to stop briefly at a store to warm himself, etc. But one spring day Johnny arrives home at nearly five o'clock, and Mother naturally asks, "Johnny, where have you been?" Johnny replies, "I've been playing in the puddles." "But Johnny," Mother objects, "don't you know that you are supposed to come directly home from school?" "Yes." "Well, why didn't you?" "Well, I just didn't want to. I wanted to play in the puddles." "Well, son, you will have to be punished for this." "But Mother," Johnny cries, "you can't punish me for that. I couldn't *want* to do anything else."

We obviously do not, and would not, consider Johnny's objection relevant. Why? Because in holding someone responsible for something we do not ask why he wants to do so-and-so, but only whether his doing so-and-so was a result of his wanting to do it. So long as Johnny's late arrival was unavoidable—so long as his wanting to be home on time was thwarted by circumstances—Johnny was not held responsible for the late arrival; but when the late arrival was the consequence of his wanting to do something that caused him to be late, he was immediately held responsible *no matter what may have been the causes* of his wanting to play rather than obey.

Let us consider a second hypothetical case. The manager of a supermarket is apprehended in the act of removing the contents of the store safe at 2 A.M. He is accordingly suspected of attempting to commit an act of theft. Investigation discloses, however, that (a) a gunman is holding the manager's wife and children hostage and has threatened to harm them if he does not comply with orders, (b) a second gunman has forced the manager to drive to the supermarket and open the safe, and (c) the manager tried unsuccessfully to attract the attention of the police (at risk of his life) by exceeding the speed limit and running through a red light en route to the market.

Knowing these facts, we would not blame the store manager—we would not hold him responsible—for the attempted theft. Why? Simply because we are satisfied on the basis of the facts that he was not doing what he wanted to do. And the reason that he was not doing what he wanted to do was that he did not have the circumstantial freedom, the opportunity, to do it.

It is significant that the only question relevant to determining moral responsibility in either of these two cases is: Was the agent, in the circumstances in which he found himself, able to do what he wanted to do? That is, did he have the *circumstantial freedom* to actualize his own wishes? Johnny had this freedom; therefore, we hold him responsible for his late arrival. The manager in our second example did not have this freedom; therefore, we do not hold him responsible.

Who was responsible, then, for the attempted robbery of the supermarket? Obviously, it was the gunmen who forced the store manager to comply with their wishes. And in this we may see what is really meant by the notion of moral responsibility. *To be morally responsible is to be the person whose motives, whose desires, need to be changed if a given kind of behavior is to be encouraged or prevented.* We do not blame people for doing what, under the circumstances, was the only thing they could reasonably have been expected to do. We do blame them if a different desire on their part would have been sufficient to produce a more desirable kind of behavior.

Reasons for Confusion

The problem of freedom and determinism has been debated vociferously and inconclusively for many hundreds of years. Why should this be so if the solution is really as simple as I have suggested? Since this question may in itself constitute an obstacle to accepting the position I am advocating, I should like to deal briefly with it.

There are two reasons why the true solution to this much-discussed problem has eluded most of those who have addressed themselves to it. The first reason, and in my judgment the most important one, is that they have misunderstood the nature of moral judgments. To be morally responsible, as we said above, is to be the person whose motives need to be changed if a given kind of behavior is to be encouraged or prevented. This is what we mean in both of the hypothetical cases cited above. I am confident that anyone who will take the trouble to reflect on any example whatsoever in which he would be inclined to regard a person as morally responsible will find that this is equally the case there. It is inevitable that this should be so because this is what we mean when we say that a person is morally responsible. Moreover, the function of moral judgments is precisely *to alter the motives of the person being judged and thus to influence his future behavior.* Praise and blame are simply mild forms of reward and punishment. The reason for employing either is always—in the case of blame or punishment—to discourage or prevent certain kinds of undesirable behavior or—in the case of praise or rewards—to encourage certain kinds of desirable behavior.

Let us now suppose that someone approaches the question concerning the conditions of moral responsibility without understanding the true nature of moral responsibility or of moral judgments. How would he be apt to construe them? In all likelihood he would construe moral judgments on the analogy of statements of fact. Accordingly, he would interpret blameworthiness and praiseworthiness as "intrinsic qualities" of the persons or acts being judged. From this mistaken starting point it is a very short step to the view—shared by Hard Determinist and Libertarian—that some obscure power ("freedom") *within the agent* is a condition of moral responsibility.

A second reason for the mistaken views of many people regarding this question involves a series of semantic confusions with respect to the terms "law" and "freedom." Our perception of the meaning of the term "law" derives largely from its use in connection with statutes and ordinances—the sorts of things enacted by city councils, legislatures, and parliaments. It is the very nature of this sort of "law" to prescribe behavior—indeed (by virtue of the threat of punishment) to coerce behavior. Implicit in every such law is the "or else" embodied in the system of fines or other punishments that await the offender. If we disobey, we become subject to the prescribed punishment; because we fear the punishment, we usually obey—whether or not the prescribed behavior is what we ourselves really want to do.

But in science the term "law" is used to designate a very different sort of thing, namely, an observed uniformity. Scientific law is merely a report about what has actually been observed to be the case in such-and-such a class of phenomena. Here there is no coercion, no "or else." Pure water (at sea level) is not compelled or constrained to freeze whenever the temperature reaches 32° Fahrenheit. It just does. And the "law" that states this is simply a description of what in fact has been observed to occur.

Had this distinction between prescriptive and descriptive law been clearly recognized, it probably would never have occurred to anyone to insist that moral responsibility requires exemption from the laws of nature. Moral responsibility does indeed require exemption from coercion—but the laws of nature do not coerce. The opposite of causality is acausality, or indeterminism, whereas the opposite of compulsion is freedom. Hence, the failure to distinguish the two different kinds of law led to the absurd view that moral responsibility requires a contracausal, or indeterministic, freedom.

Moral Responsibility Requires Determinism

Thus far I have only argued that moral freedom is consistent with the determinist hypothesis and that we do not need to conclude with Hard Determinist that man cannot be morally responsible in a deterministic world. In arguing thus, however, it may appear that I am being purely defensive—that I am trying to "salvage" what can be salvaged of human moral responsibility in a deterministic universe. By way of countering this impression, which is of course implicit in James' unfortunate labeling of my position as "soft" determinism, I should like to conclude by taking the offensive in this argument. The thesis I propose to support is this: not only is it the case that moral responsibility is consistent with the determinist hypothesis, but *moral responsibility would not be possible in anything other than a deterministic universe.*

That moral responsibility requires determinism is evident, in the first place, from my earlier argument concerning the absurdity of maintaining that a man can be responsible for only those of his acts that occur "by chance." For any event whatsoever, we can conceive of only two possibilities: either it has a cause or it does not have a cause. If it has a cause, then it is explicable within the context of the deterministic hypothesis. If it does not have a cause, then it is a "chance event." To reject determinism, therefore, on the ground that it is incompatible with moral responsibility—or, alternatively, to reject moral responsibility on the ground that it is not possible in a deterministic universe—is to adopt the absurd position referred to above.

My thesis can also be supported in another way. Let us suppose that this were not a deterministic universe—that some things that occur are not the inevitable consequences of antecedent causes and that a given set of circumstances would not, therefore, always produce a predictable effect. In such a universe it would be impossible to hold a man responsible for anything because he could never know what would be the result of any act he might perform. In such a universe the glass of water that yesterday quenched the thirst of a dying man might today poison him instead, or turn him into a giraffe, or do any one of countless other thoroughly unpredictable things. It is only insofar as we can predict what will be the effects of a given course of action that we can act responsibly; hence it follows that we can act responsibly only in a universe where certain predictable effects follow inevitably from certain causes. An indeterministic universe—a universe in which the orderly sequence of events is interrupted by more or less frequent "chance events"—would be a moral chaos. It is doubtful if life would even be possible in such a universe; but there is no doubt about the fact that in such a universe responsible behavior would be utterly impossible.

It seems, therefore, that the time has come to lay this old problem to rest. What is really of concern to Hard Determinist is the truth of the determinist hypothesis. It is this that he feels obliged to insist on, and in this he is right. What is really of concern to Libertarian is the truth of the conviction that man is morally responsible. This is what he feels obliged to insist on, and in this he is right. Where both Hard Determinist and Libertarian err—and this is the unargued assumption that has kept this debate alive for so many years—is in assuming that moral responsibility requires a contra-causal freedom in man. Once the absurdity of this assumption is perceived, the problem is solved.

STUDY QUESTIONS

1. Where precisely does Soft Determinist agree with Hard Determinist, and where does he disagree with him? Is there any difference between them as to the *method* by which each thinks this question must be decided?
2. Does it follow from Hard Determinist's position, as Soft Determinist says, that "a man is responsible for an act if and only if that act is uncaused"? How might Hard Determinist defend himself against this objection?
3. Do the two hypothetical examples offered by Soft Determinist support his claim that the only relevant question in deciding on a question of moral responsibility is whether the person in question did what he did because he wanted to? Could Hard Determinist explain these examples in a way consistent with his position?
4. What does Soft Determinist say is the meaning of "moral responsibility"? Do you think he is right about this? If not, what alternative would you suggest?
5. What considerations does Soft Determinist offer in support of his claim that moral responsibility actually *requires* determinism? Do you agree or disagree with this thesis? Why?

27

THE CASE FOR
LIBERTARIANISM

After the formidable array of arguments that Hard and Soft Determinist have presented in support of their respective positions and the devastating cross fire to which libertarianism has been subjected in these discussions, it may appear futile to attempt to construct a persuasive argument for my position. Yet I am convinced that libertarianism is true, and I welcome the opportunity to defend it and to show how the various objections raised against it can be rather easily overcome. Let me begin by stating where I agree and where I disagree with each of my opponents.

Hard Determinist has argued that determinism is true and that the freedom that is a condition of moral responsibility is not compatible with determinism. From these two premises he has drawn the unhappy conclusion that man is not morally responsible. My position vis-à-vis Hard Determinist is clear: I reject his first premise and I affirm his second. Of course, I do not accept his view that man is not morally responsible. I believe it can be established on independent grounds that man is morally responsible and that we must therefore accept the conclusion that determinism is not the case. I shall attempt to show in due time that the consequences of accepting this conclusion are not nearly so dire as some determinists would lead us to believe.

Soft Determinist offers a more elusive argument. Consequently, it is more difficult to state sharply just exactly where we agree and where we disagree. We disagree, of course, in our views with respect to determinism: he holds that it is the case; I hold that it is not. We disagree, moreover, in our respective views as to what sort of freedom is required in order to render a man morally responsible. He holds that the circumstantial freedom of self-realization is a sufficient condition of moral responsibility; I hold (in agreement with Hard Determinist) that man is not morally responsible unless he possesses also the natural freedom of self-determination.

It may seem as if Soft Determinist and I agree on one point, namely, that man is morally responsible. But anyone who is acquainted with both his position and mine will immediately recognize that our agreement is only verbal. We both say that man is morally responsible—but we do not mean the same thing. When he says that so-and-so is morally responsible, he means that so-and-so is the person whose motives need to be changed if a certain kind of behavior is to be encouraged or avoided. When I say that a man is morally responsible, I mean that he is fittingly, or deservingly, subject to praise or blame, reward or punishment. So even at this point we are not in agreement—except, of course, verbally.

I propose to proceed in two stages. I am convinced that soft determinism is not a tenable position—despite the fact that it is very widely held—and I shall begin by showing why it is untenable. This will prepare for a direct confrontation with hard determinism, a position I respect but nonetheless consider mistaken. I believe that a clear-thinking person must finally choose between libertarianism and hard determinism, and I shall do my best to show that the strongest considerations are on my side.

Refutation of Soft Determinism

I have the greatest sympathy for the kinds of considerations that led Soft Determinist to adopt his position. The conclusions that Hard Determinist draws with respect to man's moral responsibility are "hard" conclusions indeed, and it is not surprising that some determinists should have sought a way to avoid them within the context of their deterministic beliefs.

Nonetheless, the mistake that Soft Determinist makes—the mistake that vitiates his whole position—is incredibly obvious. What Soft Determinist does is to start from the assumption that determinism is true; he then (a) arbitrarily redefines "moral freedom" in such a way as to render it compatible with determinism and (b) arbitrarily redefines "moral responsibility" in such a way as to make "moral freedom" as he has defined it a sufficient condition thereof. He then announces that he has "reconciled" determinism and moral responsibility and that the traditional problem, which has divided libertarians and determinists for so many years, has at last been solved.

But all that has been accomplished by this little verbal sleight of hand is simply a blurring of the relevant concepts, a confusion of the issue. The question never was whether human moral responsibility *as arbitrarily redefined* could be shown to be compatible with determinism: any two theories can be rendered compatible if you are willing to allow one of them to be freely redefined. The question was, and still is, whether moral responsibility *as this concept is employed in our everyday judgments of praise and blame* is compatible with determinism. Soft Determinist's argument does not show in the slightest that this is so.

To illustrate, let us consider the question, Are all of the citizens of Flamenco absolutely loyal to their government, or do some of them occasionally commit acts of treason? Two straightforward answers are possible: Either (a) all of the citizens are absolutely loyal and there is no treason in Flamenco ("hard loyalism"), or (b) treasonous acts are sometimes committed and not all of the citizens are always loyal to their government ("occasionarianism"). But it would be distinctly unhelpful to have someone say, "Look, I can define treason in such a way that occasional acts of treason do not contradict the view that all of the people of Flamenco are absolutely loyal to their government." It would be unhelpful because we do not want to know whether treason *as thus redefined* can be made to square with "universal loyalism." If we must ask this question about the compatibility of the concepts, what we want to know is whether treason in its ordinary unaltered meaning is compatible with "universal loyalism"; and it is evident that it is not.

Hard Determinist has already cautioned us to remember—and his point is an important one—that if we intend to address ourselves to the real problem at issue we are not at liberty to define moral responsibility in any way that happens to suit our fancy. What we really mean by moral responsibility is implicit in the ways in which we ascribe praise and blame and in the ways in which we regard men as deserving of reward and punishment. We have, therefore, to attend carefully to our actual employment of judgments of praise and blame in order to "read off" from that employment the meaning that is implicit therein. Anyone who will do this will shortly discover, I am confident, that "being morally responsible" means more than simply "being capable of having behavior altered through an alteration of motives."

If Soft Determinist's account of moral responsibility were correct, what would follow? In the first place, it would follow that we ought to hold animals morally responsible no less than we do men—for there is every reason to suppose that reward and punishment will influence the behavior of dogs and horses just as much as they will influence the behavior of men. But it is significant that although we do indeed reward and punish animals, we do not apply judgments of moral appraisal to them; whereas on Soft Determinist's account of moral responsibility we should. Further, if moral responsibility means what Soft Determinist says it means, it would make no sense whatsoever to speak of a dead person as "responsible" for something, since on this hypothesis there is no one whose motives could be influenced in such a way as to bring about a different sort of behavior. Yet, we do blame dead persons for acts committed by them: Hitler and Stalin are examples. Again, we commonly "make allowances" in making judgments of praise and blame for such things as a poor childhood environment. The child who grew up in the slums, whose father was a petty thief, etc., "did not have the chance" (as we say) that his more fortunate fellows did, so we judge him less harshly. On Soft Determinist's ground we would have no reason to judge him less harshly, since we have no reason to suppose that his behavior is either more or less subject to influence than anyone else's. Indeed, if Soft Determinist is right, we ought, if anything, to judge such a person more harshly, since there is reason to suppose that more counteracting influences are needed if his behavior is to be brought into tolerable conformity with society's norms. Thus at a number of crucial points Soft Determinist's account of moral responsibility is at variance with our actual judgments of praise and blame. Since it is in reference to such judgments that we must decide this matter, Soft Determinist's inability to account for the cases mentioned must be regarded as decisive against his position.

Soft Determinist has argued that moral freedom consists simply in having the circumstantial freedom of self-realization and that this view is supported by the fact that in concrete cases we never inquire about anything else. "It is significant," he writes, "that the only question relevant to determining moral responsibility . . . is: Was the agent, in the circumstances in which he found himself, able to do what he wanted to do? That is, did he have the *circumstantial freedom* to actualize his own wishes?" But surely the reason for this is that we assume that all men always have the natural freedom of self-determination and so we do not need to inquire about it in each particular case. The reason Johnny's mother (in Soft Determinist's example) does not accept his objection that he "could not want to do anything else" is not that his objection, if true, is not relevant, but rather that she does not believe him. If she were to become convinced that he had suddenly been afflicted with a "puddle-playing syndrome" that literally compelled him to want to play in puddles, her attitude would be very different.

We may safely conclude, therefore, that the recent attempts of some determinists to affirm the moral responsibility of man without relinquishing their belief in determinism do not succeed. If man is to be regarded as morally responsible, it is necessary, as Hard Determinist has argued, that he have both the circumstantial freedom of self-realization and the natural freedom of self-determination (free will). And since, as Hard Determinist has shown, the latter is not compatible with determinism, the choice must rest between Hard Determinist's position and my own.

Replies to Objections

Hard Determinist has stated very cogently the arguments that he thinks make it unreasonable to deny the truth of the determinist hypothesis; since my position commits me to just such a denial, it is incumbent on me to show why I think his arguments are not convincing.

His first argument is that "every instance of regularity that is discovered in nature is evidence for the hypothesis that all macroscopic phenomena are reducible to the regular operations of natural laws" and that "the quantity of evidence now available from the many special sciences is so great as to make the contrary hypothesis exceedingly improbable."

I have no desire to belittle in any way the tremendous advances that modern science has made in its progressive discovery of nature's laws. I wish to point out, however, that the determinist hypothesis is not a "superhypothesis," progressively being established by mounting evidence; it is rather a heuristic principle that is presupposed in each particular scientific inquiry. It is important to scientific research that no limits be established in advance as to the scope of natural laws— since to do so would arbitrarily prevent inquiry beyond a certain point. It is not important to the scientific enterprise to maintain, either as a dogma or as a hypothesis, that there are no such limits.

Suppose, for example, that my view that man is free in a contra-causal sense were correct. This would not, so far as I can see, in any way hinder the scientific study of man. My view does not deny that there are laws governing human behavior: it only denies that human behavior is *completely* explicable in terms of such laws. Let the scientific study of man proceed as rapidly and as far as it can; let the independent variables affecting man's behavior be discovered and stated with as great precision as possible; there will still remain the "freedom factor," as a consequence of which man's behavior will not become perfectly predictable and as a consequence of which man is and will remain morally responsible. This factor may be more or less influential in determining a man's behavior than we now commonly suppose; outside influences may, as psychologists and sociologists are inclined to believe, play a much greater role in determining behavior than was once assumed. But unless and until laws have been discovered in terms of which *every detail* of man's behavior is explicable, there is no reason whatsoever to deny the presence of this "freedom factor." Indeed, as we shall see presently, there is excellent reason to affirm it.

Hard Determinist's admission that the principle of indeterminacy might turn out to be a case of real indeterminacy in the universe illustrates my point exactly. Physicists have lived with this concept for many years now, and it has not appeared to hinder their research in the least. They have simply been forced to accept the fact that when they are dealing with subatomic particles they have reached one of the limits of universal law, a realm where law-like regularity does not in fact obtain. That the human will should constitute another such limit would not appear to raise any new problems. I do not of course mean to suggest that the discovery of the principle of indeterminacy constitutes evidence in support of the freedom of the will: Hard Determinist is quite right in denying that this principle has any such direct relevance for the free-will problem. I do emphatically assert, however, that the fact that scientists have been able to accept with such equanimity the principle of indeterminacy, astonishing as that principle was in the context of classical physical theory, completely destroys Hard Determinist's claim that the possibility of indeterminacy such as would be required by a belief in free will would "cut the nerve of the whole scientific enterprise."

Hard Determinist's second argument in support of determinism (actually in support of behaviorism) is that we can, in a rough and ready way, predict the behavior of people whom we know well. This, he contends, supports the hypothesis that their behavior is governed by certain "laws" or "uniformities," which we vaguely discern in making our prediction.

I grant that we can, within certain limits, make some informed guesses as to how people that we know well will act in certain kinds of situations, but I fail to see how this in any way supports the behaviorist thesis. It is not my position that human behavior is always erratic and irrational, but only that it is not altogether the product of causes lying outside the agent. Such uniformity as we actually observe in people of our acquaintance may be due to either (a) controlling causes such as a behaviorist believes completely dominate human behavior or (b) habits of character acquired through many years of training and experience—or both. If (a) is the case, we can still adopt the opposite hypothesis in the absence of evidence to support the view that the whole of a man's behavior is the product of such causes. If (b) is the case, we can plausibly consider that a man's character is in part a product of his past choices freely made and that it may be further modified by future choices. Thus it seems clear that such regularity as we do observe in the behavior of individuals in no way supports the hypothesis that *all* human behavior is the product of causes lying ultimately outside the agent.

Hard Determinist's third argument is that reflection on the experience of "choosing among alternatives" makes it evident that (a) we always do that action for which we find the strongest motive and (b) what constitutes the strongest motive for any individual depends on causes lying outside himself. In one form or another, this is one of the oldest and most persuasive arguments used against the libertarian position. The refutation of it must unfortunately be somewhat complex.

The apparent force of this argument lies in the tacit adoption of a mechanical model to explain and describe human volition and action. According to this model, the self is conceived as a "thing" that is pulled (or pushed) in various directions by the "motives" and that is inevitably moved in the direction of the strongest pull (or push). But the model is not adequate, and to draw deterministic conclusions from it is to be misled by a faulty model. Selfhood cannot be conceived "from the outside," but only from within—in terms of what it means to *be* a self. The reality of responsible selfhood cannot be adequately described in the "paramechanical" language of motives-determining-acts; it can be expressed only in the personal-life categories of decision and choice.

Space does not permit the detailed development of an alternative to the mechanical model employed by Hard Determinist. However, we may observe that it is the moral freedom of man, not the indeterminacy of some "faculty" of man, that is here in question. As moral agents we know that (a) there are some situations in which we are "morally obliged" to act in a certain way—there is something that we "ought" to do—and (b) very often in such situations there is something that we "want" to do that differs from what we "ought" to do—there is some other thing that is our "desire" in that situation. I am willing to allow that man is not free to choose what shall be his strongest "desire" in any given situation: that, it seems to me, is determined by his character as thus far formed in relation to the details of that situation. What I would insist upon, however, is that in such a situation a man need not act in the way that is in accord with his strongest desire; he may, instead, choose a way of acting that contradicts his desire because he believes it to be his *duty* to do so. He alone decides whether his action shall correspond to duty or to desire; hence he alone is answerable for his behavior.

This is admittedly a gross oversimplification of the matter since in actual experience the conflict between duty and desire is seldom as sharp and explicit as this account suggests. It is, nonetheless, truer to our actual experience as moral agents than the mechanistic model we are attempting to refute. The student who desires a fuller explanation of this matter can at some later time inquire more fully into the notion of the self. For the present we must be content with the negative statement that a self is not a "thing" and its operations cannot be understood in terms of a mechanical model appropriate only to "things."

The Basis for Libertarianism

If the arguments just concluded do succeed in removing the chief objections to libertarianism, does this suffice to establish the libertarian position? Obviously not. What we still require is some positive ground for affirming the libertarian thesis. I shall conclude my argument by indicating what that ground must be.

There is one, and only one, ground upon which libertarianism rests: that we know ourselves to be morally responsible; therefore, we also know that whatever is necessary to render us morally responsible must be the case. Sometimes, indeed, we find ourselves in situations where we have only one way of action open to us, and in such situations we accept neither praise nor blame for doing what, under the circumstances, was the only thing we could do. But more commonly life presents us with a variety of alternatives, some of which are in varying degrees attractive to us (desire) and some of which may appear to make some kind of claim upon us as moral agents (duty). In such situations we must choose among the alternatives; and in the experience of choosing—of saying yes to one of the alternatives and no to all the rest—we know directly that it is *our choice* that determines what shall be done. Our choice is not arbitrary: we can always give a reason for it ("I wanted to," "I felt it was my duty," etc.). But neither is it predictable, because we alone decide whether and to what extent to follow duty or desire.

Since we are, and know ourselves to be, morally responsible, the universe must be the sort of place in which moral responsibility is possible. Therefore, it cannot be strictly deterministic, for in such a universe moral freedom and responsibility could not be. But neither, obviously, can it be a chaos since in such a universe we could never know what would be the result of any of our acts. (This last condition is the answer to Soft Determinist's claim that moral responsibility *requires* determinism. He is almost right, since moral responsibility does require that the universe exhibit sufficient uniformity to enable us to know the probable consequences of this or that act.) The universe must, therefore, be sufficiently uniform in its operations to enable us to "count on" certain actions producing certain effects and it must be sufficiently "loose" in its structure to permit men to make genuinely free and responsible decisions.

Fortunately, from my point of view, that is just how the universe appears to be. There certainly is a very large area in which perfect uniformity appears to prevail: hence, I can depend on bread to nourish and water to quench thirst, and I can give these to the hungry and the thirsty confident that my action will not produce unintended results. But the universe happily allows me to decide whether I shall feed the hungry and give drink to the thirsty; consequently, I am fittingly held responsible for what I do or fail to do. Because there is a considerable degree of uniformity, science is possible; and I would not want to set any a priori limits to the extent of that uniformity. But because there is a certain amount of "looseness" in the universe, moral freedom and responsible behavior have also found a place; and I would be equally reluctant to set any a priori limits to the extent of man's moral responsibility. In a strictly deterministic universe science would presumably be possible, but moral freedom and responsibility would not. In a chaotic universe neither science nor morality would be possible. But in the universe as it is, highly uniform but not strictly determined, there is ample room both for scientific knowledge and for moral freedom and responsibility. To abandon either would be to err in our understanding of man and his world.

STUDY QUESTIONS

1. Where exactly does Libertarian agree, and where does he disagree, with each of the two previous writers? Where on each of these points do your own sympathies lie at the present time?
2. How, according to Libertarian, has Soft Determinist accomplished the apparent reconciliation of determinism and moral freedom? Is this an accurate description of what Soft Determinist has done? If not, where does it go wrong?
3. Libertarian offers a *reductio ad absurdum* of Soft Determinist's account of moral responsibility. Summarize the argument. Does it succeed in your opinion?
4. What is a "heuristic principle"? How does the suggestion that the determinist hypothesis is a heuristic principle tend (if it does) to weaken Hard Determinist's case?
5. Summarize Libertarian's replies to Hard Determinist's arguments in support of determinism. Which of them, if any, do you find most convincing? Which least convincing?
6. What does Libertarian say is the "one and only one ground upon which libertarianism rests"? Do you find his argument at this point convincing? Why or why not?

FOR FURTHER READING

Adler, Mortimer, *et al. The Idea of Freedom.* New York: Doubleday, 1958.

Ayers, M. R. *The Refutation of Determinism.* London: Methuen, 1968.

Beardsley, Elizabeth L. "Determinism and Moral Perspectives," *Philosophy and Phenomenological Research,* 21 (1960), 1–20.

Bergson, Henri. *Time and Free Will.* New York: Harper & Row, 1962 (paperbound).

Berofsky, B. (ed.). *Free Will and Determinism.* New York: Harper & Row, 1966. A valuable collection of writings from many sources.

Campbell, C. A. *In Defense of Free Will.* London: G. Allen & Unwin, 1967. A collection of essays by a prominent proponent of libertarianism.

————. "Is 'Free Will' a Pseudo-problem?" *Mind,* 60 (1951), 441–465.

————. *On Selfhood and Godhood.* New York: Humanities Press, 1957.

Cranston, M. *Freedom—A New Analysis.* London: Longmans, Green, 1953.

Eddington, A. S. *The Nature of the Physical World.* Ann Arbor: University of Michigan Press, 1958 (paperbound), chap. XIV.

Edwards, Jonathan. *Inquiry Concerning the Freedom of the Will,* ed. by Paul Ramsey. New Haven: Yale University Press, 1957.

Farrer, Austin. *The Freedom of the Will.* New York: Scribner, 1960.

Franklin, R. L. *Freewill and Determinism.* London: Routledge and Kegan Paul, 1968.

Halverson, W. H. "The Bogy of Chance," *Mind,* 73 (1964), 567–570.

Hook, Sidney (ed.). *Determinism and Freedom in the Age of Modern Science.* New York: New York University Press, 1958.

Hospers, John. "Free-will and Psychoanalysis," in W. Sellars and J. Hospers (eds.). *Readings in Ethical Theory.* New York: Appleton-Century-Crofts, 1952.

Hume, David. *A Treatise of Human Nature.* Many editions. See Book II, Part III.

James, William. "The Dilemma of Determinism," in *The Will to Believe and Other Essays in Popular Philosophy and Human Immortality.* New York: Dover Publications, 1956 (paperbound), pp. 145–183.

Laird, John. *On Human Freedom.* New York: Hillary House, 1947.

Lehrer, Keith. "Can We Know That We Have Free Will by Introspection?" *The Journal of Philosophy,* 57 (1960), 145–157.

MacMurray, John. *The Self as Agent.* New York: Humanities Press, 1957.

Matson, W. I. "On the Irrelevance of Free-Will to Moral Responsibility," *Mind,* 65 (1956), 489–497.

Pears, D. F. (ed.). *Freedom and the Will.* New York: St. Martin's Press, 1963.

Rankin, K. W. *Choice and Chance: A Libertarian Analysis.* Oxford: Basil Blackwell, 1961.

Rashdall, Hastings. *The Theory of Good and Evil.* Oxford: Oxford University Press, 1924, bk. III, chap. III.

Schlick, Moritz. *Problems of Ethics,* tr. by David Rynin. Englewood Cliffs, N. J.: Prentice-Hall, 1939 (Originally published in German in 1931), chap. 7.

Sidgwick, Henry. *The Methods of Ethics,* 7th ed., rev. by Constance Jones. Chicago: University of Chicago Press, 1962.

Skinner, B. F. *Science and Human Behavior.* New York: Macmillan, 1953, chap. 1.

Smart, J. J. C. "Free Will, Praise and Blame," *Mind,* 70 (1961), 291–306.

Stebbing, L. S. *Philosophy and the Physicists.* New York: Dover Publications, 1958 (paperbound).

Stevenson, C. L. *Ethics and Language.* New Haven: Yale University Press, 1960 (paperbound), chap. XIV.

Wilson, John. "Freedom and Compulsion," *Mind,* 67 (1958), 60–69.

PART VI

MIND
AND BODY

28

THE MIND-BODY PROBLEM

The debate over the problem of freedom and determinism touched briefly on a very puzzling question that may serve as a convenient starting point for the present section. The question that Libertarian asked but did not really answer is: What, precisely, is a "self"? There appears to be something terribly mystifying about such concepts as "self," "mind," "soul," "psyche," and the like. These terms appear to denote something, but precisely what? And how is whatever they denote related to the body of the individual who is said to have that mind, or soul, or psyche? Let us, in order to get at this very puzzling question, review some of the apparent facts about body and mind that give rise to the problem.

Mental Events and Physical Events

We are all acquainted with a class of events that it seems natural and proper to describe as "mental" events. We know what it is like, for example, to have pleasurable and unpleasurable *feelings*: a cool shower after a hard day of work provides an example of the former; a dentist drilling too close to a nerve, an example of the latter. We know, moreover, what it is like to experience *emotions*: love, hate, affection, concern, jealousy, and so on. Certain sorts of *activities* also appear to be mental, or at least partly mental, such as perceiving, remembering, imagining, deliberating, and inferring. Finally, *volition* is a mental occurrence: willing or deciding to do something in preference to something else.

   Events of the kinds just mentioned appear to be different in a number of ways from "physical" events. The most obvious difference is that mental events, unlike physical events, do not appear to be publicly observable. If I am in pain, for example, nobody but me feels the pain. Other people may, of course, infer that I am in pain from the way I act (I may grimace, cry out, or perhaps clutch the part of the body that has been injured), but they cannot feel the pain that I feel. Indeed, I can fool other people about pain: I can pretend to be in pain and lead them to infer that I am in pain by going through the motions of someone who is in pain; but I cannot fool myself on this score. Either I feel pain or I do not; it makes no sense at all to say, "I thought I felt a pain, but I was mistaken."

At this point we need not raise the question, How are we aware of such mental events? The question is worth discussing, and it will be considered incidentally in the discussion that follows; but it is not the question upon which we shall focus our attention. We may observe, however, that the name that philosophers use for this process by which we appear to be directly aware of our own mental states is *introspection*. We know our own mental states by introspection and the mental states of others (if at all) by inference.

Another feature of mental events distinguishing them from physical events is that they cannot properly be said to be locatable in space. With respect to a physical event it is always meaningful to ask, Where, exactly, did it occur? But with respect to a mental event, such a question (unless it is construed to mean, Where were you when you felt, or decided, thus-and-so?) has no precise meaning. A volition, an emotion, or a recollection is not the sort of thing that can occur, say, "on the sidewalk in front of the White House, about six feet in front of the main gate"—though an explosion, a collision, a demonstration, or anything else that we classify as a physical event could.

Most people would not remain puzzled very long over these differences. The differences, they would say, result from the fact that the subjects of physical events are *bodies*, whereas the subjects of mental events are *minds*. Bodies occupy space and are locatable in space; hence, the events in which they participate are also locatable in space. Minds, however, do not occupy space (they are neither round, nor square, nor any other shape, nor do they come in various sizes) and are not, properly speaking, locatable in space; consequently, the events of which they are the subject are not locatable in space.

What, precisely, is this notion of "mind" (or "consciousness" or "self") that is so deeply embedded in the commonsense view of man? It is difficult to say precisely. It involves, certainly, the idea of something that is the subject of what we call mental events—feeling, willing, desiring, thinking, etc.—and it involves the denial that it can be described in terms of shape or size or other qualities applicable only to bodies. It is evidently closely associated with the brain, but since the brain is locatable in space (and for other reasons), the mind is not considered to be identical with the brain. It probably does no injustice to the commonsense view to say that each mind "inhabits" a particular body; in any case it is clear that each mind is believed to be intimately related in some way or other to some particular body.

We do sometimes use "spatial" language in talking about certain mental phenomena. We say things like "I can't seem to get this idea *into my head*," or "Intentions are hard to detect because they occur *in a person's mind* where no one else can see them"; but when we speak in this way, we are using spatial language metaphorically. We could, without altering the meaning of these statements, say instead, "I can't seem to comprehend this idea" and "Intentions are hard to detect because they are mental events and thus not publicly observable." It seems very doubtful, in any case, that the commonsense view of the nature of mind would allow that spatial categories are properly applicable to it.

There is something else about bodies and minds that is a part of the commonsense view, however, and that is that a given mind and the body with which it is associated mutually influence one another. The mental event that we call "seeing a flash of lightning," for example, seems to be related causally to a series of physical events involving an event in the sky, light waves, the optic nerve, and so on. The mental event that I call "feeling a pain" seems to be causally related to (a consequence of) certain physical events occurring in my body: the flame touching my finger, the bee stinging my ear, the dentist drilling my tooth, and so on. I cannot, indeed, always infer a physical event from the mental event of feeling a pain. Some pains are "psychosomatic"; they do not appear to be caused by the organic disturbances normally causing such pains. In very many cases, however, the mental event that we call "feeling a pain" does seem to be caused by a physical event that we might call "receiving an injury"; and this supposition—that some mental events are caused by some physical events—seems clearly to be a part of the commonsense view.

It is also commonly supposed that some causal series run in the opposite direction—that some mental events cause, or at least partly cause, some physical events. At the present moment, for example, I am engaged in writing, which obviously consists of a series of physical (publicly observable) events. But it seems very natural to say that at least part of the cause of my writing now is the fact that some time ago I decided to spend this day in this way, and an act of deciding is precisely the sort of thing that we call a mental event. Our thoughts, our wishes, our decisions seem to make a difference in the way we speak and act, and speaking and acting are physical events. These, in turn, sometimes cause other physical events to occur; so it appears that at least some mental events are related to some physical events as a cause is related to its effect.

These various beliefs about body and mind may be stated in two simple propositions: (1) bodies and minds are two distinct sorts of entities, neither of which can be adequately explained simply as a special form of the other, and (2) bodies and minds are capable, nonetheless, of causally acting on each other. The first proposition states the central thesis of what is called *anthropological dualism*. The second, which presupposes the first, states the central thesis of the view called *interactionism*. Interactionism, then, is simply the technical name for the "plain man's" view regarding the relation of body and mind.

Some Questions Regarding the Commonsense View

To most people the facts that we have just recounted seem commonplace enough, and for them the mind-body problem never arises. Many philosophers, however, find some features of the commonsense view extremely puzzling, and a great deal of effort has gone into the search for a satisfactory solution to the problem to which these puzzling features give rise. What, then, is the problem, and how has it arisen?

Let us consider the second question first. The problem has arisen because of (a) the unclearness of our notion of "mind," (b) certain difficulties in the way of knowing that any such entities exist, (c) the difficulty of understanding how there can be causal relations between physical and nonphysical entities, and—more recently—(d) the belief of some philosophers that the interactionist account presupposes metaphysical views that they regard as incorrect. The effect of these problems is to raise doubts about the correctness of the commonsense (interactionist) account and subsequently to initiate a search for a more adequate alternative.

The mind-body problem may be considered in terms of two related questions arising out of the commonsense view regarding body and mind, namely: Are bodies and minds two distinct sorts of entities neither of which can be explained as a form or function of the other? and, How are the apparent two-way causal relations between them to be understood? The first part of the problem calls in question the dualism implicit in the commonsense view. The latter part asks for some explanation of the fact that bodies and minds appear to be involved in mutual causal relations.

Historically, it was the latter part of this problem that first caught the attention of philosophers; the dualism implicit in the commonsense view was simply taken for granted. During the sixteenth and seventeenth centuries the question that philosophers debated was: How are we to understand the apparent mutual causation between bodies and minds? To this question a number of interesting (and sometimes far-fetched) answers were given.

René Descartes (1596–1650), whose reflections on the problem really launched the modern discussion, advocated the interactionist view. Body and mind, said Descartes, are radically distinct sorts of entities, two different kinds of substances, neither of which is reducible to the other: body is "extended, unthinking substance" and mind is "thinking, unextended substance." Nonetheless, Descartes thought it evident that body and mind interact and even conjectured that the precise point where this interaction occurs is in the pineal gland—for which, it may be said in his defense, nobody had previously been able to find any worthwhile function.

Descartes' successors by and large accepted his dualistic account of man, but some of them found his "pineal gland" theory rather unconvincing. A number of alternatives to interactionism were therefore proposed. Gottfried Wilhelm von Leibniz (1646–1716), for example, advocated a theory known as *parallelism*. Bodies and minds do not interact, said Leibniz, but they appear to do so because God has created the world in such a way that there is a perfect "preestablished harmony" between any given series of mental events and corresponding series of physical events. Mental events are always caused by prior mental events and physical events by prior physical events, but thanks to God's thoughtful provision for a perfect harmony between the two kinds of events the appearance of interaction results. Nicolas de Malebranche (1638–1715), a contemporary of Leibniz, advocated a special form of parallelism known as *occasionalism*, which might be described as harmony on the installment plan: God, said Malebranche, did not establish perfect harmony between physical and mental events "in the beginning," but as the occasion arises (presumably rather frequently) He does what needs to be done to keep the two series parallel. The result is the same, except that Malebranche's theory provided for the possibility of a certain kind of freedom for minds that Leibniz's theory did not. Benedict de Spinoza (1632–1677) advocated what has been called a "double-aspect" theory, the details of which we shall not pause to recount. Suffice it to say that none of these proposals has commended itself to more than a few of those who have concerned themselves with the problem, and it seems safe to conclude that anyone who wishes to maintain the dualism that is inherent in the commonsense view must be prepared to maintain interactionism—mutual causation—as well. In the discussion that follows, in any case, we shall ignore all except the interactionist version of the dualistic account.

The Alternatives

If we turn our attention to the first part of the problem, we shall find that the central focus of our concern must be the question, Are body and mind two distinct sorts of entity, neither of which can be understood as a form or function of the other, or are they not? To this question only three answers appear to be possible.

First, it is possible to deny that they are radically distinct and to argue that mind is explicable in terms of body—that mind is, so to speak, a purely physical phenomenon that is governed by, and explicable according to, the same sorts of laws as any other physical phenomenon. Mind, in this view, is not ontologically unique: it is not a "spiritual substance," a nonphysical reality, that acts apart from and independent of the laws of nature. It is a part of nature, even a product of nature, and wholly subject to its laws. The collective name for views that attempt to account for the relationship between mind and body in this way is *identity materialism*.

Second, it is possible to take a position just opposite to that of identity materialism—to reject the dualism implicit in the commonsense view and to argue that body is explicable in terms of mind rather than the reverse. It would be tempting, for the sake of terminological consistency, to call this view "identity mentalism," or something of that sort, but common usage dictates otherwise. We shall, accordingly, refer to this view as *panpsychism*.

Third, it is of course possible to hold that the commonsense view in this matter is the correct one and to maintain the interactionist position, which we have already described. It then is necessary to show that the interactionist position, with whatever problems it may involve, has at least as much to commend it as either of the other two alternatives.

All three positions have one task in common, however, and that is to give some account of the apparent inter-causal relations between mind and body. Whether we adopt the identity materialist, the panpsychist, or the interactionist position, the problem with which the philosophers of the sixteenth and seventeenth centuries wrestled so unsuccessfully remains a genuine problem that demands some kind of answer.

A Word About Metaphysics

We may as well recognize at the very outset of our consideration of this problem that we cannot hope to proceed very far without venturing into the rather forbidding area of metaphysics. None of the views we shall be considering really stands by itself: each is integral to a particular metaphysical position and can scarcely be made intelligible apart from the more inclusive view. Identity materialism, for example, is not just one view among many that we may take with respect to the mind-body problem; it is the view of man, and especially of mind, that is implicit in *monistic materialism*—the view that the whole of reality consists of matter and its determinations. Panpsychism, on the other hand, is the view of man, and especially of body, that is implicit in the more inclusive metaphysical view known as *monistic idealism*—the view that the whole of reality is explicable in terms of mind and its determinations. And interactionism, or at any rate the anthropological dualism that it presupposes, is the view of man that is implicit in *ontological dualism*—the view that matter and mind are ontologically distinct and that reality includes both. It is possible to carry on the discussion for a greater or shorter period of time without explicitly bringing in these wider metaphysical views, but they are always hovering in the background when the problem of mind and body is being discussed.

It has been said that the mind-body problem has given rise to more "isms" than any other problem in the history of philosophy, and this is probably true. The problem is a complex one. The more variables there are, the greater are the possibilities for a unique combination of views—each of which eventually gets christened some kind of an "ism." We have attempted in this introductory chapter to narrow the problem down somewhat in order that we may concentrate on just three theories—identity materialism, panpsychism, and interactionism. Any theory on the nature of body and mind, it would seem, must be reducible to one of these three types, and a comprehension of them will enable an understanding of related matters with little difficulty.

STUDY QUESTIONS

1. Give some examples of what are here called "mental events" and "physical events." Do you in practice have any difficulty in distinguishing the two? By what criterion do you make the distinction?
2. Summarize what you understand to be the commonsense view regarding body and mind. Is this also your view? What "puzzles," if any, seem implicit in this view?
3. What exactly is identity materialism? panpsychism? interactionism? Do these three exhaust the logically possible alternatives with respect to the mind-body problem? Explain.
4. Is anything of importance at stake in the discussion of this problem? Do you see any possible implications for psychology? for sociology? for ethics? for religion? Be specific.

29

IDENTITY MATERIALISM

Philosophers call the commonsense theory about the nature of body and mind, and of the relations between them, dualistic interactionism. In view of its wide prevalence, it must be capable of support by fairly persuasive considerations. We could, no doubt, distinguish between the reasons that have led people to adopt the view and the additional reasons that philosophers have invented to support the view once it was called in question. No doubt for some purposes this would be an illuminating distinction. For the present, however, I propose to ignore this distinction. By way of preparing for what I hold to be the correct view on this matter I wish to state, first, what I believe are generally regarded as the most persuasive reasons in favor of the interactionist account. I shall then offer several reasons for doubting the correctness of this account and shall conclude by attempting to present the case for a materialistic view of mind.

Reasons for Holding the Dualistic View

There are four main reasons why people generally have adopted—or perhaps unconsciously presupposed—the dualistic view. First, the apparent irreducibility of "mental events" and "physical events" seems to imply that they occur, respectively, in "minds" and "bodies." Thinking, feeling, desiring, wishing, willing, and the like appear to be different in kind from moving, being moved, accelerating, decomposing, and so on. The most plausible explanation of this difference, it is then asserted, is that minds are the subjects of the one set of events and bodies the subjects of the other. Hence, it is concluded, minds and bodies must be regarded as two distinct sorts of entities.

Second, the fact of personal continuity seems to favor the dualistic account. Not one single particle of the matter of which my body is now composed was in my body twenty years ago. Yet, it seems there is some sense in which I am the same "person" that I was twenty years ago. The only acceptable explanation of this fact, it is held, is that there is something that remains unaltered by these physical changes, namely, my "mind" or "soul." So on this ground, too, it appears that "mind" or "soul" must be something different from body.

Third, certain facts alleged to be discoverable by introspection—for example, our awareness of acting "deliberately" or "purposively"—are sometimes said to demonstrate that conscious activity cannot be adequately described simply as physical process. In the act of "weighing alternatives," for example, it seems that I am directly aware of the fact that I am not simply observing a process that is going on, say, in my brain: I am actively doing something, and this something that I am doing, it is held, is irreducibly "mental." The point of this argument is that we are directly aware of the uniquely "mental" character of such activities in the act of performing them; hence, they are not reducible to some other kind of process different from what we allegedly know them to be.

For many people the same conclusion is strongly reinforced by a fourth and very different sort of consideration. In Western culture a widespread belief in, and hope for, life after death prevails. This evidently presupposes a "soul" capable of existing apart from the body, for it is evident that after the event that we call "death," the body decomposes and is eventually reduced to its basic elements. If, then, we are to give any meaning to the phrase "personal immortality," something must be presupposed in the constitution of man that is not subject to the process of decomposition; and this something is called the "soul," "mind," or "consciousness." The emotional fervor with which the dualistic account is sometimes maintained is largely a result of this consideration.

These, then, are what I take to be the chief grounds upon which the dualistic theory of body and mind has been erected. Some of these reasons are very persuasive since they exhibit the dualistic theory as an explanation of certain undeniable facts—facts that must obviously be accounted for in some way or other by any theory that may be proposed. Nonetheless, a number of other considerations provide strong grounds for doubting the correctness of this account, and I propose now to indicate in some detail what they are.

Reasons for Doubting the Correctness of the Dualistic View

The theory is suspect, in the first place, because it is impossible to form a clear concept of what is meant by "mind," "soul," or "consciousness." We have here a case parallel to that of the now thoroughly discredited idea of a "material substratum," which John Locke defined as "something I know not what that thinks, feels, decides, etc." [1] It is the name for our ignorance concerning the true nature of mental events. To infer minds as the causes of mental events is equivalent to inferring "wind gods" as the causes of the blowing of the wind: the inference, in both cases, is false.

In addition, whatever it is that is supposed to be meant by "mind" or "soul," there seem to be insuperable difficulties in the way of our knowing that any such entities exist. That some organisms are capable of perception and feeling seems evident: more or less definite criteria can be established to determine when such an event is or is not occurring. But there appear to be no criteria on the basis of which we could say in any given instance, "There is a mind." There is nothing that we can see, feel, taste, touch, or smell—no observational evidence, in other words—that is in any way relevant to confirming or not confirming the statement, "A mind exists." To the purely conceptual difficulty of trying to understand just what it is that is being affirmed to exist when minds are being affirmed to exist, we must, therefore, add the epistemological difficulty that there seems to be no conceivable way by which the existence of these elusive entities could ever be known.

Even if it were possible to give conceptual clarity to the notion of "mind," and even if some evidence could be adduced to render the existence of minds probable, there remains the further difficulty that it is quite impossible to conceive how they could be involved in causal relations with bodies. Let me illustrate. Given a minimal knowledge of the laws of physiology, I can understand without too much difficulty how the movement of an arm, say, can be caused by the contraction of certain muscles, how the contraction of those muscles can be caused by certain nerve impulses, and how the nerve impulses can be caused by certain neural events—events occurring, that is, in the brain. All of these, it will be noted, are physical processes that are theoretically observable by anyone who approaches them with the proper instruments and the requisite knowledge. But how are we to understand these neural events as being "caused" by an allegedly nonphysical event called a "volition"? Is this a sort of causation—perhaps an instance of pushing or pulling, or the passage of an electrical current, or what? No answer given to this question would be intelligible; that is what I mean when I say that it is impossible to conceive how bodies and minds can be involved in causal relations. The same difficulty arises, of course, whether it is minds that are alleged to act

---

[1] John Locke, *An Essay Concerning Human Understanding*, II, xxiii (New York: Dover, 1959).

causally upon bodies (as in volition) or bodies upon minds (as in sensation).

Moreover, what we know about the structure of the nervous system makes it extremely unlikely that the process of deliberation, for example, and the purposive behavior that commonly follows upon it are different in kind from other processes that are universally admitted to be nonmental. All of the higher animals, for example, exhibit a process known as "reflex action," the detailed workings of which are quite thoroughly understood. It seems very likely that purposive activity is fully explicable as a process that differs only in complexity from reflex action. It is only because of the lapse of time between the stimulus and the response that we regard purposive behavior as something different in kind from a reflex action. Since this lapse of time is readily explicable in other ways, the similarity of such allegedly "mental" occurrences to some clearly nonmental occurrences must be regarded as a serious problem by anyone who would maintain the dualistic view.

Finally, there is a very serious objection of a purely scientific nature against the interactionist view. The interactionist account, if true, would violate the principle of the conservation of energy. We have a great deal of evidence to show that this principle is true, and even experimental evidence in support of the view that it is not violated in the case of human activity. To the extent that we are convinced of the truth of this principle, therefore, we must with equal surety conclude that the interactionist account of mind and body is false.

A few words of explanation may be in order in connection with this last point. The principle of the conservation of energy may be stated thus: in all physical processes, the total amount of energy in the universe remains constant; its form may be altered, but never its quantity. Moreover, every instance of causation known to us involves the transference of energy from the cause to the effect. If, then, it is said that some events in bodies have effects in minds, there must be some transfer of energy from the body to the mind. Since minds are allegedly unperceived, this energy should supposedly "disappear" for a time: the measurable energy in the body should decrease. And if minds cause effects in bodies, the amount of energy in the body should then increase. This does not appear to be the case. Thus, either body-mind interaction does not occur or body-mind interaction is a remarkable exception to the principle of the conservation of energy.

I think it must be conceded that the objections to which I have called attention constitute very substantial grounds for doubting the correctness of the dualistic theory and thus justify the search for a more adequate alternative. Such an alternative is to be found, in my opinion, in the materialistic view of mind.

A Materialistic Theory of Mind

One difficulty of a purely semantic nature stands in the way of the general acceptance of a materialistic view of mind, and I should like to do what I can to remove it. The difficulty is that the term "materialism" has strong negative connotations for many people that derive in large part from the association of that term with some rather crude theories advocated about a century ago. Let me at the very outset state, then, that I do not propose to account for mind in terms of tiny nuggets of matter that act and react upon one another according to Newton's Laws of Motion: nothing except a few fairly simple macroscopic phenomena can be accounted for in this crude way. Nor is it my intention, in this account of mind, to "dehumanize" man in any way. Man is clearly a noble and fortunate creature, whatever may be the correct account of mind and body, and his capacity for intelligent behavior remains his most noble endowment, however we are to understand it.

I am not advocating either (a) that mental phenomena are reducible to physical phenomena in the sense that a feeling of pain is "nothing but" the occurrence of certain neural events or (b) that mental events are simply "epiphenomena" of physical events in the way that a flickering light is cast off by an unsteady flame. Some materialists have held one or both of these views, but I do not hold them and do not propose to defend them. I agree with most dualists in holding that mind is exceedingly important in the constitution of man; but I think they are mistaken in their account of its status.

Any account of the nature of mind must begin with the fact that human beings (and, in an analogous sense, some of the higher animals) are capable of intelligent behavior. Restricting our attention exclusively to man, however, it is evident that man does not respond in an obviously mechanical way to his environment in the way that a stone or a plant does. Man is capable of sensation, feeling, memory, imagination, desire, reflective thought, and willing; stones and plants are not. It is facts such as these that have led common sense (not to mention some philosophers) to posit mind as the subject of such activities.

The thesis that I should like to establish is that mind is related adjectivally and adverbially, not substantively, to body. *Intelligence denotes some of the ways in which human beings behave, not an unperceived nonspatial entity that is somehow "within" man.* The dualistic account of body and mind has been aptly called "the dogma of the ghost in the machine." [2] Identity materialism is sometimes thought to consist simply in exorcising the ghost, leaving only the ma-

---

[2] Gilbert Ryle, *The Concept of Mind* (New York: Barnes & Noble, 1949), p. 15 and elsewhere.

chine. I am arguing, on the contrary, that man is neither a ghost nor a machine: he is a complex psychophysical organism capable of a peculiarly complex type of behavior that we call "intelligence."

A complete exposition and defense of this view would require an extensive analysis of each of the types of events commonly called "mental" events: thinking, feeling, desiring, willing, and so on. Limitations of space make this impossible, and we must accordingly be selective. Let us select the mental process that we call "thinking." If we can show that thinking is analyzable without having recourse to a substantival theory of mind, we may justly claim to have defended our view in what must be regarded as a crucial test case; for thinking is without doubt the activity *par excellence* of which minds are supposed to be the subjects.

A typical example of what we call "thinking" is the case in which a student attempts to solve a problem. It makes no difference, for our purposes, what the problem may be. Let us suppose that it is the mathematical problem of finding the square root of 196. What does a student do? If he knows the procedure for finding square roots, he will simply apply that procedure, presumably with the help of pencil and paper. If he does not know that procedure, he will have to tackle the logically prior problem of finding out how to do square roots. If he is a bright student and if he has had a lot of practice solving problems of this sort, he may even be able to dispense with paper and pencil and do it, as we say, "in his head."

What is it, then, that is going on "in his head" when he is attempting to solve this problem? The answer seems to be that certain processes are occurring in his brain. He may, as an aid to these processes, put some numbers down on paper, but this is not absolutely essential to the process itself. What is essential to the process is only that the answer he comes up with should in fact be the square root of 196—that he should end up by "knowing" what is the square root of 196.

It is not absolutely essential to such a process that the person engaged in it should be directly aware of what he is doing: mathematicians frequently are able to give the answer to a problem without consciously and deliberately going through the steps by which the answer is deduced. The same conclusion can be drawn from the fact that we sometimes wake up knowing the answer to a problem that we tried unsuccessfully to solve the night before: the relevant "thinking" occurred, apparently, during sleep.

A number of further considerations may be adduced in support of the view that thinking consists in a physical process that presumably occurs in the brain. For one thing, we are able to do it better at some times than at others: when we are fatigued, for example, we do not do it nearly so well as when we are rested. Also, our ability to think can be enhanced or decreased by administering certain drugs. Drugs and fatigue do have certain effects on the body, including the brain; hence, it seems likely that the process itself is a process occurring in the brain.

It may be objected that *awareness* of thinking is not itself a process going on in the brain. Perhaps. But this awareness, as we have already noted, does not always accompany the process that we call "thinking" —though sometimes, admittedly, it does. Moreover, to explain this awareness we should have to analyze introspection; and this, too, is a physiological process, as are all of the phenomena we call "mental events."

Replies to Objections

The most serious objections that could be raised against the materialistic view of mental occurrences are precisely those considerations that led in the first place to the adoption of the dualistic theory. The apparent irreducibility of "mental events" and "physical events" amounts, in my opinion, to little more than the irreducibility of the *language* of personal experience to the *language* of objective occurrences. We recognize that the sentence, "I am seeing a blue object," is not translatable into a sentence of the form, "Such-and-such processes are occurring in my brain," and we conclude from this that the two sentences are not about the same thing. That we have these two kinds of language to describe mental events is undeniable, but no conclusion about the status of such events follows from this fact.

The notion of personal continuity is something of a puzzle. That it is not to be accounted for by positing a "soul" or "self" that persists throughout all bodily changes is evident, however, when we consider that institutions and other complex existences are also said to exhibit continuity. Consider, for example, a university that has been in existence for a century or more. None of the original faculty, students, administration, or regents is now associated with the university. It is very possible that none of the original books is any longer to be found in the library and that no building now on the campus was there in the beginning. Yet, in some sense, it is said to be the "same" university. In what sense? In the sense, surely, that over relatively short spans of time at least some of the elements that constitute the university remain unchanged. Within any given year some features of the university are changed: some new faculty and students come, a building is razed, a new building is erected, and so on. But during that year other elements remain relatively constant: some of the same old teachers, the same old students, the same old buildings are to be found. The continuity, then, does not consist in the fact that some one element remains throughout, but that change occurs in the context of a relatively stable structure.

It may well be that continuity in the case of persons ought to be understood in much the same way. My continuity with the self of yesterday consists in the fact that in looks, in habits, in faults, in abilities, in physical structure, etc., I am for the most part identical with that person—but only "for the most part." Changes do occur— witness the fact that we are sometimes shocked (and amused) to see pictures of ourselves taken ten or twenty years ago. Must some *one thing* be posited to establish the continuity of the person we now are with the person who was born on such-and-such a date and at such-and-such a place so-and-so many years ago? I think not. It is enough to establish continuity that the changes that do occur should occur within the context of a relatively stable organizational structure.

No conclusion about the status of mind can be drawn, it seems to me, from the fact that we are allegedly directly aware on occasion of acting "deliberately" or "purposively." We are apparently in a position to know our own mental states in a way that others are not (although it is to be noted that fairly precise criteria can be established for judging someone's behavior to be "deliberate" and/or "purposive"), but it can scarcely be argued that this puts us in a position to know that a mental state consists in some determination of a nonphysical entity that we call our "mind." It is just as plausible to hold that this awareness is simply one of the by-products of the occurrence of a neural process of such-and-such a kind.

On the question of life after death, it can hardly be said that a hope for such a thing constitutes a valid reason for holding that the conditions for it do, in fact, obtain. It is indeed a consequence of the materialistic view of mind that when death occurs, mind perishes no less than body; for, in this view, it is as meaningless to talk of the continuation of mind after the deterioration of the brain as it is to talk of the continuation of running after the deterioration of someone's legs. "Mind" is the collective—and misleading—name for those dimensions of human behavior that we call "intelligent"; when the human organism dies, it ceases to behave at all, and so intelligent behavior also ceases. When running stops, "swiftly" cannot continue by itself; when behavior ceases, "mind" no longer has any meaning.

The old puzzle about how minds and bodies could interact, or how the appearance of interaction was to be accounted for, is evidently a consequence of the mistake of separating body and mind in the first place and regarding the latter as a substantial entity that has then to be re-related to body in some odd way. Mind is minding; it is adjectivally, adverbially, related to the body and its behavior. But body is explicable in terms of the laws governing matter, particularly matter as organized in complex living organisms; hence mind, too, is explicable in terms of those self-same laws.

STUDY QUESTIONS

1. What are suggested in this chapter as the main reasons why people generally have tended to favor the interactionist view of body and mind? Can you think of any additional reasons for this? How would you rank these reasons, from "strongest" to "weakest"?

2. Summarize Materialist's reasons for doubting the correctness of the dualistic view. Which list of reasons—this list or the one written in answer to the previous question—strikes you as being the most convincing?

3. What exactly is the view of mind that Materialist is proposing? What arguments does he use to support this view?

4. What are Materialist's answers to what he regards as the chief arguments in favor of the interactionist view? Which do you personally find more convincing—the arguments in support of the interactionist view or Materialist's replies to them?

30

PANPSYCHISM

If we are to arrive at some acceptable view with respect to the relation of mind and body, it is important to distinguish carefully between (a) the considerations that might lead to rejecting the dualistic interactionist account and (b) the considerations that are sometimes offered in support of a materialistic theory of mind. It is often assumed that if the dualistic theory can be shown to be inadequate, then we shall be able to see without difficulty that the materialistic account of mind is correct. This, I am convinced, is erroneous. There is at least one other alternative—that body, or "matter," is to be understood mentalistically. I believe that this is the correct view.

I should like to begin by reinforcing an observation made incidentally in the introductory chapter. Although the problem of the relation between body and mind appears to be a straightforward problem about how we are to understand *man*, at root it is a metaphysical problem. It is not plausible to argue that mind is simply a particular determination of matter: no one, I think, who confined his attention to the known facts about the relevant physical and psychological phenomena would ever be tempted to subscribe to such an account. The reason that some philosophers, nonetheless, attempt to account for mind in this way is that they approach the problem with a prior conviction that *all* phenomena are ultimately explicable in terms of matter and its laws: they approach it, in other words, with a prior commitment to the metaphysics of monistic materialism. The existence of mental phenomena, therefore, constitutes an embarrassing problem for them; they are accordingly compelled to try to "reduce" mind to matter on pain of having their metaphysical theory discredited. This is true whether the metaphysics that inspires the attempt is overt, as in the case of the nineteenth-century materialists, or covert, as it is with some philosophers at the present time.

The materialistic account of mind is not at all convincing. For this reason I am almost inclined to simply ignore it and proceed directly to an exposition of what I am convinced is a far more plausible alternative. However, many people today find monistic materialism very attractive. Consequently, I dare not assume that everyone who has read Materialist's account will have found it as unconvincing as I do. I shall, therefore, point out some of the most serious inadequacies of identity materialism. However, since identity materialism is needed to maintain the metaphysics of monistic materialism, my critique of the materialistic theory of mind may also be construed as a *reductio ad absurdum* of that metaphysical theory.

Critique of the Materialistic Theory of Mind

The materialistic theory of mind is inadequate in at least four respects. First, this theory does not provide a believable account of what is happening when we are thinking, feeling, perceiving, remembering, desiring, willing, and the like. Let us consider "thinking," since this is the example that Materialist has briefly discussed. It seems evident that (a) whether or not a neural process of some unique sort is occurring whenever a person is thinking of some particular thing, this certainly has never been shown to be the case and (b) even if it should be the case that thinking of a determinate sort is always accompanied by some corresponding neural process, it does not follow that thinking simply *consists in* this neural process. The question of what neural processes are correlated with what mental states is, surely, an empirical question. It can scarcely be claimed that the investigation of this matter has proceeded to the point where anyone can with any assurance claim a one-to-one correspondence between the two. Even if this were to be established, it is extremely implausible to hold that thinking is the *same thing* as the neural process that accompanies it. A well-designed and properly programmed computer, for example, is capable of solving certain sorts of problems far more quickly and efficiently than even the brightest of mathematicians; yet, we should not (except in metaphor) describe the process by which it does so as one of "thinking." What is the difference? The difference is that to say that something is an instance of "thinking" is to posit a mind, a consciousness, as the subject of the thinking; nothing other than metaphysical prejudice could ever induce someone to give a different answer.

Materialist has, in a way, attempted to answer this objection. He says the apparent irreducibility of mental events and physical events amounts to little more than the irreducibility of the language of personal experience to the language of objective occurrences. But this way out of the difficulty is not open to the materialist. If the materialistic account of mind is correct, then a sentence like "I am seeing a blue object" *ought to be* logically equivalent to the sentence, "Such-and-such processes are occurring in my brain." The statement, "Rutabagas do not taste good," for example, is translatable into the statement, "So-and-so does not like rutabagas," since these statements are *about* the same thing—the likes and dislikes of some particular person or persons. Alternative languages that are descriptive of the same state of affairs are always translatable into one another. If, then, it is conceded that in the present case the two languages are not mutually translatable, the conclusion is inescapable that the two languages are not descriptive of the same state of affairs: mental states are not *equivalent to* neural processes.

The only way that Materialist could get around this difficulty would be to recant his rejection of epiphenomenalism. Consciousness, he would then have to say, is not exactly identical with neural processes, but is an accidental and inconsequential by-product of those processes —like a flickering light cast off by an unsteady flame. To argue in this way is to take on a host of absurdities that few materialists are willing to accept—for example, that conscious intention has absolutely nothing to do with the production of poetry, novels, philosophical treatises, or scientific hypotheses.

Materialist's account of personal continuity is also quite obviously inconsistent with what we know about this phenomenon in the one case that each of us knows best—*our own* continuity. My knowledge that I stand in a relation of continuity with a certain person born on such-and-such a date and at such-and-such a place rests, surely, on the fact that I have recollections of experiences that are related to one another in such a way that I cannot but regard them as members of a single series. I know that I am the "same person" who last evening watched a baseball game, last year took a trip to Chicago, some years ago attended a certain university, and before that lived in a certain city because I *remember* having the experiences that constitute these several events. It may well be that the "stuff" of which my body is now composed has been completely changed during this long span of time; but certain patterns, a certain more or less constant organization of this "stuff" and certain serially related memories have endured. It is to these that I have reference when I say that throughout this time I have been the "same person."

It seems grossly misleading, therefore, to explain personal continuity on the analogy of the continuity of a nonorganic complex like a university. The analogy, if there is one, must surely be applied in the other direction. An institution has, admittedly, a kind of fictional unity that bears some analogy to the unity of a person (as does a nation, a club, a political party, etc.); and the recorded history of an institution might be compared in some ways to the remembered experience of a human being. We can even "personify" a university and sing "her" praises in song and verse, but we know well enough that the "person" we thus posit does not really exist except in a metaphorical sense. It is not nearly so evident that Materialist is aware of the fact that he is using a metaphor, and a misleading one at that, when he attempts to "thingify" our experience of personal continuity.

One final objection. The materialistic theory of mind implies that men never act in terms of conscious purposes freely chosen by them, but only in the ways resultant from the mechanical causes operative upon them. In our own experience, at least, we know that this is not true. Despite Materialist's disavowal of the older mechanism, his position involves a mechanistic view of human behavior; and mechanism, old or new, is a bitter pill to swallow. We surely believe ourselves to act freely and purposively a good deal of the time—indeed, I should say that we know ourselves to do so. Unless we are to regard this knowledge as no knowledge—as illusory, in other words—we must reject the materialistic account of mind. If we do adopt that account, we must not hesitate to accept its mechanistic consequences.

Another Alternative

The position at which we have now arrived in our consideration of the problem of mind and body is the following: we have agreed with Materialist that the dualistic account of body and mind—the view that body and mind are two distinct kinds of entities involved in mutual causal relations—is untenable; and we have rejected the materialistic alternative of attempting to account for mind as a peculiar determination, or set of determinations, of matter. There appears, then, to be only one possibility remaining, and that is to regard *mind* as fundamental and body as explicable in terms of mind. What kind of a case can be made for this alternative? Since we have acknowledged that any way of resolving this problem presupposes some metaphysical theory, let us begin by noting some of the more important features of such theories.

Metaphysics consists in the attempt to elaborate a system of concepts in terms of which every phenomenon that we encounter is capable of being interpreted and understood. The requirements that a metaphysical system must meet are: (a) some phenomena shall be explicable in terms of it, (b) no phenomena shall be inexplicable in terms of it, (c) it shall be internally consistent, and (d) it shall not be productive of implications that are absurd or contrary to fact. The method by which such systems are elaborated consists in (a) generalizing some concepts that are known to have application in some limited sphere and (b) attempting to apply the concepts thus developed to all phenomena—attempting, in other words, to give them a universal application. Monistic materialism, for example, is a metaphysical system whose central concepts were originally adapted from the science of mechanics. My criticism of it is based on the fact that it does not provide a plausible explanation of mental, or psychological, phenomena.

Suppose, then, that we relinquish the idea that everything that occurs is explicable in terms of tiny units of lifeless matter that act and react upon one another according to certain laws. Suppose that we say instead that the ultimate constituents of which the universe is composed are to be conceived on the analogy of *mind.* Let us see if we can give a better account of things in this way. Everything is to be conceived as being composed of a greater or lesser number of "droplets of experience," or "atoms of consciousness," each of which is in some degree aware of the environment that constitutes its world, and each of which accordingly takes account of its environment in a way that is appropriate to its particular level of awareness. Let us, following Alfred North Whitehead (1861–1947), call such a center of experience an "actual occasion." [1]

Since the idea of an actual occasion is derived from our direct awareness of our own selfhood, it is natural that we should develop the idea in terms of other concepts derived from there as well. We know, for example, that our own lives are describable as careers in which we are constantly obliged to choose among alternative possibilities. Our past and the constitution of the rest of the world severely limit the possibilities open to us, but there are some possibilities for each of us—a variety of alternatives from which we must choose. Let us say, then, that the life of every actual occasion is a career in which it must choose, among the possibilities available to it, what it is to become. Its possibilities, like ours, are determined by (a) its past, (b) the constitution of the rest of the world that it has to take into account, and (c) its own level of awareness. Every actual occasion, then, will experience something—something appropriate to its own level of awareness—analogous to what in man is called perception, feeling, remembering, willing, and so on.

What is a "material object" according to this account—for example, a stone? Let us call it a "society of actual occasions"—an aggregate of actual occasions united together in a quasi-unity analogous to that of a society of persons. No doubt the level of awareness of the actual occasions that compose a stone is of a very low order—lower, for example, than that of the lowest organism—and the alternatives open to them are so severely limited that so far as we can see they do little more than perpetuate themselves virtually unchanged from moment to moment. So unvarying are their choices, in fact, that we can observe statistical uniformities in the behavior of the society—can

---

[1] See Alfred North Whitehead, *Process and Reality* (New York: Harper & Row, 1960), p. 113.

formulate, in other words, certain laws descriptive of the behavior of the aggregate. We can do the same thing, it is to be noted, with respect to a colony of ants or bees.

Our way of "taking account of" such aggregates is by way of what we call "perception"—in the case of our perceiving a stone, by means of sight and touch. Its way of taking account of us is to resist our efforts to penetrate it, to allow itself to be moved on occasion, and so on.

The level of awareness of actual occasions appears to vary greatly, and the options available to an actual occasion seem to widen as the level increases. In inorganic substances, the level appears to be at its lowest: we cannot even begin to imagine what it would be like to be a grain of sand or a particle of calcium. With the simplest organisms, we reach a higher level: the very simplest plants are able to exercise a degree of freedom that is unknown to any particle of inorganic matter. The level increases when we come to insects, still more when we come to the higher animals, and reaches its highest realization in man. So high is it in the case of the higher animals—dogs, horses, monkeys and the like—that we can almost imagine what it would be like to be such a creature; in any case, we cannot seriously doubt that they have a consciousness in many ways similar to our own.

How, then, ought we to conceive of man? As a society of actual occasions of varying levels of awareness. Some one of these dominates and gives unity to the society; this we call our "mind" or "soul." In the experience that we call perception—feeling a pain, for example —the pain is experienced by the finger, say, as a pressure or a piercing, by the nerves as an electrical current, by the brain as certain brain waves that occur in it, and by the mind as the feeling of pain. The experience that we call willing is experienced by the mind as deliberation and decision, by the brain as a directive to enact such-and-such an alternative, by the nerves as electrical impulses of a certain kind, and by the appropriate muscles as a directive to contract in such-and-such a way. The society, when it is healthy, is a cooperative society, each member doing its part to ensure the welfare of the whole under the guidance of its dominant member. When a hostile "foreigner" enters (as in infection), or when some members of the society become uncooperative (as in cancer), the whole society suffers; and if it cannot repel the invaders, or get rid of the uncooperative members, the whole society may be destroyed.

Limitations of space have permitted only the very briefest sketch of the metaphysical scheme in terms of which, I believe, the relation of body and mind can be correctly understood. Much more should be said by way of filling in the details; countless additional examples of its explanatory power would have to be provided before I could hope to persuade many of my readers that what I am proposing is at least in the direction of the truth. Since space does not permit this, I must be content to let the plausibility of my proposal rest for the present on its ability to solve the familiar puzzles in connection with the problem of the relation between body and mind in man. These puzzles may be summarized as follows: (a) the alleged impossibility of forming a clear concept of "mind," (b) the alleged difficulty of knowing that any such entities exist, (c) the difficulty of trying to understand how unthinking bodies and unextended minds can interact, (d) the problem of how we are to conceive of personal continuity in the case of conscious organisms, and (e) the problem of how certain "mental events" are related to the so-called "physical events" with which they are associated.

My answer to each of these puzzles is as follows. First, there is no difficulty whatsoever in forming a perfectly clear concept of mind unless we demand that the concept be formed in spatial terms. The question, What kind of a body is a mind? is not a proper question and deserves no answer. I cannot form an "image" of a mind because a mind is not the sort of thing that occupies space, and only things that occupy space can be "imaged." But I know as clearly as I know anything what a mind is: a conscious center of feelings, perceptions, thoughts, and volitions.

There is also no difficulty in knowing that minds exist. In the very act of thinking, feeling, doubting, etc., I know that I exist. In the intelligent behavior of other organisms, especially in the intelligible communication that I have with other minds, I know that other minds also exist.

There are no unthinking bodies; hence there is no "gap" between body and mind that has to be bridged by some half-mind/half-body "connecting link." There are only minds of varying levels of awareness; and every mind is able to take account of those that constitute its world in ways appropriate to its level of awareness. (Minds at a relatively low level of awareness, for example, take account of one another by means of what we call "mechanical causation.")

Personal continuity in the case of any organism—whether or not it is "conscious" in the strict, unextended, sense of that word—consists in the persistence of its structural unity and its unique relation to its past history, which past history it must take into account in choosing the next stage in its career. Something analogous to memory, therefore, must characterize the experience of every actual occasion.

There are no such things as purely physical events properly so-called. Everything that occurs is an event in the career of some actual occasion or society of actual occasions. It is only when we abstract from this and view it, so to speak, "from the outside" that we get the derivative notion of a "physical event." A given event may be perceived by the actual occasion (mind) that is dominant in the society constituting a human brain as a feeling of pain; the same event may be perceived by a neurosurgeon as the occurrence of certain neural processes. It all depends on the way that one actual occasion takes account of the experiences of other actual occasions; and that way depends in large part on the particular ways in which that actual occasion happens to be related to them.

STUDY QUESTIONS

1. What inadequacies does Panpsychist claim to find in the materialist theory of mind? Do these seem to be serious objections to the materialist theory? How might Materialist attempt to answer them?
2. What precisely is panpsychism? How well, in your opinion, does it measure up to the "requirements that a metaphysical system must meet" as itemized by Panpsychist?
3. What theory of man does Panpsychist propose? How is this theory supposed to provide a solution to the mind-body problem?
4. What at this point seem to be the strongest arguments in favor of the panpsychist theory of body and mind? What seem to be the strongest arguments against it?
5. Write a critique of panpsychism from the point of view of a materialist, answering the objections raised by Panpsychist against the materialist theory and raising appropriate objections to the panpsychist theory.

31

DUALISM
RECONSIDERED

This is hardly the place to launch a detailed critique of the metaphysical scheme that has been briefly intimated in the preceding chapter; that would obviously be premature until more of the details of the scheme have been provided, and it would hardly be germane to the immediate task at hand. However, I want to mention one small problem with the theory that is frequently glossed over by those who advocate it. The problem is: If, as the theory allows, minds do not occupy space, how does it come about that bodies, which are held to be aggregates of minds, do? This is very much like the shopkeeper who claims to lose money on every sale but "make it up on the volume." If a single actual occasion occupies no space, then a society of actual occasions —however many members it may have—must also occupy no space. But I do not wish to press this particular point. Let us consider instead the more limited question whether the panpsychist account really does succeed, as it claims, in solving the many puzzles inherent in the problem of the relation between body and mind.

On at least two points I am in very close agreement with Panpsychist. First, I think he is quite right in saying that there is no special difficulty in forming a clear concept of "mind" and that those who have felt some difficulty at this point have been looking not for a *concept* but for an *image*. No nonspatial entity can be "imaged" since "image-ing" is modeled after visual perception and visual perception is always spatially determined. Any attempt to form an "image" of mind or soul—such as Plato's famous word picture (in the dialogue *Phaedrus*) of the two horses and the charioteer—is clearly metaphorical in character. It is, at best, a pale reflection of reality itself. I find nothing obscure, however, in the concept of mind as a conscious center of feeling, perception, thought, and volition.

Second, I agree with Panpsychist that there is no special difficulty in the way of knowing that minds exist. Descartes was essentially right, I think, in saying that our own existence as a thinking being (*res cogitans*) is the most indubitable fact that it is possible for us to know. Even if we should doubt that anything else exists, we must exist in order to do the doubting. As for the existence of other minds, no doubt we do have to do a bit of analogical reasoning: we have to infer from the outward behavior of the other person that he or she is in a mental state such as we know ourselves to be in when we behave in that way (tears when we are sad, grimaces when we are in pain, laughter when we are happy, etc.). But our inferences in such cases are as warranted, surely, as any inference can be.

I am not at all persuaded, however, by Panpsychist's suggestion that the problem of how minds and bodies can interact, or appear to interact, is to be solved by simply disallowing that there is any such thing as body. I can understand two processes well enough—well enough, in any case, so that I do not normally feel puzzled about them. These are (a) communication between minds by means of intelligible discourse and (b) communication between bodies by means of mechanical causation. Whatever it is that goes on between minds and bodies—in perception and in volition—does not seem to be reducible to either of these. Panpsychist, who suggests that it is to be understood as an instance of communication of the former type, therefore, seems to be talking nonsense just as surely as Materialist, who proposes to reduce it to the latter type. We must look further for our explanation of body-mind intercausality.

Is it, indeed, even meaningful to say that the ultimate constituents of which a stone, for example, is composed are "minds with a very low level of awareness"? It makes sense, I think, to talk about animals and insects having something like a human consciousness because something like the behavior that we know to be associated with consciousness in man is to be observed in the behavior of animals. We have, in this case, three points of reference in relation to which we can fill in the fourth: human consciousness is to certain kinds of human behavior as x is to somewhat similar animal behavior. But in the case of stones—and in the case of individual parts of the human body—we lack the "similar behavior" that would permit us to work the sum. What, then, does it mean to posit "low-level consciousness" in such things? We must conclude that it means nothing at all.

With respect to the question concerning the nature of personal continuity, I am not sure that I understand what Panpsychist is suggesting; consequently, I am not sure whether I agree or disagree with his view. It seems clear to me, in any case, that our awareness of our own personal continuity is tied up with our awareness of having a mind that is one and the same mind from the beginning to the end of our life. In the strict sense of the word, therefore, I do not think that we should attribute personal continuity to any beings except those who have minds like ours. In an analogous sense, however, we can attribute continuity to animals on the ground that they possess a consciousness somewhat similar to our own, and we can attribute organic continuity to any organism so long as it maintains its organic structure and unity. Aggregates of inorganic matter—stones, for example—have continuity only in the sense that they have a relatively stable structure, but this is very loose: a piece of a stone is itself a stone and has as much structure as the larger one from which it came.

Finally, it appears wholly gratuitous to say, as Panpsychist does, that there are no such things as physical events "properly so-called." In one sense of this statement, it is obviously false: there *are* lightning flashes, thunder-claps, planetary motions, and things of that sort. These are surely more properly described as "physical events" than as anything else we might be inclined to call them. But this, obviously, is not what Panpsychist means to deny. He means to deny, rather, that we should think of such events as the consequences of the actions and reactions of bits of lifeless, unconscious matter operating according to certain invariable laws. What is really the case, he wants to say, is that everything that exists—including electrons, protons, etc.,—is composed of tiny "droplets of consciousness" and everything that occurs—including what we call "physical events"—is, properly understood, an experience in the career of some such droplet or droplets. This whole account seems to me, for reasons already given, altogether gratuitous, fantastic, and meaningless; it is, as someone has said, so incredible that no one but a very learned man could ever have thought of it.

Therefore, the attempt to reduce body to mind must be regarded as a failure, just as the attempt to reduce mind to body has been shown to be a failure. There appears to be no viable alternative to the dualistic view of body and mind that has seemed to so many to involve insuperable difficulties. In view of this, we should look once again at these alleged difficulties to see if they cannot be removed in a way that does not do violence to our sense of what is credible. The prima facie evidence certainly must be conceded to be on the side of dualism: it is only the difficulties that are supposed to attend this view that have led to the fruitless search for a monistic alternative. Let us see whether on this matter common sense cannot, for once, be vindicated.

The Alleged Difficulties of the Dualistic View

The difficulties alleged to be inherent in the dualistic view of body and mind have been nicely summarized by Materialist as follows: (a) the conceptual difficulty of trying to understand what the term "mind" is supposed to denote; (b) the epistemological difficulty that there seems to be no way we can know anything about such entities, if there are any; (c) the alleged impossibility of conceiving how bodies and minds could interact; (d) the alleged impossibility of distinguishing between purposive behavior and "reflex action" behavior in view of the fact that the same nervous system is apparently involved in both; and (e) the suggestion that interaction, if it occurred, would violate the principle of the conservation of energy. We shall consider each of these difficulties in turn.

To what I have already said regarding the first two points I should like to add that it is only materialistic dogmatism that creates the first-mentioned difficulty and only empiricist dogmatism that creates the second. On the first point, enough has already been said; anyone who is able to distinguish between a concept and an image should have no difficulty forming a precise concept of mind. On the second point, I can only say, "*Of course* we cannot see, feel, taste, touch or smell minds: they are not the sort of thing that can be perceived in that way." But we have already discussed this point sufficiently in our earlier remarks.

Let us leave the interactionist puzzle for a moment and consider the two quasi-scientific arguments. With respect to what I shall call the "nervous system argument," there surely must be *some* difference between deliberate actions and reflex actions that leads us to make the distinction in the first place. It is not necessary to go into the laboratory to discover, at least at one level of analysis, what this difference is. We can readily observe it firsthand in our own behavior. What is it, then, that leads us to call some instances of behavior— blinking, sneezing, flinching, etc.—reflex actions? The answer, surely, is that these actions occur without deliberation or decision on our part: there is a stimulus (a thrown object, a tickle in the nose, a loud noise) and the response follows immediately—"automatically," as we say. We do not have to decide to do something in such cases; we just do it. Reflex actions are, as it were, natural habits of the human organism. With deliberate actions, the situation is different. In such cases we must decide both what we shall do and when we shall do it; and the process of deliberation may be as brief or as protracted as we choose to make it.

It is not at all plausible to argue that the difference between these two kinds of behavior is due only to the relatively greater complexity of the neural processes involved in behavior of the latter kind. Even if it should be the case that the neural processes involved in deliberate action are more complex than those involved in reflex action (whatever "complexity" means in this context), it does not follow that this is the only difference. Certainly the same nervous system must be employed in the two cases: it is the only nervous system we have. But our own experience tells us that there is, nonetheless, a qualitative difference between the two. The most plausible explanation of this difference (most plausible because it accords with our actual experience) is that in the one case mind is active and in the other case it is not; in the one case mind is agent and in the other it is only a spectator. The "nervous system argument," therefore, has no force whatsoever as an objection to the dualistic view.

Nor, I think, is the "conservation of energy" argument any more convincing. There are, actually, two different forms of this argument. It is sometimes argued that (a) the dualistic theory implies that in man the principle of the conservation of energy is violated, but we know that this principle is universally valid, therefore the dualistic theory is false. At other times it is argued that (b) the dualistic theory implies that in man the principle of the conservation of energy is violated, but we have experimental evidence to show that this is not the case; hence, the dualistic theory must be false. The argument, in either form, is usually put forward with a great show of scientific learning, leaving the impression that either the dualist or Albert Einstein must be mistaken—and there is little doubt, in such a contest, who will be the winner.

Whether or not the principle of the conservation of energy is universally valid is a question for physicists to decide, and neither Materialist nor I have any basis for an opinion. Be that as it may, however, the argument cannot succeed unless it can also be shown that the interaction of body and mind, if it were to occur, must involve the transference of energy from one to the other. This has never been demonstrated: it has only been presupposed. It may well be that every instance of purely physical causation involves such a transference of energy; this, again, is a question for the physicist, not the philosopher, to decide. But it is surely begging the very question at issue to simply presuppose that body-mind interaction, if it occurs, must be an instance of physical causation and must therefore conform to the laws governing such events.

Both the "nervous system argument" and the "conservation of energy" argument are thinly veiled attempts to bring not scientific facts but scientific *prestige* to bear against the interactionist view. Neither argument arises because of any puzzles inherent in the dualistic view: they are arguments invented for the purpose of discrediting the dualistic view after that view has already been rejected on other grounds. These grounds, as I think Panpsychist has amply shown, are metaphysical ones: the dualistic view of body and mind is distinctly uncongenial to the metaphysics of materialism. The arguments must, of course, be considered on their own merits, but it helps to understand why such patently weak arguments should have been proposed if we are aware of the motivations behind them.

We are left, then, with only one difficulty in the way of adopting the dualistic view of body and mind, and that is the difficulty of understanding how bodies and minds can interact. What is it about this phenomenon that strikes us as being so odd?

Why Interaction Is Puzzling

Perhaps the reason that mind-body interaction appears so puzzling is that minds and bodies seem to be so dissimilar to one another. How can a nonspatial and nonphysical entity like a *mind* be involved in mutual causal relations with an unthinking physical entity like a *body*? But this question does not really locate precisely the source of our bewilderment, for there are innumerable examples of causation between dissimilar entities where we feel no such puzzle to exist. We believe without difficulty that there is a causal relation between a mosquito bite and malaria, between the throwing of a switch and the blowing of a siren, between the pressure on an accelerator and the increasing speed of an automobile; yet the two terms in each of these examples are highly dissimilar. We must look further for the source of our bewilderment.

Perhaps the reason that we are mystified about apparent instances of mind-body interaction in a way that we are not mystified by instances of intra-physical causality is that in cases of the latter kind we conceive of the cause and the effect (however dissimilar they may be) as being parts of a *single system,* governed by the *same laws.* We assume that there is some coherent set of laws—chemical, physical, biological, etc.—in terms of which the several series of events from the mosquito bite to the malaria, the throwing of the switch to the blowing of the siren, and the pressing of the accelerator to the increase in velocity of the automobile are all explicable. If we are mystified at this level, it is because we are puzzled as to which laws are relevant to the phenomena in question. (Compare: How do mosquitoes cause malaria? How do burns cause feelings of pain?) In the case of mind-body interaction it seems that we have to deal with two "systems," and the laws governing the interaction of body and mind do not seem to be assimilable to either.

Let me illustrate. We can explain a burn—up to a point. We can, with the help of the relevant physical laws, relate the occurrence of the flame to the increase of temperature on the surface of the skin; this increase in temperature to the occurrence of tiny electrical impulses in certain nerves; and the occurrence of these impulses to the occurrence of a certain pattern of brain waves. But then we reach a "gap" in our explanation: we have no laws—none that are coherent with, or a part of, the system of laws we have been using thus far—that will enable us to relate the occurrence of the brain waves to the feeling of pain in the consciousness of the injured person.

Once we posit the feeling of pain in that consciousness, however, we have no difficulty understanding subsequent mental events: the injured man "deliberates" between going to the doctor and treating himself; he "remembers" that his wife warned him to be careful about lighting camp stoves; he "decides" to attempt treating the burn himself; and so on. Once we get to *mind,* we can "lock in" on the other system, and everything is all right. But then there is volition and the ensuing behavior (brain waves, nerves, muscles, etc.), and once again we encounter the "gap."

Our puzzlement about the interaction of body and mind is, therefore, an expression of our desire to reduce all phenomena to some single unitary system, with one set of laws applicable to all events. But this desire, it appears, cannot be fulfilled in the present case. The only possible way of fulfilling it would be to explain mental phenomena in terms of physical laws (identity materialism), or physical phenomena in terms of mental laws (panpsychism), and neither of these is adequate to the facts. We are left, therefore, with an ultimate and irreducible dualism—a dualism that may leave us puzzled and dissatisfied but must, nonetheless, be accepted.

Although we cannot understand mind-body interaction either in terms of the laws governing physical phenomena or in terms of the laws governing mental phenomena—cannot construe it, that is, either as a physical phenomenon or as a mental phenomenon—we have the best possible evidence that interaction does occur, namely, our own experience. Physical events do cause mental events: we know this from countless instances of what we call perception. Mental events do cause physical events: we know this from countless instances of willed, deliberate behavior. These are the facts, and they cannot be denied, however puzzled we may be about the *modus operandi* of that unique mode of causality that occurs in the mutual relations of body and mind.

To realize why we are puzzled about mind-body interaction, however, is in some degree to rid ourselves of the puzzle. We then understand why this particular sort of causality seems so odd, and we are free to look at it without being tempted to deny the obvious in order to assimilate it to some other mode of explanation; we are no longer "bothered" by its oddness. It is only in this sense that an informed dualism constitutes a "solution" to the mind-body problem. The odyssey that begins with common sense and that seeks a solution to its puzzles in either materialistic or mentalistic monism reaches its culmination in a view that might be best described as common sense made sure of itself. To accept such a view is to accept the puzzle of how minds and bodies interact in preference to the even more bewildering puzzles that result if the reality of either is denied.

STUDY QUESTIONS

1. On what points does Dualist agree with Panpsychist? What objections does he raise against Panpsychist's position? Could Materialist, without abandoning his own position, join Dualist in urging these same objections?
2. Write a defense of panpsychism against the objections raised by Dualist. Which of Dualist's arguments do you find most difficult to refute?
3. What is the "nervous system argument" against dualism, and how does Dualist attempt to answer it? Who do you think has the strongest case on this particular point?
4. What is the "conservation of energy argument" against dualism? What is Dualist's answer to this argument?
5. What is it, according to Dualist, that makes apparent mind-body interaction so puzzling? Do you think he is right about this? Are you satisfied with his final answer to the puzzle?

FOR FURTHER READING

Armstrong, D. M. *A Materialist Theory of the Mind*. London: Routledge and Kegan Paul, 1967.

Aune, Bruce. "Feelings, Moods, and Introspection," *Mind*, 72 (1963), 187–207.

————. "The Problem of Other Minds," *The Philosophical Review*, 70 (1961), 320–339.

Borst, C. V. *The Mind-Brain Identity Theory*. London: Macmillan, 1970. A collection of important papers pro and con.

Broad, C. D. *The Mind and its Place in Nature*. Paterson, N. J.: Littlefield, Adams, 1960 (paperbound), chaps. III and XIV.

Dewey, John. *Experience and Nature*. LaSalle, Ill.: Open Court, 1958 (paperbound).

Ducasse, C. J. *Nature, Mind and Death*. LaSalle, Ill.: Open Court, 1951.

Evans, C. O. *The Subject of Consciousness*. London: G. Allen & Unwin, 1970.

Ewing, A. C. *The Fundamental Questions of Philosophy*. New York: Macmillan, 1951, chap. 6.

Feigl, Herbert, *The "Mental" and the "Physical."* London: Oxford University Press, 1968 (paperbound).

————. "The Mind-Body Problem in the Development of Logical Empiricism," in *Readings in the Philosophy of Science*. M. Brodbeck and H. Feigl (eds.). New York: Appleton-Century-Crofts, 1953, pp. 612–626.

Grossman, Reinhardt. *The Structure of Mind*. Madison: University of Wisconsin Press, 1965. Detailed critique of arguments for phenomenalism from a realist perspective.

Hume, David, *A Treatise of Human Nature*. Many editions. See Book I, Section VI.

Joske, W. D. "Behaviorism as a Scientific Theory," *Philosophy and Phenomenological Research*, 22 (1961), 61–68.

Krikorian, Y. "A Naturalistic View of Mind," in Y. Krikorian (ed.). *Naturalism and the Human Spirit*. New York: Columbia University Press, 1944, pp. 242–269.

————. "The Publicity of Mind," *Philosophy and Phenomenological Research*, 22 (1962), 317–325.

Lachs, John. "Epiphenomenalism and the Notion of Cause," *The Journal of Philosophy*, 60 (1963), 141–146.

Laird, John. *Our Minds and their Bodies*. London: Oxford University Press, 1925.

Laslett, Peter (ed.). *The Physical Basis of Mind*. Oxford: Basil Blackwell, 1951.

Lewis, H. D. *The Elusive Mind*. London: G. Allen & Unwin, 1970. Defends mind-body dualism against its major contemporary critics.

Locke, Don. *Myself and Others: A Study in Our knowledge of Minds*. London: Oxford University Press, 1968. Current and lucid.

Malcom, Norman. "Knowledge of Other Minds," *The Journal of Philosophy*, 55 (1958), 969–978.

Russell, Bertrand. *The Analysis of Mind*. New York: Humanities Press, 1958.

Ryle, Gilbert. *The Concept of Mind*. New York: Barnes & Noble, 1965 (paperbound).

Shaffer, Jerome. "Could Mental States be Brain Processes?" *The Journal of Philosophy,* 58 (1961), 813–822.

Skinner, B. F. *Science and Human Behavior.* New York: Macmillan, 1953. See "The Self," Pages 283–294.

Smythies, J. R. (ed.). *Brain and Mind.* London: Routledge and Kegan Paul, 1965. A valuable collection of essays by various writers.

Strawson, P. F. *Individuals.* New York: Doubleday, 1959, pp. 87–116.

Vesey, G. N. A. *The Embodied Mind.* London: G. Allen & Unwin, 1965. A Cartesian view in modern dress.

Wiggins, D. *Identity and Spatio-Temporal Continuity.* Oxford: Basil Blackwell, 1967.

Wisdom, John. *Other Minds,* New York: Philosophical Library. 1952.

———. *Philosophy and Psychoanalysis.* New York: Philosophical Library, 1953.

———. *Problems of Mind and Matter.* New York: Cambridge University Press, 1963 (paperbound).

PART VII

A PRIORI KNOWLEDGE

32

THE ISSUE
BETWEEN RATIONALISTS
AND EMPIRICISTS

Whatever may be the nature of the human mind and its relation to the body, it is an admitted but nonetheless remarkable fact that man is able to acquire knowledge of the world around him. Each of us has come to know a great many things and would have little difficulty in writing down a long list of statements that he knows to be true. Indeed, knowledge is so plentiful among men, and its acquisition so commonplace in this era of universal public education, that most of us have probably never paused to consider that this capacity to acquire knowledge is a truly remarkable fact about man.

Philosophers, whose business it is to ask questions about some things that many people simply take for granted, have long been interested in the phenomenon of human knowledge. There is, in fact (as was noted in Chapter 3), a division of philosophical inquiry called *epistemology* (from the Greek *episteme,* meaning to know) that is devoted exclusively to a study of the nature and limits of human knowledge. The problem with which we shall be dealing in this section is one of the central problems in epistemology. We shall begin with a brief analysis of the concept of knowledge.

Knowledge

What does it mean to "know" something about the world? Suppose, for example, that we say "Johnny *knows* that if you put your hand into a flame you will get burned." Just what does this mean? It appears to mean three things: (1) it is the case that if you put your hand into a flame, you will get burned; (2) Johnny believes that if you put your hand into a flame you will get burned; and (3) Johnny has reasonable grounds for so believing. Let *p* be any statement about the real world, and let *A* be any person whatsoever. When *A* knows *p*, then (1) what *p* asserts is the case, (2) *A* believes that *p* is the case, and (3) *A* has reasonable grounds for believing that *p* is the case. If any one of these conditions were not present, we would not say that *A knows p*. If (1) were absent, we would say that *A* mistakenly believes *p*. If (2) were absent, we would say that although *p* is true, and *A* ought to know it (since he has reasonable grounds), he does not. And if (3) were absent, we would probably say that *A* just "had a hunch" or "made a lucky guess."

It is important to note that what we are talking about at present is knowledge of the real world, which accordingly is expressed in statements about the real world. A statement about the real world is one that asserts that something is the case, that some state of affairs exists. If what it asserts really is the case, then it is a true statement; if not, it is false. Some philosophers speak of such statements as "statements asserting some matter of fact." Another common name for them is simply "empirical statements."

Statements about the real world should be clearly distinguished, however, from statements that only tell us something about the meaning of some word or phrase. The statement, "All bachelors are bald," is a statement about the real world: it asserts that something is the case, and it can be shown to be false by producing the appropriate evidence —a bachelor who is not bald. But the statement, "All bachelors are unmarried," is not a statement about the real world: it is simply an elucidation of a part of the meaning of the term "bachelor." We do not have to produce a single spouseless adult male human being in order to support the statement that all bachelors are unmarried, for it is not a statement about human beings at all—it is a statement about the meaning of a word. Construed as a statement about the real world, it is redundant: it says that all unmarried adult male human beings are unmarried. Hence, we know better than to construe it in this way.

The Sources of Knowledge

It is evident that there are many statements about the real world that we know to be true, that is, we have a good deal of knowledge about the real world. How did we acquire this knowledge? What are the ways by which we come to know something about the world?

One source of our knowledge, obviously, is our own experience. We have, in the course of our lives, seen and heard and touched and tasted many things; on this basis we can say many things about the world. We know, in this way, many simple facts about ourselves: that we have two arms, two legs, eyes, ears, and so on. We know, moreover, many general truths about the world in which we live on the basis of our own experience: that unsupported objects tend downward, that fire burns, that rain makes things wet, etc. The list of things that each of us knows by direct experience would be very long indeed, and since every person's experience is in some ways unique, no two lists would be exactly alike.

But if each of us knew only what we ourselves had directly experienced, our knowledge would be vastly more limited than in fact it is. By far the greater part of what we know we have learned from others. Through listening and reading we have learned many things about history, geography, literature, and the sciences—things that in all probability we would never have been able to discover for ourselves.

In reality, however, there is not much difference between these two sources of knowledge. It is as if ten men set out together to inspect a ten-room house and in order to save time and effort agreed to inspect just one room each and report to the rest. Each man, then, would know about one room by direct experience and about the other nine by indirect experience. The information that we get from teachers and from books is what we might call "secondhand experience." But, if we trace this information to its source, we will inevitably find someone whose experience has taught him what he is now teaching us.

Rationalists and Empiricists

Apart from a minor quibble over whether what we have been talking about really deserves to be called "knowledge" or not (Plato, for example, called it mere "opinion"), most philosophers would have no quarrel with what has been stated so far. It is obvious that we have some kind of cognitive rapport with the world by means of direct and indirect experience, and it is perfectly consistent with ordinary usage to say that what we acquire in this way is *knowledge* of the real world.

At this point there arises, however, one of the most controversial and important issues in philosophy. The issue is: Do we or do we not have any knowledge of the real world that is in any degree independent of experience? Is there or is there not such a thing as "direct apprehension" of empirical truths? Is experience the whole and only source of our knowledge of the real world, or is the human mind capable of grasping some truths about the world in such a direct way that experience functions only as the occasion for this insight? This is a central problem of epistemology.

Some philosophers hold that the human mind is capable of a direct apprehension of some empirical truths and that we in fact do have some knowledge of the real world that is in a certain way independent of experience. This view is called *rationalism*, and a person who holds this view is accordingly called a *rationalist*. Other philosophers deny this possibility and maintain that our knowledge of the real world arises entirely out of experience. Such men are called *empiricists*, and the position that they represent is called *empiricism*. With respect to this question rationalism and empiricism are the only alternatives, and they are mutually exclusive. You can be a rationalist or you can be an empiricist, but you cannot be both and you cannot avoid being one or the other.

In order to discuss this issue with maximum precision, however, we need a vocabulary that is somewhat more technical than the language we have been using thus far. Let us pause, therefore, to define a few terms and then attempt to state our problem in a more precise way.

Analytic and Synthetic Statements

We may begin by making a distinction between *analytic* and *synthetic* statements. An analytic statement is one in which what is affirmed in the predicate is already contained in the concept of the subject. An example of such a statement would be "All circles are round." In order to test the truth of such a statement, it is not necessary to examine any circles to see whether in fact they are all round. Being round is part of what is meant by the term "circle"; consequently, we know without making any inspection that all circles are round, that if anything is a circle it must be round. We need only "analyze the subject" of the statement, and there we shall find the notion of roundness. To call something a circle and to deny that it is round would be a contradiction: it would be equivalent to saying that some round things are not round.

A synthetic statement is one in which what is affirmed in the predicate adds something to the concept of the subject. A house, for example, may be defined as an enclosure within which human beings live and find shelter. If, then, I say, "Some houses have pink shutters," I am uttering a synthetic statement: the idea of having pink shutters is not contained in the idea of a house. I cannot produce my statement simply by analyzing the subject (house); it is, rather, a synthesis of two different concepts (house and pink shutters)—in short, a synthetic statement.

Strictly speaking, the definitions of "analytic" and "synthetic" given here apply only to analytic and synthetic statements *of the subject–predicate type*. But if the distinction is understood, it can be easily generalized to apply to statements of other types. An alternative—and broader—definition of "analytic statement" would be: a statement whose truth is determined solely by the meaning of its terms; and of "synthetic statement": a statement whose truth or falsehood is not determined solely by the meaning of its terms. A statement whose *falsehood* is determined solely by the meaning of its terms is said to be "analytically false."

A Priori and A Posteriori Knowledge

The second pair of terms for which we shall shortly have use are the terms *a priori* and *a posteriori*. Something is said to be known a posteriori if it is known on the basis of experience. How do we know that lemons are sour? We know it a posteriori: we have tasted them. How do we know that too long an exposure of skin to the sun causes sunburn? We know it a posteriori: we have been sunburned, or we have seen others who have been sunburned. All of the things we talked about a few moments ago—all of the things we know by direct or by indirect experience—we know a posteriori. Experience (either our own or someone else's) is the whole and only source of such knowledge, and if such knowledge is challenged it is to experience, and experience alone, that we must appeal for confirmation. A posteriori knowledge is only as secure as the factual evidence upon which it rests.

With a priori knowledge the situation is different. Here factual evidence is not relevant—though some philosophers would say that many a priori truths are constantly exhibited in experience. What, then, is an a priori truth? It is a statement the truth of which is evident apart from the facts of experience. To know something a priori is to know it immediately, directly, without recourse to factual evidence. In a certain sense, it is to know something "prior to experience" —in the sense, namely, that all subsequent experience must conform to what is thus known. What is known a priori is seen, as Immanuel Kant said, to be necessary and universal: once grasped, its untruth is inconceivable, and it is then immediately evident that it must be true at all times and in all places.[1]

The Problem Restated

Now it is perfectly evident that we know a great many synthetic truths a posteriori. No one—not even the most enthusiastic of rationalists—denies this, and it is a caricature of Rationalist's position to say that he does.

It is equally evident that all analytic truths are known a priori. No one—not even the most incorrigible of empiricists—denies this, and it is a caricature of Empiricist's position to say that he does.

The question is, however (and this is where the rationalist and the empiricist part company), Do we or do we not have any a priori

[1] Immanuel Kant, *Critique of Pure Reason*, Intro., II, Norman Kemp Smith (tr.) (New York: St. Martin's, 1965), pp. 43–44.

knowledge of synthetic truths? The rationalist says we do, the empiricist says we do not. That is the issue.

There is much, therefore, about which the rationalist and the empiricist are in agreement. This should not be overlooked. But there is one major issue upon which they are in disagreement, and that is whether we do or do not have any a priori knowledge of synthetic truths. It is upon this one issue that we must focus our whole attention in the chapters that follow. The controversy might be represented as follows:

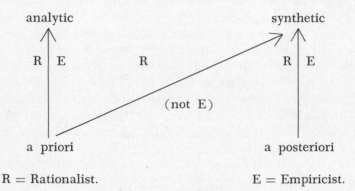

It should be apparent that we now have before us a rather more precise statement of the problem posed earlier in a somewhat different way. We talked earlier about "knowledge of the real world," and we asked whether we can have any such knowledge in a way that is in any degree independent of experience. Now we are asking whether we can have any a priori knowledge of synthetic truths. To know a synthetic truth is to know something about the real world; to know something in a way that is in any degree independent of experience is to know it a priori. We have before us, therefore, a nontechnical and a technical formulation of the same problem. The technical formulation, as we shall see, permits us to talk about it with greater precision than the other.

The Issue Behind the Issue

It may be well to say a few words at this point about what is at stake in this celebrated controversy. If empiricism is right in affirming that all of our knowledge of reality (as opposed to our knowledge of analytic truths) is a posteriori, then it is clear that our knowledge of reality is limited to that which falls within or can be definitely inferred from the realm of our experience. Now if this is the case, it seems clear to most philosophers that speculative metaphysics is impossible, for metaphysics consists precisely in the attempt to acquire knowledge of things that are "beyond" (the Greek *meta* means "beyond" or "behind") the world of our experience. Any talk about God, or the soul, or a transcendent good is ruled out as meaningless.

Bear in mind, then, that when Rationalist offers examples drawn from such sources as geometry and logic to build his case, what he is basically trying to do is to establish the principle that an a priori knowledge of synthetic truths is possible. If he can establish this principle, then he may hope to employ it in his metaphysical inquiries; if not, his whole procedure—the very possibility of doing metaphysics—is highly suspect.

How the Argument Must Proceed

If we have understood the issue upon which the rationalist and the empiricist are at such loggerheads, we shall not have any difficulty in seeing how they will have to go about supporting their respective positions.

Consider a simple analogy. Suppose that I am of the opinion that there are some pink-tufted owls in captivity and my opponent is of the opinion that there are none. How can we proceed with our dispute? Quite obviously, in order to support my position I must produce some examples. Indeed, if I can produce just one example of a pink-tufted owl, I shall have won my case. And my opponent, what must he do? Clearly, he must attempt to show that any example that I bring forth is not really an example of a pink-tufted owl. This he may do in either of two ways. He may show that (a) although the bird I am offering as an example of a pink-tufted owl is indeed pink-tufted, it is not an owl, or (b) although it appears to be an owl, it is not pink-tufted. If he can make good his claim to either of these points, my example ceases to be an example.

Just so with the rationalist and the empiricist. It is up to the rationalist to bring forward examples of synthetic truths that, as he believes, we know a priori. If he can produce a single convincing example of such a truth, he will have won his case: we then have some a priori knowledge of synthetic truths.

The empiricist, on the other hand, must attempt to show that the examples offered by the rationalist are not, after all, examples of synthetic truths known a priori. This he may do in either of two ways. He may attempt to show that although a particular example is a synthetic truth, it is not known a priori at all: it is, he may say, an a posteriori synthetic truth. Or, alternatively, he may attempt to show that what is offered as an example of an a priori synthetic truth is not synthetic at all: it is, he may say, an a priori analytic truth. For the empiricist is convinced of two things: that all statements that are known a priori are analytic and that all statements that are synthetic are known a posteriori. Empiricists may disagree among themselves as to which of these two categories a given statement belongs in, but they are agreed that every statement whose truth is knowable by us belongs in one or the other.

The empiricist, it should be noted, cannot fairly be expected to produce an independent argument to prove his contention that all synthetic truths (all truths about the real world) are known a posteriori. In the very nature of the case, this is not possible. The burden of proof lies, as in a formal debate, with the affirmative—with the one who says "there are some so-and-sos." In the present instance, therefore, the burden of proof rests with the rationalist. All that we have a right to expect of an empiricist is that he present a convincing refutation of anything that a rationalist may offer as an example of a synthetic truth known a priori.

In attempting to enter into the discussion of this issue, therefore, we must reflect very carefully on the examples that are offered by the rationalist. Concerning each example that is given, we must ask ourselves two simple questions: Is this a synthetic truth? Is it known a priori? If with respect to any example that is given we answer both questions in the affirmative, then we are agreeing with the rationalist. If we find no example that, after due reflection, seems to be both synthetic and a priori, then we are agreeing with the empiricist.

STUDY QUESTIONS

1. Are you satisfied with the analysis of "knowing" suggested in this chapter? Can you think of any instance that fails to meet the criteria here suggested that you would be inclined to call an instance of knowing? or an instance that satisfies these criteria that you would not be inclined to call an instance of knowing?
2. Make a list of the several ways in which the problem of a priori knowledge is stated in this chapter. Then check your understanding of the problem by restating the problem in your own words.
3. Are you convinced that rationalism and empiricism are the only possible positions to take with respect to this question? Is it true that "you cannot be both and you cannot avoid being one or the other"? Explain.
4. What is the difference in meaning between "analytic" and "a priori"? between "synthetic" and "a posteriori"? As you understand these terms, is it correct usage to speak of a statement as being a priori or a posteriori? Is it correct to speak of a statement being known analytically or synthetically?
5. Why must the argument between rationalists and empiricists proceed by way of considering examples brought forward by the rationalist? Why is it impossible for the empiricist to construct an independent "proof" of his position?

33

THE RATIONALIST THESIS

The introductory chapter has presented an excellent statement of the problem about which my empiricist friends and I are in such complete disagreement. It is now my turn to enter the discussion and to present what I consider to be the correct answer to the problem there stated, that is, the rationalist answer. I believe that we do have some a priori knowledge of synthetic truths, and I propose shortly to offer a number of examples that I should like to think will prove convincing to any fair and open-minded reader.

Before I do that, however, there is one point in connection with my position that I should like to make clearer than it has been made thus far. The point is, I admit, somewhat subtle, but an understanding of it is absolutely essential to an understanding of my position.

The Two Roles of Experience

Let me state unequivocally, then, that I am not maintaining that we have any knowledge of any kind (of either analytic or synthetic truths) in a way that is *totally* independent of experience. It seems obvious that if we now know something, there must have been some time at which we learned it, and that the occasion on which we learned it was for us an experience of some kind. I am not a proponent of a theory of "innate knowledge." I do not think there are some bits of knowledge that we are born with and therefore have prior to all experience. There have been philosophers who have maintained this, but it is not the position that I hold or propose to defend.

What I wish to maintain is that experience does not always play the same role in learning. For much of our knowledge, experience is the whole *source* of what we come to know: this is knowledge a posteriori. But sometimes experience functions in another way: it is only the *occasion* for our coming to know, and what we come to know on that occasion vastly transcends the particular situation in which that learning occurs. We consider some statement about the world, we ponder it, and then we "see"—directly, immediately—that it is, and indeed *must be*, true. It is when we come to know something in this way—when experience is only, so to speak, a window through which we look—that we have a case of a priori knowledge.

Perhaps the difference can be clarified by the use of a pair of contrasting examples. Let us first consider an example of something that is known a posteriori. A teacher is talking to her class about various kinds of birds and particularly the subject of crows. "What color are crows?" she asks; and the little boy in the fourth row who always likes to be the first to answer a question pipes up, "They're black." Little Suzie is not quite convinced, so she asks, "Is that right, Miss Twaddle? Are all crows black?" And Miss Twaddle says, "That's right, Suzie. All crows are black." But Suzie still is not convinced, so she presses a little further. "Miss Twaddle," she asks, "how do you know that? How do you know for sure that some place, some time, there may not have been a white crow? How do you know that *all* crows are black?"

How could our poor hard-pressed teacher go about answering Suzie's question? One way, of course, would be to play a little trick on Suzie. She could say, "Suzie, if you come across a bird that is just like a crow except that it is white instead of black, it isn't a crow—you'll have to invent some other name for it." But if Miss Twaddle wants to deal fairly with Suzie, she will have to proceed in a rather different way. She might ask, for example, whether anyone in class had ever seen a crow that was not black. She might report that she herself had seen thousands of crows in her lifetime and that as far as she could recall each and every one of those thousands of crows was black. She might send the class to the library to see whether they could find any reports of non-black crows. She might consult a bird expert and report to the class that as far as he knew there had never been an authenticated case of a non-black crow.

What would be the point of all this? The point is that the statement, "All crows are black," is only as secure as the factual evidence on which it rests. The statement is a summary of the experience of many people, and if it is called in question, the only way that it can be supported is to point to that evidence. Suzie, if she is wise, will not be completely convinced. It is still possible, she may point out, that somewhere, sometime, a non-black crow—perhaps an albino—will hatch from the egg of a normal crow. And in this, of course, Suzie would be right.

But now let us consider a second example. Our class has gotten a few years older and has graduated from a study of birds to a study of geometry. A Mr. Twiddle is their instructor. "Class," he begins, "let us briefly review yesterday's lesson. What is a triangle?" And the young man in the fourth row, who still likes to be the first to answer any question, replies, "A triangle is a closed plane figure having three straight sides." "All triangles?" asks Mr. Twiddle. "All *Euclidean* triangles," our hero replies. "How big must the angles be?" asks Mr. Twiddle. "They can be any size you like," comes the reply, "provided only that you have a closed plane figure with just three straight sides. That, and that alone, is enough to make it a triangle—no matter how big it is or how big the angles are or anything else."

"Very well," says Mr. Twiddle, "but today I want to show you something else about triangles"—whereupon he demonstrates the theorem that the interior angles of a Euclidean triangle total 180 degrees. The class struggles briefly with the theorem. One by one they "catch on," and by the time the hour is half over they have all apparently gotten the point and are able without difficulty to "prove" the theorem for themselves.

But Suzie is still with us, and she still wants to make sure that she is getting the straight information. So she asks, "Mr. Twiddle, how do you know that *all* Euclidean triangles have interior angles that total 180 degrees?" Now in this instance it would be utterly pointless for Mr. Twiddle to round up evidence to show that of all the Euclidean triangles that he or anybody else had ever seen, none had ever been found to have interior angles that totaled either more or less than 180 degrees. He can only return to the proof of the theorem and try to help Suzie see that the very nature of triangularity is such that anything that is a Euclidean triangle *must* have interior angles totaling 180 degrees. Furthermore, once Suzie really "sees" this, once she really has hold of this truth about triangles, nothing in the world can ever dissuade her from assenting to it. To know something a priori is to know it with a directness and with a certainty that experience alone can never give.

Kant once put the matter as follows.[1] All knowledge, he said, clearly *begins* with experience—both knowledge a priori and knowledge a posteriori—but not all knowledge *arises out of* experience. It is only a posteriori knowledge (as in the case of the example about crows) that arises out of experience. Accordingly, it is to experience alone that we can turn if a statement that is affirmed on that basis is called in question. But there is also an a priori knowledge of the world (as in the example about triangles). And it is characteristic of such knowledge that we must turn not to empirical evidence for support, if a statement whose truth is known in this way is called in question, but rather to an inspection of the nature of the thing about which the

---

[1] Immanuel Kant, *Critique of Pure Reason*, Intro., II, Norman Kemp Smith (tr.) (New York: St. Martin's, 1965), p. 41.

statement is made. You may parade before my eyes as many black crows as you like: I shall still retain some doubt about whether in fact all crows are black. But I know beyond the shadow of a doubt that if anything is a Euclidean triangle, its interior angles total 180 degrees. What is the difference? The difference is that in the one case we are dealing with a posteriori knowledge and in the other with a priori knowledge. In the one case the knowledge arises out of experience; in the other experience is only the occasion for my coming to know.

Examples of Truths Known A Priori

It is hoped that these few remarks will have clarified what rationalists mean when they talk about knowledge that is acquired in a way that is in some degree independent of experience. The point is so important to a fair appraisal of my position, and so easily and so often misunderstood, that I want to urge my readers to ponder it very carefully —so that they are absolutely sure they see the point of it—before considering the rest of the discussion.

The remainder is relatively simple. I want to offer a few examples of synthetic truths that we know a priori. This is not difficult, for there are countless examples at hand—truths about the world that all of us know, truths that we know not a posteriori but a priori.

One large class of truths that we know in this way is *arithmetical* truths. Any true arithmetical statement will do. Let us consider the statement, $7 + 5 = 12$. This, of course, is simply a brief and convenient way of saying what could be said in ordinary language: seven things added to five things give you a combined total of twelve things.

The first fact to notice about this statement is that it is synthetic: it is a statement about the real world. It is, of course, a very general statement about the world: it applies to apples and oranges and pennies and kittens and anything else that we might have occasion to count and add together.

Consider what would have to be the case, however, if this statement were analytic. We would then have to say that by simply analyzing the subject ("seven things added to five things") we could find the predicate ("twelve things") already present. But we cannot do this. What we find, when we analyze the subject, is this: (a) the concept seven, (b) the concept five, and (c) a direction to perform the intellectual operation involved in combining seven and five into a single total ("added to"). In order to get our predicate we have to perform the prescribed intellectual operation. To do this we must leave off analysis and consider the natures of the numbers involved. Only when we do this—only when we consider the nature of "seven" in conjunction with "five" and perform the intellectual act of combining them—can we get our predicate. In order to do this, we must add to our subject the quite different concept "twelve" in the synthetic statement, "seven things plus five things are twelve things." Arithmetical statements are one and all synthetic.

The second fact to notice about this statement is that its truth is not known a posteriori. It is not like the example of the crows: we are not more or less confident that seven things added to five things equal twelve things, depending on how many times we may have added seven and five. We *know*—absolutely, certainly, without the slightest doubt—that any time, any place, if seven things are added to five things the total will be twelve things. There is a necessity, a universality, a self-evidence, a certainty about this statement that no statement whose truth depends upon the facts of experience can ever have. It may be exhibited in experience, but experience can never contradict it. Its truth is known a priori: we learned it, indeed, through experience, but not by way of summarizing the facts of experience.

Here, then, are as many examples of synthetic truths that are known a priori as anyone could ever ask for. What is true of $7 + 5$ is equally true of $8 + 9$ and $4 - 2$ and 6×7 and every arithmetical statement that ever has been or will be made. Each of them, it will be seen, is a synthetic truth whose truth, if it is to be known at all, must be known a priori.

A second large class of synthetic truths known a priori consists of the truths of geometry. We have already had an illustration about the triangle. Let us consider that example more closely.

Geometry is what we might call the science of physical space. Since any object that could ever appear to us must appear in space, we know a priori that it must conform to the truths of geometry. If, therefore, someone tries to tell us that one time—perhaps, say, in the jungles of Africa—he saw a Euclidean triangle whose interior angles totaled only 160 degrees, we are simply not going to believe him. We may suggest that he made an incorrect measurement, or that the sides of what he thought was a Euclidean triangle were not straight, or even that he is lying to us or trying to fool us. But we know that his report cannot be true because we know a priori that Euclid's theorem is true. And because this is so, experience—wherever, whenever, and to whomever it occurs—must conform to it. Geometrical knowledge is knowledge a priori.

A third class of synthetic truths that are known a priori consists of a very large class of statements that, for lack of a better name, we shall call *logical* truths. An example of such a truth is the statement, "Anything that has shape has size." Another example would be the statement, "A thing cannot both have and not have the same characteristic at the same time."

Consider, for example, the statement that anything that has shape has size. Surely it is evident that this is a synthetic statement. It asserts a fact about the world—it may or may not be an important fact, but it is a fact, and one that we know to be true—namely, that in each and every instance in which there is an object that has shape there is also an object that has size. Now shape and size are not the same thing: I can know that something is round, for example, without having the slightest idea how big it is. Shape and size are diverse characteristics that an object may have. But—and this is the point of the statement—the nature of shape is such and the nature of size is such that whenever one characteristic is present, the other must be also. There is, we might say, a necessary connection between the characteristic that we designate by the term "shape" and the characteristic that we designate by the term "size"; it is this connection that we are affirming when we say that anything that has shape has size.

But it is equally clear that the truth of this statement is known a priori. We directly "see" the necessary connection to which we have just referred, and seeing this, we know without the slightest doubt that the statement is necessarily and universally true. We know, with a certainty that empirical evidence could never give us, that there never has been and never will be an instance of shape without size, or of size without shape. In knowing this, we know a logical truth, and experience cannot fail to exhibit this truth.

Or consider the statement, "A thing cannot both have and not have the same characteristic at the same time." It is true, of course, that we have observed that as a matter of fact objects do not both have and not have the same characteristic at the same time: an object is not simultaneously hot and cold, or colored and uncolored, or big and small, or what-have-you. But our statement goes beyond this. Our statement affirms not merely that as a matter of observable fact things *do* not simultaneously have and not have a given characteristic, but that they *cannot*. The rational mind perceives a necessity and a universality in this truth that experience could never provide, thus certifying it as a truth that is known a priori. And yet it is a truth about the world, a truth indeed that has been exhibited in our experience countless times. It is on the basis of our certainty regarding this statement that we know with equal certainty that contradictory statements (one affirming and one denying that a certain object has a given characteristic) cannot be simultaneously true. Logical truths are synthetic truths that are known a priori.

The fourth class of synthetic truths known a priori that I should like to mention is *ethical* truths. Numerous examples come to mind, but let us confine our attention to the statement, "The infliction of needless pain is evil."

There can be no question, it seems to me, that this statement is synthetic. The notion involved in the infliction of needless pain is undoubtedly highly complex, but this much at least is clear: we can analyze that notion as thoroughly as we please, and we will not discover that the idea of being evil is a part of it. What we mean by "the infliction of needless pain" are such things as a boy torturing an animal "just for the fun of it" or someone mauling a younger and weaker person in order "to show how tough he is." What we are saying about such instances is that, in addition to being instances of animal or human suffering willfully caused by some responsible agent, they have the additional character of being evil. In so saying we are adding to the concept of the subject something not a part of that concept—we are connecting them in our synthetic judgment, "The infliction of needless pain is evil."

What sort of evidence could possibly be adduced in support of such a statement? Evidence could, of course, heighten our awareness of how painful such acts can be, or how absurd and pointless they are, but that is beside the point. What we are affirming is that the infliction of needless pain is not only needless and painful (that *is* analytically true), but that it is also something else, namely, evil, reprehensible, morally blameworthy. Not all the evidence in the world could either confirm or disconfirm our judgment; if its truth is known at all, it is known a priori.

And its truth is known, is it not? We are not moral ignoramuses—though we may not always act in accordance with the moral truths we do perceive. We know, even if we ourselves should be the agents who inflict needless pain, that what we do is evil. We see directly, with an immediacy and a certainty that empirical evidence could never give us, that this act has the moral quality of being evil. And so it is with all ethical truths.

Let me conclude by presenting a small but important disclaimer. In arguing as I have for the possibility and the reality of an a priori knowledge of synthetic truths, I have not meant to disparage in any way the importance of a posteriori knowledge. There are things that can only be known a posteriori, and due credit should be given to the scientists, historians, and others who, through careful observation and experimentation, have contributed so greatly to the sum of human knowledge. The point of my remarks is simply this: however great the quantity of knowledge gained in this way, it does not constitute the whole of our knowledge of reality. We have, in at least the four areas mentioned, countless instances of truths about the real world that are known a priori. It may or may not be important for us to be aware of this—that is another matter. But important or not, it is the case, and that is all that I have tried to show.

STUDY QUESTIONS

1. What difference or differences do you see between the theory of "innate knowledge" and the theory that Rationalist attempts to defend in this chapter?
2. Is there a difference between the role that experience plays in our knowledge about crows and that which it plays in our knowledge of geometrical truths? Has Rationalist succeeded in identifying a real difference here—however one might wish to account for it?
3. List the four classes of truths that Rationalist offers as examples of synthetic truths that are known a priori. What evidence does he offer in each case that the truths to which he has reference are synthetic truths? that they are known a priori?
4. Can you think of any examples in addition to those offered by Rationalist that might plausibly be considered as examples of synthetic truths that are known a priori? Which of Rationalist's own examples do you find most convincing? which least?

34

AN EMPIRICIST RETORT

There is some danger, I think, that readers of Rationalist's account may have gotten a somewhat mistaken view of empiricists, namely, that they are a group of rather stubborn and close-minded individuals who are so enamored of empirical methods of acquiring knowledge that they simply refuse to recognize the knowledge acquired in another way. Rationalists, it may appear, are more open and broad-minded. They allow that there is a great deal of knowledge that is acquired by way of observation and experimentation (a posteriori knowledge), but they do not limit man's knowledge to this: they go on to assert that the human mind is capable of a direct apprehension of some empirical truths and that in fact we know many things about the world in this direct, a priori, way.

This impression of empiricists is quite mistaken, and I shall begin my defense of empiricism by attempting to dispel it. Let me state plainly that I am an empiricist for one reason only, and that is that I have never encountered a single example of an alleged a priori synthetic truth that did not prove upon closer inspection to be either analytic (hence not a truth about the real world at all) or else a posteriori. I am, however, willing to be shown, and if I ever do encounter an example of such a truth I will concede immediately to the rationalists. Until then I must honestly state that every synthetic truth known to me is known a posteriori, and every statement that I have ever seen that could with any degree of certainty be said to be known a priori is clearly analytic. Pending evidence to the contrary I must, therefore, continue to maintain that as far as I can make out all of our knowledge of the real world is a posteriori.

This much, however, I will concede to the rationalists: I think it would be very nice if it were possible to acquire knowledge of the world in an a priori manner. The method of careful observation and experimentation—of observing, measuring, and trying one hypothesis and then another—is painfully slow and laborious. It would be most pleasant if it were possible just to think and by mere thinking to "see" truths about the world in the way that Rationalist seems to think we can. But we have no right to demand that things be the way we want them to be: we have to take things the way they are. Unfortunately, they are not the way Rationalist says they are, as I shall now attempt to show.

Arithmetical Truths

Let us begin by reconsidering Rationalist's account of arithmetical truths. Such truths have long been the favorite examples to which rationalists have had recourse whenever challenged to defend their position. If we are successful in refuting these examples, we may be reasonably confident that those remaining will prove no more difficult. If it can be shown that arithmetical truths are not a priori synthetic, then the chief citadel of rationalism will have been destroyed.

It is my belief—and this view is shared by some but not all empiricists—that arithmetical truths are synthetic truths known a posteriori. I am, therefore, in agreement with Rationalist in affirming that the truths of arithmetic are synthetic truths, but I am disputing his claim that they are known a priori.

My reasons for holding that the truths of arithmetic are synthetic truths are the same as those of Rationalist. It seems evident that when we know some arithmetical truth—for example, that $7 + 5 = 12$, or $4 - 2 = 2$, or $6 \times 7 = 42$—we know something about the real world: we know that whenever you add seven things to five things, you will get a combined total of twelve things; that whenever you subtract two things from a group of four things, you will have a remainder of two things; that whenever you combine six groups of seven things each (or seven groups of six things each), you will have a total of forty-two things. It also seems evident to me that, as Rationalist maintains, the notion "twelve" cannot be found by analyzing the subject term, "$7 + 5$." If I know that $7 + 5 = 12$, as I do, then what I know is a synthetic truth.

The crucial question, then, is *how* do I know this? My answer is that I know it by experience. I did not know this when I was born. I did not learn it in some ecstatic moment of insight, when the eternal truth of this statement suddenly flashed into my mind. I learned it in the way I have learned everything else that I know about the world: by experience and nothing else. First I learned to count. In so doing, of course, I was simply learning the meanings of the words "one," "two," "three," and so on. Then I began to notice certain relationships —for example, that I had five fingers on each hand, and that five fingers plus five fingers made ten fingers; that I had five toes on each foot, and that five toes plus five toes made ten toes; that if I had one penny, and my father gave me another one, I had two pennies, and so on. Every way I turned, no matter what objects I had to deal with (fingers, toes, pennies, playmates, apples, kittens, everything), certain numerical relationships impressed themselves upon me. My experience, your experience, everyman's experience has been thoroughly pervaded by numerical facts since the moment we first began to be aware of the world around us. It is this experience that has given us our knowledge of arithmetical truths.

What makes some people think that there must be something unique and wonderful about arithmetical truths is, I suppose, the remarkable certainty that such truths seem to have. We are, as Rationalist says, sure about these truths in a way that we are not sure about the statement, "All crows are black"—no matter how many crows we may have seen. So much is this the case that "mathematical certainty" is for most people, as it was for the philosopher Descartes, a model of the highest degree of certainty that it is possible for us to have. How are we to account for this certainty?

The answer, I believe, is very simple: we are supremely sure of the truth of arithmetical truths because of the overwhelming amount of evidence that we have observed in support of these truths. Every day of our lives, in thousands and thousands of different ways, experience has crowded in upon us, exhibiting the truths that we express in our arithmetical equations. With all of this evidence, and never a scrap of evidence to the contrary, we at length become convinced: we *know* that $7 + 5 = 12$ (and $4 - 2 = 2$, etc.); our certainty reflects the unbroken uniformity of our experience.

Why, then, are we less certain about crows—even if we have never seen a crow that was not black? There are, I think, two reasons. The first is that the quantity of experience upon which this inference is based is infinitesimal in comparison with that upon which our inferences regarding arithmetical truths are based. Practically everything that we experience exhibits arithmetical truths, whereas it is only on relatively rare occasions that we happen to see crows. Furthermore, experience has taught us that in many species of living things color is a variable characteristic. Perhaps we have seen a black sheep in a flock of white sheep, or an albino mouse, and so we find it easy to conjecture that there might be an exception with respect to color among crows as well. Hence, it is not surprising that we are less than certain that the statement "all crows are black" will stand the test of further experience.

It may be noted that there are other empirical truths, which everyone agrees are known a posteriori, about which we are much more certain than we are about the color of crows. We know with a high degree of certainty, for example, that at sea-level barometric pressure pure water freezes at a temperature of 32° Fahrenheit. We know this by experience. Many individuals, in many different parts of the world and at many different times, have had an opportunity to observe this phenomenon, and never has a case been reported in which these conditions failed to bring about the stated result. With all of this evidence in support of the statement, and no evidence to the contrary, we make the statement with a high degree of confidence that our experience in the future will conform to what we have observed to be the case in the past.

If we imagine an example in which we have even more supporting evidence than we have regarding the freezing of water, it is not difficult to see that the result would be a kind of knowledge that is so certain that it would be natural to call it an instance of "absolute certainty." This is the case with arithmetical knowledge. The evidence in the case of freezing water is so great that it is virtually inconceivable to us that there should ever occur an exception to it. But the evidence in support of arithmetical truths is greater yet—so great, indeed, that for most of us an exception to one of these truths is totally inconceivable. It is this inconceivability of an exception that we are expressing when we say that we know these truths with absolute certainty.

Geometrical Truths

The account that I should be inclined to give of geometrical truths is identical to the one I have given of arithmetical truths. They are, as Rationalist says, synthetic truths; but like the truths of arithmetic they are known a posteriori, not a priori.

Consider, for example, the statement, Two straight lines cannot enclose a space. This, presumably, would qualify as one of the truths that Rationalist says we know a priori. I shall argue, on the contrary, that we know it a posteriori.

In the first place (and I think Rationalist would agree with me) it is clear that we learn the meanings of the words of which this statement is composed by experience. We learn the meaning of the phrase "straight line" in the same way that we learn the meanings of words like "table" and "chair": by hearing the words applied to certain kinds of objects. We learn that matches are "straight," but barrel staves are not; that knitting needles are "straight," but the edge of a dish is not; that a pencil, or the edge of a ruler, is "straight," but a dog's nose, or a cat's ear, is not. This, surely, is how we learn the meanings of words. If we did not have any experience of this kind to tell us the meanings of certain words, those words would be nothing to us but meaningless sounds.

The question, then, is this: once we know the meanings of the words in the statement in question, how do we come to know that the statement is true? I am arguing that we learn this by experience.

What kind of experience is it that teaches us that two straight lines cannot enclose a space? The question need not puzzle us long: our experience is replete with evidence to support this general truth. We may have seen the roofs of houses and noticed that the two lines that intersect to form the peak of the roof never (by themselves) enclose a space. We have observed the parallel sides of a road, the parallel tracks of a railroad, the intersecting lines of a leg and rung of a chair, and so on. And never—not once—have we seen an instance when two straight lines have by themselves enclosed a space. We do not, perhaps, consciously formulate the *statement* at first, but the statement is, nonetheless, a true generalization about our experience. When, therefore, we study geometry and come upon this axiom (as it is called), it may strike us as being "obviously" or "self-evidently" true. Indeed, we may be so impressed with the obviousness of it that we are tempted to say with Plato that it is not really a case of learning at all, but a case of "recollecting" an "eternal truth" that has been present within our soul ever since its creation. But is it really surprising that a truth so lavishly exhibited in our everyday experience should seem obvious when we see it formally stated for the first time? It does not seem so to me.

What is true of this particular example is equally true of all other geometrical truths—with one proviso. Many of the more complex and unobvious theorems of geometry are not directly exhibited in our experience, but they are deducible from those that are. What I mean is this. If proposition *A* and proposition *B* are learned from experience, and proposition *C* can be validly deduced from propositions *A* and *B*, then proposition *C* has ipso facto been learned from experience as well. Geometry is a science wherein the more remote and complex truths are deduced from those that are simpler and closer at hand; these latter, as I hope I have made clear, are gathered from the vast data of our everyday experience.

The certainty of geometrical truths, as of arithmetical truths, rests upon the vast quantity of evidence upon which the foundational truths of the science of geometry are based. It is not necessary, therefore, to repeat what has already been said on this point in connection with arithmetical truths.

Logical Truths

If I have succeeded in showing that the truths of arithmetic and geometry are a posteriori synthetic truths, my readers should have no difficulty in seeing that the truths of logic are of the same sort. Rationalist's first example—the statement that anything that has shape has size—is a perfect example of a fact about the world that has been exhibited in our experience so many times that it is now inconceivable that there could ever occur an exception to it. With all this experience upon which to base our statement, what need have we for a special theory about a remarkable human capacity whereby we are supposedly able to "immediately apprehend" this homely, everyday truth? The same may be said with respect to his second example—that an object cannot both have and not have the same characteristic at the same time. The "necessity" that Rationalist finds in this statement is nothing more than our psychological certainty that a truth so lavishly and so consistently exhibited in our experience will continue to be exhibited without exception.

One type of logical truth, which a man might pardonably suppose to be a priori, would be one that states a set of circumstances in which a particular conclusion may be drawn from certain premises—for example, any statement of the form, "If all A's are B's, and all B's are C's, then all A's are C's." There is, admittedly, a certain self-evidence about such a statement. We certainly cannot imagine the possibility of going wrong in asserting the conclusion if we are granted the premises—no matter what meanings may be assigned to A, B, and C.

The explanation of this certainty is, nonetheless, the same as in the previous examples. When Aristotle set about the task of formulating and systematizing the rules of logic, he did not just sit down and think—or, rather, wait for "direct apprehensions" to occur. Rather, he paid attention to the actual arguments that people used, and he noted the conditions under which arguments succeeded in establishing their conclusions and the conditions under which they did not. The conditions under which they did succeed he called "rules of inference"; the conditions under which they did not succeed he called "logical fallacies." But the data from which he began—and the data on the basis of which other logicians have modified and augmented his work—are the actual arguments, successful or unsuccessful, that people employ. Logical truths are derived from the data of experience. The certainty of these truths is due to the large quantity of evidence upon which they are based.

Ethical Truths

Only ethical truths remain to be considered. The problem is how to construe ethical statements in a way consistent with empiricism. I admit that there is something unusual about ethical statements, and it is understandable why Rationalist would appeal to this class of statements in support of his position. I am not sure that I understand just what makes ethical statements so unique, but I am quite sure that it is not (as Rationalist claims) the fact that they are synthetic truths known a priori.

It is worth noting that we do not know "ethical truths" with the kind of certainty that is supposedly characteristic of a priori knowledge. To affirm an ethical statement is to affirm a belief, a conviction. It is as if we were saying, for example, "I don't know for sure what is right or wrong in this matter (perhaps no one does) but I will take my stand on this, that the infliction of needless pain is evil." What is affirmed as an ethical statement is not something that we know: it is something that we believe, something that we venture. And if it is not known at all, it is obviously not known a priori.

There are, it seems to me, two features of ethical statements that might explain their unusual character. The first is that they are typically affirmed in this venturing, convictional way. An ethical statement is not a report: it is a statement recording our intention to act in certain ways and encouraging others to do the same. The second is that such statements, unlike all of the others we have been considering, speak not of what *is* the case but of what *ought to be* the case. It may be the connotation of "oughtness" that makes ethical statements seem so very different from all other statements.

There are, as a matter of fact, numerous ways in which an empiricist can construe ethical utterances without compromising his empiricism. The subject is a very complex one, however, and has already been discussed in detail in another place (see Part IV). For the present, then, we may be content to leave the status of ethical statements an open question. What is quite clear is that they are not synthetic truths known a priori; and this, so far as the refutation of rationalism is concerned, is the only point of importance.

STUDY QUESTIONS

1. Empiricist has argued that our knowledge of arithmetical truths, like our knowledge about crows, is a posteriori. How does he explain the fact that we are much more certain about the one sort of truths than we are about the other? Are you satisfied with his explanation?
2. What evidence does Empiricist offer in support of his claim that geometrical truths are known a posteriori? Do you think he is right on this point?
3. Suppose that it is true that Aristotle worked out the "rules of logical inference" in the way that Empiricist says. Is this sufficient to establish that they are truths known a posteriori? Could Rationalist allow this account and still claim that they are truths known a priori?
4. Is there something unusual about ethical statements, as Empiricist says there is? Does it seem plausible to you that this is due to the fact that ethical truths are synthetic truths known a priori? Do you find Empiricist's explanation of this alleged uniqueness more or less persuasive than Rationalist's?

35

ANOTHER ALTERNATIVE FOR EMPIRICISTS

I hope that my disagreement with the author of the last chapter does not obscure the fact that on the main issue of the present controversy he and I are in perfect agreement: all our knowledge of synthetic truths arises out of experience. We are, therefore, united in our opposition to rationalism since we cannot allow the claim that there are some synthetic truths—some truths about the real world—that are known a priori. Whatever we know about the real world we have learned from experience—our own and that of others. And whatever is known apart from experience (a priori) is not a truth about the real world at all but merely an analytic truth.

Granting this common ground of all empiricists, however, and granting also our common opposition to rationalism, there remains some disagreement among empiricists as to whether certain classes of statements are to be construed as analytic a priori or as synthetic a posteriori. My colleague has argued that arithmetical, geometrical, and logical truths are all synthetic a posteriori. In my opinion he is mistaken about this, and I shall attempt to show that, except for logical truths, they are actually analytic a priori truths. I shall also have something further to say about ethical truths, though not so much in disagreement with as in addition to what was said at the conclusion of the last chapter.

Arithmetical Truths

Statements about the real world—synthetic statements—have one distinguishing feature in common: it is always possible to specify some state of affairs which, if it were the case, would make the statement in question false. The statement, "All crows are black," is made false by the supposition that there exists a white crow; hence, it is evident that in this case we have a synthetic statement. This test, carefully applied, should enable us to distinguish without difficulty between synthetic and analytic statements.

Our test, it should be noted, is not an arbitrary one: it follows from the definition of a synthetic statement as a statement about the real world. A synthetic statement asserts that the world is so-and-so: it asserts that something really is the case. Consequently, it must be possible to specify a state of affairs in which this would not be the case—in which, accordingly, our statement would be falsified.

Let us now apply our test to an arithmetical statement. What would have to be the case for the statement "7 + 5 = 12" to be false? Let us suppose that I put what I believe to be seven objects (oranges, say) into a bag, and then I put in what I believe to be five more. I bring them to the grocery clerk to be priced. He counts them and finds—to my surprise—that the bag contains only eleven oranges. I count them again, he counts them again, and finally I am convinced: there are only eleven oranges in the bag.

Does this state of affairs falsify the statement, "7 + 5 =12"? Obviously not. We might adopt any one of several explanations of what happened: perhaps I miscounted the first time, perhaps one of the oranges that I counted did not get into the bag, or perhaps someone removed one of the oranges after I had put it in the bag. But note: we would not think of adopting the explanation that this was a remarkable exception to the statement, "7 + 5 = 12." The state of affairs just described does not falsify our arithmetical statement.

What state of affairs would falsify our statement? None. The only way the statement "7 + 5 =12" could be rendered false would be to change the meaning of one or more of the symbols of which the statement is composed. If the symbol "7" were defined to mean what is ordinarily meant by the symbol "8," then the statement would, of course, become false. But then we are no longer describing a state of affairs in the real world to which the statement in question refers: we are altering the meaning of the statement itself.

The truth about arithmetical statements is that they are, one and all, analytic truths. What tends to mislead us is the fact that a number has meaning only in the context of the whole number system. The meaning of a number consists, partly, in its relation to every other number in the system. Part of the meaning of the number "7," for example, is that it is one more than "6" and one less than "8," that it is two more than "5" and two less than "9," and so on. Hence, it is a part of the meaning of "7" that it is five less than "12." Consequently, when we affirm that 7 + 5 = 12, we are only stating explicitly some of the meaning relations that obtain in the system between the numbers 7,

5, and 12. Were this not the case, mathematical reasoning would not have the certainty that it has.

If we look, now, at the reasons that the previous two writers have given for holding that arithmetical truths are synthetic, it is not difficult to see where and why they have gone wrong. First, they have failed to note that the concept of a number is exceedingly complex, that it involves the relations of that number to every other number in the number system. If we think of 7 and 5 as simple concepts—visualizing seven dots and five dots, or some such thing—then it seems very natural to conclude that we cannot get the predicate 12 by analyzing the complex symbol 7 + 5, but only by "performing the prescribed intellectual operation." But as soon as we realize the complexity of the concept of a number—as soon as we realize that its meaning includes its relations to the other numbers in the number system—the error becomes apparent.

Second, these writers have been misled by what I shall call the "quasi-empirical" character of arithmetical truths—a character they share with many analytic truths. Many analytic truths look, at first glance, as if they were "about the real world"; that is why we cannot decide on the status of a given statement simply on the basis of whether or not it "seems" to be about the real world. The statement, "All bachelors are unmarried," for example, seems to be a statement about real bachelors. It is only when we apply the test—when we try to specify a state of affairs which, if it were the case, would falsify the statement—that it becomes evident the statement is not really about bachelors at all, but only about the meaning of the word "bachelor."

So it is with arithmetical truths. They seem, admittedly, to be about the real world—about "apples and oranges and pennies and kittens and anything else that we might have occasion to count and add together," as Rationalist says. But this appearance is deceptive, as we have already shown. When the crucial test of *falsifiability by empirical facts* is applied, it becomes evident that arithmetical statements are purely analytic. No state of affairs can be imagined which, if it were the case, would render an arithmetical truth untrue, for the very good reason that an arithmetical truth is not a statement about the world; it is a statement about the relations between numbers in a number system.

Therefore, arithmetical truths are analytic truths known a priori by anyone who understands adequately the meanings of the symbols. The certainty of such truths is, as Rationalist asserts, due to the fact that they are known a priori; but because they are analytic truths our knowledge of them does not constitute an a priori knowledge of the real world.

Geometrical Truths

It is not surprising that many philosophers have believed that the truths of geometry are synthetic truths known a priori. It seems plausible to hold, as Rationalist does, that geometry is "the science of physical space" and that a geometrical statement is therefore about the real world. If we hold this and then reflect on the peculiar certainty with which we are able to "demonstrate" the theorems of geometry, it is also natural to conclude that geometry consists of a remarkable collection of a priori truths about the real world.

It must be said, however, that today there is less reason to draw this conclusion than in the time of Plato, or Descartes, or even Kant. Today we know that Euclidean geometry is not the only possible geometry; we know that what can be "demonstrated" in any geometry depends not on a correspondence to the real world, but on the definitions with which we begin. We may or may not be able to use a given geometry to explain physical space: that is an empirical question to be decided only by trial and error. What is known, therefore, when we have demonstrated a geometrical theorem, is not anything about the real world at all but only some consequence implicit in the definitions with which the demonstration began.

One reason so many people have been persuaded that the truths of geometry are synthetic rather than analytic is that in studying geometry we have the impression that as each new theorem is demonstrated we are discovering (or "grasping") a new truth. We learn, for example, that a triangle is a closed plane figure having three straight sides, and subsequently we "discover" a truth that does not seem to be contained in this definition (for example, that its interior angles total 180 degrees). But the truth is that this latter theorem is implicit in the definition of a triangle together with the other definitions (some of which are called axioms) of Euclid's system. If this were not the case, it would not be possible to construct a valid proof of the theorem. Were it not for the fact that our intellects are limited, we would never have a sense of discovery when we first succeed in proving a complex geometrical theorem: we would immediately see all of the logical consequences of our definitions and would have no need for a formal demonstration. But this human limitation should not be allowed to obscure the fact that geometrical reasoning always begins with gratuitously assumed definitions and concludes with theorems having the same gratuitous character. Geometrical truths, without exception, are analytic.

Logical Truths

I am uncertain as to what Rationalist intends to include in the class of what he calls "logical truths." It may be that some of the truths he has in mind would require one explanation while others would require somewhat different ones. I shall, however, deal briefly with his two examples and shall add a few remarks that I hope will eliminate any possible misunderstanding on this point.

One example that Rationalist discusses in some detail is the statement, "Anything that has shape has size." To me this is rather obviously an analytic statement. The concept of a "thing"—or of an "object," as Rationalist says later—includes both the idea of having some shape and the idea of having some size. Shape and size are, indeed, diverse characteristics, but both are implicit in the idea of a spatial object, which is what Rationalist has in mind. Fully stated, Rationalist's statement should read, "Anything that occupies space has both shape and size." Rationalist has been misled by the elliptical character of his own statement.

Rationalist's second example is a rather confused statement of the Principle of Noncontradiction, which simply stated asserts merely that a statement and its contradictory cannot both be true. There is, to be sure, something very puzzling about the status of this principle, and it deserves to be pondered with some care. It is puzzling, I think, in the same way that the certainty of statements of the form, "If all A's are B's, and all B's are C's, then all A's are C's" is puzzling. Let us try to unravel the puzzle.

The Principle of Noncontradiction, in my opinion, is nothing more than a linguistic convention: it plays the same role in language that rules play in a game. There are, in fact, many such rules. One of the rules of any language "game" is that every simple proposition is either true or false. Another rule is that if a proposition is true, then it is not false; and if it is false, then it is not true—the Principle of Noncontradiction. As linguistic conventions these rules are neither analytic nor synthetic, since they are not statements at all: they are merely rules that we must follow if we are to use language intelligibly.

Much the same kind of account can be given of rules of inference, of which one example has been given ("If all A's are B's," etc.). It has been argued that rules of inference are empirical generalizations based upon analyses of the actual arguments, successful or unsuccessful, that people employ in the attempt to establish their conclusions on the basis of certain sorts of premises. This position contains some truth, but on the fundamental question of the logical status of the rules of inference I think it is incorrect. It rightly asserts that these rules were determined by Aristotle and others through a process of inductive reasoning. But what Aristotle discovered in this way were not truths about the real world (in any significant meaning of that phrase), but rather the rules by which, in our language, we can reason successfully from premises to conclusions. Aristotle might be compared to a man who, never having read or heard anything about the rules of baseball, figured out the rules for himself by watching how the game was actually played. Such an observer would, quite obviously, employ inductive reasoning; but what he would discover in this way would not be a group of synthetic truths, but a system of rules prescribing what players may and may not do in the game of baseball. Just so with the rules of inference. They are not synthetic truths, since they are not truths at all: they are rules governing logical inferences in our language. To know these rules is not to know some truths about the real world: it is to know how to speak intelligibly within the context of the remarkable game that is human discourse.

Ethical Truths

I have already indicated that I am quite in agreement with the remarks about ethical truths made by the author of the last chapter, and I have no wish to discuss at this time the many ways in which an empiricist might handle such utterances. I would like, however, to make just one suggestion as a kind of footnote to those remarks, and then I shall conclude.

We found, in the case of what are commonly called "logical truths," that properly speaking they are not "truths" at all, but simply rules, linguistic conventions governing the use of language. Once this is recognized, the question as to whether they are synthetic or analytic disappears: since they are not truths at all, they are neither synthetic nor analytic. Perhaps an analogous account can also be given of ethical truths. Perhaps they are not "truths" at all; hence neither analytic nor synthetic. I suggest that they might be linguistic expressions of a quite different type. Three possibilities come to mind: (a) statements of intention, (b) veiled commands, or (c) expressions of feeling. Since the question as to the logical status of ethical discourse is still a very controversial one, I do not wish to commit myself to any one of these options or to attempt a defense of one. I would, however, suggest that in view of this controversy it seems extremely hazardous to rest any part of the case for rationalism on an appeal to examples drawn from this source.

STUDY QUESTIONS

1. At what point or points does the author of this chapter (Empiricist B) claim to be in agreement with the author of the previous chapter (Empiricist A), and at what point or points does he claim to be in disagreement? Would it be inconsistent for someone to agree with

Empiricist A's account of some of Rationalist's examples and Empiricist B's account of others?

2. What is the "falsifiability test" that Empiricist B proposes as a method for distinguishing between analytic and synthetic truths? Does this seem to you to be a valid test? What use does Empiricist B make of this test in his subsequent discussion?

3. What account does Empiricist B give of "rules of inference"? Do you think he is right? In your judgment, would it be plausible for Rationalist to argue that these are examples of synthetic truths that are known a priori?

4. What do you think of the suggestion that what Rationalist calls "ethical truths" are not "truths" at all? Is Empiricist B right in saying that if this is the case, it is not proper to ask whether they are analytic or synthetic? Why?

36

A RATIONALIST REPLY

I suppose it would be excessively unkind to whisper the suggestion that our two empiricist friends, in their respective efforts to defend an embattled empiricism, have rather effectively canceled each other out. Empiricist *A* has allowed that most of what I have offered as examples of synthetic a priori truths (all except ethical truths) are indeed synthetic, and he has attempted to show that the certainty with which we hold these truths to be true is due to the vast amount of experience upon which they are based. Empiricist *B* has recognized that this attempt is a failure, and he has tried the other alternative of interpreting these statements as analytic a priori. I cannot resist the temptation to play the role of peacemaker in the present dispute. I think each of our empiricist friends is half right: Empiricist *A* is right in holding that the truths in question are synthetic and Empiricist *B* is right in holding that they are a priori. It is scarcely necessary to point out that this also means that each is also half wrong.

There would be little point in rehashing all of the arguments in support of the view that arithmetical, geometrical, logical, and ethical truths are all synthetic a priori. I have already stated what I consider to be the most convincing reasons for so regarding them, and I have little to add by way of augmenting what I consider to be a strong positive case. Our empiricist friends have raised a number of interesting points, however, and since I have been given the last word, I should like to use the opportunity to defend my position against the criticisms that have been stated.

The Status of the Argument

Perhaps we should begin by stating once again the status of the argument. There is always some danger, when arguments become numerous, that the main point at issue will become obscured, and should this happen, the whole point of the discussion would be lost.

The question at issue is this: Do we or do we not have any a priori knowledge of synthetic truths? I have argued that we do and have offered four classes of examples in support of my view. Our two empiricists have argued that we do not and have attempted to show that my several examples can all be interpreted in some other way.

Some readers may have come to the conclusion that my account of ethical truths, for example, is not correct. What effect would this have on the argument? Simply this: it would remove one group of examples of synthetic a priori truths, leaving the others intact. But note: it would still be the case that we have some a priori knowledge of synthetic truths, and my basic position would remain unscathed. *Only if every plausible example of synthetic truths known a priori has been shown to have some other status has rationalism been shown to be mistaken.*

I do not mean, in what I have just said, to withdraw my claim that ethical truths are in fact synthetic truths known a priori. I will stand by all the examples I offered earlier. My point is simply that if someone were to disagree with me about the correct interpretation of some of my examples, while agreeing with me with respect to others, he would still be on my side insofar as the fundamental issue in the rationalist-empiricist controversy is concerned. Rationalists have some differences, too—but it only takes a single example of an a priori synthetic truth to clinch the case for rationalism. I turn now to a consideration of some of the points raised by my opponents.

Necessary Truths and Empirical Generalizations

Empiricist A has argued that arithmetical, geometrical, and logical truths are synthetic a posteriori, and he has attempted to account for the certainty with which we hold these truths to be true by saying that they are based on a very large quantity of experiential data. I think he is mistaken on this point, and I want to present one final argument in support of this opinion.

An empirical generalization is only as strong as the evidence on which it rests. If a generalization is based on scanty evidence, we are very uncertain about its truth. If it is based on quite a bit of evidence, we are more certain of its truth. And when the evidence from which our generalization is drawn is extremely voluminous, so that we have good reason to believe that if there were ever an exception to the statement it would in all likelihood have been observed, our confidence in the truth of the generalization may reach a very high degree of certainty. When we are dealing with empirical generalizations, there is a perfect parallel between the quantity of evidence upon which the generalization is based and the degree of certainty with which it is held to be true.

But surely it is evident that the certainty with which we hold arithmetical, geometrical, and logical truths to be true is out of all proportion to the quantity of "evidence" upon which, if they were empirical generalizations, they would have to be based. There are, admittedly, some simple truths of this sort—such as simple combinations of numbers up to ten or so and simple geometrical axioms such as the one about the impossibility of two straight lines enclosing a space—that are confirmed by our experience almost every day of our lives. But consider for a moment some more complex examples. How many times in your life have you multiplied 762 by 316? Perhaps never. Yet you know, *with absolute certainty*, once you work the problem, what the answer is. How many triangles have you measured to find the sum of the interior angles? How many triangles have you inscribed in a semicircle? Yet you know, once you have understood the proof of the relevant theorems, that the interior angles of a Euclidean triangle total 180 degrees and that any triangle inscribed within a semicircle must be a right triangle.

There are, on the other hand, many truths that are really empirical generalizations, for which there is a great deal of supporting evidence, but to which we can readily conceive exceptions—though we may never in fact encounter an exception. I can readily imagine, for example, that on some occasion pure water at sea-level barometric pressure might fail to crystallize at 32° Fahrenheit as the law says it will. I am highly confident that this will not happen, but I do not have the absolute certainty that I have about a priori truths: the most that I can have with even the best-documented empirical generalization is a very high degree of probability. If, then, I encounter a truth that I see to be necessarily true, and which I therefore know to be true with absolute certainty, I know that what I have before me is an a priori truth. And if, in addition, this truth is about the real world, so that in knowing it I know not just the meanings of certain terms but something about reality, then I know that I have to do with a synthetic a priori truth. Let anyone who remains in doubt on this point compare any one of the examples I have given with the best-documented empirical generalization that he can think of. I am confident that he will not fail to see the difference. There is much, very much, that we know by observation and experimentation; but what we know in this way we do not know with the absolute certainty that is the hallmark of a priori knowledge.

The Falsifiability Test

Empiricist *B* has recognized that the truths of which we have been speaking cannot be accounted for in the way that Empiricist *A* attempts to account for them, and he accordingly tries to account for them in yet another way. Contrary to what may seem to be the case, he argues, arithmetical and geometrical truths are not synthetic truths at all: they are analytic. And the proof of this, he goes on to say, is that it is not possible to describe a state of affairs that, if it were the case, would render one of these statements false. This "falsifiability test," as he calls it, is the big weapon in his attack on synthetic a priori truths. We will do well to inspect it closely to see just how lethal it really is.

Although I would not go so far as to deny that the falsifiability test may be of some occasional value in helping us decide whether a given statement is analytic or synthetic, it is not the infallible test that Empiricist *B* thinks it is. The reason is that a *logically impossible* state of affairs cannot be consistently described. If, therefore, we find ourselves unable in some instance or other to describe a state of affairs that, if the case, would falsify the statement in question, there are two possibilities: the statement may be, as Empiricist *B* says it must be, an analytic statement, or it may be a synthetic truth to which there are no logically possible alternatives.

Consider once again the statement, "Anything that has shape has size." I freely grant that neither I nor anyone else can imagine or describe a state of affairs that, if it were the case, would falsify this statement. (I can, of course, construct a sentence that appears to contradict the statement. I can say "Some things that have shape do not have size"—but Empiricist *B* and I both know that in saying this I would not be describing a possible state of affairs.) The reason that I cannot describe a state of affairs that, if true, would falsify the statement in question is not that my statement is analytic, but rather that there is no logically possible alternative to the synthetic truth it expresses. We can see that although size and shape are different characteristics of spatial objects, they are, nonetheless, related in such a way that where one is present the other must be also.

Even if the falsifiability test were taken at face value, however, it would not do the job that Empiricist *B* wants it to do. I noted with great interest that he himself, as a matter of fact, did not make use of the test in his discussion of geometrical truths. And with good reason: even by this measure geometrical truths turn out to be synthetic truths. For it is not at all difficult to describe a state of affairs that, if true, would falsify almost any geometrical theorem we can think of. It is perfectly conceivable that the interior angles of a Euclidean triangle, for example, might have totaled 160 or 190 degrees instead of 180, or that a triangle inscribed on the base of a semicircle might always have had one obtuse angle instead of one 90° angle. It just happens to be the case that Euclid's theorems with respect to these matters are true, and if we have studied a little geometry we know that they are true. But to know that they are true is not, in this case, to render the alternatives inconceivable.

Third, even the one application that Empiricist *B* does make of the falsifiability test—to arithmetical truths—is not very convincing. Certainly we would not, in the example of the oranges, adopt the explanation that the reason we only had eleven oranges in the bag is that we had here a remarkable exception to the general rule that $7 + 5 = 12$. But surely the reason we would not adopt this explanation is that we know a priori that $7 + 5 = 12$. Because we know this, and know it with absolute certainty, we quite naturally seek some other explanation for the fact that the bag does not contain as many oranges as we expected it to; for to know something a priori is to know also that experience must conform to what is thus known.

Let us suppose, however, that (in spite of his unfortunate reliance on what has turned out to be a faulty weapon) Empiricist *B* were right in his interpretation of mathematical truths. What would be the consequences?

In the first place, it would remain a gigantic puzzle that we are able to use arithmetical and geometrical reasoning to draw conclusions about the world at all. It is a remarkable fact that we are able to calculate all sorts of things—budget deficits and satellite orbits and a million other things—by applying the appropriate mathematical formulae to the data with which we begin. But remarkable though this is, it is, nonetheless, a fact. On Empiricist *B's* account, however, this fact is not only remarkable: it is inexplicable. For on his account mathematical truths are not truths about the world at all: they are purely vacuous statements that do nothing more than make explicit some of the meaning relations that have, apparently quite arbitrarily, been assigned to the various symbols in our number system. It is difficult to take seriously a theory that forces us to the conclusion that the applicability of mathematical reasoning to the real world is nothing but a happy coincidence.

In the second place, if the applicability of mathematical reasoning to the real world were, as Empiricist *B* holds, a matter of simply "trying it out to see if it works," then we ought to be in doubt about whether it will work when it is applied to phenomena with which we have had no previous experience. We should then entertain some doubt, for example, whether the arithmetical and geometrical truths with which we are familiar on earth will hold on the moon or on Mars.

But we do not in fact entertain any such doubts, and the reason we do not is that we know that the truths that we express in our equations are necessarily and universally true.

Logical Truths

I am delighted that Empiricist *B* has seen fit to bring up the matter of the status of the so-called laws of thought and rules of inference because they constitute some of the most convincing examples in support of my position. I hold, of course, that the laws of thought and the rules of inference are synthetic a priori truths. It seems to me that whatever plausibility my opponent's account of these truths has depends on the unargued assumption that speaking a language is very much like playing a game, and that the rules governing the use of language are, like the rules in a game, altogether a matter of convention. This is hardly the place to enter into a full-length discussion of the question concerning the relation of language to reality, but we should be aware of the fact that the account of logical truths with which we are now dealing presupposes a view regarding the status of language that is extremely implausible.

My own view—and I only have space to state it and hope that my readers will be able to see for themselves that it is correct—is that language has evolved out of the encounter of the human mind with reality, and that it therefore incorporates a certain logical structure that corresponds to the structure of reality. The laws of thought and rules of inference, in this view, are not at all a matter of convention: they are grounded in the very structure of reality—are, in fact, universal and synthetic truths about reality. They may be ignored not simply at the cost of speaking unintelligibly, but of speaking falsely. If I or someone else should attempt to ignore the Principle of Noncontradiction—should say, that is, that some simple propositions are both true and false—we would not be guilty of breaking one of the rules that people happen to have adopted in order to play the language game: we would be guilty of uttering a statement that is not true. A proposition cannot be simultaneously true and false, and the reason for this is that a given state of affairs cannot both be the case and not be the case at one and the same time. It is reality, not merely conventional rules, that determines the truth or falsity of what we say. A so-called language that did not mirror the structure of reality in its own logical structure would be no language at all.

A Word About Ethics

Perhaps it was unwise to bring ethical truths into the present discussion since I might have anticipated that it would only lead to confusion. So much has been written of late on the status of these truths, and so many theories have been propounded, that many philosophers hesitate even to mention the matter for fear that they will be compelled to defend their position against a vast number of opposing theories.

It is interesting to note, however, that this question did not become a matter of serious controversy until early in the present century when British and American philosophers began to rally in large numbers around the banner of empiricism. This strongly suggests a fact that is evident to anyone who is acquainted with the recent literature on this matter: the question of what to do with ethical truths is and remains one of the thorniest problems for an empiricist to handle. If there are, as Empiricist A has said, "numerous ways in which an empiricist can construe ethical utterances without compromising his empiricism," it is not because these various ways are all so plausible, but rather because no one of them is sufficiently plausible to win very many adherents. But this is a matter that has been discussed elsewhere at some length (see Part IV), so we need not enter into it here.

My position, in any case, remains unchanged and, for that matter, virtually unchallenged by the few remarks my opponents have made on the subject of ethical truths. If anyone is absolutely determined to be an empiricist, I have no doubt that he will be able to find among the many empiricist accounts of ethical truths one that is to his liking. If, however, I have succeeded in persuading some of my readers that we do in fact have some a priori knowledge of synthetic truths, I think they will have little difficulty in agreeing that ethical truths are among those known in this way.

STUDY QUESTIONS

1. Is Rationalist right in saying that "it only takes a single example of an a priori synthetic truth to clinch the case for rationalism"? Explain.
2. Is Rationalist right in saying that (a) our certainty of the truth of an empirical generalization varies according to the amount of evidence on which it rests, and (b) the certainty with which we hold arithmetical, geometrical, and logical truths to be true is out of all proportion to the quantity of "evidence" upon which, if they were empirical generalizations, they would be based? If so, how does this affect Empiricist A's position? Empiricist B's?
3. What considerations does Rationalist bring forward in his attempt to show that the falsifiability test is not capable of doing the job that Empiricist B wants it to do? How might Empiricist B answer Rationalist on this point?
4. State briefly Rationalist's attempted *reductio ad absurdum* of Empiricist B's account of mathematical truths. Does it succeed? Explain.

FOR FURTHER READING

Blanshard, Brand. *The Nature of Thought,* vol. 1. New York: Humanities Press, 1939, chaps. 28–30.

———. *Reason and Analysis.* LaSalle, Ill.: Open Court, 1962, chaps. 6 and 10.

Cassirer, Ernst. *The Problem of Knowledge,* tr. by W. H. Woglom and C. W. Hendel. New Haven: Yale University Press, 1950, chaps. 1–4.

Kant, Immanuel. *Critique of Pure Reason.* tr. by Norman Kemp Smith. New York: St. Martin's Press, 1965 (paperbound). See Introduction, Sections 1–5.

Leibniz, G. W. *New Essays Concerning Human Understanding.* Many editions. See especially Book I and Book IV, Chapters 1–9.

Lewis, C. I. *An Analysis of Knowledge and Valuation.* LaSalle, Ill.: Open Court, 1947, chaps. 1–6.

———. *Mind and the World Order.* New York: Scribner, 1929, chaps. 7–9.

Locke, John. *An Essay Concerning Human Understanding.* Many editions. See especially Book I and Book IV, Chapters 1–9.

Pap, Arthur. "Are All Necessary Propositions Analytic?" *The Philosophical Review,* 58 (1949), 229–320.

Plato. *Meno.* Many editions.

Quine, W. van Orman. *From a Logical Point of View,* 2nd. ed., rev. New York: Harper & Row, 1961 (paperbound). See especially "Two Dogmas of Empiricism."

Reichenbach, Hans. *The Rise of Scientific Philosophy.* Berkeley and Los Angeles: University of California Press, 1958 (paperbound).

Russell, Bertrand, *Introduction to Mathematical Philosophy.* New York: Humanities Press, 1960, chaps. 1, 2, 13, and 14.

Ryle, G., K. Popper, and C. Lewy. "Why are the Calculuses of Logic and Mathematics Applicable to Reality?" *Proceedings of the Aristotelian Society,* Supplementary 20 (1946), 20–60.

PART VIII

THE
PROBLEM OF
INDUCTION

37

THE LEGACY
OF HUME

Rationalists and empiricists agree, as we have seen, that we have a good deal of a posteriori knowledge of synthetic truths. It is obvious to everyone concerned that it is in this way that we know many particular facts—such as the color of the house in which we live, the name of the street on which our house is located, and so on. (Note that these are particular facts, not general truths: I know the color of my house and you know the color of your house, but neither of us knows from this anything about the color of houses in general. A particular fact has to do with some particular state of affairs that obtains in some particular place at some particular time. Such particular states of affairs, we are saying, are known a posteriori.) It is evidently in this way that we also come to know a great many general empirical truths. Some of these are common everyday truths that any normal person assents to without question—for example, that fire burns, water wets, and ice is cold. Others, like the generalizations at which scientists arrive after conducting elaborate experiments, are much more abstruse and unordinary.

The process by which we proceed in our thinking from the particular facts of our experience to the general truths that seem to be exhibited in experience is called *induction*. How did we come to know the general truth that fire is hot? Presumably, somewhat like this: we tried putting our hand near a fire and discovered to our pain that it was hot. We then knew the particular truth that *that* fire was hot. On some other occasion we again tried putting our hand near another fire and discovered that it, too, was hot. How many experiments it took to persuade us of the general truth that all fire is hot depended on how clever we were and, perhaps, on how hot the fires were upon which we conducted our experiments. But we did, in any case, come to know this general truth; and the process by which we concluded from the painful facts of our experience to the general conclusion is what is called induction. A general truth that is arrived at in this way is called an *empirical generalization*. This all seems simple enough, and for a long time it never occurred to anyone that the phenomenon of inductive reasoning presented any special problems of a philosophical nature. Then came David Hume.

Hume's Question

The question that Hume raised concerning induction was: "What is the nature of that evidence which assures us of any real existence and matter of fact beyond the present testimony of our senses or the records of our memory?" [1] What, in other words, is the justification for affirming a general empirical truth on the basis of our knowledge of some few particular facts? By what logical right do we claim to know that some empirical generalizations are true?

It is evident, Hume argued, that we do not know a priori what properties belong to an object that comes within the range of our experience:

> Adam, though his rational faculties be supposed, at the very first, entirely perfect, could not have inferred from the fluidity and transparency of water that it would suffocate him, or from the light and warmth of fire that it would consume him. No object ever discovers, by the qualities which appear to the senses, either the causes which produced it or the effects which will arise from it; nor can our reason, unassisted by experience, ever draw any inference concerning real existence and matter of fact.[2]

It must be, then, by experience that we know these things. But what, asked Hume, are we warranted in asserting on the basis of experience? Only that *in the past*, or *in all cases thus far observed*, such and such has been the case. Hume asserted:

> These two propositions are far from being the same: *I have found that such an object has always been attended with such an effect*, and *I foresee that other objects which are in appearance similar will be attended with similar effects*. I shall allow, if you please, that the one proposition may justly be inferred. But if you insist that the inference is made by a chain of reasoning, I desire you to produce that reasoning.[3]

---

[1] David Hume, in Charles W. Hendel (ed.), *An Inquiry Concerning Human Understanding* (New York: Liberal Arts, 1955), p. 41.

[2] *Ibid.*, p. 42.

[3] *Ibid.*, p. 48.

Hume was convinced that no acceptable answer to his question was possible. He accordingly adopted the position that induction is not logically justifiable because every inductive generalization presupposes a proposition that can never be proved—namely, that the future will resemble the past and that "similar powers will be conjoined with similar sensible qualities." "If there be any suspicion that the course of nature may change," he concluded, "and that the past may be no rule for the future, all experience becomes useless and can give rise to no inference or conclusion." [4] No doubt we cannot avoid, as a matter of habit, drawing inferences of this kind and planning our affairs as if these inferences were trustworthy; but such inferences, Hume was convinced, have no satisfactory logical warrant.

A Restatement of Hume's Question

In light of the subsequent discussion of the problem so effectively raised by Hume, it is desirable to restate the problem in a somewhat different form. It is evident that two separate but closely related questions are involved. The first question might be stated thus: Is induction a valid logical procedure? Have we any logical right to draw general conclusions on the basis of our limited observation of some particular facts? The second question is: If induction is a valid logical procedure, does its validity rest on any a priori principles? Thus amplified, the question becomes: *Is induction a valid logical procedure and, if so, does it involve any a priori principles?*

Before turning to a preliminary characterization of the alternative positions that may be taken with respect to this question, let us look briefly at two commonsense reactions to Hume's puzzle. Both of these reveal a failure to grasp the point of Hume's question.

A common reaction of people who encounter the problem for the first time goes something like this: Everybody knows that inductive reasoning is warranted; this is evident from the fact that everybody does it—including philosophers who ask sophistical questions. As a matter of fact, it would not be possible to perform any of the normal activities of life if we could not assume that the empirical generalizations drawn from our past experiences are well founded and, indeed, true. It is only in this way that we know such essential everyday truths as that bread nourishes, water quenches thirst, and so on. If we could not depend on these, all activity and all life would have to cease.

This objection, which is a very natural one, misses the point of Hume's question. As a practical matter, Hume was well aware that we all do and indeed must make inductive inferences. "As an agent," Hume said explicitly, "I am quite satisfied in the point; but as a phi-

---

[4] *Ibid.*, p. 51.

losopher who has some share of curiosity, I will not say skepticism, I want to learn the *foundation* of this inference." [5] After it has been acknowledged that all men do in fact employ inductive reasoning and live their lives on the assumption that the empirical generalizations thus established are well founded, the question still remains: By what logical right, if any, do we make such inferences? It was his inability to find an answer to this question that drove Hume to the conclusion that inductive reasoning has no logical warrant at all.

It is also suggested that Hume's problem disappears if we bear in mind that all we have a right to ask of an empirical generalization is that it be more or less *probable*. Hume's error, it is sometimes said, consists in his failure to recognize the difference between deductive and inductive reasoning. Deductive reasoning leads to conclusions that are as certain as the premises: in a valid deductive argument, if the premises are true the conclusion must be true. But with inductive arguments, this is not the case. However many instances of a given phenomenon are observed, it is only more or less probable that the observed uniformities will hold for all phenomena of that type. Once this is recognized, it is suggested, Hume's problem disappears.

Unfortunately, Hume's problem cannot be wished away in this facile manner. Hume was well aware of the fact that empirical generalizations are not certain since, as he pointed out, "the contrary of every matter of fact is still possible." [6] His point was not the truism that inductive reasoning does not establish its conclusions with the certainty and the necessity that deductive reasoning does. His point was the far more radical one that *what we call inductive reasoning is not reasoning at all*, that we have no logical right to affirm on the basis of our past experience that it is even *probable* that such-and-such will be the case in the future. No doubt the most that we can ask is that inductive reasoning be allowed to establish its conclusions with varying degrees of probability. The effect of Hume's question is to raise serious doubt as to whether even this much can be allowed.

Alternatives to Skepticism

Hume's own position with respect to this question is commonly referred to as *inductive skepticism*. It consists in affirming that induction is not a valid logical procedure—that, as Hume said, "even after we have experience of the operations of cause and effect, our conclusions from that experience are *not* founded on reasoning or any process of the understanding." [7] Our propensity to believe that the future

---

5 *Ibid.*, p. 52.

6 *Ibid.*, p. 40.

7 *Ibid.*, p. 47.

will be more or less like the past, that what has been observed to be the case in the past is therefore a reliable guide to the future, is nothing more than an interesting psychological fact about ourselves. Induction itself—as a logical procedure, as a species of reasoning—remains unwarranted and unjustified.

Many philosophers, though they acknowledge the legitimacy and the importance of Hume's question, have been unwilling to accept Hume's negative and skeptical answer to that question. They have held, on the contrary, that induction is a valid logical procedure and have attempted in various ways to show how inductive inferences are warranted. Most of these attempts may be divided into two general classes, which we shall call *constructive empiricism* and *rationalism*.

Constructive empiricism consists in the assertions that (a) induction is a valid logical procedure and (b) its validity does not depend on an appeal to any a priori truths. The first proposition distinguishes this position from that of the inductive skeptic; the second distinguishes it from that of the rationalist. Any empiricist who wishes to maintain the logical validity of inductive reasoning must be prepared to defend both. Chapter 38 represents one such attempt to answer Hume's question along these lines.

The rationalist's solution to the problem, as has been intimated, consists in affirming that (a) induction is a valid logical procedure but (b) its validity depends on an appeal to some truth that is known a priori. The embarrassment of empiricism with respect to the problem of induction, in the view of many rationalists, is only one more proof of the inadequacy of the empiricist epistemology. If even general empirical truths cannot be established in a way that is consistent with empiricism, they argue, then it is quite clear that empiricism leaves much to be desired. This view is developed in some detail in Chapter 39.

It should be noted that it is not absolutely incumbent on a rationalist to adopt the "rationalist" solution to the problem of induction. A man might be a skeptic with respect to the problem of induction and still be a rationalist by virtue of the fact that he holds that there are some other synthetic truths that we know a priori. Thus someone could conceivably be a rationalist without accepting the "rationalist" position on this point; but if he does accept the rationalist position on this point, he is by that a rationalist, no matter what other views he might hold.

If we take Hume's problem at face value, inductive skepticism, constructive empiricism, and rationalism are the three possible positions. A number of philosophers, however, have found themselves unconvinced by the attempts of both rationalists and empiricists to solve Hume's problem on its own terms, and yet they have been unwilling to draw Hume's skeptical conclusion with respect to our supposed knowledge of general empirical truths. Therefore, various attempts have been made to discover some incorrect assumption in Hume's statement of the problem (and in its discussion since) that, if eliminated, would show the problem not to be as serious as it appears. These attempts to solve the problem by dissolving it have taken a variety of forms.

One such attempt is represented by *pragmatism*. What is wrong with the traditional problem, according to the pragmatist, is its presupposed view concerning the nature of truth. How the pragmatist theory of truth is supposed to be of assistance in solving the problem of induction is explained in Chapter 40.

Another way of attempting to lay this old problem to rest has been advocated by the distinguished contemporary philosopher Karl Popper. Popper's position involves two main parts: (a) an acceptance of Hume's refutation of induction, together with (b) a denial that this has any serious consequence so far as our knowledge of empirical truths is concerned. This position is advocated in Chapter 41 from Popper's point of view that, once the status of scientific knowledge is understood, the traditional problem of induction will no longer be considered a problem.

A student who is considering the problem of induction for the first time should approach it with the supposition that it is a genuine and important problem to which skepticism, rationalism, and constructive empiricism are the only available solutions. In this way he will be able to judge whether the other two attempts are as successful as they claim to be in solving the problem by, so to speak, circumventing it.

STUDY QUESTIONS

1. What precisely is the difference between a particular empirical fact and a general empirical truth? Give several examples of each.
2. What exactly is the problem of induction? Test your understanding of it by attempting to restate the problem in several different ways.
3. How do the two "commonsense" reactions mentioned in this chapter miss the point of Hume's question? Do they attribute to Hume some assumption that he did not make, or do they address themselves to some question other than the one Hume was asking?
4. Give two or three examples of inductive arguments that you yourself have used, or have heard used by someone else. Does it seem to you that the premises (in your examples) provide some warrant for affirming the conclusion? If so, how? Are you, or are you not, making some a priori assumption?

38

EMPIRICISM
AND THE PROBLEM
OF INDUCTION

Hume did no great favor to science, empiricism, or common sense in raising the problem of induction. Both science and common sense are outraged at the thought that the generalizations affirmed on the basis of observation should have, as Hume said, no logical foundation; and it *is* a problem that is not congenial to empiricism. Yet it is unthinkable that we should resort to ad hoc theories of a priori knowledge in order to account for such a homely thing as the belief that the sun will rise tomorrow. Hence, we may be sure that if the matter is only considered in the proper perspective, it will become clear that the problem of induction is not the stumbling stone for empiricism that it is sometimes believed to be.

I think we should be aware, particularly in view of some suggestions that have been made from time to time, that this is no mere pseudo-problem. A number of disastrous consequences would follow if it should be concluded that induction is not, after all, a valid logical procedure. It would be profitable to begin our consideration of the problem by considering some of the consequences that we shall be compelled to accept if, with Hume, we come to a skeptical conclusion.

Consequences of Inductive Skepticism

It should be apparent, in the first place, that our knowledge of many everyday empirical truths rests on a basis of inductive inference. We know, for example, that unsupported bodies fall toward the earth, that air-breathing animals cannot long survive under water, that bread nourishes and water quenches thirst, and so on. If inductive reasoning is not well founded, we have no logical basis, no rational foundation, for believing these things. Then, so far as the logic of the matter is concerned, we might with as much justification hold the contrary—that unsupported bodies (evidence to the contrary notwithstanding) sometimes fly upward, that some air-breathing animals flourish under water, that bread and water sometimes injure rather than nourish a hungry and thirsty man.

In the same way many of our particular expectations with respect to the immediate future would turn out to be rationally indefensible if induction is overthrown, for these are but particular instances of, or particular deductions from, general truths. I believe that the dinner I shall eat tonight will nourish my body, not poison it. Why? Because I believe in the truth of the general proposition that food nourishes. I believe that if I were to leave my third-floor office by way of the window rather than by way of the elevator or stairs I would be, at the very least, severely injured. Why? Because I believe in the truth of such general propositions as these, that unsupported bodies fall toward the earth at an accelerating rate of speed and that a fall of three stories is extremely likely to seriously injure the human body. Yet, if induction is not a valid logical procedure, I have no rational basis for these expectations.

What is even more incredible, however, is that the whole enterprise of natural science would be without a logical foundation if induction is not defensible. All of the reasoning of the scientists, from Galileo and Newton and Kepler to Einstein and Heisenberg and Bohr, would have to be regarded as no *reasoning* at all, but simply as so many exercises of the "inference-drawing propensity" of the human psyche. This, I submit, is simply absurd. And a view of induction that compels us to draw such a conclusion is similarly absurd.

A sober consideration of what is at stake in the controversy over induction makes it evident, therefore, that Humean skepticism cannot be the last word on this matter. Simply to list the consequences of the skeptical position is at the same time to construct a powerful *reductio ad absurdum* of that position. Somehow it must be possible to establish the logical validity of induction; and if we are empiricists, we will seek a way to do this consistent with empiricism.

Induction and the Principle of the Uniformity of Nature

It is hardly necessary to give an elaborate description of what we are doing when we "draw an inductive inference," since every one of us is familiar with it from personal experience. We observe some phenomenon—the sun rising in the east, for example—and then we observe another instance of that same phenomenon, then another, and another, until at length we draw our inference—that the sun always rises in the east, or whatever the inference might be. We proceed, that is, to affirm *universal* regularity on the basis of *observed* regularity. And, in the case of a true inference, our general conclusion is constantly confirmed by our subsequent experience.

It is quite evident that in reasoning in this manner we are tacitly assuming what is sometimes called the Principle of the Uniformity of Nature. This principle may be stated in a variety of ways, of which the following are representative. P_1: The universe is so constructed that everything that occurs may be viewed as an instance of some general law or laws. P_2: The universe is not a chaos of random events; some uniformities, or laws, are exhibited in phenomena widely separated in space and time. P_3: Nature operates according to some uniform laws; what has occurred in the past, therefore, is a reliable guide for the future.

I do not wish to discuss in detail the differences that are evident in these three versions of the principle of uniformity. P_2 and P_3 are, I think, virtually identical, the only significant difference being that the latter specifically mentions the reliability of the past as a guide for the future. P_1 differs from the other two in that it appears to affirm universal determinism; since we do in fact employ inductive reasoning even though we may have serious doubts about whether or not determinism is true, it is evident that we do not necessarily assume the principle as stated in P_1 when we are reasoning inductively. I think we can say that *if* we had some way of knowing that P_2 is true, we would have no difficulty in understanding the logical foundation of inductive reasoning.

A brief explanation of the logical structure of inductive reasoning, *if we assume the Principle of the Uniformity of Nature* (P_2), might prove helpful at this point.

A typical instance of inductive reasoning would be the familiar one in which we infer, from the fact that all the crows we have observed are black, that all crows are black. The reasoning by which we arrive at this general conclusion is as follows:

Major premise: What is true of Crow 1, Crow 2, Crow 3, etc., is true of all crows.

Minor premise: Crow 1, Crow 2, Crow 3, etc., are black.

Conclusion: All crows are black.

Upon what basis, then, do we affirm the major premise? It should be clear that it is the general conclusion of a higher-level argument, the structure of which is as follows:

Major premise: The universe is not a chaos of random events; some uniformities are exhibited in phenomena widely separated in space and time.

Minor premise:	Crows are among those phenomena that exhibit such uniformities.
Conclusion:	What is true of Crow 1, Crow 2, Crow 3, etc., is true of all crows.

It is important to note that the conclusion of our argument—all crows are black—is only more or less probable and that this is exactly what we should expect if the logical structure of the argument is as I have said. The premises from which the conclusion is drawn are known with something less than absolute certainty; this uncertainty —or, as I should prefer to say, this *varying probability*—that attaches to the premises is accordingly passed on to the conclusion.

But how do we know with any degree of certainty that the universe exhibits some uniformities? How does this ultimate major premise of all inductive reasoning get established? This is the question that now has to be answered.

Two Kinds of Induction

We may make a beginning toward unraveling this puzzle if we make a distinction between what I shall call *informal* induction and *rigorous,* or *scientific,* induction. The former must have been practiced by man since the very emergence of the human species upon earth, and even man's prehuman ancestors must have employed something analogous to it; the latter has been practiced only within the last few hundred years.

Informal induction may very well be, as Hume said it was, nothing more than the habit of generalizing from our experience. Every human being, including the most primitive people on earth, believes a vast number of general truths on this basis. The general truths that an Eskimo knows in this way, it is evident, will be on the whole quite different from those known by a tribe that lives in equatorial Africa or a family of Australian aborigines. The Eskimo will know, for example, that snow is cold, that seals are good for food, that seal oil may be used for such-and-such purposes, and so on. A member of an African tribe will know that the midday sun is to be avoided, that certain sorts of animals are to be feared, that such-and-such berries are poison, and the like. And still other general truths will presumably be known by the aboriginal inhabitants of Australia.

Some of the things that people believe they "know" in this way may turn out to be false. Many generations of Africans must have believed, for example, that all men are black, and the Eskimos of the far north may have believed that all men live in houses made of snow. Informal induction, therefore, is not an entirely reliable procedure; but it is the starting point from which better things may come.

Let us suppose, now, a civilization in which a reasonably high level of culture has been achieved and in which there is, for some members of the society at least, sufficient leisure to cultivate intellectual pursuits. What materials would the thinkers of this culture have to work with? According to our account, they would have (a) a stock of general truths, or at any rate general beliefs, arrived at in the informal way described above and (b) as a strict correlate of this, a belief that nature exhibits some uniformities—the uniformities expressed in the particular set of beliefs that summarize the common experience of the people of that society.

In such a situation, it is natural that the following question should be asked: May there not be other, less obvious, uniformities in nature that no one has yet taken the trouble to observe? We know that nature exhibits some uniformities. Let us see if we can find others.

It is when this step is taken that we pass from the primitive to the scientific attitude toward the world and from informal to scientific inductive reasoning. To look for uniformity is quite a different thing from simply noting the uniformity that is obvious to everyone. In the case of informal induction, we are scarcely (if at all) aware of the fact that we are drawing an inference: we simply act *as if* certain uniformities obtain, without consciously considering the general truth that is therein implied. With scientific induction, however, the situation is different. Here we deliberately, carefully, painstakingly *attempt* to find some general truth that will tie together the apparently diverse data of experience.

Scientific induction differs from informal induction in at least four ways. First, in every instance of scientific induction we are quite consciously taking a risk. We are not simply summarizing what we have observed: we are deliberately going beyond what we have observed to affirm as a general truth a proposition that may, for all we know, be erroneous.

Second, in the case of scientific induction we actively try to disprove the generalization that is the conclusion of our inductive reasoning. When we engage in scientific inductive reasoning, we are not simply "reading off" the obvious general truths exhibited in the world; we are seriously attempting to discover uniformities that are not obvious to everyone, trying to find uniformities that hold without exception. Informal induction reveals nothing that is parallel to this.

Third, in the case of scientific induction we continue to maintain a critical, not-quite-convinced attitude toward even those uniformities that survive our best efforts to disprove them. The conclusion of a scientific induction, however impressive the evidence upon which it rests, is always subject to modification. With informal induction this is not the case.

Fourth, scientific induction, unlike informal induction, proceeds according to fixed rules. These rules, which were first given formal expression by John Stuart Mill (whose nomenclature is still in common use), specify the ways in which inductive reasoning can proceed with the minimum possibility of error. Mill's Methods, as they are called—the Method of Agreement, the Method of Difference, the Joint Method of Agreement and Difference, etc.—represent scientific induction fully conscious of its own procedures. It is these methods, implicit in the procedure of rigorous thinkers of every age and explicit in the work of Mill, that have produced the impressive results that make the modern era the age of science *par excellence*.

The situation, therefore, seems to be this. The Principle of the Uniformity of Nature appears to be the product of informal inductions that are themselves nothing more than the "reading off" of certain rather obvious uniformities exhibited in the everyday experience of man. The Principle of the Uniformity of Nature must, therefore, be a product of what Hume called our "habit" or "propensity" of looking for regularity amongst the diverse data of our experience. Once the principle of uniformity becomes known in this rather informal way, however, it serves as the major premise in the rigorous forms of inductive reasoning and is itself subjected to the same critical appraisal to which all of the conclusions of inductive reasoning are exposed. It therefore becomes more and more firmly established with each successful induction. Thus, the principle itself and the informal inductions upon which it was originally based are justified and rendered secure by the rigorous methods to which they have given rise.

If, as we have argued, the major premise of all scientific inductive reasoning rests on merely informal inductions, then it might appear that the reasoning that proceeds from that premise must itself share in the insecurity of that foundation. This objection, which it is natural to raise at this point, has been effectively answered by Mill, who stated:

> The precariousness of the method of simple enumeration is in an inverse ratio to the largeness of the generalization. The process is delusive and insufficient, exactly in proportion as the subject-matter of the observation is special and limited in extent. As the sphere widens, this unscientific method becomes less and less liable to mislead; and the most universal class of truths, the law of causation for instance, and the principles of number and of geometry, are duly and satisfactorily proved by that method alone.[1]

In spite of the fact that the Principle of the Uniformity of Nature rests on the foundation of the informal inductions of prescientific man, it is saved from insecurity by two factors: the extreme breadth

---

[1] John Stuart Mill, *A System of Logic*, III, xxi, 8th ed. (New York and London: Longmans, Green, 1956), p. 373.

of the principle itself and the fact that it has been subsequently tested and confirmed according to the critical spirit of the scientific mind. Thus it is able to function as a secure foundation for all subsequent inductive reasoning.

Hume's error, it appears to me, consists in the fact that he failed to analyze carefully enough the logical structure of inductive reasoning. He failed to make the all-important distinction between informal and scientific induction. Hume saw, correctly enough, that inductions of the scientific type presuppose the principle of uniformity, and from this he concluded that the principle itself must simply be gratuitously assumed. It required a century or more after Hume to bring to light the distinction he did not see and by which the problem of induction is solved.

STUDY QUESTIONS

1. What "disastrous consequences" does Empiricist say would follow if we were to accept Hume's skeptical conclusions regarding induction? Do you think he is right? If so, does this constitute a *reductio ad absurdum* of inductive skepticism, as Empiricist says it does?
2. What is the principle of uniformity? Is Empiricist right in saying that this principle constitutes "the ultimate major premise of all inductive reasoning"? Is it true that we would have a logical warrant for making inductive inferences if we could somehow establish the truth of this principle?
3. What exactly is the distinction that Empiricist makes between "informal" induction and "scientific" induction? What use does he make of this distinction in his subsequent argument?
4. How does Empiricist attempt to answer the objection that if the principle of uniformity is established by the relatively insecure method of "informal" induction, then all of the reasoning based upon this principle must be equally insecure? Are you convinced by his answer? Can you present a better one?

39

THE RATIONALIST'S WAY OUT

It is a continuous source of interest to observe the various ways in which empiricists twist and squirm in their vain attempts to find an acceptable alternative to the inductive skepticism of Hume. Hume's question has been, as Empiricist has hinted, a distinct embarrassment to empiricists—so much so that I suspect more converts to rationalism may have been won in this single point than on any other point to which rationalists commonly appeal in support of their position.

The empiricist is in a serious predicament. On the one hand, he is aware that inductive skepticism does lead to disastrous and, indeed, unacceptable consequences with respect to the status of a good deal of our knowledge of the world. On the other hand, he is committed to the proposition that empiricism is true—and Hume appears to have shown that on empiricist premises his skeptical conclusions cannot be avoided. But on empiricist grounds, Hume still has the final word; two centuries of effort have not produced a single convincing defense of inductive reasoning that does not violate the central tenet of empiricism. On the problem of induction, the only viable alternatives are skepticism and rationalism.

Critique of Constructive Empiricism

It should be apparent to everyone who is not blinded by empiricist dogmatism that the argument set forth in the preceding chapter does not succeed in its attempt to show that induction is a valid logical procedure. It is inadequate, as a matter of fact, in several different ways.

In the first place, it fails to grasp the true purport, the really radical character, of Hume's argument. Hume did not say, as Empiricist implies in the latter part of his essay, that it was only the reasoning of *scientists* that was placed in jeopardy by his critical questioning of the validity of induction. *All* inductive reasoning, he argued, proceeds on the assumption that nature is uniform, that the future will be like the past. This means, therefore, that anyone who would answer Hume must do one of two things: either he must show that Hume was mistaken in his claim that all inductive reasoning presupposes the Principle of the Uniformity of Nature or he must show that that principle is not itself a product of inductive reasoning. Since Empiricist has done neither of these, it is apparent that he has not really understood the radical character of Hume's question.

From this it is also clear, in the second place, that Empiricist's argument turns on a distinction that is more apparent than real. Inductive reasoning, like anything else, can be done either carelessly or carefully, and there is no harm in calling attention to this difference by calling the one "informal" and the other "rigorous" or "scientific" induction. But as soon as we recognize that this is all the distinction amounts to, it becomes apparent that we cannot make the use of it that Empiricist has attempted to make. Even "informal" induction, according to Hume's analysis, presupposes the principle of uniformity; unless Empiricist can exhibit the logical structure of "informal" induction in a way that escapes Hume's criticism, it will not be of any help to him as a foundation for "scientific" induction.

It is fair to say, therefore, that in the last analysis Empiricist's argument is circular. The very principle that he hopes to establish by means of "informal" induction—the Principle of the Uniformity of Nature—must be presupposed before the first such inductive generalization can be made.

Empiricist seems to have realized that his argument leaves something to be desired, and near the end of his essay he tries to patch it up as best he can. This he does by (a) a vague reference to the subsequent "purification" of the principle of uniformity once it has given birth to "scientific" induction and (b) gratuitously assuming the general principle that "the wider the generalization the more certain it is."

I do not rightly know how to distinguish between a "purified" and an "unpurified" principle, but I think I know what Empiricist has in mind. The Principle of the Uniformity of Nature, according to his account, still carries the taint of its unscientific past: it is not, in its natural state, a suitable principle for "scientific" use. It needs, therefore, to be "purified"—or, to put it more prosaically, to be reestablished by scientific induction. But this, quite obviously, cannot be done, since on Empiricist's own account "scientific" induction presupposes the unbaptized principle. It is no wonder that the reference to "purification" was rather vague!

Nor is Empiricist's case rendered any more convincing by the introduction of Mill's suggestion that the broader the generalization is, the more certain it is. This does not even appear to be true: it rather seems to be the case that the more cautious we are about generalizations—the closer we stay to what we actually observe—the more confident we may be about the correctness of those generalizations. But let us assume, for the moment, that Mill is right in this. How does he claim to know that it is true? Is it a priori? Obviously, no empiricist can allow this. Is it, then, the product of inductive reasoning? Then the validity of induction must already be assumed, and no principle that is established thereby can be called in to enhance its validity.

The Logical Premise of Inductive Reasoning

There are, I have suggested, only two possible ways to counter Hume's attack on inductive reasoning. One is to show that the Principle of the Uniformity of Nature is not itself the product of inductive reasoning. The other is to show that Hume was mistaken in his belief that all inductive reasoning presupposes the Principle of the Uniformity of Nature.

Some rationalists have attempted the first of these two alternatives as a way of reestablishing the validity of inductive reasoning, but not successfully in my opinion. It seems evident, in the first place, that we do not know a priori that the Principle of the Uniformity of Nature in its "strong," or deterministic, form (P_1, see p. 291) is true. I myself have grave doubts about the truth of the principle when it is stated in this way; hence, I cannot justly be said to "know" it either a priori or a posteriori. A defense of inductive reasoning that depends on an appeal to a priori knowledge at this point seems, therefore, to be very weak. On the other hand, we do know that the principle in its weaker form (P_2 or P_3) is true, but it is quite obvious that the principle in this form is itself an inductive generalization—is, in other words, known a posteriori. Our knowledge of the principle in this form, therefore, presupposes the validity of inductive reasoning, and the ground of that validity must be sought in some other place.

A clue to the correct solution of this problem may be found in the way by which we are able to proceed from premises to a conclusion in deductive reasoning. Our ability to do so depends on certain rules of inference that we know a priori (see Chapter 36). May it not be, then, that in inductive reasoning it is some *logical principle* that enables us to make our inferences? Let us reexamine the logical structure of an inductive argument to see whether this is not in fact the case.

We may take as our example the well-worn one about the crows. We start, in this case, with what we shall call the observational premise—that N crows have been observed, and all of them have been black. From this we feel justified in inferring the probable but not certain conclusion that all crows are black. The argument appears to be this:

Observational premise: N crows have been observed, and all of them have been black.

. . . .

Inductive conclusion: It is more or less probable that all crows are black.

If we are on the right track, we ought to seek for some logical principle—some rule of inductive inference—that will enable us to draw the general conclusion. The principle should be such as to (a) provide a warrant for our drawing the inference and (b) account for the fact that the inference is only probable, never absolutely certain.

The principle for which we are seeking might be stated: "The more often two things have been observed to be conjoined in nature, the more probable it is that they are always so conjoined." Putting this principle—which I shall call the logical premise—in the place of the elliptical dots in our argument, we get the following:

Observational premise: N crows have been observed, and all of them have been black.

Logical premise: The more often two things have been observed to be conjoined in nature, the more probable it is that they are always so conjoined.

Inductive conclusion: It is more or less probable that all crows are black.

There are three observations that I should like to make regarding this principle. First, it should be noted that when this premise is supplied, it is no longer a mystery how we are able to draw our inductive conclusion. The reasoning that is involved is, in fact, deductive: the conclusion is validly inferred from the premises, as in any sound deductive argument.

Second, the principle does account for the fact that inductive generalizations are made with varying degrees of certainty. The conclusion—that it is more or less probable that all crows are black—follows rigorously from the premises and is known with the same certainty that the premises are known. The proposition that all crows are black is itself only more or less probable (as is the case with any empirical generalization), and this probability is explicitly stated in the conclusion.

Third, the argument, thus stated, exhibits the fact that the probability of the empirical generalization that appears in the conclusion varies directly with the quantity of evidence upon which it is based. If I have seen one crow, my generalization has a very low degree of probability. If I have seen a hundred, the probability increases. And if I have seen thousands and have checked the reports of others who have seen thousands more, the probability becomes very high. The principle as stated does, therefore, correspond to our intuitive conviction that the greater the quantity of evidence upon which a generalization is based, the greater the probability that it is true without exception.

I spoke just now about "our intuitive conviction" with regard to the quantity of evidence upon which a generalization is based. It seems clear to me that we do in fact have such a conviction—indeed, that we *know* that this is the case. What we have called the logical premise of all inductive reasoning, however, is nothing more nor less than a statement in slightly different terms of this very truth. To say that something is known intuitively is to say that it is known a priori. In identifying this logical premise, therefore, we may plausibly claim to have discovered the a priori ground of the validity of inductive reasoning.

Hume's chief error, if this analysis is correct, consists in his assertion that inductive reasoning always involves an appeal to the Principle of the Uniformity of Nature. This principle, he correctly observed, is itself a product of inductive reasoning, and he accordingly drew the conclusion that all inductive reasoning is circular—is, in fact, no reasoning at all. Empiricist accepted Hume's analysis of the structure of inductive reasoning and attempted unsuccessfully to show that the Principle of the Uniformity of Nature could be established without appealing in the process to that very principle. It is only when this initial assumption as to the structure of inductive reasoning is rejected that the correct solution to the problem becomes apparent.

I do not suppose, however, that the solution I have proposed will be of any comfort to empiricists, because it carries with it the rather surprising conclusion that there is an a priori element even in most a posteriori knowledge—in all that goes beyond the particular data of direct observation. This includes, obviously, all of the general findings of the natural sciences as well as the everyday truths that we all take for granted every day of our lives. To an empiricist, however, this conclusion is not only surprising, it is totally unacceptable; for to accept it is to concede that empiricism is a misguided epistemological theory.

It seems fair to say in conclusion, therefore, that properly understood the *reductio ad absurdum* argument that Empiricist directed against inductive skepticism is an equally effective demonstration of the absurdity of empiricism itself. The real merit of Hume's argument is to have shown precisely that skepticism with respect to inductive reasoning is an inevitable consequence of empiricism. It follows, therefore, that anyone who wishes to maintain the empiricist position must be prepared to accept the consequences of inductive skepticism, and, if those consequences are indeed absurd—as Empiricist and I both believe they are—then empiricism itself is an absurd and untenable position. When this is clearly understood, the correctness of the solution here proposed may become even more apparent.

STUDY QUESTIONS

1. Rationalist suggests that anyone who would answer Hume on the problem of induction "must do one of two things." What are they? Are these the only ways of answering Hume? Is it true that Empiricist has done neither?
2. Is Rationalist right in saying that the difference between "informal" and "scientific" induction is nothing more than the difference between careless and careful reasoning? Is the *logical structure* the same in both instances? If so, does this seriously damage Empiricist's argument?
3. What "clue" to the solution of the problem of induction does Rationalist claim to find in "the way by which we are able to proceed from premises to a conclusion in deductive reasoning"? Does this strike you as a promising way to approach this problem? Do any of the conclusions you have drawn in your study of earlier problems prevent you from pursuing this approach?
4. Which of the "two things" that Rationalist says one must do to answer Hume does Rationalist himself attempt to do? Does he succeed? How would you expect Hume to reply to Rationalist's argument?

40

THE PROPOSAL
OF PRAGMATISM

Whenever the discussion of a philosophical question reaches a complete impasse, as the discussion of the problem of induction appears to have done, it is a good idea to ask whether there is not something wrong with the question itself—whether, for example, some incorrect assumption is not being made or some impossible requirement being set up for any answer that is to be regarded as acceptable. Should this prove to be the case with regard to some particular dispute, it is not surprising that all of the parties to the dispute should end up by proving nothing at all and that their attacks and counterattacks should serve no other purpose than to convince saner men that the disputants simply do not understand the business that they are attempting to prosecute with such ostentatious vigor.

That the three-way discussion of the problem of induction has indeed reached an impasse cannot be seriously doubted by any impartial observer. The absurdity of inductive skepticism and the inadequacy of what is quaintly called "constructive empiricism" have already been sufficiently demonstrated, and, if Rationalist appears for the moment to have the upper hand in the argument, it is only because for the time being he has had the opportunity to speak last. It is an easy matter to show, however, that his position is as untenable as the other two, and by way of clearing our minds for a fresh and more promising way of looking at this old problem, we shall begin by pointing out what is wrong with the rationalist position.

Critique of Rationalism

We may begin by observing that the principle that "the more often two things have been observed to be conjoined in nature, the more probable it is that they are always so conjoined" is hardly a very promising candidate for an a priori truth, even according to the criteria that rationalists themselves commonly employ in identifying such truths. Most rationalists are in the habit of following Immanuel Kant on this point, and the two criteria of a priori knowledge to which they customarily point are what Kant called the "necessity" and the "universality" of such truths. Kant said:

> If we have a proposition which in being thought is thought as necessary, it is an *a priori* judgment, and [if] a judgment is thought with *strict universality,* that is, in such manner that no exception is allowed as possible, it is not derived from experience, but is valid absolutely *a priori.*[1]

It may be argued with some plausibility that Rationalist's "rule of inductive inference" has the requisite universality, though we could raise a question as to whether it really does exhibit the "strict" universality of which Kant spoke. It does not seem that an exception to this principle is inconceivable in the way that an exception to an arithmetical truth is inconceivable; but I shall not press this point. What is clear is that this principle does not exhibit the necessity that is alleged to be the hallmark of truths known a priori. There is nothing self-evidently true about this principle, as there is, for example, about the axioms of geometry. If we are reasonably sure that the principle is sound, the reason is, surely, because we have found that it *works.* And this has certain implications for our whole understanding of this problem that we shall have to develop shortly. For the present, however, we may be content to have shown that even on Rationalist's own terms it cannot be plausibly maintained that what has been offered as the principle of all inductive reasoning is known a priori.

In addition, I do not think that Rationalist has succeeded in disengaging inductive reasoning from the assumption that nature is uniform, for the logical principle is, after all, only as secure as our belief that nature does not behave in a way that is wholly capricious—as secure, in short, as the Principle of the Uniformity of Nature. Hume's objection is equally as devastating in its effect on Rationalist's position as Rationalist has perceived it to be on constructive empiricism: "If there be any suspicion that the course of nature may change, and that the past may be no rule for the future, all experience becomes

---

[1] Immanuel Kant, *Critique of Pure Reason*, Intro., II, Norman Kemp Smith (tr.) (New York: St. Martin's, 1965), pp. 43–44.

useless and can give rise to no inference or conclusion." [2] To doubt the Principle of the Uniformity of Nature is at the same time to doubt the validity of the proposed rule of inductive inference. Thus, Rationalist's solution to the problem is no better than that of Constructive Empiricist whom he so roundly criticizes.

We are left, therefore, with three positions—inductive skepticism, constructive empiricism, and rationalism—all of which are seen to be untenable. Yet these are the only positions that it is possible to take with respect to the question that has been stated. Something, evidently, has gone wrong. There is something artificial, something incorrect about the assumptions upon which the whole argument thus far has been proceeding. Let us try to locate the error and raise the discussion to a new and more fruitful level.

Truth

There is one assumption that all three previous writers on this question share in common, and that is that a statement is true if and only if what it asserts to be the case really is the case. They have all assumed the *correspondence* theory of truth. Proceeding on this assumption, they have asked: How can we possibly know that reality corresponds to the assertions that we make when we utter an empirical generalization? We know, indeed, that reality corresponds to the simple observational statements with which we begin; but how can we know that it corresponds to the statement with which we conclude—a statement that leaps far beyond what we have observed and purports to describe phenomena that we have not observed and perhaps never shall observe?

To ask this question is, I submit, to ask a question that cannot be answered. That is why none of the illustrious philosophers who have tried to do so have been able to answer it. To show why this is an unanswerable question is our task in the remainder of this essay.

William James provided the key with which we may hope to unlock this old puzzle when he said:

> There can *be* no difference anywhere that doesn't *make* a difference elsewhere—no difference in abstract truth that doesn't express itself in a difference in concrete fact and in conduct consequent upon that fact, imposed on somebody, sometime, and somewhere . . . Ideas . . . become true just in so far as they help us to get into satisfactory relation with other parts of our experience, to summarize them and get about among them by conceptual short-cuts instead of following the interminable succession of particular phenomena.[3]

---

[2] David Hume, in Charles W. Hendel (ed.), *An Inquiry Concerning Human Understanding* (New York: Liberal Arts, 1955), p. 51.

[3] William James, *Pragmatism* (New York and London: Longmans, Green, 1959), pp. 49–50, 58; also see pp. 197–234.

Let us examine these ideas and see how they can help us in coming to some satisfactory view with respect to the problem of induction.

"There can be no difference that doesn't make a difference." This means that the meaning of any idea *consists* precisely in the consequences that it is supposed to have for either our own experience or that of someone else. The meaning of the idea that there are tigers in India, for example, consists simply in—to quote James again—the "procession of mental associates and motor consequences that follow on the thought, and that would lead harmoniously, if followed out, into some ideal or real context, or even into the immediate presence, of the tigers." [4] The notion that there could be two different ideas that have identical practical consequences is simply meaningless.

Another way to put this is to say that ideas are "plans for action." We never desire to know just for the sake of knowing. We desire to know in order that we shall be able to get about in the world of our experience, in order that we shall be able to pursue our purposes in the world (no matter what those purposes might be). It is only in this way that we are able to choose, from among the infinite things that we might conceivably attempt to understand, those things that we do in fact seek to understand; it is *our interests, our purposes*, that determine the selection.

To say, then, that an idea is true is not to say that it is an exact "copy" of reality. It is to say, rather, that it works, that it enables us to move about in the world of our experience. "True ideas are those that we can assimilate, validate, corroborate and verify. False ideas are those that we can not." [5] This is the only sense of truth and falsehood that has any relation to the purposes for which we wish to distinguish the two—the only meaning, therefore, that this distinction can possibly have for us.

Truth, therefore, is always truth for someone. What was true for medieval man—the ideas that were adequate to enable him to get around in the world of his experience—is not necessarily true for us. Experience, as James so aptly put it, has ways of "boiling over," thus compelling each generation to modify what was received from the previous generation as the truth—to make its own truth, so to speak. But the idea of a purely objective truth, a truth that has no practical consequences for human experience, is an empty and meaningless concept. The reasons that lead us to call an idea true are precisely the reasons that make it true.

The idea of an "absolute truth," therefore, can be nothing other than the idea of a truth that would be adequate to all possible experience, a truth that no experience could ever require us to modify or reject.

---

[4] William James, *The Meaning of Truth* (New York and London: Longmans, Green, 1910), pp. 44–45.

[5] James, *Pragmatism, op. cit.*, p. 201.

Such truth may be the ideal goal toward which all of our attempts to know the truth are aiming, but it is not the quality of those provisional and temporary truths that constitute the truth-for-us. The truth-for-us is simply the truth that works, the truth that enables us to get about in the "booming, buzzing confusion" that is the world of our experience. It is, as James said, "the expedient in the way of our thinking."

Let us now return to the problem of induction and see how the ideas we have just been considering can aid us in reaching its correct solution.

The Problem of Induction Revisited

Suppose a man speaks to us as follows: "In all of my experience thus far, I have observed nothing but black crows. It seems to be true, therefore, that all crows are black. But how can I be sure that this is true absolutely? How can I be sure that the future will be like the past, that all 'future' crows will be black just as all 'past' crows have been? How can I infer from the observed to the unobserved?"

If we have understood the ideas set forth in the preceding pages, we shall have no difficulty in responding to such a query. We shall have to say, obviously, that our puzzled friend cannot be sure that the generalization that summarizes his past experience will hold in the future, but that, until experience itself contradicts him, he would, nonetheless, be well advised to regard his generalization as true. And what we would mean by this is, quite simply, that so long as no *facts* arise to compel him to alter his generalization it will serve to enable him to get around within a certain segment of his experience (to tie together, for example, what he sees in the forest, what he reads in books, and what he hears in the conversation of others). If something occurs within the field of his experience that gives the lie to his belief, then and only then will it cease to be true; then, too, he will be compelled to seek for a new generalization that is sufficient to encompass this new experience as well as the old.

All parties to the dispute about the validity of inductive inferences have been obsessed with the idea of "absolute truth." It is this idea of truth that they have in mind when they ask, How can we know that the generalizations that are the products of our inductive inferences are true? They have sought, accordingly, to find a logical method that would somehow guarantee their truth. Hume, at least, saw that this was not possible and drew the skeptical consequences with which we are all familiar. Those who came after him continued the search for a method, with the inconclusive results that have made this problem the scandal of philosophy.

It is interesting to note that both rationalists and empiricists who have addressed themselves to this problem have attempted to validate induction by exhibiting it as, after all, a concealed form of *deductive* reasoning. The assumption has been, apparently, that deductive reasoning somehow "guarantees" the truth of its conclusions and that if induction could be shown to be deduction, then somehow the "absolute truth" of its conclusions could be conclusively established.

The truth of the matter is, however, that the mere form of a man's reasoning can never guarantee the truth of his conclusion. The conclusion of a valid deductive argument must, of course, be true if the premises are true, since the conclusion does nothing more than to assert explicitly what has already been asserted implicitly in the premises. But the form of the argument tells nothing at all about the truth of the premises. To determine that, you must go to experience; to go to experience is, in the last analysis, to invoke the pragmatic criterion of truth.

The way of wisdom in this matter, therefore, is to refuse to answer Hume's question on its own terms. The question, Is induction a valid logical procedure? presupposes that it is the validity or invalidity of the procedure that must decide whether or not we are warranted in believing that our empirical generalizations are true and that the truth of our generalizations consists in their being exact "copies" of reality. Both of these assumptions, we have argued, are mistaken. The truth of our generalizations consists in the fact that they work (in the sense already described), and our warrant for believing them is also simply the fact that they work. To see this is not, obviously, to answer Hume's question; it is, on the contrary, to see that no answer is required.

The root of the difficulty, actually, is the failure to recognize that intelligence is simply a tool with which man has been endowed through the evolutionary process, the precise function of which is to enable man to cope with a highly complex environment. The function of reflective thought is to transform a situation in which we experience obscurity, doubt, conflict, or disturbance of some sort into one that is clear, coherent, settled, and harmonious. Insofar as in our experience we do not encounter obscurity, doubt, conflict, etc., our habitual patterns of behavior serve us adequately and intelligence does not come into play. The business of intelligence, then, is to find suitable behavior patterns when experience confronts us with a situation containing some novel elements. The "problems" that intellect is equipped to solve are, therefore, profoundly practical problems.

Now the problem of induction is not a practical problem. Hume himself admits this when he says, "As an agent, I am quite satisfied on the point." [6] It is a purely theoretical problem that arises only if we try to press intelligence into a task for which it was never intended,

---

6 Hume, *op. cit.*, p. 52.

namely, the disinterested pursuit of abstract truths having no practical bearing on the conduct of life. To recognize this, and to draw the appropriate consequences from this recognition, is at last to find an answer to Hume—not, indeed, the answer he sought, but the only answer to which his question is entitled. For the best answer to this question, as indeed to many philosophical questions, is the one that satisfies us in such a way that we are no longer inclined to bother ourselves about it.

STUDY QUESTIONS

1. What criticisms does Pragmatist direct against Rationalist's attempted solution of the problem of induction? Can you think of any way that Rationalist might defend himself against these criticisms?
2. Are you inclined to agree with Pragmatist that the discussion of the problem thus far has reached an impasse and that the reason for this may be that all of the parties to the dispute have been making some incorrect assumption? Are you equally persuaded that the assumption in question is the one Pragmatist says it is? Explain.
3. What is the theory of truth that Pragmatist offers as an alternative to the "correspondence" theory? Does this strike you as a correct description of what we ordinarily mean by "truth"? Or is Pragmatist not suggesting that this is what we *do* ordinarily mean, but rather what we *ought* to mean?
4. How, according to Pragmatist, does the pragmatic theory of truth aid in the solution of the problem of induction? How do you think a Humean skeptic might respond to Pragmatist's proposal?

41

A FOOTNOTE
TO HUME

Although I find myself in general agreement with the sentiments expressed in the opening paragraphs of the last chapter, I am not at all convinced that Pragmatist has succeeded in putting his finger on whatever it is that makes the problem of induction, as he says, "artificial." Pragmatist writes with the enthusiasm and the disdain of a man who has just taken in hand a new and, to him, exciting principle, by means of which he proposes to lay low all sorts of problems that have troubled able minds for centuries. The precise connection between the pragmatist theory of truth, however—even if we accept that theory— and the problem of induction is, to say the least, somewhat difficult to discern; and it is far from having been proved that that theory itself is one that it would be wise or prudent for us to accept.

Rather than attempting to assess the strengths and weaknesses of Pragmatist's argument, however, I propose that we return to the original problem as stated by Hume. Hume, as I shall hope to show, was not right in everything that he said about this problem, but his analysis is still more perceptive than any of the subsequent attempts that have been made to find a satisfactory answer to him. If we find that we are able to answer Hume without adopting the questionable theory of truth that is advocated in the previous chapter, I think we may safely ignore what is there proposed.

I spoke just now about finding an "answer" to Hume. Strictly speaking, however, I do not intend to propose an answer to Hume but to show, on the contrary, that his question ought not to trouble us in the way that it is usually supposed to do. I shall, as a matter of fact, agree with a great deal that Hume has said. My comments, therefore, should not be construed as an attempt to refute Hume; they are, rather, only a footnote to Hume's own penetrating remarks on induction that appear in Section IV of *An Inquiry Concerning Human Understanding*.

Where Hume Was Right

Hume argued, it will be recalled, that there is no possible way of showing that induction is a valid logical procedure. Induction depends, said Hume, on the assumption that nature is uniform and that what has been observed to be the case in the past is, therefore, a safe guide as to what may be expected to occur in the future. This assumption, as Hume correctly perceived, can in no way be established. It is evidently not known a priori, nor can it be established inductively (since we could not reason inductively without assuming the very principle that is to be proved). We must conclude, therefore, said Hume, that induction is not a valid logical procedure and that our propensity to draw inductive inferences is nothing but a habit that is itself a product of the repeated observation of "constant conjunction."

It seems to me that after two full centuries of more or less vigorous discussion of this problem, Hume remains triumphant on each of the following points:

1. *Inductive reasoning does presuppose the Principle of the Uniformity of Nature.* Constructive empiricism, as we saw, does not even attempt to deny this; what it attempts to do, with notorious lack of success, is to establish the principle by a kind of "preinductive inference" in order that induction proper can get under way. Rationalist's attempt at a defense of induction does indeed pretend to deny the necessity of this assumption, but it has already been sufficiently shown that the "logical principle" that Rationalist attempts to put in its place derives whatever plausibility it has from this very assumption. On this point, therefore, Hume must be judged to have been correct.

2. *The Principle of the Uniformity of Nature cannot itself be established by inductive reasoning.* Hume wrote:

> We have said that all arguments concerning existence are founded on the relation of cause and effect, that our knowledge of that relation is derived entirely from experience, and that all our experimental conclusions proceed upon the supposition that the future will be conformable to the past. To endeavor, therefore, the proof of this last supposition by probable arguments, or arguments regarding existence, must be evidently going in a circle and taking that for granted which is the very point in question.[1]

---

[1] David Hume, in Charles W. Hendel (ed.), *An Inquiry Concerning Human Understanding* (New York: Liberal Arts, 1955), pp. 49–50.

Constructive Empiricist's essay, with its obvious circularity, is the best possible demonstration that on this point also Hume was right.

3. *The Principle of the Uniformity of Nature is not known a priori.* This is a point that is not susceptible of direct proof, since the statement that something is or is not known a priori can never be either proved or disproved. It is significant, however, that even many rationalists are far from convinced that this principle is known a priori, and they have directed their efforts toward finding some other principle upon which to ground the validity of induction. If anyone is disposed to hold, therefore, that the Principle of the Uniformity of Nature is known a priori, I can think of no argument that might change his mind; but the majority of philosophers who have struggled with this question, rationalists and empiricists alike, are united in their judgment that in so saying he would be simply mistaken. On this point, too, the decision must be in favor of Hume.

The conclusion appears inescapable, therefore, that induction is based on a principle that is known neither a priori nor a posteriori; consequently, it is not known at all. Induction must, therefore, be judged to be incurably irrational. This was Hume's conclusion, and since it follows from the three propositions that we have just considered, we must also agree with Hume on this. *Induction is not a valid logical procedure.*

Where Hume Was Wrong

It seems to me, however, that there are two points on which Hume was clearly mistaken, and it is the failure of most of Hume's critics to see these mistakes that makes his attack on induction appear to have such devastating consequences.

First, Hume was mistaken in his view that our propensity to believe that nature operates according to certain invariable laws is nothing but a habit that, like other habits, is a product of repetition—repetition, in this case, of the repeated observation of what Hume called "constant conjunction." "From causes which appear similar," he said, "we expect similar effects." [2] Induction has no logical foundation, but it has a psychological foundation in the phenomenon that we call "habit."

The reduction of the process of induction to habit does not agree completely with what we know about the way that habits become established. What typically occurs when a habit is getting established is that things that at first have to be done quite consciously and deliberately come at length to be done effortlessly and, as we say, almost

---

2 *Ibid.*, p. 50.

automatically. In learning to drive, for example—or to type, or to ski —we begin by applying certain rules, certain "laws" if you will; but when the operations in question have become a matter of habit, we are scarcely aware of applying rules: we simply do what we have learned to do. Nothing comparable to this appears to occur in the case of induction. We do not at first "induct" deliberately and with effort, and then perform with less and less conscious effort as we become better at doing it. It seems highly unlikely, therefore, that our propensity to draw inductive inferences is, as Hume said, a habit established by repetition.

Even if Hume's account of our inductive propensity as a habit established by repetition were psychologically sound, it is inadequate in yet another respect. There is no such thing as "repetition" pure and simple: repetition must be repetition *for someone,* there must be someone who interprets some event as a repetition of some earlier event. This means, however, that there must be some point of view, some system of expectations or interests that leads us to note certain similarities between what is happening now and what happened at some earlier time. It is our point of view—the interests and the expectations that we bring to an event—that determines what is to count as a repetition of some earlier event or events. It is evident, therefore, that these expectations are *prior to,* and not *products of,* repetition. Hume's attempt to explain our expectation that the future will resemble the past as a product of repetition must, therefore, be regarded as a failure.

This brings us to Hume's second error: his uncritical and mistaken assumption that it is by induction that we arrive at interesting general conclusions regarding the laws that govern empirical phenomena. Hume assumed that the everyday general truths that we all take for granted in ordering our lives, as well as the more subtle generalizations that we claim to establish in the natural sciences, are one and all "inductive inferences"; and having shown that induction is not logically valid, he concluded that we have no rational basis for believing these generalizations to be true. It is because these truths appear threatened, and because we cannot tolerate the thought that so much of our supposed knowledge should turn out to be no knowledge at all, that we are so upset at the thought that induction is not a valid logical procedure. It is the rationality of our belief in these truths, not the logical credentials of induction itself, that we feel obliged to defend. If, therefore, we can succeed in showing that our knowledge of general empirical truths is indeed obtained by a noninductive procedure, we should have no difficulty in accepting with equanimity Hume's negative conclusion regarding the rationality of induction.

How General Empirical Truths Are Known

It is my contention that the correct account of the origin and status of our knowledge of empirical truths is as follows:

1. Our aim, in seeking empirical knowledge, is to achieve a true description of the world. The ideal goal of all science is to achieve a description that is so accurate and so complete that everything that occurs can be understood as an instance of some general law or laws. (It will be noted that in saying this I am disagreeing with the so-called "pragmatic" or "instrumentalist" theory of truth set forth in the preceding chapter.)
2. We can never be sure that the description of the world that at any time we suppose to be true really is true, though we can sometimes be reasonably sure that in some respects it is false.
3. The method by which we replace inadequate descriptions of the world with more adequate ones is not the method of induction, but the method of *conjecture and refutation*. All our knowledge of general empirical truths is at best hypothetical; to say that some empirical generalization is true is only to say that despite our best efforts to do so we have thus far been able to discover no counter-examples.

To hold a certain hypothesis about the world, to believe that certain phenomena are governed by such-and-such laws, is to have a certain set of expectations about what will happen under such-and-such conditions. In science we express this by saying that on the basis of this or that law we can "make predictions," and our predictions are descriptions before the fact of what we expect to occur whenever a given set of conditions is fulfilled. Contrary to what is sometimes said, it is not the case that an empirical hypothesis is only as secure as the evidence on which it is based; a hypothesis is secure in direct proportion to the amount of effort that has been expended in the attempt to disprove it. Any number of hypotheses may be invented to account for almost any set of empirical facts; it is not the hypothesis that is supported by the greatest number of favorable examples, but the one that survives our best efforts to find counter-examples that wins the right to be admitted to the fund of human knowledge.

Our knowledge of empirical truths, therefore, is nothing but the set of beliefs about the world that we have adopted in order to account for our expectations with respect to the world. There is nothing infallible, nothing final, nothing definitive about such knowledge. A hypothesis that seems adequate for a time may at length have to be revised, as phenomena are discovered that do not conform to the expectations (predictions) we were led to have (make) on the basis of our supposition that the hypothesis was true. Then we must seek to devise a new hypothesis, one that will account for the new phenomena as well as the old, and the search for counter-examples to the new hypothesis must begin anew.

Advances in our knowledge of general empirical truths, accordingly, always come about by way of revising our earlier hypotheses, of replacing less adequate hypotheses with more adequate ones. Every hypothesis that we propose will, of course, have been preceded by observations—the observations it was invented to explain. But those observations, in turn, must have been made within the context of an earlier hypothesis or set of hypotheses: it was precisely because the earlier hypothesis did not explain the observations in question that the new hypothesis had to be devised.

Where, then, does the whole process begin? The answer must be that it begins with the inborn expectations with which we enter the world. A newborn child expects the world to serve his needs—to feed him when he is hungry, warm him when he is cold, and so on. His initial hypothesis, we might say, is that the world is always just as he wants it to be. This is not a very adequate hypothesis, but it (or something like it) must be the starting point for every human being. And from that point to the affirmation of the most subtle and sophisticated theory in nuclear physics the process must lead through countless revisions and refinements of hypotheses successively advanced and discarded. Every instance of learning is a modification of what was previously known.

Among the expectations with which every child enters the world is, apparently, the expectation that he will find some uniformity among the diverse phenomena that occur in the world of his experience. The experience of finding regularity does not create the habit of expecting it, as Hume said: on the contrary, the expectation that we shall find regularity gives rise to the habit of looking for it, of demanding it, of searching for it even when it is not obviously present. This is a most fortunate habit, for without it scientific inquiry could never flourish—but that is another matter.

It is time to conclude. Hume argued, as we have seen, that induction is not a valid logical procedure. In this, according to our view, he was right. Hume also believed, however, that in demonstrating the invalidity of inductive reasoning he was demonstrating the irrationality of our supposed knowledge of general empirical truths. In this, if our account is correct, Hume was mistaken. The true import of Hume's analysis of induction does not consist in the questions it raises about the status of empirical generalizations: it consists rather in the convincing demonstration that induction cannot in fact be the method by which scientific inquiry is carried on. It is one of the ironies of intellectual history that so much effort should have been devoted to the futile effort to find a suitable defense for induction instead of being directed toward a more searching analysis of the true nature of scientific inquiry.

STUDY QUESTIONS

1. The author of this chapter mentions three specific points on which, in his judgment, Hume was right. Do you agree? What is the view of each of the previous writers with respect to each of these points?
2. What objections does the author of this chapter raise with respect to Hume's account of induction as a "habit"? Are his objections sound? (Consider, for example, poor study habits. Do they get established in the way described? How about driving habits? eating habits? shaving habits?)
3. What exactly does the author of this chapter propose as an alternative to induction? Is he right in saying that this method, rather than induction, is the method by which advances are made in our knowledge of general empirical truths? Does this account really avoid the difficulties raised by Hume?
4. Would you classify the author of this chapter as a rationalist or an empiricist? On what basis?
5. Which of the views set forth in this chapter are you inclined to agree with? Which do you disagree with? About which, if any, are you still in doubt?
6. If you had now to take some position with respect to the problem of induction, what would that position be? What seem to you to be the strongest reasons in favor of this position? What do you regard as the most serious objections that might be raised against it?

Black, Max. *Problems of Analysis*. Ithaca, N.Y.: Cornell University Press, 1954, chaps. 10–12.

Feigl, Herbert. "The Logical Character of the Principle of Induction," in H. Feigl and W. Sellars (eds.). *Readings in Philosophical Analysis*. New York: Appleton-Century-Crofts, 1949.

Hume, David. *An Inquiry Concerning Human Understanding*. Many editions. See Sections IV and V.

James, William. *Pragmatism and Other Essays*. Cleveland, Ohio: World Publishing Co., 1965. See Lecture VI, "Pragmatism's Conception of Truth."

Mill, John Stuart. *A System of Logic*. Toronto: University of Toronto Press, 1966. See especially Book III, Chapters 1–5.

Nagel, Ernest. *Logic Without Metaphysics*. New York: Free Press, 1956. See Part II, Chapter 7, "The Ground of Induction."

Popper, Karl. *Conjectures and Refutations*. New York: Basic Books, 1963. See especially Pages 33–59.

Russell, Bertrand. *Human Knowledge*. New York: Simon and Schuster, 1962 (paperbound). See Part VI, "Postulates of Scientific Inference."

Strawson, P. F. *Introduction to Logical Theory*. New York: Wiley, 1952, chap. 9.

Wright, Georg Henrik von. *Treatise on Induction and Probability*. Paterson, N.J.: Littlefield, Adams, 1960 (paperbound).

PART IX

THE ONTOLOGICAL STATUS OF THE PHYSICAL WORLD

42

COMMONSENSE REALISM AND ITS CRITICS

"Ontological status" is a phrase that is not used in ordinary conversation. It is, rather, a part of the technical vocabulary of philosophers. Let us begin our discussion of the problem of the ontological status of the physical world by trying to make clear what philosophers are talking about when they use this rather forbidding-sounding combination of words.

To talk about the ontological status of something is to talk about the kind of being that it has. To say that the ontological status of X is this or that is to say something about X's *mode of existence:* it is to say in precisely what sense it is true to say that there *are* X's. Let us consider a few examples.

It makes sense to say that there are such things as dreams. The word "dream" does not denote a nonentity. It denotes something real, some real occurrence. But what sort of occurrence? What really are dreams? What is their ontological status? Someone might reply that a dream is an experience that a person has in his astral body while his physical body is asleep. Most of us would probably say that a dream is a series of occurrences that take place in our imagination while we are asleep. To reply in either of these ways is to say something about the *kind* of reality that a dream has. The disagreement that is apparent in these two answers is a disagreement about the ontological status of dreams, a disagreement about what sort of thing the item in question is.

Consider the case of angels. What really are angels? Someone might say that angels are rational, sexless, winged creatures existing in heaven and serving God in a variety of ways. Someone else might say that angels are mythical beings, once imagined to exist in an imaginary heaven, with no more existence in reality than the elves and fairies in the familiar children's tales. Once again, the disagreement is over the ontological status of angels. To affirm either position is to hold a particular view as to the kind of being or mode of existence of whatever it is that is denoted by the term "angels."

Let us consider a third example. Someone remarks, "I was at the theatre last night and saw Othello kill Desdemona. What a bloody sight!" A bystander exclaims (not in jest), "How terrible! Did they catch the murderer? Is he in jail now? Will you have to be a witness at his trial?" The bystander, in this example, has mistaken the ontological status of the event in question. He has interpreted a scene in a play, a fictitious murder, as if it were an actual murder; he has treated Othello and Desdemona as if they were real people instead of fictitious characters in a dramatic production.

Three observations may be made at this point. The first observation is that what we are prepared to regard as "live options," with respect to questions of ontological status, depends in part on our world-view, on the kind of picture of reality we have. The "astral body" theory of dreams is not a live option unless our picture of reality includes a theory about "astral bodies" that are able to leave their physical counterparts on occasion, participate in various adventures with other people who are also wandering about in their astral bodies, and so on. The same is true of the theory that angels are real inhabitants in a real heaven. Some disputes about ontological status, therefore, resolve themselves in the last analysis into disputes about the credibility or incredibility of this or that world-view.

The second observation is that within any given world-view there can still be genuine disagreement as to the ontological status of this or that particular class of phenomena. By and large, it is only insofar as people share a relatively common world-view that they can fruitfully discuss questions of ontological status; otherwise some of the parties to the dispute will be proposing answers that are not considered by the others to be live options.

The third observation is that the number of ontological categories available within the context of any given world-view is fairly large and not capable of exhaustive enumeration. There are—to take some fairly noncontroversial examples—bodies and properties of bodies; minds and their ideas; living creatures and their behavior; and so on. To "place" something ontologically is to assign it to its proper place in a world-view—to interpret it as belonging to such-and-such a kind of being. To ask about the ontological status of something is to ask what is its proper "place."

Ontological Dependence

Some things could not exist without other things upon which they may accordingly be said to be "dependent" for their existence. Dreams, for example, could not exist without dreamers. It is ridiculous to talk of dreams as if they were the sort of thing that could wander about on their own looking for someone to "have" them.

To say that something *A* is dependent on something else *B* for its existence is to affirm a relation of *ontological dependence*: it is to say that *A* is ontologically dependent on *B*. Thoughts are ontologically dependent on thinkers, dreams on dreamers, actions on actors, and so on. If the ontological status of *B* is assumed to be known, the question as to the ontological status of *A* may be satisfactorily answered by pointing out its ontological dependence on *B*. If the ontological status of *B* is itself in question, then the ontological status of everything held to be ontologically dependent on it is also in question.

The Physical World

The question considered in this section concerns the ontological status of a very large class of objects that we designate by the collective phrase "the physical world." It includes all those things that we perceive by means of our five senses: the totality of varicolored, varishaped, varisounding objects that we see, hear, taste, touch, or smell.

There is no serious disagreement, either among philosophers or among nonphilosophers, about how the world appears to us, about how we perceive it to be. It appears to consist of a vast number of individual objects—trees, stones, birds, animals, men, etc.—that exhibit a wide variety of colors, shapes, sounds, smells, temperatures, tastes, textures, and so on. Were anyone to deny that this is how the physical world appears to him, we would be inclined to think that either he is not being honest with us or else he is lacking some of the normal facilities for sense perception (as in the case of a person who is deaf or blind).

But is the physical world really the way we perceive it to be? Is the physical world *as we perceive it* an exact copy of the physical world *as it really is*, or is the reality "out there" different in some ways from our perception of it? To ask such questions is not yet to ask about the ontological status of the physical world; it is only to call in question the trustworthiness of our perceptions. But it is a very short step from this to the ontological question.

The specific question that we shall be considering is: Is the physical world in any degree dependent on a perceiver for its existence?

Does this varicolored, varishaped, varisounding reality that we perceive exist even when someone is not perceiving it, or is it in some sense constituted by and therefore dependent on perception? The point of the question may be made clearer by a brief preliminary survey of the possible answers.

Four Alternatives

The commonsense answer to this question, and certainly the view held by most people prior to any sophisticated reflection on it, goes something like this: There is a real physical world that causes us to have the perceptions that we have, and our perceptions are more or less exact copies of the qualities that are really present in those objects. An object that appears to be brown really is brown; one that is perceived to be hard or cold or smooth really is hard or cold or smooth; and so on. In short, the physical world *exists* quite independently of our perception of it and is in no way dependent on our perception for its existence. If all perceivers were annihilated, the varicolored, varishaped, varisounding world that we now perceive would still be there —though there would not, of course, be anyone around to perceive that it was there.

The view that we have just stated is usually called "naïve realism" by philosophers who address themselves to this problem. The name seems a somewhat unfortunate one, however, since the term "naïve" has connotations that suggest that any position so named is obviously not worthy of serious consideration. In the discussion that follows, therefore, we shall refer to this position as *commonsense* or *direct realism* and to someone who holds this position as a *commonsense* or *direct realist*.

A second position that may be taken with respect to this question is the view known as *subjective idealism,* or *phenomenalism.* The former name is rather closely associated with the name of George Berkeley, an early eighteenth-century Irish philosopher, and is not in general use at the present time. Although today the position goes by the name of phenomenalism, and the grounds upon which it is commonly held are somewhat different from those upon which Berkeley first maintained it, it is essentially Berkeley's position.

Phenomenalism stands at the opposite extreme from commonsense realism in the scale of possible answers that may be given to the question concerning the ontological status of the physical world. It explicitly rejects the "copy" theory of perception and asserts that the being of a physical object consists in its being perceived, that the physical world is accordingly completely dependent on the perceptions of a perceiver for its existence. Berkeley's classical formula for this view was *"Esse est percipi"*—to be (a physical object) is to be perceived. Strange as this position may appear when encountered for the first time, it can be supported by a number of very powerful arguments, and it is held by many philosophers at the present time.

In addition to commonsense realism and phenomenalism there remains only one other way in which it is possible to answer this question, and that is to say that the physical world is partly dependent on a perceiver for its existence and partly independent of a perceiver. What is perceived is in some ways like and in some ways unlike what is really "out there." There is both similarity and dissimilarity between the world as we perceive it and the world as it really is. This view is called *critical realism*.

Critical realists, however, exhibit significant differences among themselves, depending upon whether the view they advocate emphasizes the similarity between our perceptions and the real world (thus staying fairly close to the realist end of the scale) or the dissimilarity between the two (thus coming closer to the phenomenalist view). We shall, in the discussion that follows, make a semantic distinction between these two forms of critical realism, calling the more mild form *critical realism* and the more radical form *hypercritical realism*. The difference between them, it must be remembered, is only one of degree.

There is one term that occurs rather frequently in philosophical writings on this problem. The term is *sense-datum* (plural, *sense-data*). Sense-data, according to philosophers who use the term in discussing this question, are what we immediately perceive whenever we are ordinarily said to be perceiving something. Thus a person who is hallucinating, for example, and who "sees" a pink elephant is said to have the same sense-data as people who are not hallucinating and who see a real pink elephant.

Employing this term, we can distinguish the four positions defined above in the following way. Commonsense realism is the view that the sense-data that normal people have, when their senses are not impaired, are accurate copies of the real characteristics of the physical world and accordingly the physical world is not constituted by our sense-data in any way whatsoever. Phenomenalism is the view that what we call the physical world is simply the inferred totality of our actual and possible sense-data and does not exist apart from these sense-data. Critical realism (in any form) is the view that the sense-data that we directly have when we are perceiving the physical world are in some respects similar to the characteristics objectively present in the physical world and in other respects dissimilar. Hypercritical realism is simply a variant of this view that places the greater emphasis on the dissimilarity between the two.

There is a special form of phenomenalism—some philosophers would say it is a logical implication of phenomenalism—known as *solipsism*. The view is difficult to state with precision, but a fair approximation is the following: it is the view that *I* alone exist in the primary or fundamental sense of "exist" and that everything else that exists does so only in the secondary sense of being my perception or thought. Just as my dreams do not exist unless I am dreaming them, so, according to this view, nothing exists unless *I* am having the perceptions or thoughts that constitute its existence. This view, though difficult to refute, is universally regarded as being highly implausible. To the best of my knowledge it has not been seriously advocated by any major philosopher in the whole history of Western philosophy. It stands, however, as the fantastic limit to which skepticism can be carried regarding the inferences made from the data of sense experience, and it does come up occasionally in discussions of the problem of the ontological status of the physical world.

It is possible to discuss many of the matters in this section in terms of a slightly different question: Can our senses be trusted to give us accurate information about what the world is really like? Many philosophers prefer to discuss these matters in relation to this question, partly because discussions of ontological status are more or less out of style at the present time. However, the classical discussions of perception—those of John Locke, George Berkeley, David Hume, Immanuel Kant, and others—were quite openly directed toward a determination of the ontological status of the physical world. Moreover, it seems evident that any view we might adopt with respect to the veracity of our perceptions would have important implications for our view of the ontological status of the physical world. For these reasons we shall focus our discussion on the ontological question.

Chapters 43–45 may be viewed as three successive critiques of commonsense realism, each one progressively rejecting more of what commonsense realism affirms concerning the ontological status of the physical world. The discussion moves from a mild form of critical realism to hypercritical realism and then to phenomenalism. Finally, a defender of direct realism is given an opportunity to show what, if anything, can be salvaged of the commonsense view.

STUDY QUESTIONS

1. What ontological status would you be inclined to assign to each of the following: a hunch, a plan, redness, temperature, weight, Huckleberry Finn, Abraham Lincoln, a headache?
2. What precisely is the main question posed for consideration in this chapter? Restate it in at least three different ways (without changing the point of the question!).
3. What, in brief summary, are the answers to this question offered by the "four alternatives" defined in this chapter? As you understand

the problem, do these four alternatives exhaust the logical possibilities?
4. Do you find anything odd about the following statement? "The arguments in favor of solipsism are so convincing that I find myself compelled to adopt the position; I am surprised that more people do not come to the same conclusion."

43

CRITICAL REALISM

It cannot be denied that most people trust their sense perceptions and accordingly believe that the world is really very much as they perceive it to be. Most people would also grant, I suppose, that they can err in *judgment*: for example, that they might judge an object seen some distance away to be a dog when it is really a stone. But they would not, on this account, mistrust their senses; they would realize they have judged too hastily and perhaps would make a resolution to suspend judgment on some future occasion until they have had an opportunity to make a closer inspection. Once they have identified the object in question as a stone, however, they would not doubt that the stone really is hard, rough, heavy, porous, and gray, as it appears to be. And if we were to ask them how they *know* that the stone really has these characteristics, they would reply with some indignation: "Because I have seen it with my own eyes, and felt it with my own hands!"

However, this view that the world really is as we perceive it to be, that it really has all of the characteristics we perceive it to have, is one that cannot survive critical reflection. However accustomed we may be to thinking of the world in this way, it is a view that cannot be seriously maintained, as will be evident from the following considerations.

Critique of Commonsense Realism

That commonsense realism is not a defensible position is evident, in the first place, from the fact that we sometimes have illusory perceptions. A straight stick immersed in water, for example, looks like it is bent: there is no point of view we could adopt that would make it look any other way. It is only because such a stick does not feel bent and again looks straight when removed from the water that we have learned not to rely on our visual sense-data in this kind of situation. Or consider a mirage. A traveler in the desert who sees a mirage sees it just as surely as we can see real water and real trees; it is only because the mirage recedes or disappears as he approaches it—only because he can never reach it, drink its water, be cooled by the shade of its trees—that he calls it an illusion. The "phantom pains" of persons who have suffered the loss of a limb may also be mentioned as a case in point.

There is no reason to conclude that because our senses deceive us at times they deceive us all the time. It is only on the assumption that they do not deceive us all the time, as a matter of fact, that we can identify our perceptions of the bent stick, the mirage, and the phantom pains as illusory. But we must conclude that we cannot reasonably maintain that the physical world *exactly corresponds* to our perception of it. In view of these examples of illusory perception, the most that can be maintained is that the world is like the majority of our perceptions.

The same conclusion may be reinforced by a second consideration, namely, that certain changes in a perceiver produce changes in his perceptions of the physical world. Suppose, for example, that a quantity of water is kept at a constant temperature. On one occasion I come from a hot bath, immerse my hand in the water, and pronounce it cold. On another occasion I come from having handled ice, immerse my hand in the water, and pronounce it warm. The water was not really cold in the first instance and warm in the second, but of the same temperature. It was my perception that varied, not the water itself.

As another example, consider what happens when we wear colored glasses—pink, brown, green, or what have you. The world, as we all know, then appears more pink, more brown, more green than otherwise. How can we be sure that the wearing of colored glasses does not enable us to see more clearly what the world is really like? Another example: persons under the influence of certain drugs perceive the world in a way different from that in which they perceive it when they are not under its influence. Which perceptions are correct? Which set of perceptions provides an accurate copy of the real world?

A particularly interesting phenomenon to consider with regard to this question is color-blindness. Two observers, *A* and *B,* look at some patches of color. *A* perceives some patches to be red and others to be green; *B* perceives them to be all the same color. *B,* accordingly, is said to be color-blind. But note: it is only because most people are, like *A,* able to make the distinction that the few unable to do so are said to be color-blind. Were the statistics reversed, persons who perceive a distinction would perhaps be regarded by the majority to be subject to a strange illusion. Whose perception is to be regarded as an accurate copy of the real world? We cannot say, "those who are normal," since normalcy is here defined in terms of the perceptions of the majority. It is not reasonable to decide a question of this sort by means of a referendum.

We could, of course, save some vestiges of the commonsense view by making a number of arbitrary decisions at this point. For example, we could say that it is the majority of the perceptions of people who have normal perception—people who have suffered no accident or injury affecting perception, who are not color-blind, who are not wearing colored glasses, who have been for some time in a room whose temperature is exactly 68° Fahrenheit, etc.—that tell us what the world is really like. But it is apparent that such decisions are purely arbitrary, and with each new difficulty that appears a new requirement must be introduced. To realize this is to realize that something other than commonsense realism must be adopted.

How far must we go, then, in our departure from the commonsense view? Not very far. Let us see upon what basis such an answer might be both rendered precise and supported.

The Case for Critical Realism

The principle that should guide us in determining what is real about what we perceive is the one enunciated by Locke. Such qualities as are utterly inseparable from a physical object, such that a particle of matter however small could not be conceived to exist without it, are real qualities of that object; everything else that we perceive, though it indeed may appear to us to be a real quality in the object, is in truth nothing but a modification of our faculty of perception.[1] We shall, following Locke, call these respectively *primary qualities* and *secondary qualities*. We shall say, accordingly, that primary qualities are really in the object and, in respect to these, the object is as we perceive it to be. Secondary qualities, however, are not in the object at all, but are only modifications of our faculty of perception caused by the object through its primary qualities. Let us see what account of the physical world can be given on the basis of this distinction.

Every object that we perceive appears to have the following qualities: color, shape, size, temperature, degree of hardness (texture), and either rest or motion; some objects, but not all, also have some odor, some taste, and some sound. These are the qualities that our various senses perceive to be present in the objects that come before us.

Which of these qualities really are present in the object? Applying

---

[1] See John Locke, *An Essay Concerning Human Understanding*, II, xxiii (New York: Dover, 1959), pp. 390–423.

our rule, we get the following: shape, size, temperature, texture, solidity, and either rest or motion. Take any object you please and divide it up into as many and as tiny parts as you will: each part will still have some shape, some size, some temperature, some degree of solidity, and some texture, and it will be either in motion or at rest. These, therefore, are the primary qualities of an object.

What remain to be accounted the secondary qualities of an object are, therefore, its color, its odor, its taste, its sound, its warmth or coldness. These, it is apparent, depend on the sense apparatus of the percipient and consist in nothing more than a modification of that apparatus by the object. Were the senses associated with our eyes, our ears, and our nose capable of being affected differently, things would appear to have different colors, different sounds, different odors than they now appear to have; were our body temperature higher or lower than it is, things would not be perceived to be warm or cold in the proportions that they now are.

The qualities that are objectively present in an object are, therefore, according to our view, shape, size, temperature, texture, solidity, and either rest or motion. These cause, via the mechanism of our sense apparatus, (a) impressions that are like the qualities themselves, which we call impressions of primary qualities, and (b) impressions unlike the qualities, which we call impressions of secondary qualities.

There is one further point that must be made in order to render our account complete. It is impossible to conceive of an object as being made up simply of its several qualities randomly thrown together. An object has a certain unity, a certain coherence, for which our account thus far has made no provision. In a former day it was possible to posit a "substance" or a "substratum" that underlay and supported the qualities—an admittedly vague concept that Locke, for example, disparaged as merely "the supposed but unknown support of those qualities we find existing, which we imagine cannot subsist . . . without something to support them." [2] With the much more sophisticated knowledge of matter that we have now, however, it is impossible to account for the unity and coherence of objects in this way. We say, therefore, that the unity that we perceive in objects is simply the natural consequence of the laws of nature acting upon the particular piece of matter in question. In the case of inanimate objects the relevant laws are physical and chemical laws, and the resultant unity is merely structural. In the case of living things this account must be supplemented by citing certain relevant biological laws, and the resultant unity (so long as the organism is alive) is organic as well as structural.

In order to come to a decision on the question concerning the physi-

---

[2] *Ibid.*, p. 391.

cal world we can safely ignore, I think, the more recondite facts about matter that have been reported by modern science. Whatever science may conclude concerning the nature of the physical world at the atomic and subatomic level, at the macroscopic level this world exhibits real qualities of shape, size, temperature, texture, solidity, and either rest or motion. These are real, and while they may indeed be dependent on atomic and subatomic processes for their reality, they are in no way dependent on us as human perceivers.

Critical realism's answer to the question, Is the physical world in any degree dependent on a perceiver for its existence? is "Yes, in some degree." Color, sound, taste, smell, warmness, and coldness—the secondary qualities of objects—are dependent on a perceiver; they are, in fact, nothing but modifications that occur within the perceiver. If there were no perceivers capable of being modified in this way, there would be no color, sound, taste, odor, warmness, or coldness in the world. But the primary qualities are in no way dependent on a perceiver. They would continue to exist even on the supposition that all perceivers were annihilated.

The chief reason for adopting critical realism is that it enables us to solve the puzzles about perception that originally caused us to question the commonsense view. This view enables us to explain the fact that alterations in a perceiver result in certain changes in that person's perception. It is no longer a puzzle that what is perceived to be cold at one time may, without any change in the object, be perceived by the same person to be warm at another time (or even simultaneously, if one hand is warm and one cold), since the impressions of warmness and coldness are seen to be dependent on certain conditions in the perceiver. Similarly, the puzzles that arise in connection with our perception of color are easily solved: things appear to be colored differently to persons who are color-blind, under the influence of certain drugs, or wearing colored glasses, because these things alter our visual sense apparatus and because color is nothing but a modification of the appropriate sense organ.

There are other puzzles in connection with perception that can also be solved easily in the context of this view. For example, some people are able to hear high-pitched signals that are completely inaudible to others. From the point of view of commonsense theory, is a signal that is inaudible to all but a few people really a sound or is it not? For critical realists, this phenomenon causes no difficulty. Sound is nothing but a modification of the audial apparatus of some perceiver. Some people are capable of being affected by air vibrations of a higher frequency than others—hence, the difference. Any such modification is a sound, and so the difficulty disappears. Individual differences with respect to taste and smell can be accounted for in the same manner.

Some Remarks About Perception

It is evident, then, that we must reject the commonsense view regarding the ontological status of the physical world, and with it must go also the "copy" theory of perception. The real world is not exactly as it appears to be; if our sense impressions are a "copy" of the real world, they are a very poor copy indeed. What shall we say of the status of our sense impressions? How are sense-data related to the objects in the real world that are their causes?

The answer implied in the position I am advocating is that the sense-data *represent* the real objects before our minds. We directly perceive the sense-data, and we make certain inferences about the objects that they represent. What we see, hear, taste, touch, and smell, we really do see, hear, taste, touch, and smell: here there is no error. But what we infer about the objects that are represented to us by these various kinds of sense-data may be in error. Commonsense realism is thus seen to consist in the view that for every sense-datum that appears in our perceptual field there is something *just like it* in the physical world. And this view, as we have seen, is one that is not consistent with the facts.

We must take care, however, not to depart further from the commonsense view than the facts require us to do. The facts that led us to reject the commonsense view do not, so far as I can see, require us to reject any more of that view than we have here suggested. There are, I am aware, certain considerations that seem to favor the phenomenalist view on this matter, and these obviously are worthy of being considered on their own merits. That view, however, involves certain difficulties that I do not think can be resolved without returning to something like the view here proposed. It seems to me that every argument that tends to support the phenomenalist position is equally valid, if it is valid at all, as an argument in support of solipsism—a view so patently absurd that the arguments in its support must be regarded as highly suspect. That we must depart as far from the commonsense theory as I have proposed seems obvious; but it seems equally obvious that to depart any further would be neither wise nor prudent.

STUDY QUESTIONS

1. What considerations does Critical Realist bring forward to support the view that "commonsense realism" is not a defensible position? Can you think of any way to defend commonsense realism against this critique?
2. What is the criterion by which Critical Realist proposes to distinguish between "primary" and "secondary" qualities? Does he apply it consistently in drawing up his two lists? In your opinion, is the criterion itself a valid one?

3. What, according to Critical Realist's account, are the "primary" and "secondary" qualities, respectively, of each of the following: a red brick? a book? a bowling ball? a siren? a mirage?

4. What reasons does Critical Realist give for adopting his theory regarding the status of the physical world? Do you find his reasons convincing? Can you think of any way that his case might be strengthened?

44

HYPERCRITICAL REALISM

I think my readers should know that the name "hypercritical realism" is not one that they are apt to find in any philosophical writings prior to the early 1960s. The name was originally coined by Herbert Feigl, and I think it is quite obvious that he used it only in jest. However, it is remarkably suggestive of what I hold concerning the relation of our percepts (what we perceive) to the physical world, and I would not object if it were to come into general use as a descriptive title for the position that I represent.

Anyone who is at all familiar with the advances that have been made in the science of physics during the past few decades will recognize immediately, I think, that we cannot stay as close to common-sense realism as Critical Realist has urged us to do. This rough-and-ready description of the world in terms of primary and secondary qualities may have deserved some credence a century or two ago, but it deserves no such credence today. We have learned a good deal since the days of Locke. It is now a matter of common knowledge that the particles of which material objects are composed are not little nuggets of matter, each retaining the "primary qualities" of which Critical Realist speaks—shape, size, motion, and all the rest. We know, or at least we think we know, that everything in the physical world is a compound of some few basic elements; every element is reducible to molecules; every molecule to atoms; every atom to protons, neutrons, electrons, and numerous other even smaller particles. To try to understand the relation of our percepts to a world thus conceived in terms of Critical Realist's theory is like trying to do fine etching with a pick axe: the tool is simply not adequate for the job to be done.

We need not plunge into the complexities of modern physics, however, in order to see that we cannot be satisfied with so minimal a departure from the commonsense theory as Critical Realist has proposed. A number of far less recondite facts are as evidently fatal to his theory as the facts he does mention are to the commonsense theory. Let us consider in some detail the "damaging" facts that Critical Realist has overlooked.

Some Paradoxes of Perception

Critical Realist has called attention to a number of rather unusual perceptual phenomena—the refraction of light as it passes through a transparent liquid (the example of the bent stick), mirages, "phantom pains," and the like—and has rested the case for his view on the claim that he is able to account for them. However, a number of paradoxes arise in connection with some far less spectacular and unusual perceptual phenomena that cannot be easily accounted for in the context of his theory.

The first group of paradoxes to which I should like to call attention arises in connection with what I shall call the "perspectification" that accompanies all visual perception. Consider, first, the quality of an object that we call its shape. The shape that an object appears to have depends entirely on the point of view from which it is viewed. A sheet of typing paper, for example, appears to be a rectangle if you view it from a point directly above its center; each of its four corners, accordingly, appears to be a right angle or very nearly so. Turn it at a slight angle, however, step away from it a few feet, and two of the corners will appear to be acute angles and two obtuse. The same phenomenon occurs in all cases of visual perception: the apparent shape varies depending on the point of view of the observer and is constantly changing as the observer moves in relation to the object being viewed (or vice versa). A lake that looks round when viewed from the air (directly above its center) looks like a wide oval when viewed from the top of a nearby mountain and like a very long and thin oval when viewed from any point along its shore. A penny looks round from one point of view, oval from another, and rectangular from yet another, and so on.

Which of these many shapes that every object appears to have is supposed to be really present in the object? Why should the "top-side" view of a printed page, or the "air" view of a lake, or the "front and center" view of a penny be granted a privileged status? To do so is rather obviously to make an arbitrary choice. To say that something is "round," for example, is only to say that it will appear to be round if you look at it from such-and-such a point of view. No reason can be given, however, for saying that this point of view rather than some other is the one from which we can see what shape the object "really" has. In the case of three-dimensional objects there is in fact no point of view from which an object appears to have the shape that it is usually said to "really" have.

Consequently, if we wish to maintain Critical Realist's position, we must be prepared to do one of two things. Either we must say that an object has many shapes and that the one you see depends on the point of view from which you happen to observe it; or, quite arbitrarily, that this or that point of view puts us in a position to see its "real" shape. If we are not willing to accept one or the other of these alternatives— and I for one am not—then we must give up the view that objects have a "real" shape that corresponds to our perception of their shape.

The same perplexities arise in connection with size. From a long distance, a tractor-trailer truck may appear the size of a child's toy, but as it speeds closer its size may become disproportionately large. So it is with all visual perception: the size that an object appears to have depends on how close you are to it when you are looking at it. I have yet to meet a person to whom the moon, when viewed from earth with the naked eye, does not *appear* to be about the size of a basketball. Through a telescope, of course, or from a space ship near its surface, it looks much larger.

Which of the apparent sizes of an object is to be accounted its "real" size? Is it the close-up view? How close? We are faced, evidently, with alternatives comparable to those that we had to contend with in connection with shape: either we must hold that an object really has many sizes, and that the one you perceive depends on how far you are away from it; or we must claim to know that there is some precise distance from which we are able to perceive its "real" size. Or we must give up the view that objects have a "real" size to which some perception of ours exactly corresponds.

What, then, can be retained of Critical Realist's account? Is temperature a real quality in objects? Perhaps. But we do not perceive temperature, we merely infer it from what we see on a thermometer. What we perceive is only impressions of warmness and coldness, and these even Critical Realist admits to be modifications in the perceiver. Can texture be retained as real quality in objects? Here, too, difficulties arise. What feels smooth to the touch looks rough when viewed under a microscope: hills and valleys then appear on a surface we thought to be perfectly smooth. Which is it "really," rough or smooth? Or is it both? We are back in our old dilemma.

It is scarcely even necessary to discuss the paradoxes that arise if we try to regard rest and motion as real qualities objectively present in objects. We are all sufficiently familiar with the fact that motion is relative to realize that whether a thing is to be regarded as being in motion or at rest depends entirely on what you assume to be at rest in making your judgment. If the earth is asumed to be at rest, then a boulder lying on a mountainside is also at rest; if you assume the sun to be at rest, then the earth and everything on it, including the boulder, are in motion. To an observer on earth, the earth appears to be at rest, and the sun, the moon, and the stars appear to revolve around it. To an observer on the moon, or on Mars, the surface on which he stands would be judged to be at rest, and everything else would appear to be in motion in relation to himself. Whether a thing is perceived to be in motion or at rest depends on the point of view of the observer. Our alternatives are (a) to say that every object in the universe really has many motions, (b) to say that only one of these is its "real" motion and give some reason for so saying, or (c) to concede that rest and motion are not real qualities of objects at all, but only part of the way in which objects appear to an observer.

There remains of Critical Realist's list of primary qualities only solidity, and by this time I suspect we are prepared to concede that it, too, is unlikely to stand up under close scrutiny. It seems evident, in the first place, that "solidity" can only mean the tendency that an object has to resist another object and that this must vary depending on the size and strength of the invading object. To a fly a piece of balsa wood must appear quite solid; to a man it does not. To a small child a piece of stiff paper appears quite solid; to an adult it appears soft and malleable. Which is it "really"? Any answer that we might give would be completely arbitrary.

In point of fact, we know that nothing in the whole world is "really" solid. This desk upon which I am writing appears to be solid, to have such-and-such a shape, such-and-such a size, such-and-such a color and texture, and to stand absolutely motionless here in the center of my office. In reality it has none of these qualities. All of these qualities are relative to my faculty of perception, the particular senses with which I happen to be equipped and the particular point of view from which I happen to observe the desk. What really is "out there" is quite different, radically different, from what I perceive to be out there. What, then, are we justified in believing about the real qualities of physical objects?

Appearance and Reality

In order to solve these paradoxes, we must make a clear distinction between the world of our percepts and the world as it really is—or, to use a terminology that is very old in the history of philosophy, between appearance and reality. The world appears to us to consist of a multiplicity of objects of various sizes, shapes, colors, textures, temperatures, and so on. On the basis of these appearances, common sense constructs a theory of a real three-dimensional space in which all of these objects are believed to exist and ascribes to them the various characteristics that they appear to have. It is this whole common-sense theory about the world that collapses when it is subjected to close scrutiny.

What is really "out there," however—the physical world as it really is—is being discovered with greater and greater accuracy by the natural sciences, especially by the science of physics. This is hardly the place to begin to summarize all that we now know about the constitution of the universe, but a brief sketch may indicate how we ought to think about an object if we want to conform in some degree to what physics tells us it is really like. A good example is the above-mentioned desk.

According to modern physics, the desk on which I am writing is not, as it appears to be, a solid block of "matter" that occupies some particular position or series of positions in a fixed three-dimensional space. It consists, rather, of several series of events occurring in a four-dimensional manifold that physicists call "space-time," these several series being interrelated in a vast variety of ways. What I call my desk is, in short, something that happens; it is, in fact, a vast conglomeration of happenings that occur in the particular region of space-time that it occupies. None of the particles involved in the events constituting my desk—the protons, neutrons, electrons, etc.—is solid, or colored, or warm, or cold, or anything else that we perceive when we perceive the desk. The language that is appropriate to the desk as I perceive it is absolutely inappropriate for a description of the atomic events of which it is really composed.

It is logically possible, of course, that the atomic events of which my desk is composed should be occurring without my being aware of them in any way—just as radio waves are constantly passing through the region of space-time that I occupy without my being aware of them in any way. It happens to be the case, however, that as a result of the atomic events that constitute my desk, and as a result of certain other atomic events that are related in various ways to the atomic events that constitute my desk, radiations are emitted that, when I am properly situated, cause a series of occurrences in my brain that I call "perceiving the desk."

Consider, for example, the perception of solidity. I perform the activity that I call "pressing my hand against the desk" and say that it is "hard" or "solid." In reality, however, no particle that is involved in the events of which my hand is composed comes in contact with the particles involved in the events of which the desk is composed. What really happens is that an electrical force is created by the nearness of the former to the latter, and this force—through a complicated process involving my nerves and my brain—causes the event that I call perceiving the "hardness" or "solidity" of the desk.

Or consider color. My desk looks brown; according to the commonsense view it really is brown. Physics, however, tells us otherwise. What is really happening when I am "perceiving brown" is that electromagnetic waves of various frequencies are being emitted from the sun and (after a journey requiring roughly eight minutes) are streaming through my window and striking my desk. Some of these waves enter the desk, causing certain changes in it that we describe as an increase in its temperature. Others are scattered by the particles that constitute the surface of the desk, and some of these (by way of my eyes, optic nerve, and brain) create the event in me that I call "perceiving brown." And so on for all sensible qualities.

Hypercritical realism's answer to the question concerning the ontological status of the physical world is that the physical world is dependent on a perceiver for the existence of all of what we may call its commonsense qualities: color, sound, taste, odor, shape, size, solidity, and all the rest. It is only because of the constitution of our faculty of sensation—the particular modifications of which it happens to be capable—that the world appears to us to have these qualities. If we, or beings having a faculty of sensation like ours, were to be annihilated, all such qualities would accordingly disappear. What would not disappear, however, are the atomic and subatomic events that constitute the physical world and cause us to have the particular perceptions we do have. To that extent, the physical world has a real existence of its own and is in no way dependent on a perceiver for its existence.

Perception

I find myself, therefore, in agreement with old-fashioned critical realism on two important points: (a) there is something "out there" that constitutes the real world and (b) it is what is "out there" that causes us to have the perceptions we have. Perceptions do represent realities in the external world, but they do not represent them as they really are. To infer that the physical world is just like, or somewhat like, the world as it appears to us is to ignore most of what science has taught us and to become involved in endless paradoxes. The way to solve these paradoxes is to make the distinction we have made between appearance and reality and to allow that the perceptions that represent physical realities to us are in no way like the realities they represent.

In conclusion I should like to state that I am well aware that it is not easy for any of us to relinquish the idea that the physical world really is as we perceive it to be. As I look now at the desk that I have recently been so busy dissolving into atomic and subatomic events, I am as powerfully tempted as the most unconvinced commonsense realist to think that it really has the solidity, the color, the smoothness, etc., that I perceive it to have. It is only when I attend carefully to the arguments, only when I consider the difficulties involved in saying this, that I know it cannot be so. As a *theory*, commonsense realism or anything very close to it simply will not do; but as a way of looking at the world, as an attitude that governs our everyday commerce with the world, none of us is able to divest ourselves of it. For the world that we must take account of in most of our affairs is the world of appearance, not the world of reality.

STUDY QUESTIONS

1. What "paradoxes" does Hypercritical Realist mention which, according to him, cannot be explained in the context of a mild form of critical realism? Can you think of any way that Critical Realist might be able to defend his position against this attack?
2. What is Hypercritical Realist's general answer to the question posed in this section? What, if anything, makes his position a form of "realism"?
3. What, according to this theory, is the ontological status of color? of sound? of temperature? of electrons? of atoms? of molecules?
4. What criterion does Hypercritical Realist use in distinguishing between "appearance" and "reality"? Is it, in your opinion, a sounder criterion than that employed by Critical Realist?

45

PHENOMENALISM

Phenomenalism is the view that the existence of a physical object is dependent upon its being perceived by some percipient, that a physical object is nothing but a construct made up of the percepts that are the immediate objects of perception. It follows directly from this that the physical world is completely dependent on some perceiver(s) for its existence and that, if all perceivers were to be annihilated, the physical world would accordingly cease to exist.

The task of explaining and defending this view is rendered easier than it might otherwise be by the fact that much of what I ordinarily would have to say in order to build my case has already been said by the two writers who have preceded me in this discussion. The last writer has, indeed, brought us to the very borders of phenomenalism. I propose to show that the very considerations that have brought the argument to this point require us to take a further step that leads to the phenomenalist position.

The Inconsistency of Hypercritical Realism

Hypercritical Realist has argued, quite rightly, that we cannot validly infer from the fact that the world appears to us as a multiplicity of objects of various colors, shapes, sizes, textures, etc., that it really is so. If we try to say this a host of puzzles arise, and we cannot solve these puzzles without departing rather far from the commonsense view. Next, he goes on to suggest that we know, nonetheless, that there is something "out there" that causes us to have these sensations and that what this something is can be learned by studying physics. He then proceeds to give us a short course in atomic physics and supposes thereby that he has persuaded us that so much at least can be retained of the realist view.

But surely it is fair to ask, How do we know that the atomic events that we do not see are objectively real, when we evidently do not know that the size, shape, color, etc., that we do see are objectively real? How have the physicists come by this esoteric knowledge—this knowledge of what is supposed to lie behind the appearances?

We know the answer, of course: they have inferred it from certain observed phenomena. Commonsense realism is the consequence of an unsophisticated inference from some more or less obvious facts of observation; hypercritical realism is the consequence of a sophisticated inference from some less obvious facts of observation. But if the inference is not justified in the first instance, neither is it justified in the second. There is no more reason to say that the latest theory of the physicists is an accurate description of something real "behind the appearances" than there is to say that the description of a commonsense realist is accurate. The two differ considerably in their respective degrees of sophistication, but so far as validity is concerned, they are on the same ground. Realism is equally naïve, whether it is maintained in a commonsense or in a scientific version.

It is worthy of note that scientists themselves do not make the mistake that Hypercritical Realist has made of regarding scientific theories as descriptions of anything at all. What Andreas Osiander said in his preface to Nicolaus Copernicus' treatise *On the Revolutions of the Heavenly Bodies* may be said of all scientific theories: There is no need for these hypotheses to be true, or even to be at all like the truth; one thing is sufficient for them—that they should yield a calculus that agrees with the observations. Scientific hypotheses are, in short, nothing more than instruments that are useful for purposes of calculation. Their function is not to tell us what the world is really like, but to aid us in controlling the world as it appears to us.

It seems clear, therefore, that the very arguments that have been used in the preceding chapters to establish some form of critical realism really tend to support instead the phenomenalist view. We have no basis upon which to infer a universe of signaling stations beyond or behind the perceptual signals that we constantly receive: the only world of which we have or can have any knowledge is the world of our perception. But this is precisely what we mean by the phrase, "the physical world"; hence, it is clear that the physical world is altogether dependent on perceivers for its existence.

A Commonsense Argument for Phenomenalism

Let us return again to the example of the desk. If I want to teach a child the meaning of the word "desk," what I have to do is obvious. I have to show one to him and let him see it and touch it—in short, I have to put him in a position to receive certain sense-data, and I have to pronounce the word "desk" so that he will associate it with those sense-data. If he then learns the meaning of this word, what can he possibly understand it to mean but the impressions of hardness, brownness, flatness, etc., that he was taught to associate with the word "desk"? It is in this way, surely, that all of us have learned the names of such familiar objects as desks, chairs, tables, stones, trees, and so on.

What does it mean, then, to say that something—a desk, say—exists? It can only mean that if you go to such-and-such a place (where the desk is said to exist) you will have percepts of the sort that you have learned to associate with the word "desk." If the statement "there is a desk in my office" is true, then you will have desk-like percepts if you go into my office; if it is false, you will not. A statement affirming the existence of something is always a statement about percepts.

But what happens to things when nobody is perceiving them? Do they exist? Yes they do; but to say that something exists when nobody is perceiving it is still to say something about percepts, namely, that if someone were to go to such-and-such a place (where the thing is said to exist), he would have such-and-such sorts of percepts. Every statement to the effect that something exists is a statement about actual or possible percepts. Any meaning that we try to ascribe to the word "existence" in addition to this is simply unintelligible.

If, then, someone says that something exists behind the percepts, and that this is the cause of our having such-and-such percepts, he is saying something that has no meaning. It makes sense to say that there are real actors in a real studio that cause us to have the particular percepts we have when we look at television, because we know what it is like to have the percepts that constitute the set of events we call "actors in a studio." Here we can "go behind the scenes," so to speak, without forsaking the realm of percepts. But to talk about a reality behind the appearances, a nonperceptual something that causes us to have percepts, is to talk nonsense. The appearance *is* the reality. If there is anything beyond the world as it appears to us (whatever that might mean), we must remain forever in ignorance of what it is.

The physical world, therefore, exists only in our percepts. If there were no perceivers there would be no percepts and hence no physical world. Berkeley was right: to be a physical object is to be perceived.

Objections and Replies

I do not think that the phenomenalist view of the ontological status of the physical world is really very vulnerable to attack by opposing views. The various forms of critical realism that have been proposed are, I am convinced, nothing more than temporary stopping places for "backsliding realists": philosophers who have failed to follow all the way along the route that leads to phenomenalism have done so more by default than by acute philosophical argument. There are, however, a few commonsense objections that are sometimes raised against the phenomenalist view. To demonstrate just how strong the case for phenomenalism really is, I should like to state these objections and show how easily they can be met.

It is sometimes objected, for example, that it is silly to say things like, "I had some corn-flakish percepts for breakfast this morning," or "Help! Someone has stolen my new-car-ish percepts," but that according to the phenomenalist view this ought to be a perfectly proper way of speaking. However, the phenomenalist theory does not commit a supporter to the view that talk of this sort is proper. Indeed, it is never proper to mix ordinary language and technical theory in this way. It would be equally absurd to say, "I had a bowl of corn-flakish protons, neutrons, and electrons for breakfast," or "Someone stole my new-car-ish atoms." What constitutes proper usage for purposes of ordinary discourse cannot decide questions of physical or philosophical theory. The objection is quite beside the point.

A second objection that is sometimes raised is that phenomenalism provides no basis upon which to distinguish between valid and illusory percepts. If to be is to be perceived, then mirages and other things which even common sense regards as illusions must be as real as anything else, for a mirage is obviously something that is perceived. Because we can distinguish between illusory and nonillusory perceptions, phenomenalism must be in error.

In answer to this objection it is only necessary to point out that the difference between illusory and nonillusory perceptions is a difference among perceptions. The reason that we call some perceptions illusory is that they lead us to have certain expectations that are not fulfilled. We regard a mirage as illusory, for example, precisely because it leads us to expect certain other perceptions—those constituting what we call "drinking water" and "resting in the shade of a tree"—that are not forthcoming. To say that something is real and not illusory is not to posit an unperceived metaphysical reality "behind" our percepts: it is to say that the expectations that our percepts create in us can be fulfilled—that we shall not be disappointed if under such-and-such conditions we count on having such-and-such additional percepts. Try as we will, I do not think we shall find any further reason for making the distinction. If the water-and-shade percepts that we anticipate when we see a mirage were forthcoming, we would not call it a mirage; it would then be identical with what we call an oasis.

It is sometimes argued that according to the phenomenalist account physical objects—trees, stones, freight trains, skyscrapers, and other such apparently solid and substantial things—are constantly popping in and out of existence: when someone is perceiving them they exist, when nobody is perceiving them they cease to exist. And this, it is

said, is absurd. Even Berkeley, it may be pointed out, found this idea
so preposterous that he advanced the idea that things exist continually
in the omniscient perception of God; and this, to say the least, seems a
bit farfetched. The absurdity of Berkeley's view is beautifully reflected
in this oft-quoted limerick:

> There was a young man who said, "God
> Must think it exceedingly odd
> If he finds that this tree
> Continues to be
> When there's no one about in the Quad."

> Reply

> Dear Sir:
> Your astonishment's odd:
> I am always about in the Quad.
> And that's why the tree
> Will continue to be,
> Since observed by
> *Yours faithfully,*
> God.[1]

My form of phenomenalism, however, can easily account for the
continued existence of objects during those times when they are not
being perceived—and I do not have to invoke a "perpetual perceiver"
in order to accomplish this. According to my view, to say that something continues to exist even when it is not being perceived is simply
to say that if someone fulfilled such-and-such conditions, he would
have such-and-such perceptions. Physical objects, as John Stuart Mill
once said, are permanent possibilities of sensation. A physical object
consists of percepts, actual and possible; the intervals of time during
which the object is not actually being perceived are filled in by the
continuing "possibilities of sensation" that remain.

Even after hearing this explanation, however, we may be inclined
to ask: How is it that common sense comes to take it for granted that
objects continue to exist when they are not perceived, in exactly the
same way that they do when they are perceived? Where does the commonsense idea of an objectively real, ontologically independent physical world come from? The answer, I think, is that certain features of
our perceptual experience induce us to posit such a world. The most
important of these features are (a) the resemblance between the various percepts that we call percepts of the "same thing," (b) the occurrence of these similar groups of percepts in the context of a relatively
stable perceptual environment, (c) the fact that we can, within certain limits, predict what sorts of percepts we shall have under such-
and-such conditions, and (d) the fact that the perceptions we have

---

[1] Ronald Knox, as quoted by Bertrand Russell in *A History of Western Philosophy* (New York: Simon and Schuster, 1945), p. 648.

can be varied in a more or less systematic way depending on our own movements. The idea of an independently existing world of physical objects, which appear to us in the vast variety of ways evident in our actual perceptions, is an ingenious hypothesis that common sense has erected to account for these features of our perceptual experience; but it is, as we have seen, a hypothesis that does not stand up under close scrutiny.

How are we to account for the consistency and the order that obtain among our percepts, if there is no independent physical world that is the cause of them all? Phenomenalism cannot satisfactorily answer this question, but neither can the realist theory. The realist theory only pushes the problem one step back: it accounts for order among our percepts by positing an ordered world and either takes the order of the world for granted or leaves it unexplained. Phenomenalists say that the order that evidently obtains among our percepts *is* the order in the world because the only world of which we have any knowledge is the world of our percepts. If there is some explanation of why there is order in the world, then that is why there is order among our percepts; if there is no explanation, then there is none for the order among percepts either. The discussion about order, in any case, in no way favors the realist view.

Therefore, it is not to the point to argue that the phenomenalist view is refuted by the fact that people in the same general vicinity have more or less the same sense-data. Of course they do; if they did not, they would not be able to speak and act as if they lived in a common world. That our percepts are more or less alike and systematically related in a wide variety of ways is simply an ultimate fact that has to be taken for granted. To try to "explain" it by positing an ordered world "behind" the percepts is like trying to explain the sleep-producing effect of some drugs by saying they have in them a "soporific power." Such a statement is not only an inadequate explanation: it is not even a meaningful combination of words.

The final objection against phenomenalism with which I should like to deal concerns our knowledge of the existence of other minds. If phenomenalism were true, it is sometimes said, we could never know that other minds exist. If to say that something exists is to say that we are having, or could have, such-and-such percepts, then—since no actual or possible percepts can warrant our saying that another mind exists—they do not exist. By this argument it is concluded that phenomenalism must lead to skepticism regarding the existence of any mind other than our own and in the end to solipsism.

The question concerning our knowledge of the existence of other minds has always been a difficult one for empiricists, and I shall not pretend that I am able to give a definitive answer to it. I may say, however, that neither I nor any other phenomenalist known to me is a solipsist; therefore it is evident that being a phenomenalist does not entail accepting the solipsist position. But it is not easy to say how it is that we know of the existence of other minds.

A great part of the difficulty consists in the obscurity of the very notion of a "mind." In some senses that have been given to that word, I do not think we know of the existence of any minds, including our own. What we really want to know when we ask, Do other minds exist? is: Do other conscious and sentient beings exist? It seems to me that the phenomenalist can answer as follows: (a) our own existence as conscious and sentient beings is immediately evident to us (our existence consists, as Berkeley said, in perceiving, not in being perceived); (b) we perceive beings that look, talk, and act in ways very similar to ourselves; and (c) by analogy we infer that they, too, are conscious and sentient beings just as we are. Common sense, in my opinion, can do no better.

Phenomenalism and Empiricism

In conclusion I want to state briefly what I conceive to be the relation of phenomenalism to some of the epistemological questions discussed earlier. Anyone who intends to be absolutely consistent in his adherence to empiricism must in the end adopt the phenomenalist view with respect to the ontological status of the physical world. If we are serious about the view that all we know is what comes to us in experience, then it is clear that all we know is our percepts. To posit an unseen world "behind" the world of our percepts is to claim that by means of experience we can go beyond experience; and this is just what an absolutely consistent empiricism will not permit us to do. The point, briefly put, is this: phenomenalism is the ontology of empiricism. Let phenomenalism be overthrown and rationalism will have won the day.

STUDY QUESTIONS

1. What argument does Phenomenalist use to enforce his conclusion that hypercritical realism is no more tenable than commonsense realism? Is his argument sound? Can you think of any way to defend Hypercritical Realist's view against this argument?
2. How does Phenomenalist attempt to establish his position? Is this a sound argument in your opinion?
3. Summarize the "commonsense objections" to his position that Phenomenalist mentions, and his reply to each. Are you satisfied with his replies? Can you think of any other difficulties with this theory that Phenomenalist may have neglected to mention?
4. Phenomenalist says: "Neither I nor any other phenomenalist known to me is a solipsist; therefore it is evident that being a phenomenalist does not entail accepting the solipsist position." Is this a good argument?

46

RETURN
TO REALISM

A wise old professor of mine once said, "There are times in the study of philosophy when you must listen very carefully to that still, small voice that whispers insistently in your ear: 'Poppycock'!" That time has come. From the simple commonsense view that we live in a world that exists, whether or not we perceive it—a world whose features we are able to discern (to some extent, at least) by means of our five senses—we have been led step by step to the preposterous view that (a) the physical world "exists only in our percepts," (b) "to be is to be perceived," and (c) the idea of an independently existing world is nothing but a mistaken hypothesis for which there is no evidence at all. Now this conclusion is perfectly and utterly absurd, and I propose to begin this essay by pointing out some of the most glaring absurdities inherent in the phenomenalist position.

Critique of Phenomenalism

Let us begin by taking another look at the "commonsense objections" to which Phenomenalist has attempted to reply in order to fortify his position. He states five such supposed objections to his position and offers answers to each. The first two of these—the ridiculous descriptive expressions phenomenalism allegedly leads to and the problem of distinguishing valid and illusory percepts—are not valid objections to phenomenalism, in my opinion, and so I propose to say no more about them. The other three arguments, however, are quite decisive, and I want to show how inadequate Phenomenalist's replies are.

First, it is absurd to say, as Phenomenalist does, that *physical objects* are hopping back and forth between the status of being "possible percepts" and that of being "actual percepts," depending on whether or not someone is perceiving them. Phenomenalist makes light of Berkeley's view that the world is saved from an intermittent existence because it is perceived at all times by God, and takes obvious delight in reciting Knox's famous limerick about the tree that, thanks to God's perpetual observation, "Continues to be diagonal When there's no one about in the Quad." I suggest that Phenomenalist's position is really no more believable than Berkeley's:

> "I wish," said a possible tree
> "That someone would come *stare* at me;
>   For to be very factual,
>   I'd like to be actual:
> I am tired of mere possibility."

> "Be patient," replied an old stone,
> "You trees really ought not to moan;
>   Why, for billions of years
>   There were no eyes or ears:
> We survived on possibility alone."

Let me put my point very simply. When I say that a physical object exists even when I am not perceiving it, I do not mean that God is perceiving it, and I do not mean merely that if someone fulfilled such-and-such conditions he would have percepts of a certain kind. I mean, quite simply, that it *exists*. Now it is true that if something exists, then a person who gets himself into a position to perceive it will in fact perceive it. The existence of the object is a factual precondition of its being perceived; but the statement that it exists is not logically identical with the statement that it is being perceived.

Note that in order to sustain his view Phenomenalist must hold that prior to the evolution of sentient life in the universe nothing at all existed except, of course, potentially. The generally accepted view that the universe existed—really existed—for billions of years prior to the emergence of life becomes unintelligible on this view. In studying the samples of rocks recently brought back from the moon we are not trying to determine what kinds of "percepts" an observer might have had four and a half billion years ago if he had been on the moon: we are trying to determine what really happened there (and elsewhere in the solar system) during those eons of time prior to the emergence of life.

Phenomenalist argues, further, that the realist theory is no more capable of explaining the fact of order in the world than is the phenomenalist theory; hence, he says, the fact that phenomenalism has no explanation for "the consistency and order that obtain among our percepts" ought not to count against it. I think, on the contrary, that the consistency and order of what we perceive does count—decisively

—against Phenomenalist's view. Note that there are two sorts of facts that have to be explained. First, there is the fact that each individual perceiver perceives the world as being relatively ordered: objects appear to be more or less permanent, change usually occurs in an orderly and intelligible way, and so on. Second, there is the fact that people in the same general vicinity perceive the same world—to use Phenomenalist's language, they "have more or less the same sense-data." Now it is totally unconvincing to say that the "order and consistency" that are thus perceived are "ultimate facts" to be "taken for granted." These facts are easily explained within the context of a realist ontology; they only become inexplicable from the phenomenalist position.

Consider a simple analogy. Most of us have had the experience of standing in a television display room and observing a number of sets that all display what we call "the same picture" and emit what we call "the same sounds." Now suppose that someone who knows nothing at all about television were introduced into this situation. What hypothesis would he be justified in forming to "explain" these identical pictures? He could, of course, hypothesize that for no reason at all the sets just happen to be displaying the same pictures—but that would hardly satisfy him, no matter how primitive he might be. Surely, he would be inclined to say, there must be some *common source* of these pictures. And in so saying he would, of course, be right. Just so with respect to the present point—except that in the present case it is the consistency of the perceptions of hundreds of millions of people that has to be explained. Phenomenalism has no explanation for this, whereas realism does. I consider this a decisive argument against phenomenalism.

The last objection that Phenomenalist attempts to refute is that a completely consistent phenomenalist ought to be a solipsist, since no actual or possible percepts warrant our saying that another mind exists. What is Phenomenalist's reply to this objection? That "neither I nor any other phenomenalist known to me is a solipsist; therefore it is evident that being a phenomenalist does not entail accepting the solipsist position." Now I submit that the fact that Phenomenalist and his friends are not in fact solipsists does *not* demonstrate that solipsism does not follow logically from their position: it proves only that they do not have the courage to draw this particular logical inference. It is not by logical argument but by mere fiat that Phenomenalist rejects the solipsist dilemma. Phenomenalism implies solipsism: this is the ultimate *reductio ad absurdum* of phenomenalism. Phenomenalist acknowledges the absurdity of solipsism and attempts to escape the *reductio* by pleading that his position does not really commit him to solipsism. But the crucial question—crucial for Phenomenalist, that is—remains unanswered: if on the basis of our percepts we are not justified in affirming the existence of a real world that is the cause of those percepts, how on the basis of those same percepts can we be justified in affirming the existence of minds other than our own? Until Phenomenalist answers this question, we are justified in holding that he is saved from solipsism not by rational argument but by a small residuum of common sense.

Further absurdities, which Phenomenalist did not mention, follow if we adopt his position. If phenomenalism is true then it follows, for example, that some merely *possible* things are the causes of some *actual* things. The collisions that are believed to have created the craters on the moon, for example, were (so far as we know) observed by no one. The supposed collisions, on the phenomenalist theory, are nothing but some possible percepts that were not actualized: their existence is purely hypothetical and nonactual. But the craters on the moon are actual (at least part of the time) since they are from time to time observed by astronomers, astronauts, and people who visit observatories. Now according to the phenomenalist theory, the statement that "the craters on the moon were caused by the impact of meteors that strayed into the moon's gravitational field" means, roughly, "the actual crater-percepts that you get when you look at the moon through a sufficiently powerful telescope are the result of some possible collision-percepts, the conditions for which existed some billions of years ago when, unfortunately, there were no perceivers to actualize them." To say the least, this statement is more than a little difficult to swallow. I am not even sure that it makes sense to say that one set of actual percepts (rain-percepts) cause another set of actual percepts (wet-pavement-percepts); but I am completely convinced that it makes no sense at all to say that some actual percepts are caused by some merely hypothetical possible percepts that nobody ever actually had. Phenomenalism reduces the notion of causality to utter nonsense.

One final objection. Phenomenalism implies that if there were no perceivers nothing would actually exist, since all that exists is minds and their perceptions. The annihilation of all sentient life is, however, logically conceivable and is in fact a ghastly empirical possibility that we have been forced to think about since the advent of the atomic age. But surely it is absurd to say that the annihilation of all sentient life would terminate the actual existence of the whole physical universe? I think it makes more sense to say that in the event of such a tragedy the sun, the moon, the stars, and the planets would continue to exhibit the motions they now exhibit; that on this sad old planet that we call Earth the winds would still blow, the snow and the rain would still fall, and perhaps in time grass would grow and flowers would bloom once more; but no one, sadly, would be here to observe these occurrences. Phenomenalism tells me that such a statement makes no sense, or that it makes a kind of sense (the possible-percepts story) that is about as close as you can come to no sense at all. Thus we may add this argument to a long list of reasons for rejecting the phenomenalist position.

Realism Reconsidered

Where, then, has Phenomenalist gone wrong? If phenomenalism is really as vulnerable as the preceding argument has shown it to be, how can so many able philosophers be persuaded of its truth? Most important of all, what view are we warranted in holding about the ontological status of the physical world?

I suggest that the initial error that has sent so many philosophers down the "slippery slope" to phenomenalism is the innocent-looking claim that the immediate objects of perception are sense-data. I shall argue, on the contrary, that the immediate objects of perception are sights, sounds, tastes, smells, tactual qualities, etc. I shall, in short, defend the view known as *direct realism*. In order to defend this view I must refute the argument from illusion, which is the principal argument on which the erroneous claim that the immediate objects of perception are sense-data has been erected.

What, exactly, is an illusory perception? It is nothing more than the mistaken belief that something exists together with the mistaken belief that we are immediately perceiving it. A mirage, for example, is the mistaken belief that at a certain place in the desert there is an oasis and the mistaken belief that I am immediately perceiving the oasis I mistakenly believe to exist. Were these two beliefs not mistaken, I would not be the victim of a mirage but would instead be having the experience called "seeing an oasis."

What, then, is a man perceiving when he is "seeing a mirage"? Nothing at all. Normal perception is the true belief that an object exists together with the true belief that we are immediately perceiving it. Illusory perception is the false belief of these same propositions. The immediate object of normal perception is the object that we believe we are perceiving—sounds, color patches, shapes, etc. Since in the case of illusory perception there is no real object, it follows that nothing is being perceived. What occurs in the case of illusory perception is *not* the perception of "sense-data" to which nothing corresponds in reality, but the holding of certain *beliefs* that happen to be false. "Sense-data" are mere phantoms introduced in order to provide an object for perception in those cases in which someone is said to "see" something that does not really exist. My analysis of illusory perception shows that no such object is required; thus we can simply dispense with the whole concept of "sense-data."

The immediate objects of perception, *when perception is actually occurring,* are the colors, shapes, sounds, tastes, odors etc., that we perceive by means of our senses. The term "immediate" here means simply that these are the phenomena that appear directly in our perceptual field: they present themselves to us, and under appropriate conditions we perceive them. In a derivative sense, however, we may say that what we perceive are not colors, shapes, sounds, tastes, etc., but trees, stones, automobiles, steaks, etc. That is, we may add to the immediate perception the *judgment* that the sound we just heard was from an approaching airplane, or that the object we see in the distance is a tree—and in this we may be mistaken. It seems perfectly proper to say, however, "I hear an airplane," "I see a tree," or "I smell a steak"; in such cases we are expressing what I should call *mediate* or *indirect perception.* The *immediate* objects of perception are colors, shapes, sounds, tastes, odors, etc., and the *mediate* objects of perception are the objects that have those colors, shapes, sounds, tastes, odors, etc.

Is the physical world, then, in any degree dependent on a perceiver for its existence? No. The physical world is altogether independent of the perceptions of any perceiver. It existed for billions of years before the emergence of sentient life and may well exist for billions of years after all such life has vanished from the scene. In the meantime, however, our unaided senses reveal to us some of the shapes, colors, sounds, etc., that are really there; by the use of various instruments that magnify the powers of our senses—microscopes, telescopes, etc. —we are able to perceive features of the world that are not discernible to the unaided eye or ear. But these qualities, too, are really there: the account of the physicist supplements but does not conflict with the account of common sense. To say that the observations of physicists are valid while those of plain men are not (hypercritical realism) is purely arbitrary.

I would observe in conclusion that there is no need to develop a constructive argument in support of direct realism in order to establish the truth of this position. Commonsense realism is the position from which everyone sets out in this controversy: men become critical realists or phenomenalists (or even solipsists) only because they are persuaded by some argument or other that they must abandon their "naïve" or "commonsense" realism. In order to reestablish the realist position, we have only to refute the arguments that led to its abandonment in the first place. Direct realism is only commonsense realism that has become sure of itself through having defended itself against its critics. Hence the arguments of direct realists are typically directed not toward the positive fortification of their position but rather toward the refutation of the arguments commonly leveled against it.

STUDY QUESTIONS

1. "The existence of the object is . . . a factual precondition of its being perceived; but the statement that it exists is not logically identical with the statement that it is being perceived." Explain.

2. Does the fact that "people in the same general vicinity perceive the same world" count against the phenomenalist position? Defend your answer.

3. "Phenomenalist is saved from solipsism not by rational argument but by a small residuum of common sense." Do you agree? Explain.

4. What, according to Realist, is an illusory perception? Do you agree with his analysis?

5. "Sense-data are mere phantoms introduced in order to provide an object for perception in those cases in which someone is said to 'see' something that doesn't really exist." Does this seem plausible to you?

6. "There is no need to develop a constructive argument in support of direct realism in order to establish the truth of this position." Attack or defend this statement.

Adams, E. M. "The Nature of the Sense-Datum Theory," *Mind*, 67 (1958), 216–226.

Armstrong, D. M. *Perception and the Physical World*. New York: The Humanities Press, 1961.

Austin, J. L. *Sense and Sensibilia*. London: Oxford University Press, 1962 (paperbound).

Ayer, A. J. *The Foundations of Empirical Knowledge*. New York: St. Martin's Press, 1958 (paperbound), chaps. I, II, and V.

————. *The Problem of Knowledge*. New York: St. Martin's Press, 1956, chap. III.

Barnes, W. H. F. "The Myth of Sense-Data," *Proceedings of the Aristotelian Society*, 45 (1944–1945), 89–117.

Bergmann, Gustav. *Logic and Reality*. Madison: University of Wisconsin Press, 1964, chap. 14.

Chisholm, R. M. "The Problem of Empiricism," *The Journal of Philosophy*, 45 (1948), 512–517.

Dewey, John. *Essays in Experimental Logic*. New York: Dover Publications, 1960 (paperbound), pp. 1–74 and 250–302.

Eddington, A. S. *The Nature of the Physical World*. Ann Arbor: University of Michigan Press, 1958 (paperbound).

Ewing, A. C. *The Fundamental Questions of Philosophy*. New York: Macmillan, 1951, chap. 4.

Garnett, A. C. *The Perceptual Process*. London: G. Allen & Unwin, 1965. Short, highly readable, critical realist view.

Gibson, James J. *The Senses Considered as Perceptual Systems*. London: G. Allen & Unwin, 1968.

Joske, W. D. *Material Objects*. New York: Macmillan, 1967.

Lewis, C. I. *An Analysis of Knowledge and Valuation*. LaSalle, Ill.: Open Court, 1947 (paperbound), chap. VII.

Locke, D. *Perception and our Knowledge of the External World*. London: G. Allen & Unwin, 1967.

Mandelbaum, M. *Philosophy, Science, and Sense Perception*. Baltimore: Johns Hopkins Press, 1964. Defends critical realism.

Price, H. H. "The Argument from Illusion," in H. D. Lewis (ed.). *Contemporary British Philosophy*, Third Series. New York: Macmillan, 1956, pp. 391–400.

————. *Perception*, 2nd ed. New York: Dover Publications, 1950.

Russell, Bertrand. *Human Knowledge*. New York: Simon and Schuster, 1962 (paperbound). See Part Three, "Science and Perception."

————. *The Problems of Philosophy*. New York: Oxford University Press, 1959 (paperbound), chaps. 1–4.

PART X

THE EXISTENCE OF GOD

47

ON PROVING
GOD'S EXISTENCE

There are a number of questions about God that philosophers have been inclined to ask at various times in the history of Western philosophy. Many of these have been concerned with the *nature* of God: Is God rightly described as a "person"? Is God absolutely eternal and immutable, or does He in some sense participate in change? If God does not change, how is it possible for Him to experience love, or solicitude, or compassion? These, and dozens of other questions of this kind, figure prominently in the writings of such Christian philosophers as St. Augustine, St. Anselm, St. Thomas Aquinas, and Duns Scotus. To modern ears, such questions often sound exceedingly strange, even unimportant; but to the philosophers of the Middle Ages they were questions of the first importance. One measure of the distance that modern thought has traveled from the thought of the Middle Ages is the infrequency with which such questions are discussed today.

There is another question, however, that has been of interest to at least some philosophers in every age. That is the question, Does God exist? Some philosophers—for example, St. Augustine—thought the existence of God was so self-evident that it did not even require to be proved (though St. Augustine does offer one such proof in his treatise *On the Free Will*). Others, like St. Albert the Great, St. Thomas Aquinas, and René Descartes, thought the existence of God required proof, but they considered it a relatively simple matter to construct such a proof. Aquinas, for example, offers no less than five such "proofs" in the space of just two or three pages. Most philosophers today are at least in agreement on this, that the proof of the existence of God, if it is possible at all, is no easy matter; and it is probably true to say that the majority of them regard it as impossible.

The Problem of Definition

Before we can discuss intelligently the various arguments that have been offered as proofs of the existence of God, it is necessary that we consider carefully a prior question, namely: What is the meaning of the term "God"? Let us see why, in connection with the arguments concerning the existence of God, this is such an important question.

Suppose that someone proposed for discussion the question, Do *snergs* exist? Now it would be obviously futile to begin to construct arguments for or against the existence of "snergs" until some agreement had been reached as to what was *meant* by the term "snergs." Indeed, confusion would most surely occur, for those who affirm the existence of "snergs" might have one sort of thing in mind, and those who deny their existence might have another sort of thing in mind. As a result their disagreement would be merely verbal rather than real (see Chapter 5). Unless there is agreement on this key point, and thus agreement as to what is the point of the question that is being asked, the question itself cannot be intelligently discussed.

Even philosophers, unfortunately, have not always understood clearly the crucial importance of this prior question, and as a consequence a good deal of confusion has been created in the discussion of this problem. Some philosophers have supposed, for example, that the question, Does God exist? is equivalent to: Does there exist, some place beyond the reach of even our most powerful telescopes, a very wise and powerful being who once upon a time brought the world into existence, who occasionally even now interferes in its orderly operations, and who will some day reward the righteous and punish the wicked? They have supposed, that is to say, that it is God *as conceived by popular unsophisticated Christian piety* whose existence is in question; and they have relatively little difficulty in showing that none of the arguments that have been offered in an attempt to "prove the existence of God" succeed in proving the existence of such a being. They do not always realize, however, that no philosopher who has seriously proposed an argument for the existence of God has ever intended to prove the existence of a being so conceived.

What, then, have those philosophers who have attempted to prove the existence of God meant by the term "God"? It is very difficult to answer this question with the precision that might be desired. It seems, however, that those philosophers who have entered most seriously and profoundly into the discussion of this question—philosophers such as St. Anselm, Aquinas, Descartes, and Immanuel Kant (who are far from agreeing on the soundness of the various arguments for the existence of God)—have meant by the term "God" at least the following:

1. A reality that transcends space and time.
2. The ground of being and value.
3. A reality worthy of man's worship.

The question, Does God exist? means, therefore, Is there a reality that transcends space and time, is the ground of being and value, and is worthy of man's worship? To answer this question in the affirmative is to affirm that God exists. To answer it negatively is to deny that God exists. To affirm or deny the existence of any other sort of being is to miss the point of the question, Does God exist?

There are in this formulation of the question, however, certain terms that are unclear, notably the terms "reality" and "ground." Let us try to clarify them. Perhaps the best way to get at the meaning of the term "reality" as used in this context is to note the reasons for using this term instead of the term "being." To speak of God as "a being" would not do justice to what philosophers who have attempted to prove the existence of God have meant by the term "God." Why? Because our notion of "a being" is the notion of a spatiotemporal something that exists alongside other spatiotemporal somethings. To speak of "a being" is to speak of something that exists in some places but not in others, at some times but not at others. Philosophers who have believed that God exists, and that His existence could be proved, have not intended to assert the existence of *a being* occupying some particular region of space-time. They have meant to assert, rather, the existence of a reality that is not subject to the categories of space and time—a reality, in other words, that transcends space and time. Hence, we must speak of God not as a being, but as a reality.

To say that God is to be conceived as a reality that transcends space and time is to say that God is not to be conceived simply as a natural object, as one of the many objects that we might encounter within the realm of nature. No telescope will ever be constructed, no space journey ever undertaken, that will reveal God's habitation—not because the distance is too great, but because the question of God's existence does not concern distance at all. If we cannot attach some meaning to the phrase, "a reality that transcends space and time" (and many philosophers today insist that they cannot), then we simply cannot enter into the discussion of the question, Does God exist?

Next, what is meant by the term "ground" in the above formulation? Why do we not use instead the word "cause"? The reason is the same as in the previous case: the term "cause" is (in contemporary usage) too closely tied up with the notions of space and time. A "cause" is a spatiotemporal something that stands in a certain relation to something else that we call its "effect." But the notion of God, we have said, is the notion of a reality that transcends space and time:

hence, we must not speak of God in such a way as to suggest "a spatiotemporal something." We want, however, to affirm something like the relation of cause and effect between God and being and value. How shall we do this? Philosophical usage has given us the term "ground," which means roughly (in philosophical usage) "nonspatiotemporal cause." Let us say, then, that God is the "ground" of being and value.

What, finally, does it mean to say that the idea of God is the idea of a reality "worthy of man's worship"? This is in many ways the most puzzling of the three statements. Something like this must be said, however, to take account of the fact that the term "God" is in the first instance a *religious* term—so much so that we would not be too far from the truth if we were simply to define "God" as "the object of the act of worship." The supposition is, however, that the object of worship is somehow worthy of man's devotion, which in our philosophical tradition at least has meant that God is conceived to be holy, just, good, merciful, and so on. Many philosophers (Aquinas, once again, is an excellent example) have attempted to construct proofs of a number of such "attributes" of God, but it seems clear that the very notion of God includes in embryonic form the idea that He possesses in an eminent degree those virtues that we normally admire in one another. It is this notion that we are including in the idea of God when we say that God is to be conceived as "a reality that is worthy of man's worship."

The question whether God exists—whether there exists a reality that transcends space and time, is the ground of being and value, and is worthy of man's worship—is no trivial question. I think most people would agree with the sentiments of the philosopher who said (though he himself rejected all of the arguments for the existence of God):

> If we found that any of the traditional arguments for the existence of God were sound, we should get out of our one hour this . . . afternoon something of inestimable value, such as one never got out of any hour's work in our lives before. For we should have got out of one hour's work the answer to that question about which, above all, we want to know the answer.[1]

Many philosophers who, like the one just quoted, believe that none of the traditional arguments for the existence of God is sound, believe, nonetheless, that the question of the existence of God is an exceedingly important question. In fact, some of those who have come to the

---

[1] J. J. C. Smart, "The Existence of God," a public lecture given at the University of Adelaide in 1951, published in Antony Flew and Alasdair MacIntyre (eds.), *New Essays in Philosophical Theology* (London: S.C.M. Press; and New York: Macmillan, 1955), pp. 28–46; see p. 28.

conclusion that God does not exist (for example, Friedrich Nietzsche and Jean-Paul Sartre) have recognized that this conclusion must profoundly alter a man's understanding of himself, his fellows, and his world. It is probably safe to say that anyone who does not regard the question of the existence of God as a serious and important question has not really understood the point of the question.

A Related Question

To the question, Does God exist? there are just three possible answers: "Yes" (theism), "No" (atheism), and "I don't know" (agnosticism). Philosophers, however, are not just interested in people's opinions on this matter: they are interested primarily in the reasons that might be given in support of an opinion. The philosophical discussion of the existence of God has, therefore, had a slightly different focus than we have suggested thus far.

Let us approach the question of the existence of God by asking a slightly different question. Let us consider the question, Are there any *rational grounds* for believing in the existence of God, and if so what are those grounds? Are there any *good reasons* for believing that the proposition "God exists" is true, and if so what are those reasons? Such a question may be answered in a number of ways.

One way of answering this question is to say that there are some rational grounds for believing in the existence of God—in which case we ought to be prepared to say what those grounds are. What this means in practice is that an *argument* for the existence of God is put forward and an attempt is made to show that the argument succeeds in establishing the truth of the assertion that God exists. Chapters 48–50 attempt to do this in terms of three of the traditional arguments for the existence of God.

It should be noted at this point that what is to be allowed to count as "rational grounds" in this connection depends very much on a man's epistemological persuasion. If a man is an empiricist, for example, he cannot go along with the proponent of the cosmological argument when he makes an appeal to "rational insight" (Chapter 49). If, on the other hand, someone is persuaded by the cosmological argument, then he must be prepared to draw the epistemological consequences. Here, as with every philosophical problem, intricate and important interrelationships with other philosophical issues are evident.

A second way of answering this question is to say that none of the arguments offered in support of the existence of God is sound and to draw the conclusion that God does not exist. It is evident that philosophical naturalism cannot allow the existence of God (as defined above). It is, therefore, incumbent on a naturalist to take this position with respect to the proposed arguments. A critique of the arguments from this perspective is offered in Chapter 51.

Not all of those who deny the soundness of the traditional arguments for the existence of God are philosophical naturalists, however. Some theologians, for example, deny that the existence of God can be established by rational argument; yet they obviously do not draw the conclusion that God does not exist. This position—the view that there are no sound arguments by which the existence of God can be proved, but that God nonetheless exists and His existence is certified in certain (presumably) nonargumentative ways—represents a third way of responding to the question posed in this section. Chapter 52 attempts to build the case for such a view.

A Preliminary Look at the Arguments

Since the question as to whether or not God exists is one in which many people have been extremely interested, it is not surprising that a rather large number of arguments have been constructed in an attempt to prove that the proposition "God exists" is true. No less than five types of arguments have been put forward. Let us survey them briefly before proceeding to a more detailed consideration of three such arguments.

It is possible to argue, first, that the *existence* of God can be correctly inferred from the *idea* of God. Such an argument is termed an *ontological* argument for the existence of God. This type of argument, the most famous example of which was formulated by St. Anselm of Canterbury (1033–1109), is considered in some detail in Chapter 48.

Second, it is possible to argue that the existence of the world presupposes, implies, or points to the existence of God. This type of argument is called a *cosmological* argument for the existence of God. Among the best-known arguments of this type are those of Avicenna (980–1037) and St. Thomas Aquinas (1225–1274).

A third type of argument begins with the fact that there is order in the world and attempts to reason from this fact to the conclusion that God exists. An argument of this type is called a *teleological* argument. Arguments of this type have been advocated by such men as William Paley (1743–1805) and F. R. Tennant (1866–1957).

The *moral* argument for the existence of God attempts to reason from certain features of moral experience to the conclusion that God exists. Immanuel Kant (1726–1806) defended a version of this argument, as did also the British philosophers W. R. Sorley (1855–1935) and A. E. Taylor (1869–1945).

A fifth type of argument is the *argument from religious experience*. Such an argument begins with certain features of religious experience and attempts to reason from these to the conclusion that God exists.

This type of argument is rarely encountered in serious philosophical discussion, but it is attacked from time to time—apparently on the supposition that there are people who endorse some version of it.

There are few areas of philosophical inquiry in which the poverty of language is more evident than in the discussion of the arguments for the existence of God. The "five ways" of Aquinas, for example, are stated in the language of Aristotelian metaphysics and are quite unintelligible apart from an understanding of that metaphysical system. Since Aristotelian metaphysics does not inform the conceptual vocabulary of most people today, an intelligent appraisal of Aquinas' arguments is simply impossible for these people. It will be evident in the essays that follow that the advocates of the various arguments for the existence of God are groping for a terminology that is both adequate to express the ideas they are trying to express and intelligible to modern ears.

STUDY QUESTIONS

1. Why is it necessary to come to some agreement about the meaning of the term "God" before engaging in a discussion of arguments purporting to prove the existence of God?
2. Does the definition of God here proposed agree with what you have ordinarily understood the term to mean? If not, how would the definition have to be altered in order to express what you have understood it to mean?
3. What are the reasons given for using the terms "reality" and "ground" rather than "being" and "cause" in the definition of God? Do these strike you as being sound reasons? What difference would it make in the discussion if the terms "being" and "cause" were substituted for "reality" and "ground"?
4. What is an ontological argument for the existence of God? a cosmological argument? a teleological argument? a moral argument? an argument from religious experience?

48

THE ONTOLOGICAL
ARGUMENT

The history of Western man's struggles with the problem of the existence of God during the past sixteen hundred years provides an interesting commentary on the development of Western thought during
this period of time. At the first stage in this development—in the
thought of St. Augustine—the existence of God is simply taken for
granted: it is regarded as a matter so self-evident that a proof of God's
existence would be simply superfluous. At the present stage of this
development (I do not say the last), it is the *non*existence of God that
is commonly taken for granted: any attempt to prove the existence of
God today is, in the view of many of our contemporaries, anachronis-
tic and futile. The intervening chapters in this history, marked by the
explicit formulation of the ontological argument (St. Anselm), the
rejection of the ontological argument in favor of the cosmological argument (Aquinas), and the rejection of both of these in favor of the
teleological argument (Deism), indicate the course by which our culture generally has moved from an implicit belief in the existence of
God to an implicit disbelief in the existence of God. An advocate of
any argument for the existence of God today has little reason to be
optimistic about his prospects for winning a substantial number of
adherents for his point of view.

Moreover, the task is rendered even more difficult by the incredible
ignorance of many people regarding what is to be proved. A reasonably well-educated person should know that philosophers who believe
it is possible for us to demonstrate that God exists emphatically do *not*
believe in the existence of "the Old Man in the Sky" of primitive
supernaturalism. Even St. Augustine, who might have been excused
for holding what we would regard as "primitive" ideas, knew better. If
the only alternatives before us were naturalism and supernaturalism,

then it is clear that the only honest choice anyone could make would have to be naturalism. Supernaturalism, with its demons and its angels, its throne in the heavens, and its Old Man in the Sky, belongs to the childhood of our culture. These things may survive indefinitely in the symbolism of religious communities and as the picture language of simple religious faith, but they have no place in the serious discussion of the question concerning the existence of God. It would be better if the problem of the existence of God were never discussed at all than to have it discussed in such a childish and superficial way.

There is, happily, an alternative, and that is to enter seriously and passionately into a consideration of what it means to affirm that God exists, to try to grasp this great affirmation so profoundly and so intimately as to understand how some men—not simple and unlettered men, but some of the intellectual giants of our culture—could have regarded it as unthinkable that any man *who knew what he was doing* could refuse to affirm it. Let this question be our point of departure: How could intelligent and learned men—men like St. Augustine and St. Anselm—have been persuaded, as almost nobody is today, that the existence of God is self-evident? What did they see, or think, or feel, or understand that most men today apparently do not? Perhaps in this way we may begin to understand what a twentieth-century version of the ontological argument would be and why, even today, it deserves our attention and respect.

St. Anselm

St. Anselm of Canterbury (1033–1109) was one of the few truly original thinkers who appeared during the long interval of time between St. Augustine (354–430) and St. Thomas Aquinas (1225–1274). Like St. Augustine, whom he sought to emulate, St. Anselm conceived his task to be that of an apologist for Christian orthodoxy. All his writings reflect his theological and apologetic concerns; indeed, he did not make a hard and fast distinction between theology and philosophy. In two of his writings, however—the *Monologium* and the *Proslogium*— he advanced a number of arguments for the existence of God. These are worthy of study in themselves quite apart from the apologetic context out of which they arose.

The ontological argument was the product of St. Anselm's quest for

> . . . a single argument which would require no other for its proof than itself alone; and alone would suffice to demonstrate that God truly exists, and that there is a supreme good requiring nothing else, which all other things require for their existence and well-being.[1]

---

[1] St. Anselm, in S. N. Deane (tr.), *Proslogium (and other writings)* (LaSalle, Ill.: Open Court, 1962), p. 1.

The arguments that he had previously offered (in the *Monologium*) were, St. Anselm realized, extremely complex and, therefore, unconvincing to many readers. The argument he sought and believed he now had found was to be so simple that no one could fail to understand it, and so cogent that no one who understood it could fail to be convinced by it.

Unfortunately, the argument as developed by St. Anselm is far from simple, at least to modern ears. The crucial passage reads as follows:

> Even the fool is convinced that something exists in the understanding, at least, than which nothing greater can be conceived. For, when he hears of this, he understands it. And whatever is understood, exists in the understanding. And assuredly that, than which nothing greater can be conceived, cannot exist in the understanding alone. For, suppose it exists in the understanding alone: then it can be conceived to exist in reality; which is greater. Therefore, if that, than which nothing greater can be conceived, exists in the understanding alone, the very being, than which nothing greater can be conceived, is one, than which a greater can be conceived. But obviously this is impossible. Hence, there is no doubt that there exists a being, than which nothing greater can be conceived, and it exists both in the understanding and in reality . . . There is, then, so truly a being than which nothing greater can be conceived to exist, that it cannot even be conceived not to exist.[2]

This is a far more forceful argument than most of St. Anselm's critics have realized. In order to appreciate its cogency, however, it is first necessary to understand it; and this is not easy.

The Argument Restated

The force of St. Anselm's remarkable argument may be seen more clearly if it is restated as follows:

Proposition 1. By the term "God" is meant a being than which none greater can be conceived.

Proposition 2. Whether we affirm or deny the existence of God, a being than which none greater can be conceived exists in the understanding.

Proposition 3. It is possible to conceive of a being than which none greater can be conceived existing not only in the understanding but in reality as well; and this is greater.

Proposition 4. If, therefore, a being than which none greater can be conceived exists *only* in the understanding, it is not a being than which none greater can be conceived.

---

2 *Ibid.*, pp. 8–9.

Proposition 5. Therefore, a being than which none greater can be conceived exists also in reality.

I do not think that anyone would deny that if Propositions 1–4 are allowed to stand, Proposition 5 (the conclusion) would follow from them. Let us consider what may be said in defense of Propositions 1–4.

Proposition 1 simply asserts a minimal definition of the term "God." St. Anselm is saying, in effect, that people who believe in the existence of God believe in the existence of a being than which none greater can be conceived, that the only way to deny the existence of God is to deny the existence of a being than which none greater can be conceived. Thus far, it seems to me, St. Anselm's opponents have no reason to object. If they do, the result is only a quibble over terms since it is this definition that determines the substance of what St. Anselm means when he affirms that God exists.

Proposition 2 simply points out the obvious fact that anyone who affirms or denies the existence of God must, first, understand the meaning of the term "God." If anyone says the words, "God does not exist," but means something other than "a being than which none greater can be conceived does not exist," he is only denying the existence of something else to which he incorrectly gives the name "God." In order to really affirm or deny the existence of *God*—in order, that is, to be a party to this debate at all—we must understand what the term "God" means. And since, as St. Anselm says, "whatever is understood, exists in the understanding," Proposition 2 must be affirmed.

This brings us to Proposition 3, which is surely the crux of St. Anselm's famous argument. What is St. Anselm saying? He is saying that it is possible for us to distinguish in thought between (a) a being that exists only in our concept and (b) a being that exists in our concept and in reality; he is also stating that a being of the latter sort is greater than a being of the former sort. Let us consider this matter very carefully.

Two important questions must be asked: Can we make the distinction St. Anselm says we can make? Is it self-evidently true that a being existing in reality is on that ground alone greater than a being existing only in concept?

As to the first, it seems evident that in some cases, at least, we have no difficulty in making the distinction that St. Anselm asks us to make. We can distinguish without difficulty, for example, between an imaginary dog and a real dog; the proof that we are making a distinction between the two is that we have certain expectations in connection with the one that we do not have in connection with the other. I am thinking at this moment, for example, of a particular Dalmatian. I expect to see him occasionally as I drive by the yard where he usually is kept, I expect to observe him playing with the neighborhood children, and so on. But I can also form the concept of a dog identical with him in every respect save one: this dog exists only in my concept, not in reality. This dog, I know, will never be lying in the yard as I drive by, will never play with the neighborhood children, will never chase my car—unless, of course, I provide some *imaginary* children and cars for him to frolic with. I do not have the same expectations with respect to the latter that I have with respect to the former; and the reason is that I can and do distinguish between real and merely conceptual existents. If Kant's oft-quoted statement that existence is not a predicate means, as it is usually supposed to mean, that it is not possible for us to make this distinction, then I think we must conclude that on this point Kant was simply mistaken. We can and do make the distinction that St. Anselm is asking us to make.

Is it self-evidently true, then, that a being existing in reality is on that ground alone greater (more perfect) than an otherwise identical being existing only in concept? Here, it seems to me, we must choose among three alternatives: either (a) whatever order of excellence may be attributed to a thing in concept, some additional excellence accrues to that thing if, in addition, it is conceived to exist in reality; or (b) whatever order of excellence may be attributed to a thing in concept, that excellence is totally unaffected if, in addition, it is conceived to exist in reality; or (c) whatever order of excellence may be attributed to a thing in concept, that excellence is diminished if, in addition, it is conceived to exist in reality. I know of no way to *prove* that the first of these alternatives is to be preferred to the other two. For myself, however, I have no doubt that St. Anselm's assumption on this point is correct, and I should think that the burden of proof must lie with those who would adopt either of the other two alternatives.

I should like to urge my readers to ponder very carefully what St. Anselm is saying at this point, for if they can understand and accept Proposition 3 they should have no difficulty in agreeing with the remainder of the argument. Can we distinguish between a being that exists only in concept and a being that exists both in concept and in reality? The answer certainly is that we can. Then it makes sense to say that existence in concept and in reality is better than existence in concept alone. Peace in the world is certainly better than a mere concept of peace in our minds That God should exist in reality is certainly better than that we should merely have a concept of Him. We can and do distinguish between mere conceptual existence and real existence, and we do regard the latter as superior. It *is* possible to conceive of a being than which none greater can be conceived existing not only in the understanding but in reality as well; and this *is* greater.

It follows (Proposition 4) that if a being than which none greater can be conceived exists in the understanding only, it is not a being than which none greater can be conceived. Consider: it has already been shown (Proposition 3) that a being existing in concept *and* in reality is superior to an otherwise identical being existing in concept only. If, therefore, you say that this being exists in concept only you are contradicting yourself; for you are saying that a being than which none greater can be conceived is not in fact a being than which none greater can be conceived. Such a statement is contradictory in the same way that the statement "Some round figures are not round" is contradictory: it asserts something in the subject that is denied in the predicate.

But note well what this means: *You cannot deny the existence in reality of a being than which none greater can be conceived without contradicting yourself.* Since by the term "God" we mean a being than which none greater can be conceived, it follows that the statement "God exists" is necessarily true. Once we grasp the concept of God as a being than which none greater can be conceived, we cannot fail to understand that God's existence is a logical necessity. God, as St. Anselm says, "cannot even be conceived not to exist."

It is sometimes said by those who reject this argument that if it were a sound argument it should be possible to prove in the same way the existence of many things—for example, an island than which a more beautiful one cannot be conceived. The answer to this objection is that the reasoning is not parallel, and so the conclusion does not follow. There is no logical necessity in the existence of an island than which a more beautiful one cannot be conceived, for the concept of existence is not implicit in the concept of maximum beauty. In the one unique case of a being than which a greater cannot be conceived, however, the reasoning applies, for existence is implicit in the concept of such a being (Proposition 3). In this one case, and only in this one case, real existence follows necessarily from the mere concept of such a being.

The question before us is, Are there any rational grounds for believing in the existence of God, and if so what are those grounds? I have argued that the very concept of God as a being than which none greater can be conceived makes it logically necessary that God exists —that our belief in the existence of God rests on the very secure rational ground of logical necessity. It follows, then, that to deny the existence of God is not only to make an error of fact: it is also to be involved in a self-contradiction, to make a logical error. Thus we ask with St. Anselm:

Why, then, has the fool said in his heart, there is no God (Psalms 14:1), since it is so evident, to a rational mind, that [God] dost exist in the highest degree of all? Why, except that he is dull and a fool? [3]

---

[3] *Ibid.*, p. 19.

STUDY QUESTIONS

1. The author of this chapter seems to be rather pessimistic about the prospects for convincing many of his readers of the soundness of his (or any other) argument for the existence of God. Why? What factors in our culture does he cite as obstacles that an advocate of any such argument must try to overcome?

2. Does the "restatement" offered here accurately reproduce St. Anselm's argument? If not, how should it be revised in order to do so?

3. We are advised in this chapter that we ought to accept the first two premises of St. Anselm's argument without question. Do you agree? Defend your answer.

4. "It is possible for us to distinguish in thought between (a) a being that exists only in our concept, and (b) a being that exists in our concept and in reality." Do you agree or disagree? Defend your position.

5. "A being that exists in our concept and in reality is greater than an otherwise identical being that exists only in our concept." Do you agree or disagree? Defend your position.

6. In your opinion, is the ontological argument a sound argument? If not, where do you think it goes wrong?

49

THE COSMOLOGICAL
ARGUMENT

Anyone involved at all seriously in the discussion of the problem of the existence of God—or, more specifically, the problem of assessing the cogency of the several arguments for the existence of God that have been put forward—is painfully aware that the present-day advocate of any such argument must somehow try to overcome a number of serious obstacles. Chief among these are the following: (a) the apparently inescapable vagueness of the concept "God," (b) the anti-metaphysical bias of modern thought, and, as a corollary, (c) the absence of a vocabulary acceptable to the modern mind that is suitable for the construction of a proof of the existence of God. I am not sanguine about the prospects for overcoming these obstacles in what follows; but I do think the existence of God is capable of strict demonstration and shall do my best to state my proof in a form that will not require a modern reader to stretch his ordinary categories of thought too far.

It is not surprising that the concept of God is less precise than most of the concepts that we customarily employ; most of our concepts are of objects that exist in space and time—objects concerning which it is appropriate to ask questions like: Where is it? How big is it? What color is it? and so on. If the concept of God were to be given that kind of precision, we would no longer be talking about *God* at all; for whatever we do mean by "God," it is clear that we do not mean "one object (or being) among others in the world of space and time."

The question concerning the existence of God is, therefore, a unique question. It would be silly to try to prove the existence of a spatiotemporal object. The existence of any such object is a purely contingent fact: to convince anyone of its existence you must produce not an argument but *the object itself*. Only if it presents itself in some way to some one of our senses are we willing to say that it "exists." And rightly so.

But God cannot be presented to any one of our senses in such a way that we can know of His existence in the same way that we know of the existence of spatiotemporal objects. If we are to know of the existence of God, therefore, it must—in this one, unique case—be by way of argument, or demonstration. The question we must ask is this: Is there any feature of the world of space and time that points to a reality that *transcends* space and time, is the ground of the being and value of this world, and is worthy of man's worship? To answer this question in the affirmative is to construct (or at least to affirm that it is possible to construct) a cosmological argument for the existence of God.

St. Thomas Aquinas

"The existence of God," said Aquinas, "can be proved in five ways." [1] Thereupon, in a scant three pages, the great Angelic Doctor gave to the world five of the most famous arguments for the existence of God that have ever been formulated.

None of the "five ways" is original with Aquinas (nor, of course, did he claim that they were), and they are not equally persuasive. The first three "ways," in particular, are very similar, and all three differ markedly from both the fourth and the fifth arguments. There are reasons for regarding the third "way" as the fundamental, or centrally important, one of Aquinas' five arguments. The complete text of this argument reads as follows:

> The third way is taken from possibility and necessity, and runs thus. We find in nature things that are possible to be or not to be, since they are found to be generated, and to be corrupted, and consequently, it is possible for them to be and not to be. But it is impossible for these always to exist, for that which can not-be at some time is not. Therefore, if anything can not-be, then at one time there was nothing in existence, because that which does not exist begins to exist only through something already existing. Therefore, if at one time nothing was in existence, it would have been impossible for anything to have begun to exist; and thus even now nothing would be in existence— which is absurd. Therefore, not all beings are merely possible, but there must exist something the existence of which is necessary. [But every necessary thing either has its necessity caused by another, or not. Now it is impossible to go on to infinity in necessary things which have their necessity caused by another, as has already been proved

[1] St. Thomas Aquinas, *Summa Theologica*, I, Ques. 2, Art. 3, in Anton C. Pegis (ed.), *Basic Writings of St. Thomas Aquinas* (New York: Random House, 1945), Vol. I, p. 22.

in regard to efficient causes. Therefore we cannot but admit the existence of some being having of itself its own necessity, and not receiving it from another, but rather causing in others their necessity.] This all men speak of as God.[2]

Although I hold this to be a sound argument, I do think it suffers from one serious defect. It is more complicated than it needs to be because of Aquinas' inclusion of a multiplicity of "necessary things which have their necessity caused by another." It may have been necessary to include this for polemical reasons at the time that Aquinas was writing, but to a modern reader it appears as excess baggage that serves only to clutter up the argument. Nothing essential to the argument is lost, I think, if we simply omit this reference to a series of hypothetical "necessary beings" (everything within the brackets above) and conclude directly from the existence of "beings [that] are merely possible" to the existence of "something the existence of which is necessary . . . [that] all men speak of as God."

Both defenders and critics of this argument sometimes assert that the starting point of the argument is a fairly obvious feature of the world, namely, that something exists. I think that this assertion is incorrect and that it indicates a serious misunderstanding of the argument. The starting point of the argument is not that something exists (that *is* obvious) but that some *contingent beings* exist—and that is not obvious at all. It is precisely at this point that we determine whether or not we are going to go along with Aquinas' argument; either we share his insight into *the contingency of finite beings*, or we remain unconvinced by his argument.

Two Common Criticisms

It will be convenient to deal at this point with two criticisms that are frequently made of this argument. The words "necessary" and "contingent," it is sometimes said, are words that apply not to *things* but to *propositions*. To speak of God as a "necessary being," or "something the existence of which is necessary," must mean (if it means anything at all), "The proposition 'God exists' is a necessary proposition." But this is precisely the claim of the ontological argument. Therefore, the cosmological argument reduces ultimately to the ontological argument, and if the ontological argument is not sound, then neither, obviously, is the cosmological.

It is easy to show, however, that this is a superficial criticism. It is superficial because it starts with purely arbitrary definitions of the terms "necessary" and "contingent." It then attempts to employ these definitions to make Aquinas—or anyone else who advocates this form

---

[2] *Ibid.,* pp. 22–23. The brackets will be explained in the following paragraphs.

of the cosmological argument—say something he clearly and definitely did not say and did not mean to say. Let it be granted that in logic the terms "necessary" and "contingent" apply only to propositions (not to terms or to arguments). In logic, a necessary proposition is one the negation of which involves a self-contradiction; a contingent proposition is one the negation of which does *not* involve a self-contradiction. Does this exclude the possibility that *outside* the realm of logic—in metaphysics, for example—these same terms may have a somewhat different meaning? Of course not.

The cosmological argument, in whatever form, always moves from the *ontological contingency* of finite being to the *ontological necessity* of the ground of being. Aquinas does not, in the argument quoted above, use the term "contingent"; he speaks instead about "things that are possible to be or not to be." But that is precisely what "ontological contingency" means.

A second very common—and, in my view, mistaken—objection to Aquinas' argument concerns his claim that "It is impossible to go on to infinity," which is essential to the argument in each of the first three ways. Why can't you go on to infinity? some critics have asked. Mathematicians regularly employ the notion of an infinite series. Why should we regard it as self-evident that a series of "contingent beings" or "causes" cannot proceed to infinity?

This objection, like the first, rests on a misunderstanding of the cosmological argument. Aquinas' point is not that a particular being —a man, let us say—is dependent on his parents for his existence, and they on their parents, and they on theirs, and so on—all the way back to God. The cosmological argument has nothing to do with the relation between parents and children: it has to do with the present ontological contingency of some being and its present dependence for its existence on some noncontingent ground. The possibility of an infinite mathematical series is, therefore, totally irrelevant to the argument.

That the cosmological argument has nothing to do with this story of one generation succeeding another may also be seen in the fact that if the argument is construed in this way, it can at best prove that *at some time in the past* there was a remote ancestor of this presently existing contingent being. It is not the purpose of the cosmological argument to prove the present existence of somebody's great-great-great-great . . . grandfather. Therefore, it should be evident that to construe the argument in this way is to *mis*construe it, indeed to render it altogether ludicrous.

I have dwelt briefly on these two objections to the cosmological argument for two reasons: first, because they are commonly accepted as sound objections to the argument and for that reason seem to require some answer; second, because they reveal some of the most common misunderstandings of the cosmological argument. The discussion of them affords an opportunity to point out and attempt to remove these misunderstandings. I may be wrong in my view that the cosmological argument is a sound and convincing proof of the existence of God, but I am not wrong in insisting that any opinion with respect to this argument should be based on a serious effort to understand the argument as it is understood and intended by those who support it.

A Restatement

By way of exhibiting even more clearly the truly persuasive character of the cosmological argument, I should like to offer a restatement of the argument in what I take to be its simplest possible form. The argument can be reduced to just two premises and a conclusion. I propose to state it in this way and to indicate the grounds on which each of the premises rests; I should then hope that some of my readers may find it possible to join me in affirming the conclusion.

The cosmological argument, reduced to its simplest possible form, may be stated as follows:

Some contingent beings exist.
Contingent beings require a noncontingent ground of being in order to exist.

A noncontingent ground of being exists.

The crucial step in this argument, as I have already indicated, is the first premise. In assessing this argument the question that must be asked is: *On what basis* is it affirmed that "some contingent beings exist"?

The answer that must be given will, I fear, be disappointing to many. The ontological contingency of finite beings must be grasped directly; it cannot be demonstrated on the basis of some other more evident truths. I know only too well that the notion of "rational insight" is distinctly out of favor at present; but if we do not have such direct insight into the ontological contingency of finite things, we cannot know it at all.

Though this truth cannot be demonstrated, however, it may be possible to suggest a few things that will help to "elicit the insight." Aquinas does this, for example, when he calls attention to the fact that things in nature are subject to "generation and corruption"—they come into being and pass away. "My days," says the Psalmist, "are like a shadow that declineth, and I am withered like grass." [3] The coming-into-being and the passing-away of individuals is, of course, a fact that can be observed. This fact can, and often does, give rise to the

---

[3] Psalms, 102:11.

feeling of the transience of all things, of the tenuous and precarious character of finite existence. From here it is but a step to the rational insight into the ontological contingency of finite being upon which the cosmological argument rests.

Or we may take a slightly different approach. At the present moment you are, of course, existing. If you are like most people, you probably take your existence for granted. Concerning the future (tomorrow, for example), you do not ask Will I *be*? but What will I be *doing*? But in all seriousness, can you simply take your own existence for granted? Isn't existence a gift received anew moment by moment? It is certainly conceivable that in the next moment we, and our world, could be annihilated, we could simply cease to exist—in short, that the gift of existence could be withdrawn and in our place there should be nothing. To ponder our own existence in this way is to feel the uncertainty, the precariousness, the gratuitousness of all finite existence, including our own. To conceptualize this feeling is to grasp the ontological contingency of finite being, the rational insight with which the cosmological argument begins.

The second premise of the argument—that contingent beings require (presuppose) a noncontingent ground of being in order to exist —is analytically true. To say that something is "contingent" is to say that it is "ontologically dependent": it is to affirm a relation and therefore implicitly to posit that to which the relation refers. If we understand what we have said when we have affirmed the contingency of finite being, there is no difficulty in affirming this second premise. Its function is simply to spell out what is implied in the initial insight into the contingency of finite being, and this in such a way as to make it evident that this insight does indeed imply the existence of God.

The Object of Worship

Although in my discussion thus far I have had in mind chiefly those critics of the cosmological argument who think it tries to prove too much (that God exists), I am not unaware that there are other critics who object to the argument on the ground that it proves too little. A deeply religious person may respond to the cosmological argument with profound indignation because the "ground of being" who appears at the conclusion of the argument—this "God of the philosophers," as Blaise Pascal said—bears little or no resemblance to the loving Heavenly Father of living religious faith. "Away with these abstractions!" is the cry of such well-meaning people. What is to be said in answer to such an objection?

Part of the answer—and the only answer I shall attempt to give—is that it is not the business of the philosopher to attempt to prove everything about God that is of importance for religious faith. Faith simply presupposes the reality of God and by means of a rich symbolism seeks to worship Him in a way that is worthy of Him. Faith lives in symbolism and in imagery, not primarily in concepts; this is why all *concepts* of God—even those formulated by theologians—seem, from the point of view of faith, woefully inadequate.

But philosophers, *qua* philosophers, are not entitled to such a presupposition. For philosophy the question whether God exists is a legitimate and, indeed, inescapable question. As I have indicated, I believe that we are entitled to answer this question in the affirmative. I believe, further, that the concept of God that emerges at the conclusion of the cosmological argument is capable of considerable enrichment, when the argument is applied to a wide variety of contingent existents (as Aquinas does, for example, in the first three of his "five ways"). But the God whose existence is thus established, though surely worthy of man's worship, can never acquire by philosophical argument the rich (but profoundly anthropomorphic) connotations that religious faith ascribes to Him in poetry, prayer, and song. In comparison with the God of living faith, the God of the cosmological argument must appear highly abstract, austere, and remote. Philosophical argument cannot deal in imagery: it is limited to concepts, which it must strive to make as precise as it possibly can. Philosophical argument cannot disclose to us the richer reality that is the object of religious faith, but it can and does disclose to us the reality of God as the ground of the being of finite things. We must not expect of it more than this.

STUDY QUESTIONS

1. What is meant by the statement that the question concerning the existence of God is "a unique question"? Is it? What assumptions is one making if one holds that it is? if one holds that it is not?
2. Restate St. Thomas Aquinas' "third way" premise by premise, just as St. Anselm's argument was restated in the previous chapter.
3. What are the "two common criticisms" of the cosmological argument that our author attempts to refute? Does he succeed?
4. What is the difference between attempting to "prove a proposition" and attempting to "elicit an insight"? Why does the author of this chapter resort to the latter?
5. Who would be apt to criticize the cosmological argument on the ground that it proves too much? on the ground that it proves too little? What is your own opinion of the argument?

50

THE TELEOLOGICAL ARGUMENT

Like the two writers who are to succeed me in this discussion, I am not at all impressed with either the ontological argument or the cosmological argument for the existence of God. I have never been impressed with them in their "classical" formulations—those of St. Anselm and Aquinas, respectively—and I am no more impressed with them after reading the explanations offered by the preceding two writers. Both of these arguments are vulnerable to a really devastating and, I think, decisive critique, which I assume will be forthcoming in the chapters that follow. I shall be content, therefore, to simply state my rejection of these arguments, leaving the detailed criticism to others, and shall proceed directly to the formulation and defense of a third argument that in my estimation is far more persuasive.

The argument of which I speak is commonly called the "teleological" argument (from the Greek word *télos*, meaning "end" or "goal"). Aquinas' "fifth way" is a version of this argument, but the "classical" statement of the argument is in William Paley's *Evidences of the Existence and Attributes of the Deity.*[1] It is an argument that deserves to be studied with great care.

The Sense of Wonder

We shall be better prepared both to understand and to appreciate the teleological argument if we first consider briefly the kind of human

---

[1] William Paley, in Frederick Ferré (ed.), *Natural Theology; Selections* (Indianapolis: Bobbs–Merrill, 1963).

experience out of which, or against the background of which, the argument has come to be formulated.

All but the most pedestrian and unpoetic of human beings must, at times, be impressed by the vastness, the grandeur, the beauty, and the order of the universe. There is a feeling of awe and wonder when we stand upon the shore of a stormy sea, gaze upward on a starry night, or survey the rugged beauty of a range of mountains. Here is power, restless and profound; here is vastness, staggering in magnitude; yet here is order, beautiful to behold.

Scientists in whom the sense of poetry is still alive tell us of a similar experience when they have penetrated some of the less obvious wonders of nature. To understand the structure of the atom is to marvel at its ordered complexity; to survey the course of evolution is to view a magnificent process unfolding through millenniums of time; to grasp the genetic code is to possess a key by means of which yet further mysteries of nature may shortly be unlocked. Here, too, are wonders of the universe at which men may well marvel—and do. Here are phenomena capable of inspiring awe of which our ancient predecessors could not even dream; but the wonders they beheld—the star-filled sky, the mountains, and the sea—are ours as well. How very much there is, in the world as we perceive it, to inspire that sense of awe of which we have been speaking.

It seems very natural, when some feature or other of the universe impresses us in this way, to say that it could not be by chance or accident that the universe is the way it is. A beautiful poem, a great symphony, a particularly inspiring work of architecture, a remarkable engineering achievement—these are impressive and rightly cause us to give honor to those whose efforts brought them into being. But more wonderful still is the poetry, the harmony, the power, the beauty, the architecture, and the structure of the universe itself. Surely it, too, has an Author, an Architect, a magnificent Craftsman, whose wisdom and power are commensurate with the mighty work that He has wrought. Every person living, at some time in his life—when these remarkable features of the universe were impressed upon him in some particularly overwhelming way—must have entertained sentiments such as these.

The Argument

It is against this background that we must try to understand and to appreciate the teleological argument. The teleological argument is simply an attempt to extract and to render conceptually precise the argument that is implicit in the natural reflections to which this experience of wonder gives rise.

Paley's formulation of the argument in *Evidences of the Existence and Attributes of the Deity* does not, unfortunately, lend itself to a brief summary statement. The argument, as he says, is cumulative; his whole book is the argument. I shall try to indicate the general course of his argument, however.

Paley begins by noting that whenever we come upon something of which it is apparent that "its several parts are framed and put together for a purpose"—a watch, for example—we conclude without hesitation that it has been designed for this purpose by some intelligent designer. Nothing that we may subsequently learn about the watch (that it sometimes fails to work perfectly, that it is capable of reproducing itself, or anything else) can dissuade us from believing that it (or, if it is the product of a "parent" watch, its most remote ancestor) is the product of an intelligent and skillful designer. Paley states:

> There cannot be design without a designer; contrivance, without a contriver; order, without choice; arrangement, without anything capable of arranging; subserviency and relation to a purpose, without that which could intend a purpose; means suitable to an end, and executing their office in accomplishing that end, without the end ever having been contemplated, or the means accommodated to it. Arrangement, disposition of parts, subserviency of means to an end, relation of instruments to a use, imply the presence of intelligence and mind.[2]

So much for the first part of Paley's argument. The second part of Paley's argument is to show that the universe abounds with phenomena that, like the watch, exhibit teleological order.

> Every indication of contrivance, every manifestation of design, which existed in the watch, exists in the works of nature; with the difference, on the side of nature, of being greater and more, and that in a degree which exceeds all computation . . . The contrivances of nature surpass the contrivances of art, in the complexity, subtlety, and curiosity of the mechanism; and still more, if possible, do they go beyond them in number and variety: yet, in a multitude of cases, are not less evidently mechanical, not less evidently contrivances, not less evidently accommodated to their end, or suited to their office, than are the most perfect productions of human ingenuity.[3]

Paley's favorite example of design in nature is the eye, whose delicate and intricate mechanism he discusses in great detail. But countless other examples are to be found in nature.

The conclusion, Paley suggests, must therefore be drawn: design in

2 *Ibid.*, p. 10.
3 *Ibid.*, p. 13.

nature points to the existence of an intelligent Designer of nature, just as design in a watch or other machine points to the existence of its designer.

> Were there no example in the world of contrivance except that of the eye, it would be alone sufficient to support the conclusion which we draw from it, as to the necessity of an intelligent Creator. It could never be got rid of because it could not be accounted for by any other supposition, which did not contradict all the principles we possess of knowledge.[4]

I think that this argument is sound and convincing, and I propose to reduce it to its barest essentials and to add a few comments by way of elucidating its fundamental structure.

Elucidation and Defense of the Argument

The teleological argument contains two premises, one straightforwardly factual and the other a general principle. The factual premise is: nature exhibits a number of instances of means ordered to ends. The general principle is: the ordering of means to ends presupposes the existence of an intelligent designer whose intelligence and power are sufficient to account for the product he has wrought. The whole argument, therefore, is as follows:

> Nature exhibits a number of instances of means ordered to ends.
>
> The ordering of means to ends presupposes the existence of an intelligent designer whose intelligence and power are sufficient to account for the product he has wrought.
>
> ---
>
> The ordering of means to ends in nature presupposes the existence of an intelligent designer whose intelligence and power are commensurate with the magnitude of his product.

It is important to note, in attempting to assess this argument, that it does not say, or presuppose, that the whole universe is cooperating to achieve some single ultimate purpose. This may or may not be the case: the argument is neutral with respect to this question. Some critics of the teleological argument have unfortunately failed to grasp this point.

It should also be observed that the argument does not say, or presuppose, that the several "ends" toward which the various means are ordered are necessarily good, or such as human beings would always approve of, or such as tend to serve our needs. The ferocity of the tiger, for example, and the various endowments that make it such a dangerous animal, serve the end of *its own* self-preservation—some-

---

[4] *Ibid.,* p. 44.

times, at man's expense. This is an "end" in the sense in which that term is used in this argument, human preferences in the matter notwithstanding. Numerous other examples could be given.

The factual premise in this argument seems to me to be simply beyond dispute. The evidence is all about us, and it is overwhelming. Animals have eyes in order to see, ears in order to hear, teeth in order to chew their food, digestive organs in order to utilize their food, lungs in order to breathe, and so on. In the plant world, too, we observe the adaptation of means to ends: root systems in order to draw nourishment from the soil, leaves in order to derive the benefits of the sunlight, and so on. Look where we will, the evidence is the same: every species of living thing known to us, every plant, every insect, every fish, every mammal, is endowed with those characteristics necessary to its existence and way of life.

We know, of course—as Paley did not—that this remarkable state of affairs has come about through a long process of evolution whereby the forms of life now found in nature have developed from other forms no longer extant. But this alters the argument not at all. Consider this process at any point you will: the sort of evidence we are now considering will abound in whatever state of the universe exists at that time. However far we press our inquiry into the remote past, we find not chaos but order: means subservient to ends, processes conducive to the emergence of life, circumstances conducive to the proliferation of life, powers adapted to the preservation of life. So much for the factual premise.

The second premise—that the ordering of means to ends presupposes the existence of some intelligent designer to "do the ordering"— is an inductive generalization well substantiated by experience. It is beyond dispute that in every such instance of which we have any reasonably certain knowledge, the principle holds true: we know of no watches without watchmakers, ships without ship-builders, or planes without plane-builders. We would never allow, if we were to be shown one of these objects, that without the intelligent direction of any mind whatsoever the object in question just "happened to happen." Where we find *means ordered to ends,* "chance" is as good as no answer at all; for in every such instance of which we do have knowledge, we find mind—intelligence—behind it. Every day we observe countless examples of this principle; we have never observed, or been offered, a counter-example. The principle would seem to be as secure, therefore, as it is possible for any inductive generalization to be.

If the argument is to be attacked, it must be on the ground that the order that we find in nature is not sufficiently similar to the order that we find in human contrivances to justify applying the principle. David Hume saw this clearly and in his *Dialogues Concerning Natural Religion* (published posthumously in 1779) exercised, as he says, "all

[his] sceptical and metaphysical subtilty" in an attempt to weaken the analogy. But after doing his best, or rather his worst, to find some alternative to intelligent design as a principle of explanation, even Hume is forced to conclude (in the words of Philo, his chief spokesman in the *Dialogues*):

> In many views of the universe and of its parts, particularly the latter, the beauty and fitness of final causes strike us with such irresistible force that all objections appear (what I believe they really are) mere cavils and sophisms; nor can we then imagine how it was ever possible for us to repose any weight on them.[5]

The order that we find in nature calls for *some* explanation. The analogy between it and the order that we find in contrivances known to be the product of intelligent purpose is infinitely stronger than any other analogy that anyone has been able to suggest. Against this objection, therefore, the teleological argument stands secure.

The Wider Teleological Argument

We have, of course, learned a great deal about the world since the days of Paley and Hume, and I can well imagine a reader acknowledging that such an argument had some persuasive power prior to the work of Charles Darwin, while pointing out that the adaptation of means to ends as we find it in nature is adequately explained by the principle of natural selection. In this opinion, there is no need for explanation through "divine intelligence." Since this objection appears serious to many people, it deserves to be treated with respect—though it is by no means fatal to the teleological argument. What it does is to force us to broaden the scope of the field within which we may discern the workings of the divine intelligence.

Consider the following remarkable facts about the world as we know it:

1. The world is intelligible in a very high degree. The world, somehow or other, is capable of being understood by means of the logical and mathematical categories of the human mind.
2. The evolutionary process, which posits "chance" mutations whose survival depends on their suitability to enhance the organism in its struggle for life, has operated *as if* it were intended to produce variety, beauty, mind, and intelligence.
3. The inorganic world, which according to current theory existed for hundreds of millions of years before life emerged on our planet, is remarkably well adapted—physically, chemically, thermally, etc. —to the maintenance of life.

---

[5] David Hume, in Norman Kemp Smith (ed.), *Dialogues Concerning Natural Religion*, 2d ed. (New York: Social Sciences, 1948), p. 202.

4. Nature has developed in such a way that there are numerous phenomena that elicit in at least one creature—man—a sense of beauty.
5. The conditions of human life have developed in such a way that man is able to postulate, pursue, and in a high degree achieve moral ideals.

How are we to account for these remarkable facts? What hypothesis will do justice to the truly astonishing fact that out of a mass of inorganic matter there has emerged, through a process that might have worked in countless other directions, not only life (which is remarkable enough in itself), but a being possessing intelligence, morality, and a sense of beauty? Say, if you will, that it is all a matter of chance, that the laws of nature had to produce *some* kind of a world, and that this just happened to be the one that emerged. I for one do not believe it. If this world emerged as "a throw of the dice," then I cannot escape the conclusion that the dice were loaded: there is, as Sir Arthur Eddington once remarked, a "cheater" some place in the vicinity. The hypothesis that the world is the way it is because God has arranged it that way is, I think, strongly supported by facts such as we enumerated above. Evolution, far from destroying the teleological argument, provides new evidence of adaptation of means to ends and thus supports the God-hypothesis that it is the purpose of the teleological argument to establish.

The Limits of Philosophical Argument

It is a mistake, extremely common in our day, to expect too little of philosophical argument; it is also a mistake, more common in the past, to expect too much. The teleological argument by itself does not and cannot be expected to give us a rich, "full-blown theology," such as would satisfy the wishes of a religious community. For that is needed the images evoked and provided by religious literature, the sentiments that are nourished in various rites of worship, and the vocabulary and ideas that have life and meaning only in the context and the tradition of this or that worshiping community. Any philosophical attempt to "fill out" the concept of God in these essentially religious ways would be rightly resisted, both by philosophers and by nonphilosophical adherents of religion.

The God whose existence is proved by the teleological argument is not the Brahman of Hindu faith, the Yahweh of Jewish faith, or the Heavenly Father of Christian faith. The God of the teleological argument, strictly speaking, is simply an unknown Mind and Power, by virtue of whose workings we find order in the world about us. About this austere notion cluster the sentiments of awe and wonder at the marvels of nature—the natural precursors, perhaps, of that "sense of the holy" that is so distinctive of religious communities. Perhaps, too, the awareness of the beauty of nature and of the greatness of the privilege of being alive leads to some intimation of the goodness of God, so that He is conceived not only as Mind and Power, but also as Goodness.

Philosophical reflection on the awesome spectacle of order in nature cannot take us beyond the bare knowledge of God's existence and the faint intimation of some few of His attributes. But—and this is the chief burden of this essay—it can take us this far. Having come this far, we may or may not turn to religion to enrich our concept yet further: that is another matter altogether. Philosophy is not theology, and philosophical understanding is not religious faith; but the understanding that philosophy can give us, limited though it is, may serve as a foundation for faith.

STUDY QUESTIONS

1. What relevance, if any, does the discussion of "the sense of wonder" have for the subsequent discussion of the teleological argument?
2. Look up St. Thomas Aquinas' "fifth way" (*Summa Theologica*, Part I, Question 2, Article 3), and compare it with the argument given in this chapter. What similarities do you find between the two arguments? What differences?
3. How does one go about identifying an instance in nature of "means ordered to ends"? What right have we to say, for example, that the "end" served by the ferocity of the tiger is the self-preservation of the tiger rather than the death of its prey? Is some criterion at work here that has not been made explicit?
4. Is the analogy between "order in nature" and "order in human contrivances" sufficiently close to support the second premise of the teleological argument? How important is this alleged analogy to the argument?
5. "Evolution, far from destroying the teleological argument, provides new evidence of adaptation of means to ends and thus supports the God-hypothesis that it is the purpose of the teleological argument to establish." What is your opinion?

51

THE NONEXISTENCE OF GOD: A NATURALISTIC REJOINDER

It is a fundamental tenet of philosophical naturalism that the whole of reality consists of objects and events occurring in space and time and that the system of spatiotemporal events that we call the "world" is self-dependent and self-operating. It is an obvious negative corollary of this view that there is nothing real that transcends this world —no gods, no values, no anything. To say that something "exists" is to say that it is, or is reducible to, some spatiotemporal event or events— events, moreover, that we can perceive or could perceive under such-and-such circumstances, or (at a minimum) that are causally related to events of this kind. It makes sense to say that grasshoppers exist, because we can see them. It makes sense to say that mountains exist on Venus, because we know what it would be like to see them. It makes sense to say that electrons exist, because the event that we call the existence of an electron is causally related to other events that we perceive. It does not make sense, in any of these ways, to say that God exists.

But no sooner do naturalists point out that the statement "God exists" is, at best, exceedingly odd (and at worst meaningless), than theists turn this very observation against us. "Quite so," they say, "but the reason is that the existence of God is a unique instance. Grasshoppers, mountains, and electrons exist only *contingently,* but God's existence—and this is the only one of its kind—is *necessary.* That is why the statement 'God exists' strikes us as being so odd." On this whole question of the existence of God I would like to make just one assertion and then be done with it: the statement "God exists" has no clear meaning; it is as senseless to deny it as it is to affirm it. But in view of the rejoinder ("This is a unique case") we have no choice but to go over the worn-out old arguments to show why they do not establish the proposition "God exists" in any meaningful acceptation of those terms. What follows, then, is a *disproof of the proofs* for the existence of God.

The Ontological Argument

There is one very strong prima facie reason for doubting the soundness of the ontological argument and that is that practically everybody who has studied it carefully has in the end rejected it. St. Anselm, of course, who invented the argument, believed it to be sound; so also did René Descartes and Gottfried Wilhelm von Leibniz. But Gaunilon in the eleventh century, Aquinas in the thirteenth, Hume and Kant in the eighteenth, and nearly every major philosopher since then have rejected it. If we can decide on the soundness of an argument on the basis of the consensus of those who are most competent to judge, the ontological argument must be adjudged a failure.

The critics of the ontological argument have rejected it principally for three reasons, all of which I consider valid. First, if the reasoning contained in the ontological argument were sound, it should be applicable in other instances as well—namely, to the superlative instance of any positive quality. It should be possible to prove (by a parallel argument) the existence of an island than which none more beautiful can be conceived (this was Gaunilon's example), a mountain than which none taller can be conceived, and so on. But this is clearly absurd. It seems evident, therefore, that something is wrong with the argument.

We begin to understand just what is wrong with it when we consider, in the second place, that it really is not the case that when anyone either affirms or denies the existence of God, a being than which none greater can be conceived "exists in the understanding." Let it be granted that we can utter the *words*, "a being than which none greater can be conceived"; but we have no *concept* of a being so described. St. Anselm's statement that, whether we affirm or deny the existence of God, a being than which none greater can be conceived "exists in the understanding," is an exceedingly odd statement. If it means anything at all it must mean that he who affirms or denies the existence of God has a *concept* of a being than which none greater can be conceived. And this, I am saying, is highly questionable; indeed, I think it is false.

The third reason for rejecting the argument is the most decisive. Existence, as Kant said, is not a predicate. To assert that something is *red*, for example, is to make an assertion that requires us to alter our concept of that thing; "red," therefore, is a predicate. But the assertion that something *exists* in no way modifies our concept of that thing.

The ontological argument hinges on an alleged contrast (Proposition 3 of the summary) between (a) a being existing only in the understanding and (b) an otherwise identical being existing both in the understanding and in reality. But this is a contrast, a distinction in thought, that it is not possible for us to make. Our *concept* of a real Dalmatian differs in no way from our *concept* of an imaginary one. The difference between the two does not consist in anything found in the concepts themselves but rather in the different ways in which the two concepts are related to our (actual or possible) perceptions. Hence, even if it were possible to form a concept of a being than which none greater can be conceived (and I have questioned this), it still would not be possible to conclude to the existence of God; the crucial distinction upon which the whole argument turns is one that it is not possible to make.

The Cosmological Argument

There are many forms of the cosmological argument, and it would be a tedious job to pass them all in review and criticize each in detail. In Chapter 49 the cosmological argument has been presented in the form that most contemporary supporters regard as its most persuasive form, and I shall restrict my remarks to this version. Anyone who understands what is wrong with the argument in this form will have no difficulty in detecting the weaknesses in any other form of the argument that he may happen to encounter.

The cosmological argument as stated suffers from three very serious defects. Let us begin at the beginning: the first premise ("Some contingent beings exist") is either unintelligible, or it is a truism. If it is unintelligible, it is not deserving of serious consideration. If it is a truism, nothing of importance follows.

I am at this moment looking at an ashtray. It presumably is one of the "contingent beings" that this premise says exists. Very well. What does it mean to say that this ashtray is "contingent"? I can think of three possibilities. It may mean that (a) there was a time when this ashtray did not exist and now it does—it has "come into being" and will, presumably, some day cease to exist. Or it may mean that (b) the nonexistence of this ashtray is conceivable. Or it may mean that (c) the continuation in existence of this ashtray is dependent on certain things without which it would cease to exist. If *a*, nothing of importance follows. You may, if you wish, argue to the existence at some time in the past of an ashtray maker, but this is quite obviously beside the point. If *b*, again nothing of importance follows. We can conceive of the nonexistence of anything simply by thinking of it as occupying space and then imagining that space to be empty. If *c* is meant, the situation is a little more complicated, but the result is the same. It is apparent, for example, that the continued existence of this ashtray depends on the continued validity of certain laws of physics— the cohesion of its parts, its tolerance of the temperature levels to which it is subjected, and so on. But this does not take us any distance at all toward establishing the proposition, "God exists."

If the proposition, "Some contingent beings exist," does not mean one of these three things, I can only insist that I find it unintelligible. If there is something else that I am supposed to "see directly," I can only confess that I do not see it. Until the defenders of the cosmological argument tell us plainly and explicitly what they mean by the statement, I think we are justified in suspecting that they do not see it either. Either they mean one or more of the three things suggested above, or they mean nothing at all.

Let us, however, be as charitable as we can. Let us suppose that the supporters of this argument do mean something when they assert that "Some contingent beings exist." What might they mean? Option *c* would seem to be their most promising choice. They might insist that something of significance does follow from it because we cannot be satisfied with an infinite regress. If something Z (the ashtray, for example) is dependent on something else Y for its continued existence, they might say, then we can ask the same question about Y. Is it contingent or not? Eventually we must come to a *non*contingent cause, and this is what we mean by God.

But there is something very wrong with this argument from ashtrays to physics to God. What is it? Just this: we know that by means of physical laws we can only reason to other physical laws or to some spatiotemporal event or events. Physical laws are passports that enable us to move from one range of phenomena to another range of phenomena *in the natural world*. They do not give us an exit visa to pass outside spatiotemporal reality. Moreover, what is wrong with a series of contingent causes, even an *infinite* series of contingent causes? In this case every member of the series is contingent in the sense defined above, and there is no first member. Is this any harder to conceive of than an infinite mathematical series, or infinite space?

Finally, the conclusion of the argument is so ambiguous that it seems quite impossible to either affirm it or deny it—impossible because it is totally unclear what we would be affirming or denying. How can anyone either affirm or deny that "a noncontingent ground of being exists"? What concrete difference would it make in your experience or mine whether this statement (if it is a statement) is true or false? None whatsoever. It is a meaningless combination of ponderous words, designed to intimidate rather than to elucidate. But one thing is clear: whatever these words are supposed to mean, the premises that precede them do not establish the existence of God. We may not like it, but it happens to be the case that this world and its laws are the only "reality" there is. Any attempt to reason from this or that feature of the world to some reality not of the world is sheer fantasy.

The Teleological Argument

The third, and by far the weakest, of the traditional arguments for the existence of God—though, oddly enough, it is popularly regarded as one of the most persuasive—is the teleological argument. Since the defects of the argument have only to be pointed out to be seen, I shall restrict myself to a very summary statement of them.

The statement that "Nature exhibits a number of instances of means ordered to ends" is subtly ambiguous. What nature exhibits is a high degree of *lawlike regularity.* If this is all that is meant by "means ordered to ends," all well and good; but it seems that more than this is intended. The language suggests "purposiveness," or "ordering," and thus subtly suggests *in an allegedly factual premise* that we ought to look for a "purposer," or "orderer." We seem to have here a case of syllogistic smuggling.

Furthermore, the alleged analogy between the lawlike regularity that we find in nature (to substitute for the offending terms) and that which we find in human contrivances is notably weak. We do indeed posit a human intelligence whenever we encounter an implement that (a) serves some conceivable purpose and (b) is evidently not altogether a product of nature. But neither of these characteristics applies to the regularities that we find in nature—not even to those offered by the author of Chapter 50 as examples of the sort of thing he has in mind. On what basis, then, are we supposed to see an analogy?

It is quite beside the point to argue that "The analogy between (order in nature) and the order that we find in contrivances known to be the product of intelligent purpose is infinitely stronger than any other analogy that anyone has been able to suggest." This may well be. I am no more impressed than was Hume, for example, by the suggestion that the universe could be likened to a giant plant or to a spider web rather than to a machine. But why should it be likened to anything at all? A human contrivance, after all, utilizes in some way or other certain laws of nature that man, by careful inquiry or by good luck, has discovered. May not these laws be themselves the ultimate facts to which appeal can be made, and may not the universe itself be the model of regularity in relation to which every other instance of regularity is only a pale analogy?

Moreover, even if the argument were sound, the being whose existence it establishes would be nothing more than a finitely wise, finitely powerful, amoral (if not malevolent) architect. The inventor of a machine does not create the materials with which he works: he only shapes them. Hence the "orderer" whose existence is supposedly established by this argument is only a craftsman, not a creator. The argument, if it is sound, requires only that this cosmic "orderer" be very wise and very powerful: hence, it does not establish the existence of an *infinitely* wise and powerful being. The argument requires nothing at all in the way of goodness. Since there is evil in the world that he is supposed to have designed, it may be assumed that he is something less than perfectly good; at best he must be considered amoral, at worst malevolent. This is hardly a description of God in any religiously meaningful sense of the term.

Finally, even if the argument did establish the existence of this strange being, it would establish only his past, not his present, existence. The existence of a watch implies only the existence of a watch-maker *at the time the watch was made:* it does not in any way assure me of his *present* existence. Similarly, if the existence of an ordered universe implied anything at all (which I doubt), it would be that once upon a time, long, long ago, there was a world-maker. He may since have died or changed his occupation.

The teleological argument is not a good argument. It derives its prestige entirely, I suspect, from the fact that it unites the "natural wonder" of which we heard in the last chapter with the apparently kindred feeling of "reverence" in a way that is satisfying to religious people. It may even be that the feeling of reverence arose originally out of this feeling of natural wonder. Be that as it may, it is perfectly evident that the belief in the existence of God did not come about because of the cogency of the teleological argument.

A Final Word

None of the arguments for the existence of God is able to withstand careful scrutiny. Why, then, do so many people believe that God exists? The answer can only be that this belief is irrational—an illusion (Sigmund Freud), a personification of society (Emile Durkheim), or something else. The persistence of this belief in spite of the demonstrable fallaciousness of the arguments used to support it suggests that it must answer to some very deep emotional need of many people. Therefore, it may be thought cruel to show, as I have done, how weak those arguments are. However, it is evident that people who believe in God did not arrive at this belief by means of rational argument; it is unlikely that the removal of the arguments will by itself destroy that belief. Perhaps there are people who need this particular illusion. If so, they will probably keep it—with or without intellectual props. Second, we have addressed ourselves to this problem only in the interest of knowing the truth. Are there or are there not rational grounds for believing in the existence of God? As a convinced naturalist, I hold that there are not. I think that this is the truth. If the truth is painful, it is still the truth. Things are the way they are; the best we can do is to try to see them that way, not the way we might like them to be.

STUDY QUESTIONS

1. What objections does Naturalist bring against the ontological argument? Are they all sound objections, in your opinion? (Compare Naturalist's third objection with the defense of Proposition 3 in Chapter 48.)
2. What are Naturalist's objections to the cosmological argument? Do they apply with equal force to Aquinas' "third way" and to the shorter formulation offered in Chapter 49?
3. What are Naturalist's objections to the teleological argument? Do they apply with equal force to Paley's argument and to St. Thomas Aquinas' "fifth way"? Do you think Naturalist is right in calling this "by far the weakest" of the arguments for the existence of God?
4. Select whichever of the traditional arguments you consider to be the strongest and attempt to defend it against Naturalist's criticisms.

52

THE FAILURE OF THE ARGUMENTS: A SYMPATHETIC APPRAISAL

In the debate about the existence of God there would seem to be only two plausible positions: either (a) there is some sound argument for the existence of God, and everybody ought to believe that God exists; or (b) there is no sound argument for the existence of God, and everyone ought to hold that the existence of God is improbable or, at best, highly problematic. The absence of an argument proving that something exists does not, of course, prove that the thing in question *does not* exist. It must be admitted, however, that the burden of proof rests with those who make the affirmative claim. (For example, I cannot prove that there are not little two-headed green animals living on the planet Venus, but sanity seems to require that I assume that there are none unless, or until, some evidence is produced to indicate that there are.)

I find myself in disagreement with both positions and therefore, I fear, in a position that must, at first, seem somewhat strange. I hold, with the author of the last chapter, that there is no sound argument for the existence of God; but I also hold, with the authors of the previous three chapters, that God exists and His existence can be known by us. It is this position that I shall try to elucidate. It represents, I think, the only possible way in which the impasse between theists and naturalists concerning the problem of the existence of God can be overcome.

Arguments and Rational Grounds

One way of stating the position that I should like to defend is: there are no sound *arguments* for the existence of God, but there are, nonetheless, valid *rational grounds* for believing in His existence. Naturalists are right in rejecting the arguments for the existence of God but wrong in denying His reality; theists are right in affirming the reality of God but wrong in insisting that His reality is capable of proof.

Strictly speaking, it is not possible to *prove* the reality of anything. Reality manifests itself to us, or it does not; only in the former case is it possible for us to know it. One cannot even prove the reality of the physical world, as the futile discussions between realists and phenomenalists over this very question show. Solipsism is the only consistent alternative to a direct cognition of the reality of that which manifests itself to us as real.

Few philosophers who have addressed themselves to the realist-phenomenalist controversy have realized, I suspect, that their reflections concerning that problem are intimately related to the question of our knowledge of the reality of God. But they are. The root question, in both cases, is: How do we cognize *reality*? How do we get beyond perception and feeling to an awareness of the reality of that which seems to lie behind them? Upon our answer to this question depends the solution to both the realist-phenomenalist controversy and the problem of the reality of God.

The chief difficulty in the way of achieving a satisfactory solution to these and a number of other related problems is the very limited (and limiting) concept of *reason* that prevails in our culture at the present time. In the great classical tradition of Western philosophy—and I include all of the major figures from the Golden Age of Greek philosophy down to and including the German Idealists of the nineteenth century—reason was conceived as the structure of the conscious self by virtue of which man is able both to grasp and to shape reality. It is one and the same reason, according to this view, that seeks to know the truth, to love the good, and to appreciate the beautiful. Man, it is evident, relates to his world in a variety of ways, each qualitatively different from the others: he knows (cognition), he feels (emotion), he appreciates (aesthetics), he loves or hates (conation), he acts (practice). Reason, in the classical view, is the ground and locus of all of these; it expresses the unity of the self even as it acknowledges the multiplicity of its relations to the world roundabout.

In our culture, however, this concept of reason has been lost. Reason is conceived by most people today simply as man's capacity for *reasoning*. Its function is conceived to be purely cognitive, and all the other functions formerly assigned to reason are therefore judged to be "irrational." Feelings may be appropriate or inappropriate, but they cannot be rational; acts may be discreet or indiscreet, but they cannot be right or wrong (consistent with or contrary to right reason). Even in its cognitive function, the scope of reason's competence has been radically narrowed: to espouse a moral or aesthetic value is no longer to cognize something but simply to express a private taste. The whole business of reason is, in short, to attain scientific knowledge, and what is not scientific knowledge is not knowledge at all: it is, in other words, irrational.

If any culture were absolutely consistent in maintaining this view, the consequences would be truly appalling. The outstanding characteristics of such a culture would be an impressive degree of technical competence, that is, an ability to do an enormous variety of things exceedingly well, and a complete lack of conviction as to whether any of these things are really worth doing. People in such a culture would be (as F. Scott Fitzgerald once said of himself) like a little boy alone in a big house, who now could do anything he wanted to do, and who suddenly discovered that there was nothing he wanted to do. The whole life of man, on such a view, must be made up of technical knowledge and totally irrational feelings and inclinations. Such technical knowledge could not even include a knowledge of the reality of the world toward which it is supposedly directed.

Fortunately, no culture—not even ours—has been absolutely consistent in maintaining this view; but ours has gone far in this direction. We are more than a little embarrassed about espousing values that cannot be defended "scientifically." We are reluctant to engage in public discussion of issues that do not admit of clear-cut factual answers—such as the responsible use of atomic power or the obligations of industrialized nations toward those that are not.

No argument for the existence of God can be successful, for argument does not belong to the level of reason where the reality of God is manifest. Argument belongs to the level of "technical" or "scientific" reason; it cannot take us beyond this. On this point, naturalism is right. But neither is it possible, without making some gratuitous assumptions, to prove the existence of anything else. If we are to know of the reality of anything, reality must disclose itself to us; there is no other way.

Our knowledge of the reality of God might be described as "nontechnical," "nondiscursive," "nonargumentative," or even "nonscientific"; but it is not "nonrational." Too much of what is of value in human life belongs to the deeper levels of reason to allow scientific reason alone to determine what is rational and what is not. Scientific reason is and must be supreme in its own sphere: that is an important truth that was established only after a long and bitter struggle (witness the experience of Galileo). But the sphere of scientific reason is limited: that is also an important truth that our culture is dangerously close to forgetting. The penalty for ignoring the former was the temporary retardation of the progress of modern science, and that was most unfortunate. But the penalty for forgetting the latter is an overwhelming sense of the futility of life, and that—if it occurs—would be disastrous. Man can abide discomfort, but robbed of meaning he is reduced to nothing.

The Self-Disclosure of God

Material reality manifests itself to us in sense experience. The reality of the tree that I see through my office window is disclosed in the very process by which I see it: I do not first have sense-data and then infer that there is something "real" corresponding to them. Investigation, experimentation, and reasoning may tell me much about *what* it is: they cannot tell me *that* it is. Either its reality is immediately evident to me, or I must remain ignorant of it. Scientific reason cannot persuade me of the reality of the tree; indeed, it is only as this reality is given that scientific reason can begin its work.

Human reality manifests itself in *interpersonal communication,* notably in conversation. Scientific reason cannot demonstrate the existence of other minds: this is the inescapable conclusion of the endless discussions of this topic carried on ever since Hume. In love, in friendship, even in the casual relationships that we sustain with countless people whose lives barely touch ours in various ways, the reality of other rational selves is manifest to us. Here we are more aware, perhaps, of the limitations of scientific reason than in the case of material objects, for we know full well that the richness of a human personality defies exhaustive description; we know—but sometimes we forget.

God manifests himself to us in the event called *revelation.* I do not mean by this anything odd or unusual—nothing in the way of an "ecstatic vision" or anything of that sort. I mean simply that our longing that life shall have some significance, our desire that the future shall have some hope, and our anxiety over the transience and insecurity of everything that we perceive are somehow overcome. I do not think that any human being is without this experience. There is a need, a longing, an anxiety, a concern, an emptiness in human life. Somehow, from deep within ourselves, these are overcome, the void is filled, and we find courage. This "finding courage," or "being grasped by meanings," or "being sustained in the conviction of the significance of life," is what I mean by revelation; the source or ground of these is what we are talking about when we use the term "God."

It should be noted that in stating what I have just stated I am emphatically *not* setting forth another argument for the existence of God. I reject all arguments for the existence of God, including the argument from religious experience. What I am saying is that we are all implicitly aware of the reality of God, that at a level of our selves far deeper than that at which reasoning and argumentation occur God discloses himself to us. We may choose to call the reality that is thus disclosed by some other name—that is a very trivial matter. Or we may turn away from this deeper dimension of our self and try to live without meaning and without courage.

I have no serious quarrel with the definition of God suggested in the introductory chapter and adhered to with varying degrees of fidelity by the other writers. The reality that is disclosed to us in the way I have described does, indeed, disclose itself as the ground of being and value. There can be little doubt that if and when we are moved to an act of worship, it is this reality that is the intended object of our devotion. But precisely because we are dealing with a reality that is apprehended by reason in its depth rather than by scientific reason, this concept is bound to be obscure. Theology is an attempt, among other things, to make the concept "God" more precise; but the best theologians know that you cannot give this concept scientific precision without robbing it of its deepest meaning. "The heart has its reasons, which reason does not know." [1] The "reasons of the heart" are not blind, irrational emotions: they are a function of reason itself in a dimension of itself more profound than that with which we engage in scientific "reasoning."

This matter of the inevitable obscurity of the concept "God" deserves to be emphasized more than it has been thus far. H. D. Lewis is right when he says:

> . . . the skeptic and agnostic do not so much find themselves unconvinced that in fact there is a God as fail to see what is meant by "God"; and we cannot first tell them what we mean and then proceed to show that God is also real. If they can be induced to see what we mean when we speak of God they will at one and the same time be convinced of His existence . . .[2]

The chief difficulty in the way of acknowledging the reality of God is not the inescapable ambiguity of the concept; it is rather the fact that in popular religion the concept *has* been made precise, but in an absurd and childish way. People do not believe in the existence of a Bearded Father somewhere off in space, and so (they think) they do not believe in the existence of God. But the God who is the ground of being and value, whose reality is manifest to every man in the deepest reaches of his self, bears little or no resemblance to this Celestial Despot of popular fantasy. To deny the reality of the latter is to topple an idol and so to be on the side of God; to deny the reality of the former is impossible.

---

[1] Blaise Pascal, "Fragment 277," *Pensées* (New York: Everyman's Library, 1932), p. 78.

[2] H. D. Lewis, *Our Experience of God* (London: Allen & Unwin; New York: Macmillan, 1959), p. 44.

Another Look at the Arguments

If, now, we look at the traditional arguments from the perspective developed briefly in this chapter, it is not difficult to see why the debate concerning them has been so inconclusive. The critics of the arguments have, quite rightly, criticized their argumentative form; the defenders of the arguments have defended their implicit meaning. For reasons already given, the arguments cannot succeed *as arguments;* on this point the critics are right. But the arguments do express, inadequately, the awareness of the reality of God that is embedded deep in the consciousness of every man.

The ontological argument attempts to put this fundamental awareness of the reality of God into a form acceptable to scientific reason: it affirms, accordingly, that *the proposition, "God exists," is self-evident.* This, as the critics of the ontological argument have pointed out, is not the case; hence, the argument is no good as an argument. But the self-disclosure of God to reason in its depth is not the same thing as the alleged self-evidence to scientific reason of the proposition "God exists." As an argument, the ontological argument is a failure; but the insight that it attempts to express in this very inadequate way is both true and important.

The cosmological argument attempts to express this same insight in a slightly different way. The truth of the cosmological argument is that we are aware, in the depth of our selves, of the reality of the ground of our being and of all being. But the cosmological argument distorts this fundamental insight by attempting to exhibit it to scientific reason as a bit of propositional knowledge that can be gotten by correct syllogistic reasoning. This, as the critics of the cosmological argument have correctly pointed out, cannot be done: the cosmological argument is no good as an argument. However, the insight that it is attempting to express and that no argument can adequately express is both true and important.

This insight is most weakly reflected in the teleological argument. The teleological argument, at least in the form made popular by Paley and other writers in the eighteenth century, almost inevitably conjures up the image of a super-artisan going about the business of making a world; and this expresses little, if anything, of what is meant by the concept "God." There is indeed a sense of mystery that strikes us when we look upward on a starry night, and I do not doubt that this sense of mystery is best understood as a momentary heightening of our awareness of the reality of the ground of all being; but very little of this sense of mystery carries over into the teleological argument itself. People who find the teleological argument impressive are not usually convinced by the argument itself; as an argument it is the weakest of the three. They respond to it because it directs their consideration to certain features of the universe that tend to enhance the awareness of God that all men have. If the argument does this for some people, to that extent it is of value; but its value is that of poetry, not logic.

Former Harvard president Nathan M. Pusey once said,

> It would seem to me that the finest fruit of serious learning should be the ability to speak the word God without reserve or embarrassment, certainly without adolescent resentment; rather with some sense of communion, with reverence and with joy.[3]

To do this we must rid ourselves of concepts and images that make God into a thing among things, whose existence is accordingly open to question. Even our secular age knows, though it does not acknowledge, that there *is* a depth of reason and of reality; without this awareness there would be no sense of worth, value, destiny, or hope. When we learn once again that it is at this level of our being that the reality of God is manifest, we shall learn "to speak the word God without reserve or embarrassment, . . . [but] with some sense of communion, with reverence and with joy."

STUDY QUESTIONS

1. How does the author of this chapter propose to overcome "the impasse between theists and naturalists concerning the problem of the existence of God"?
2. What exactly is the distinction drawn in this chapter between *arguments* and *rational grounds*.
3. What do you make of the discussion in this chapter of the various dimensions of reason? Is it true that there is a tendency today to limit reason to what is here called "scientific reason"? Are you at all persuaded by the suggestion that there are other dimensions of reason than the "scientific"?
4. Is it correct to say that existence is not capable of demonstration— that either we must recognize it directly or else be ignorant of it? Is this true, for example, of our knowledge of the existence of physical objects? of other minds?
5. What does the author of this chapter mean by "revelation"? Is this, in fact, another argument for the existence of God?
6. Is there, as this writer affirms, an analogy between this problem and the realist-phenomenalist controversy?

---

[3] Nathan M. Pusey, *The Age of the Scholar* (Cambridge, Mass.: Harvard University Press, 1963), p. 145.

Alston, William P. "The Ontological Argument Revisited," *The Philosophical Review,* 69 (1960), 454–474.

Anselm of Canterbury. *Proslogium,* in S. N. Deane, *Anselm,* 2nd ed. La Salle, Ill.: Open Court, 1962.

Aquinas, St. Thomas. *Summa Theologica.* Many editions. See Part I, Question 2.

Brown, Patterson. "St. Thomas' Doctrine of Necessary Being," *The Philosophical Review,* 73 (1964), 76–90.

Ducasse, C. J. *A Philosophical Scrutiny of Religion.* New York: Ronald Press, 1953.

Ebersole, Frank B. "Whether Existence is a Predicate," *The Journal of Philosophy,* 60 (1963), 509–524.

Ewing, A. C. *The Fundamental Questions of Philosophy.* New York: Macmillan, 1951, chap. 11.

Flew, Antony. *God and Philosophy.* London: Hutchinson, 1966. Detailed critique of arguments for theism.

Harris, E. E. *Revelation Through Reason.* London: G. Allen & Unwin, 1959.

Hartshorne, Charles. *Anselm's Discovery: Re-examination of the ontological proof of God's existence.* LaSalle, Ill.: Open Court, 1966.

————. *The Logic of Perfection and Other Essays in Neoclassical Metaphysics.* LaSalle, Ill.: Open Court, 1962.

————, and W. L. Reese. *Philosophers Speak of God.* Chicago: University of Chicago Press, 1963 (paperbound).

Hawkins, D. J. B. *The Essentials of Theism.* London: Sheed and Ward, 1949.

Hick, John. "God as Necessary Being," *The Journal of Philosophy,* 57 (1960), 725–734.

Hume, David. *Dialogues Concerning Natural Religion,* ed. by Norman Kemp Smith. Indianapolis, Ind.: Liberal Arts Press, 1962 (paperbound).

Hurlbutt, Robert H. *Hume, Newton and the Design Argument.* Lincoln: University of Nebraska Press, 1966.

Jack, Henry. "A Recent Attempt to Prove God's Existence," *Philosophy and Phenomenological Research,* 25 (1965), 575–579.

Kant, Immanuel. *Critique of Pure Reason,* tr. by Norman Kemp Smith. New York: St. Martin's Press, 1965 (paperbound). See section entitled, "The Ideal of Pure Reason."

Kenny, Anthony. *The Five Ways: St. Thomas Aquinas' Proofs of God's Existence.* London: Routledge and Kegan Paul, 1969. Detailed analysis by a competent and sympathetic critic.

Lewis, H. D. *Our Experience of God.* London: G. Allen & Unwin; New York: Macmillan, 1959.

McIntyre, John. *St. Anselm and His Critics.* Edinburgh: Oliver and Boyd, 1954.

Malcolm, Norman. "Anselm's Ontological Arguments," *The Philosophical Review,* 69 (1960), 41–62.

Martin, C. B. *Religious Belief.* Ithaca, N.Y.: Cornell University Press, 1959.

Mascall, E. L. *Existence and Analogy.* London: Longmans, Green, 1949.

Mill, John Stuart. *Three Essays on Religion.* New York: Henry Holt, 1874.

Paley, William. *Evidences of the Existence and Attributes of the Deity.* Many editions. Originally published in 1802.

Plantinga, A. (ed.). *The Ontological Argument from St. Anselm to Contemporary Philosophers.* New York: Doubleday Anchor Books, 1965 (paperbound).

Smart, Ninian. *Reasons and Faiths.* New York: Humanities Press, 1958.

Tillich, Paul. *Systematic Theology* Vol. I. Chicago: University of Chicago Press, 1951, pp. 204–235.

PART XI

RELIGIOUS LANGUAGE

53

THE PROBLEM OF
RELIGIOUS LANGUAGE

One of the most prominent characteristics of British and American philosophy in recent years has been its profound interest in language. Never before has language itself been made the object of so much painstaking study as it has in the past twenty or thirty years, and there can be little doubt that some of the conclusions that have been drawn about the nature of language by those who have studied it most carefully are of considerable philosophical interest and importance.

Nor is it surprising that the careful scrutiny of language should have raised anew the problem of the meaningfulness of religious discourse, for the affinities of most philosophers today are not with the humanities and theology, but with the natural sciences, particularly physics. Philosophers today tend to be empiricists in their epistemology, conventionalists in their view of language, and skeptics with respect to the claim that the language of religion is in some way descriptive of transcendent reality. As a result of this preoccupation with language, and more especially as a result of certain negative implications drawn from a theory of language widely held by contemporary British and American philosophers, the problem of religious language has become the most widely discussed issue in contemporary philosophy of religion.

Background of the Problem

Lest we become too myopic in our approach to this problem, however, it may be well to note that the problem is by no means a new one. It is well over two thousand years since Plato wrote:

> The father and maker of all this universe is past finding out; and
> even if we found him, to tell of him to all men would be impossible.
> . . . If, then, Socrates, amid the many opinions about the gods . . .
> we are not able to give notions which are altogether and in every
> respect exact and consistent with one another, do not be surprised.
> Enough, if we adduce probabilities as likely as any others.[1]

St. Augustine, too, who wrote a great deal about God, was quite cogni-
zant of the difficulty; he even went so far on one occasion as to suggest that we speak of God "not in order to say something, but in order
not to remain silent." [2] Theologians of every age have on numerous
occasions echoed St. Augustine's sentiments.

The problem achieved what might be termed its first classical, or
definitive, formulation in St. Thomas Aquinas' great *Summa Theologica.* The question as formulated by Aquinas is: "Whether what is
said of God and of creatures is univocally predicated of them?" Trans-
lation: Do terms normally applied to finite objects have the *same
meaning* when they are applied to God? Aquinas thought that the
reply could not be in the affirmative, for when we apply a given term
("wise") to, say, a man, "we signify some perfection distinct from a
man's essence, and distinct from his power and being," whereas when
we apply the same term to God "we do not mean to signify anything
distinct from His essence or power or being." On the other hand, if we
say that terms are predicated of finite objects and of God "equivocally," that is, in such a way that the same word has a totally different
meaning in the two cases, then "the reasoning would always be exposed to the fallacy of equivocation." We would be concealing our
complete ignorance about God under a camouflage of words that appear to be meaningful only because they are meaningful in their ordinary application. Aquinas' solution is to go between the horns of the
dilemma. There is, he says, a third way, namely, the way of *analogy:*
"Whatever is said of God and creatures is said according as there is
some relation of the creature to God as to its principle and cause,
wherein all the perfections of things pre-exist excellently." [3] Thus,
Aquinas believed the problem to be solved.

Whatever we may think of Aquinas' solution to this problem, it is
important to recognize that the problem itself is much more radical as
considered by contemporary philosophers. Aquinas was making two
assumptions that most contemporary philosophers who are concerned
about the problem of religious language are not able to make. First,
although he was remarkably cautious in his claims regarding our

---

1 Plato, *Timaeus,* I, in *The Dialogues of Plato,* B. Jowett (tr.) (New York:
Random House, 1937), Vol. II, p. 13.

2 St. Augustine, *To Simplician—On Various Questions,* II, 2, 1.

3 St. Thomas Aquinas, *Summa Theologica,* I, Ques. 13, Art. 5, in Anton C.
Pegis (ed.), *Basic Writings of St. Thomas Aquinas* (New York: Random House,
1945), Vol. I, p. 120.

knowledge of God, Aquinas did assume that we know a good many things about the nature of God: the question was how our language could express this knowledge. He also assumed that somehow or other our language about God is meaningful: the question was *in what way* it is meaningful. The *way of analogy* is offered by Aquinas not as a solution to the problem of how we can speak meaningfully about God at all, but as an account of the particular kind of meaning "God-talk" is supposed to have—it being assumed by everyone concerned in his day that talk about God has some kind of meaning.

The Problem Today

The problem of religious language was raised anew in the twentieth century by the formulation of what is called *the empiricist criterion of meaning.* According to this criterion, a proposition is factually meaningful if and only if some empirical facts are relevant to determining its truth or falsity. There are, according to philosophers who defend this criterion, just three kinds of linguistic expressions: empirical statements, analytic truths, and nonsense. Empirical statements are factually meaningful according to the criterion. Analytic truths simply express certain meaning relations between the terms of which they are composed; they say nothing about any matter of fact. All other linguistic expressions, regardless of their "face value," are literally meaningless: they have no cognitive meaning whatsoever.

If we accept this criterion, however, we cannot avoid asking, Is it possible to speak meaningfully about God and, if so, how? Statements about God do not seem to be either confirmable or disconfirmable on the basis of any empirical observations: therefore, they do not seem to be factually significant. It seems evident (to most observers, at least) that they are not analytic truths. Are they, then, altogether meaningless—a particularly prevalent form of linguistic nonsense? So it seems to many philosophers.

Philosophers who hold that all sentences purporting to say something about God are literally meaningless do not mean to suggest, of course, that they are obviously so. Indeed, their point is precisely that the nonsensical character of such utterances is extremely *un*obvious —so unobvious, in fact, that well-meaning people have talked about God for centuries as if what they were saying were literally significant. These philosophers point out that it is only when we come to understand under what conditions language can be meaningful that we can see that some of these conditions are lacking in the case of language about God; hence, they say, we are driven to a negative conclusion.

Nor do these philosophers deny that sentences purporting to say something about God may have certain sorts of "meaning" for some people other than descriptive significance. The linguistic expression, "God loves His people and watches over them continually," may be emotionally comforting or aesthetically satisfying, or it may serve as a reinforcement of moral commitment. In these senses they will allow that it may be subjectively meaningful to someone who utters it. But the utterance cannot be literally significant even to a believer, say these philosophers; it does not assert anything that is capable of being either true or false.

Let us consider this example further. Philosophers who hold that sentences purporting to say something about God are meaningless frequently point out that, in order for a linguistic expression to be factually significant, it is necessary that we be able to specify a state of affairs that, if it were the case, would render the statement in question false. I may or may not be able to actually determine whether the state of affairs to which I have reference obtains: that is purely a question of empirical possibility and does not affect the logic of my statement. But if I cannot specify a state of affairs that, if it were the case (whether or not I can ascertain if it is the case), would render my statement false, say these philosophers, then I am not really saying anything.

Suppose, now, that someone were to ask a person who affirms the above sentence about God, "What would have to be the case in order for you to withdraw your statement that God loves His people and watches over them continually?" What could such a person say? We can imagine a conversation something like this:

Believer: I can't think of anything that would make me withdraw the statement. God just does love His people—we know that —and whatever happens, we have to go on believing that God loves us.

Critic: Let me see if I can help you. Surely the fact of human suffering—except, perhaps, for that inflicted by other men —counts against your statement?

Believer: No, not at all. Because, you see, God's love is not like human love. God's love is greater, more encompassing, more . . .

Critic: Wait a minute! How can you say that God's love is *greater* than human love? When men are suffering, other men usually try to do something about it. God, apparently, does not do anything at all. I should think we might be justified in concluding that God's love is inferior to human love, or even nonexistent.

Believer: You do not understand the infinite difference between God and man.

Critic: I see a difference, but the contrast, I must say, is not particularly flattering to God. And the "love of God" of which
you speak seems to mean nothing whatsoever. With or without this love, there would be human suffering—no more
and no less than there is now. With or without this love,
the world would apparently be just the way it is now. Your
alleged "assertion" about the love of God is no assertion at
all.

This question about the *meaningfulness* of statements about God
must not be confused with the quite different question as to how to
determine whether this or that theological statement is *true*. Our
question belongs to the logic of religious discourse, the other to the
epistemology of religious truth-claims. The first question, moreover, is
logically prior to the second: if the negative view on the significance
of religious assertions should be sustained, religion could make no
truth-claims, in which case the epistemological question could be ignored.

It is no answer to the present question to say, "We know God loves
His people because it says so in the Bible." The question is: What, if
anything, do sentences about God *mean*, whether or not they are au-
thorized by any religious authority? Are they factually significant at
all? Are they, can they be, assertions? And if so, how do they get their
meaning?

Some Alternatives

It is very difficult to classify the many ways in which various philosophers have attempted to deal with this problem, and it is impossible
in principle to determine forever all of the possible ways of responding to it. Many philosophers have taken the position that the empiricist criterion of meaning makes it evident that talk about God is
and always was nonsensical: people may keep on using it, but if they
think it is literally significant, or anything other than "emotive," they
are deceiving themselves. For someone who holds this view, the status
of religious language is no longer a problem: he is satisfied that the
empiricist criterion of meaning is correct, that it clearly rules out religious discourse, and that is the end of the matter.

Many others, however, have addressed themselves to the problem
out of a desire to show that the empiricist attack on religious language
need not be as fatal as the attackers seem to think it is. It is at this
point that the picture becomes rather confused because several different lines of defense have been attempted.

First, we may distinguish a group of writers who have accepted the
empiricist criterion of meaning and the conclusion that religious lan-

guage is devoid of literal significance, but who have argued (in a variety of ways) that this conclusion need not distress religious people since the meaning and importance of religious language lies in an entirely different dimension. Nor, these writers argue, are we saying anything to the point if we call these utterances "emotive": that is simply a pejorative way of describing an utterance that is not factually significant. According to these philosophers, if we examine carefully the ways religious utterances are used, we will find that they serve a useful and important function—though, to be sure, that function is not, as people may have once thought, factual description.

Chapters 54 and 55 represent two alternative ways of accounting for the nature of religious language along these general lines. The *ethical way,* developed in Chapter 54, goes back to Immanuel Kant, whose epistemological studies drove him to deal with this problem long before the empiricist criterion of meaning made its debut on the philosophical scene. The *existential way,* developed in Chapter 55, is of more recent vintage; a fairly large number of contemporary writers tend to identify themselves with this position. In both of these cases, however, the claim is made that the referent of religious language is subjective rather than objective: talk about God, correctly understood, is just a very special kind of talk about ourselves.

Other writers have insisted on the more traditional view that religious language is descriptive of objective reality and have attempted to show how this position can be maintained in the face of the empiricist attack. Some (few) writers have attempted to maintain that the empiricist criterion of meaning need not force the conclusion that talk about God is meaningless: this position is developed in Chapter 56. Others have argued that the empiricist criterion of meaning is itself inadequate and have attempted to affirm the factual significance of religious assertions in a way that, if accepted, would require the rejection of the empiricist criterion. This approach is developed in Chapter 57. It has, as the writer points out, much in common with the *way of analogy* of Aquinas.

This attempt to provide some structure for the discussion of the problem of religious language has deliberately been more tentative than that suggested for many of the previous problems discussed. In part, this is a requirement of the problem itself: it does not admit of a definitive statement of all the alternative possible answers. More than this, however, it reflects the status of the problem at the present time: this problem constitutes one of the "growing edges" of philosophy today (as a survey of a few contemporary philosophical journals will make evident). Perhaps, in time, some new consensus will be reached —possibly along one of the lines suggested here or along some line not yet suggested in the literature. The student who grasps the issues involved in this controversy may be confident that he is familiarizing himself with a problem that is sure to be widely discussed in the years ahead. In the meantime, he should keep his categories somewhat fluid and be open to possibilities that up to this moment may not have been imagined.

STUDY QUESTIONS

1. What is meant by the terms "univocal" and "equivocal"? What are St. Thomas Aquinas' objections to saying that certain things are predicated of God and of creatures "univocally"? What are his objections to saying that certain things are predicated of God and of creatures "equivocally"?
2. What is the empiricist criterion of meaning? How does this create a problem so far as religious language is concerned? Is *all* religious language placed in jeopardy by this criterion, or only certain kinds? Be specific.
3. Is the question about the meaningfulness of religious language separable from, and logically prior to, the question about the truth of religious truth-claims? Explain.
4. Formulate a concise statement of the problem of religious language as you now understand it. What do you understand to be the alternative ways of responding to this problem?

54

THE LANGUAGE
OF MORAL RESOLVE

It is more than a little misleading to call the criterion referred to in Chapter 53 a criterion of *meaning*. The criterion, to speak more correctly, is a criterion of *factual significance*. To say that a certain statement is "devoid of factual significance" is one thing; to say that the same statement is sheer "nonsense" seems like quite a different matter. The prejudicial language in which the problem of religious discourse has been discussed in recent years has done much to add confusion to an issue that is desperately in need of elucidation and, if possible, solution.

Although I regard the terminology in which much of the recent discussion has been carried on to be highly misleading, I do not think it can be denied that the empiricist criterion of factual significance (as I shall call it) is valid. No sentence can be significant—factually or otherwise—unless (a) its terms are understood and (b) it is in tolerable conformity with the syntactic rules of the language in which it occurs. ("Some drapples are snark pling" fails to meet the first requirement, "Pickle ostrich many seven" fails to meet the second.) If, however, a sentence is to be factually significant, in addition to fulfilling these two requirements it must also be the case that (c) it purports to describe some theoretically verifiable state of affairs: this, it would seem, is what we mean by calling it "factually" significant. If a person who claims to be uttering a factually significant statement can specify no state of affairs that, if it were the case, would render his statement false, it would seem fair to conclude that (despite his claim) he is not really uttering a factually significant statement. The criterion is nothing more than a definition of what we mean by "factually significant"; I do not see how we could reject it without blurring the rather obvious distinction between factually significant sentences and other sorts of sentences.

Nor can there be any doubt that according to this criterion religious language is not factually significant. The sentences, "God is three in one" or "God loves His people and watches over them continually," describe no states of affairs that are either confirmable or disconfirmable by any conceivable data. Such sentences are all right as far as their syntax is concerned. They may be all right as far as their terms are concerned. But they are not factually significant. They are descriptive of nothing. They are, therefore, neither true nor false.

This conclusion regarding the nonfactual character of religious language is regarded by many people, including some philosophers, as seriously objectionable. Most of the religions of the world claim to assert some matters of fact when they utter sentences about God, though Zen Buddhism appears to be an exception. But I think that the pseudo-descriptions into which most religions seem to have fallen are a spurious element in those religions. The supposed assertions are not, *qua* assertions, essential to religion; their real significance lies in another dimension. It is to this "other dimension," in which the true (nondescriptive) significance of religious statements is to be found, that I wish to direct attention in the remainder of this chapter.

Religion and Morality

Construed as statements of fact, sentences about God are entirely vacuous; their true meaning, I shall argue, consists in the fact that they express the *moral resolve* of the person who sincerely utters them —his sincere intention, in other words, to act in certain ways. I propose to indicate some of the reasons for adopting this view. I shall then give a few examples showing how some very common sentences having "God" as their subject ought to be construed.

We may begin with the observation that, whatever the view on the question of religious language, it is evident that morality constitutes an exceedingly important *part* of religion. What would Judaism be without the Ten Commandments, or Christianity without the Sermon on the Mount and the moral precepts of St. Paul, or Buddhism without the Noble Eight-fold Path? There are, indeed, ceremonies of various kinds—baptism, communion, regular forms of worship, and so on. Practices such as the singing of hymns and praying are common in many religions. But at the heart of every religion is a system of *moral precepts:* rules for behavior that the adherents of that religion are expected (and frequently exhorted) to observe.

Every religious group, as a matter of fact, constitutes an ethical community. Corporate worship is a solemn act in which the ethical community is reminded of its moral duty and given an opportunity to deepen and reaffirm its moral resolve. In the Christian religion, baptism and communion are also easily explicable in this context: baptism is a rite in which the young are formally inducted into the ethical community, communion a rite in which the members of the local unit of the community affirm their identity with the larger community in the pursuit of a common ethical task. Indeed, we would not be far from the truth if we were to define religion as *the solemnizing of ethical commitment.*

Parables and Other Stories

Since, as I have argued, it is the chief function of religion to encourage certain kinds of moral behavior, it is to be expected that every religion would produce a body of linguistic materials that tend to support this function. This is precisely what occurs. There are, for example, numerous stories, some that are told as if they were historical (the crossing of the Red Sea or the conquest of Jericho), others that are frankly fictional (the parables of Jesus). The question as to whether a given story is really historical, however, is not of any great importance. Whether there ever was a "rich young ruler" who came to Jesus for advice is of no more consequence than the question whether there ever was a Good Samaritan who befriended the man who had been set upon by thieves. The point, in both cases, is to encourage a certain kind of behavior; the question as to the historicity of the story is inconsequential.

The genius of such stories consists in the fact that they make vivid and thus lend powerful psychological support to the ethical duty of the adherent. The injunction to "love your neighbor as yourself" is undoubtedly an excellent summary of the Christian ethic, but it is rather abstract; the story of the Good Samaritan reveals in a vivid and concrete way what it means to love your neighbor as yourself. So also with the injunction to love your enemies and to return good for evil; it is not the general precept, but the oft-retold story of Jesus forgiving those who crucified him, even as he hung upon the cross, that moves Christians to act in a like manner. Countless additional examples could be given from the literature of man's religions.

If men are to be persuaded to act in the prescribed ways, however, it is not enough that they be shown how it is that they are to act: they must also be given some volitional support. Many of the stories with which religious literature abounds serve the purpose of supplying motives to encourage adherents to act in the desired way. Two sorts of motives seem to be promoted, in varying degrees, by these stories: gratitude and fear. In some religious communities one motive seems to predominate, in others the second. But both are present in some degree in all religions. The people of Israel are to obey the law given at Sinai out of gratitude to the God who has delivered them out of Egypt "with a strong hand and an outstretched arm"; but this God is also a "jealous" God, who will tolerate no worship of other gods and will severely punish those who disobey Him. St. Paul appeals to his readers "by the mercies of God" to act in certain ways; but the New Testament also warns of "the outer darkness" and the "weeping and gnashing of teeth" that await those who disobey. Sometimes the Buddha smiles and sometimes he frowns; but always he enjoins the extinction of desire as the key to a proper mode of life.

If we add to these stories the poems and hymns that recount these stories, that express the attitudes that the stories and the experience of the community have succeeded in creating, and that encourage the further development of such attitudes, it is apparent that a very considerable amount of the linguistic materials of religion can be satisfactorily accounted for. Even prayers, perhaps, might be accounted for as verbal expressions of the community's (or the individual's) sincere desire to achieve more fully the ethical ideal of the community, though the fact that they are customarily addressed to God calls for further explanation. A great many things that are otherwise extremely puzzling about religion fall nicely into place as soon as we recognize that a religious group is essentially an ethical community.

The Attributes of God

It is in this same context that language about God is to be understood. Sentences of the form, "God is ———," are not descriptions of an Absent Potentate; their truth does not depend on the veracity of certain esoteric sources of information. Sentences about God, like all of the linguistic materials of religion, are to be understood in terms of their function in relation to the moral resolve that is the very raison d'être of the community. The question that we must ask is: How do sentences about God function in relation to the life of such a community?

How, in fact, do religious people think of God? Chiefly, it would appear, as the giver and enforcer of the moral law. And because God is conceived to be the giver and the enforcer of the moral law, He is also conceived to embody within Himself all of the virtues enjoined in the moral law. *God is the personification of the ethical ideal of the religious community.* Every moral virtue espoused by the community, therefore, is ascribed to God: love, mercy, wisdom, forbearance, and so on.

Every statement about God is in reality an assertion of some aspect of the ethical ideal of the community and an affirmation of the community's sincere intention to act according to that ideal. "God is love" means, in a Christian community, "We value self-denying love such as that enjoined and practiced by Jesus of Nazareth and do firmly resolve to act in this way ourselves." The mercy of God, the wisdom of God, the compassion of God, the forbearance of God can easily be understood, *mutatis mutandis*, in the same way.

Let us return to the statement, "God loves His people and watches over them continually." This expresses the community's corporate concern for each of its members—its ideal, if you will, that every member of the community shall act in such a way as to serve the needs and the welfare of every other member. The concern of one person for another who is ill (or otherwise in need) *is* the "love of God" of which the statement speaks. The meaning of the statement consists precisely in the fact that it honors such concern and enjoins each and every member of the community to incarnate this concern in his everyday dealings with his fellow-men. Behind every statement about God is the implied injunction, "You shall be perfect as your Heavenly Father is perfect."

How Some Religious Language Can Be Meaningless

Although a great deal of discourse about God is, so to speak, "legitimized" in this way, it does not necessarily follow that all of it is. There are, I should say, a number of sentences having "God" as their subject that cannot be construed in this way, and there would seem to be no alternative but to regard them as being absolutely meaningless. Examples of such sentences would be, "God is three persons in one," "God is able to do anything that He wants to do," and "God knows Himself perfectly and in knowing Himself knows the world."

It is to be noted, however, that sentences such as these are not the kind that would come naturally and spontaneously to the lips of a devout member of a religious community. They are not specimens of the language of living religion; they are the products of academic theology. Many sincere laymen have, in fact, a kind of instinctive "feel" for the irrelevancy of such sentences to the real life of the religious community; they are impatient with "theological abstractions" and prefer to hear their ministers talk about things that are "relevant to life."

Theologians, however, are not a unique species of human beings, and it seems reasonable to suppose that there must be some basis for such formulations in the conceptual framework within which the language of living faith occurs. Such a basis is to be found in the personification of ethical ideals that gives rise to the very idea of God. Once the notion of a supremely perfect Person is established, it seems natural to ask, What is He like? Much of what is said will faithfully express the ethical ideal of the community, and so the community will recognize in what is said a true description of "their God." Given the supposition that talk about God is talk about a personal being, however, certain other things will follow as logical consequences: God does not change (for the ethical ideal is constant); God does not alter his plans or feel either joy or sorrow (for such would involve change); and so on. Immense efforts have been expended by theologians to achieve logical coherence in the concept of God, and innumerable things have been said about God in the interest of achieving such coherence that, according to my theory, are quite meaningless.

What our proposal really comes down to is this: the proper criterion for judging the meaningfulness of sentences about God is not the criterion of *factual* significance, but the criterion of *ethical* significance. No sentences about God are factually significant. But many sentences about God are, nonetheless, ethically significant: they express the ethical ideal of the religious community that asserts them and record the community's resolve to act in ways consistent with this ideal. To construe statements about God in this way is to preserve everything that is of importance to a religious community. It is, at the same time, to acknowledge the indisputable validity of the empiricist criterion of factual significance. It seems, therefore, a completely satisfactory solution to the problem of religious language.

STUDY QUESTIONS

1. What position does Moralist take with respect to the empiricist criterion? Does he endorse it? modify it? reject it? reinterpret it?
2. Moralist represents religion as "the solemnizing of ethical commitment" and interprets various things—rites, religious literature, and so on—in terms of this definition. Is he right about this? Can you think of any elements that are constitutive of religion that cannot be interpreted in this way?
3. What concept of God does Moralist recommend as being closest to the view held by most religious people? Why? As far as you can judge, do you think he is right on this point?
4. How exactly does Moralist propose that we construe statements about God? Apply his proposal to several examples other than those that he himself offers.
5. According to Moralist, there are some things that religious people ought to stop saying since, in his theory, they are meaningless. Make a list of things that appear to fall in this category. Are they, as he suggests, superfluous to religion—"spurious elements"?

55

THE LANGUAGE
OF HUMAN EXISTENCE

Because I agree with Moralist about the validity of the empiricist criterion of factual significance, and because I share his concern that
religious language not simply be cast aside as meaningless, it is not
surprising that I should find his account of religious language extremely attractive. Like Kant, from whom he evidently has learned
much, he presents a very plausible account of religion and of religious
language, and in so doing he preserves a kind of meaning for at least
a part of our talk about God.

We cannot hold it against this account that it dismisses much that
religious people have always supposed they were saying when they
uttered sentences about God. Popular piety unquestionably *does* conceive of God as a kind of Great-grandfather-in-the-sky, who is conceived to "have" his various attributes in the same way that Mr. Jones
has red hair; and such literally "ascriptive" meaning clearly cannot be
allowed by the empiricist criterion. Popular piety, and probably also
academic theology, want our language about God to be objectively descriptive, and this it cannot be. Any dissatisfaction with Moralist's
account that arises solely because of the fact that he does not allow
this kind of meaning to religious language is, therefore, quite illegiti-
mate.

Although I share Moralist's view regarding the nonobjective character of religious language, I am not satisfied with his positive account
of that language simply as an expression of moral resolve. Religion is
more than simply a "solemnizing of ethical commitment," and the
peculiar language of religion is more than the recording of the intention of some group of people to act in certain sorts of ways. It is my

purpose in what follows to indicate what that "more" is and to suggest an account of religious language that takes proper cognizance of this.

Religion and the Human Situation

Religion is a product of man's response to what we may call "the human situation"—the existential conditions within which his life as an existing individual is and must be lived. To say that these are "existential" conditions is to say that they are implicit in the very structures that determine human existence: they cannot be removed by any improvement in man's external environment, by any increase in his wisdom, or by any advance in his understanding of himself. They are there. They profoundly condition his existence at its very center. They can be acknowledged and accepted, but they cannot be removed. They are a part of what it means to be an existing human being.

That every human life stands under the terrible threat of total personal nonfulfillment is the first "existential fact" relevant for a proper understanding of religion. To be a human being is to know that there is a way that we ought to go, a life that we ought to live—and to know, at the same time, that we may miss it altogether. This is the threat of being "lost" of which all religions speak. It is because all men know this threat and because religion addresses itself to it that the appeal of religion is so universal.

The threat of personal nonfulfillment—the fear, deep within every man, of being utterly and irrevocably "lost"—expresses itself in a variety of ways. It expresses itself, for example, as a horror of death. What a mockery death makes of human life! Here a young man full of promise, there a mother of several little children, and there a brilliant statesman in whom millions of people had placed their hope, is taken by death. And each such event reminds us that we, too, must die. The one fact of death renders absurd the hopes, the plans, the words and works that occupy us all. To reflect upon this, to see death as the final absurdity in a life that is nothing but "a tale told by an idiot, full of sound and fury, signifying nothing," [1] is to feel at least something of the horror of death. It is one of the ways that the threat of nonfulfillment expresses itself in human existence.

It expresses itself also in a sense of guilt because of real or imagined wrongdoing. All men know this sense of guilt—whether or not it attaches itself to particular overt acts—for to be a human being is to experience the threat of nonfulfillment, to know that we may miss the way that we ought to go. The feeling of guilt is simply the recognition of having "missed the way," the recognition that our lives have

---

[1] William Shakespeare, *Macbeth*, Act 5, Scene 5.

not measured up to what they might and ought to have been. The religious term for this is "sin," which connotes a profound *lack* in human life.

The threat of personal nonfulfillment also expresses itself in a sense of meaninglessness that perpetually haunts human existence. If I have missed the way that I should be walking and if death has the last mocking word, then anything that I may set my hand to now must be utterly devoid of meaning. Nothing that I might do now can have any meaning unless there are at least some proximate values for me to pursue; and there can be no proximate values unless they, in turn, are steps toward the realization of some more ultimate values. But death robs me of the latter. I am left with drabness and weariness: an unlovely Chekhovian world in which "all is vanity and a striving after wind." [2]

However, this is only one side of the dialectic within which we must try to understand religion. It accounts for the negative, or threatening, elements in religion: the wrath of God, the threat of Hell, the possibility of remaining bound to the cycle of rebirths (Buddhism), and so on. Every religion exhibits some such elements, but no religion consists exclusively of these elements; it is precisely the claim of religion to point to a way in which this ultimate threat to human existence is overcome—a way, to use the religious term, of "salvation." "Salvation" means the complete *fulfillment* of self—the overcoming of the threat to self-fulfillment. There is, according to all religions, a grace in human existence by which this threat is accepted and conquered. Grace, too, is experienced in many forms, of which we may pause to mention just three.

It is experienced, first, as the conquest of the horror of death. There seems to be no distinctive word for this experience in our language, but religious literature abounds with references to such things as "deliverance from death unto life," "the conquest of man's last enemy," and so on. "O death," writes St. Paul, "where is thy sting? O grave, where is thy victory? Death is swallowed up in victory." [3] The doctrinal expression of this experience is the doctrine of personal immortality (and its many variants).

Grace is experienced also as forgiveness—an acceptance of oneself despite having "missed the way" and a confidence in that continued acceptance of self into an unknown future. We could call this simply a sustaining sense of personal worth; there is no particular reason for preferring the religious term "forgiveness." It is this experience that religious people mean when they talk about "forgiveness."

Third, the experience of grace is manifest in human experience as

---

2 Ecclesiastes, 1:14.
3 I Corinthians, 15:54, 55.

a sense of meaning, as a feeling that somehow the whole human enterprise is worthwhile and that an individual's part in that enterprise shares in that worth. Somehow meaninglessness and despair do not have the last word in human life: values thrust themselves upon us, tasks really worth doing lie before us, and life itself seems eminently worth living. We know the threat of meaninglessness, but we also know the overcoming of this threat.

All religions are shaped and formed by the dialectic that I have briefly described. The several religions use an infinite variety of pictures, symbols, and ideas, but their function is always the same: to assist their adherents in achieving the "way of salvation" by which the threat to self-fulfillment is overcome in all its varied forms.

Our Language About God

It is correct, as far as it goes, to say that God is conceived by religious people as "the giver and enforcer of the moral law"; but it does not go far enough. More importantly, He is conceived as the giver of life and of salvation, the conqueror of death, the forgiver, the savior. *God is the supposed source of the grace that overcomes the "lostness" that threatens and oppresses human existence.* Of course, He is also conceived as giving and enforcing the moral law, but this is only because the moral law is thought to define in part the way that God would have us walk.

What each religion sets before its adherents is not simply a distinctive moral code, but a concrete and all-inclusive *existence-possibility.* This includes, of course, a moral code of some kind, but it includes much more. It includes a distinctive set of symbols, through which adherents of a particular religion will be taught to conceptualize various dimensions of their experience. It includes certain rites, in which the peculiar religious needs developed in a religious group will find appropriate expression. A religious group is not only, or even primarily, an ethical culture society: it is a fellowship of human beings who are seeking the way of salvation together and who have learned to employ a common set of symbols to mark their progress on that way.

It is not at all difficult, against this background, to understand the ritual use of language that refers to God: God is addressed as a very exalted person not altogether unlike ourselves, and He is made the object of both prayer and praise. In prayer, the worshiper expresses both fear (which is never wholly overcome) and confidence that the Giver of salvation will supply his need. In praise, the worshiper expresses gratitude for blessings received and most especially for the incomparable gift of salvation.

But what, according to the view here developed, can be the meaning of a theological assertion of the form "God is ———— (good, wise, holy, just, etc.)"? According to the empiricist criterion of meaning, such statements cannot mean what religious people typically think they mean. What, then, is their meaning?

I think the answer is as follows. Theological statements of this kind have two elements: they express (a) the existential ideal of the community and (b) the gratitude of the community for blessings received. It is the intertwining of these two elements that gives to such statements their peculiar character.

Let us consider first the existential ideal. St. Anselm's statement is particularly apt: "God is everything that it is better to be than not to be." [4] God is conceived by the faithful to realize in His own nature all of the goodness that He looks for in them—not only moral goodness, but also such nonmoral qualities as wisdom and prudence. Much talk about God is, therefore, as Moralist says, a way of setting before the community the ideal to which the community is committed. But the ideal is not merely an ethical ideal: it is an ideal that encompasses the whole of life.

The picture is complicated by the fact that such talk about God also includes a great deal that is purely honorific. The feeling of gratitude that characterizes the life of religion leads the spokesmen of religion, the theologians, to ascribe to God, who is conceived as a very exalted person, all sorts of qualities that no mere human being could ever have or hope to have—power, majesty, might, ubiquity, and so on. Such statements have meaning not as an expression of the existential ideal of the community, but rather as an exaggerated expression of the gratitude of the community. The gratitude is real and legitimate, but the expression of it by the ascription to God of qualities such as "omnipotence" and "omnipresence" is very misleading.

Talk about God is meaningful not as a description of an Unseen Being, but as an expression of the existential ideals and the innermost feelings (of gratitude, etc.) of human beings. There may or may not be a Being who charts the way that we ought to go and gives forgiveness and salvation. But the way, forgiveness, and salvation are real components of our existence, and every moment of our existence is lived in relation to them. The meaning of our talk about God depends on the ways in which that talk reflects our experience of lostness, forgiveness, and salvation; we have these experiences firsthand and can discuss them as meaningfully as we can discuss anything else.

STUDY QUESTIONS

1. What does Existentialist mean by "existential conditions"? What "existential conditions" does he suggest are relevant for a proper understanding of religion? To what extent does Existentialist's account of

---

4 St. Anselm, in S. N. Deane (tr.), *Proslogium (and Other Writings)*. (La-Salle, Ill.: Open Court, 1962), p. 11.

religion involve a rejection of Moralist's account, and to what extent could it be construed as simply supplemental to that account?

2. Is there some connection between (a) a view of the nature of religion, (b) a concept of God, and (c) a view regarding the meaning (or lack of meaning) of religious language? Illustrate your answer by reference to the theories discussed in this and the preceding chapter.

3. What does Existentialist suggest is the "peculiar character" of religious language? Does this strike you as a plausible suggestion?

56

THE EMPIRICAL FOUNDATIONS OF RELIGIOUS LANGUAGE

A person who has gone through a substantial portion of his life complacently believing that his discourse about God is—at least in some respects—descriptive of a transcendent reality cannot but be taken aback by the suggestion that this is not so. Surely, he is inclined to think, there must be some relatively easy solution to the problem. But the empiricist criterion of factual significance is a very restricting doctrine. And so, in desperation, he is tempted to look for desperate solutions.

I think that the two proposals just presented are examples of this "strategy of desperation." There is no doubt that a "way of life," or a "pattern of existence," is an important element within the whole fabric of a religion. It is not surprising, therefore, that elements of "moral resolve," or "existential orientation," are to found in the language of religion. However, there is equally no doubt that religion is not simply a matter of moral resolve and/or existential orientation and that the language of religion cannot, as a consequence, be accounted for simply in those terms.

Suppose that I say, "My grandfather was one of the kindest men I ever knew: would that I could be more like him." In speaking this way I am, of course, expressing a wish and an intention—recording my "moral resolve," if you wish—to act in a certain way. It may well be, further, that I have been taught from childhood to feel love and gratitude for grandfather—through being told stories of things he did for me when I was small and kindnesses he performed for other people whom I love, and so on. Under circumstances such as these my statements about grandfather would take on a certain "moral" or "existential" flavor. They would, *among other things*, record my own feelings, intentions, and aspirations.

However, my statements about grandfather would also, and primarily, still be statements *about grandfather*. Whatever it may say about my own intentions, the statement "Grandfather was a very kind man . . ." is a statement about grandfather. It may be true, or it may be false. It may also, incidentally, be quite beyond verification. But whatever else it may express, it expresses primarily my belief that grandfather was a man of such and such a character.

Something of this kind must be said, surely, about religious language. No doubt it does express, among other things, the kinds of things that Moralist and Existentialist say it expresses. But this is not all. Language about God is, first and foremost, language *about God*— about a reality whose existence or nonexistence is a matter of profound importance to us and whose real possession or nonpossession of the attributes of love, mercy, compassion, and so on determines whether or not our language about Him is true. Religion is not purely a matter of moral resolve and/or existential orientation; it is also a matter of belief. Without belief, neither moral resolve nor existential orientation would be called "religion."

It seems clear, therefore, that those who today are content to adopt one or another of the "subjectivist" solutions to the problem of religious language are living on the capital of their forefathers. They revere the way of life exemplified by their elders and suppose that it can be preserved without the beliefs that created it. If this way of life should survive the rejection of the beliefs upon which it was based, however, it will not be a religion that has survived, but merely an ethic. Religion implies belief, and the language of religion is an attempt to express belief. And beliefs, all beliefs, are either true or false.

Religious Discourse and "Facts"

If we are persuaded of the validity of the empiricist criterion of factual significance, then there are only two alternatives: either to show that sentences about God are factually significant according to the criterion or to draw the unhappy conclusion that religious people are all mistaken in thinking that their language about God is expressive of beliefs. The latter alternative seems preposterous; I propose, therefore, to defend the former. I think that sentences about God are factually significant.

The empiricist criterion of factual significance, it will be recalled, requires that in order for a sentence to be accounted factually significant, some empirical data must be relevant to its truth or falsehood. That this is the case with respect to at least some sentences about God is evident, I would argue, from the fact that religious people are concerned about the problem of evil. The occurrence of evil in the world (a fact of empirical observation) is a problem for religious people precisely because it appears to be inconsistent with belief in the perfect wisdom, power, and goodness of the Creator. If God were limited in wisdom, He could be excused because of ignorance. If He were limited in power (as Plato held), He could be excused on the ground that He did the best He could. If He were limited in goodness, then the occurrence of evil together with good is just what might be expected. But if God is said to be altogether wise (omniscient), powerful (omnipotent), and good, then the occurrence of evil counts against the statement. It is, in the sense demanded by the criterion, relevant to the truth or falsity of the statement. If it were not, there would be no point in the concern with the existence of evil that religious people have always had.

Nonetheless, the occurrence of evil does not conclusively falsify the statement, "God is perfectly wise, powerful, and good." The reason it does not is that there is a vital difference between religious truth-claims (of the troublesome kind) and scientific truth-claims. It is characteristic of scientific truth-claims that (a) they yield precise predictions regarding what will occur under such and such prescribed conditions and (b) the nonoccurrence of what is predicted is allowed to falsify the truth-claim. In the case of religious truth-claims, however, the situation is different. A theological belief leads not to precise predictions, but to certain general expectations. Job believed that God, being just, rewards the righteous and punishes the wicked according to their deserts, and, being a righteous man, he accordingly expected to experience health, long life, and prosperity. When expectations are disappointed, the result—as in Job's case—is not the *falsification of a theory* but the *calling in question of a belief*: it is what religious people call a temptation to unbelief. In such a situation a person may cease to believe what he formerly believed; but when this occurs, what has happened is not the refutation of a theory, but the collapse of a faith.

The difference between religious beliefs and scientific hypotheses does not consist in the alleged fact that the latter are factually significant while the former are not. The difference consists, rather, in the radically different ways, or attitudes, in which the respective beliefs are held. Scientific hypotheses are, quite properly, held in the tentative, provisional way with which we are all familiar: they are always open to revision, and every fact not explicable in the context of the hypothesis becomes a challenge to create a better hypothesis. Beliefs about God obviously are not, and cannot be, held in this way. The belief that God is powerful, wise, and good is not a hypothesis to be discarded as soon as some untoward event occurs: it is an article of faith, and as such it can be given up only through and with great anguish. The belief is part of a total and (ideally) unconditional *commitment*—what Friedrich Schleiermacher called "absolute dependence" and Paul Tillich called "ultimate concern." To be "absolutely dependent" on or "ultimately concerned" about anything other than God is what is called "idolatry"; but whatever the object of ultimate concern, whether God or anything else, the beliefs that someone holds about that object cannot be held in the mood of detachment appropriate to a tentative hypothesis. They can only be held in the passion that is the appropriate mood for faith.

Empirical Grounds for Theological Assertions

Thus far I have been content to argue only that acceptance of the empiricist criterion of factual significance does not necessarily force acceptance of the conclusion that sentences about God are devoid of factual significance. The conclusion does not follow because empirical observations do in fact count against certain statements about God, though they do not conclusively falsify them because of the way in which theological beliefs are held.

It may be protested that this only takes us a very small part of the way toward solving the problem of religious language. It takes us beyond the empiricist criterion of factual significance, but leaves us with the problem that our language, though admirably suited to the description of ordinary objects, cannot be properly descriptive of God. It also leaves entirely unanswered the question as to what, if anything, may be adduced as counting *in favor of* theological assertions. If nothing were to be said about these two problems, there would be scant comfort in the knowledge that there are some empirical facts that appear to count *against* such utterances.

What makes the problem of theological language seem so utterly impossible of solution is that those who concern themselves with it commonly do so on the supposition that what demands to be proved is that language can be meaningfully descriptive of a *wholly transcendent* reality. To this question there is only one possible answer: it cannot. A "wholly transcendent reality" is beyond the realm of all possible experience, and what is beyond the realm of all possible experience is, according to the empiricist criterion, also beyond the realm of factual significance. Of that of which we have no experience we are altogether ignorant, and of that of which we are altogether ignorant we cannot speak.

There is, however, no good reason for such a one-sided emphasis on the transcendence of God. High religion, it is true, has always affirmed the transcendence of God—and has been healthily agnostic about our capacity to know anything about this aspect of God's nature.

But it has also spoken of the *immanence* of God, and it is at this point that our language about God can be seen to have some intelligible meaning. To say that God is immanent is to say that He *is* present in human experience and that our language can be descriptive of Him in the same way that it can be descriptive of any other reality encountered in experience.

The primary meaning of the term "God" is: a reality that saves man from the powers and processes that are destructive of his humanity and that is (as a consequence) eminently worthy of his unconditioned commitment. Such a reality is encountered by us, I maintain, in the *creative intercommunion with other men* that characterizes interpersonal encounter at its best. Here and here alone do we encounter a creative power that truly transforms us, that overcomes the guilt, the meaninglessness, and the triviality of our existence, and that enables us to fulfill our human potentialities. Here is salvation, in the only sense of that word that I can understand. Here, therefore, is God as He is experienced by us.

It is such creative intercommunion that creates and sustains the human mind and personality. It is this that saves and transforms him who gives himself to it without reservation. It is in this reality that we find that deep acceptance of ourselves in spite of ourselves that is the true meaning of forgiveness. To him who thus commits himself, this reality gives peace, courage, comfort, and renewal of mind. If this is God, then God is in very truth that omnipresent reality in whom we live and move and have our being.

How perfectly natural, then, and how profoundly meaningful (because so thoroughly interwoven in the very fabric of our experience) to say: "God creates," "God sustains," "God forgives," "God saves," "God transforms," "God loves." In this power of creative intercommunion—this power that is among us, and in us, and is infinitely more than simply the sum of our individual powers—we encounter a reality to which it seems natural and appropriate to ascribe the attributes of deity. It is not surprising that this is so: the true lovers of God have rarely been metaphysicians, but men deeply involved in the common life of man. "God" means "creative intercommunion among men"; it is to this that we offer our prayers and our praises, when we are moved to prayer or praise.

What we experience is in very large part a function of what we have been trained to notice. A symphony is experienced as one thing by a novice and as quite a different thing by a trained musician; even among trained musicians a given symphony may be experienced quite differently by a violinist and a clarinetist. The novice hears "a lot of sound" and either likes it or does not. The musician hears themes, harmonies, progressions, varying timbres, tempos, and dynamics; he discerns structure and form in what he hears and compares the interpretation with others that he has heard. Because he knows what to listen for, he hears (discerns) many things that the novice does not.

Most people today are not attuned to the kind of experience that I have been attempting to describe—the experience of God. God is a reality in our midst, but He is almost unknown. The reason He is unknown is that we do not pay sufficient heed to that dimension of our experience in which He is manifest to us. We are novices in religious experience. What chiefly occupies our attention is things: how to get them, how to manipulate them, how to derive pleasure from them. We notice objects, we notice regularities, we notice mathematical relations—but we do not notice God. Hence, it is no wonder that our experience is shallow and our talk of God is empty. We do not need an alternative to the empiricist criterion; we need to redirect our attention and enrich our experience. Otherwise all our talk of God, with or without the criterion, is empty.

STUDY QUESTIONS

1. Is Empiricist right in his contention that "religion implies belief"? Support your answer with specific illustrations.
2. What exactly is Empiricist's position on the problem of religious language? On what point or points is he in agreement with the previous two writers? On what points is he in disagreement with them?
3. What differences does Empiricist find between scientific truth-claims and religious truth-claims? Do you agree? Are there other differences as well?
4. What concept of God is suggested by Empiricist? Can one talk about God *thus conceived* in a way that is consistent with the empiricist criterion? Would this solution to the problem be apt to satisfy most religious people? Explain.
5. What, according to this account, is the meaning of each of the following: "God creates," "God sustains," "God forgives," "God saves," "God transforms," "God loves"?

57

THE SYMBOLIC CHARACTER
OF RELIGIOUS LANGUAGE

It is regrettable that so much of the philosophical discussion of religion in recent years should have been directed toward the solution of the problem posed by the empiricist criterion of factual significance. There can be no doubt that this unfortunate narrowing of the discussion has trivialized the philosophical interest in religion. In the all but unanimous endorsement of this vaunted criterion, and the resulting consternation of some philosophers (as well as theologians) about the apparent consequences for religion and theology, ancient insights of great and permanent importance have been overlooked. I shall attempt to redress the balance.

A Critique of the Criterion

Whatever the opinion regarding the status of our language about God, the empiricist criterion ought to be rejected as a general criterion of meaning (which is what its supporters usually claim it to be). Not only is theological language consigned by this criterion to the limbo of meaninglessness, but also (a) statements about events alleged to have occurred in the past (The Battle of Gettysburg occurred in 1863), (b) statements about other minds (Mr. Jones is worrying about how he is going to send his son to college), and (c) statements postulating the annihilation of all perceivers (Should a full-scale atomic war occur, all life will be destroyed). We do know what statements of these three kinds mean; yet none of them is meaningful according to the empiricist criterion.

Moreover, the status of the empiricist criterion itself is a matter of considerable embarrassment to its supporters. The most plausible account of it is that it is an *empirical hypothesis*—an inductive generalization about the conditions of meaningfulness, derived from careful observation of statements adjudged on other grounds to be meaningful. If this is the case, however, it is evident that the "criterion" is not really a criterion at all. It cannot determine what is or is not meaningful, since the method by which the theory is erected presupposes that one already knows, *on some other basis*, which statements are meaningful and which are not. It is only fair to say that the supporters of the criterion have by and large recognized this problem and have tried to deal with it. It is also only fair to say that their attempts to do so have not been very convincing even to themselves.

As a general criterion of meaning, the empiricist criterion is, therefore, grossly inadequate. What it defines is not the conditions of meaningful discourse in general, but the conditions of meaning commonly applied in the natural sciences. If we do assume that it is a correct description of the conditions of meaning required in the natural sciences (a question for the philosophy of science), it will follow that no statement which fails to satisfy this criterion will qualify as a *scientific* statement (in the narrow sense of "scientific" currently in vogue). It will by no means follow that the statement in question is completely meaningless.

A Deeper Problem

Although the preoccupation of philosophers with the problem posed by the empiricist criterion (construed as a general criterion of meaning) has trivialized the philosophical interest in religion, it cannot be denied that the discussion of this problem has produced some valuable results. It has demonstrated, for example, that there are ethical and existential dimensions to the meaning of religious language, as previous participants in the present discussion have made clear. It has demonstrated, moreover, that the question of the meaningfulness of our *language* about God cannot be separated from the question of the meaning of the *concept* "God"—as even Empiricist's account makes evident. Consequently, the discussion has not been without value.

An older and much more serious problem that has been largely overlooked in all the excitement over the apparent consequences of the empiricist criterion, however, is this: Whatever may be the general conditions of meaningful discourse, how is it possible for a language, whose form and structure are patterned after a world of finite objects, to be descriptive of an infinite and transcendent reality? This was Aquinas' problem, referred to briefly in the introductory chapter. It is an inescapable problem for any philosophy that seriously affirms the possibility of meaningful discourse about God.

Aquinas' own proposal vis-à-vis this problem, as has already been pointed out, is the classical answer to it. He said that God the Creator stands as "principle and cause" in relation to the things He has created and that "all the perfections of things pre-exist excellently" in Him. Thus, according to Aquinas, it is permissible to ascribe the perfections that we perceive in creatures to God, provided that we bear in mind that in God they exist fully and perfectly, whereas in creatures they exist only fragmentarily and imperfectly. In the two sentences, "God is wise" and "Socrates is wise," the meaning of the predicate "wise" is neither absolutely identical (univocal) nor absolutely diverse (equivocal): it is analogical. Socrates is wise in the way that wisdom is appropriate to a finite and imperfect being; God is wise in the way that wisdom is appropriate to an infinite and perfect being. "In analogies," said Aquinas, "the idea is not, as it is in univocals, one and the same; yet it is not totally diverse as in equivocals; but the name which is thus used in a multiple sense signifies various proportions to some one thing." [1]

The theory of analogical predication is both ingenious and profound, and it is worthy of great respect. It provides, as any adequate theory of theological language must, for both continuity and discontinuity between God and the world. It allows us to affirm both the transcendence of God (by virtue of which our language is not *properly* applicable to God) and the immanence of God (by virtue of which our language has *some* meaning when applied to God). It permits us to say the kinds of things that we want to say about God (as none of the theories presented in the previous three chapters do), yet it preserves a healthy agnosticism about the propriety of our language—it reminds us that no description of God is really adequate to the reality of the divine mystery. It seems evident, therefore, that any theory that (a) presupposes that "God" means an immanent-transcendent reality as conceived in classical theism and (b) affirms the possibility of meaningful discourse about this reality must in the last analysis be something very similar to, or perhaps only a variant of, this theory.

Analogical predication consists, actually, in a very clever combination of positive and negative predication. It is evident that some statements about God are purely negative: they do not affirm that God is thus and so, but rather they deny that God is thus and so. It seems appropriate, for example, to say that God is not composite, not corporeal, not finite, and not subject to change, and these assertions are commonly expressed by saying that God is simple, incorporeal, infinite, and immutable. There is evidently no mystery about how such God-talk can be meaningful since the predicates employed are all being used in their proper everyday sense.

---

[1] St. Thomas Aquinas, *Summa Theologica*, I, Ques. 13, Art. 5, in Anton C. Pegis (ed.), *Basic Writings of St. Thomas Aquinas* (New York: Random House, 1945), Vol. I, p. 120.

The "analogical way" of talking about God is in very large measure a further extension of this "negative way." To be sure, in analogical predication we are attempting to make a positive statement about God —to say something about what God *is* rather than about what He is *not*. But the negative way continues to function by attempting to remove from the positive meaning of the predicate whatever it would not be appropriate to attribute to a being who is not composite, not corporeal, not finite, and so on. This is what is involved in saying that God is wise "in the way that wisdom is appropriate to an infinite and perfect being": by applying the negative way we *rid* the concept of those features that would make it inappropriate for a description of the divine reality.

Thus stated, however, the theory of analogical predication is open to one very serious objection. If the analogical meaning of a given predicate as applied to God is just its ordinary meaning minus those elements that render it incapable of describing the divine reality, it follows that the relation between a given term as applied to God and the same term as applied to creatures is in part equivocal and in part univocal. Insofar as "wise" connotes finitude, corporeality, etc., it refers only to creatures: to this extent "wise" as applied to God and "wise" as applied to creatures are *equivocal* terms. But what of the meaning that remains once the objectionable elements have been removed? To that extent, "wise" as applied to God and "wise" as applied to creatures are *univocal* terms. And so, it would seem, all of the objections to "univocity" apply with equal force to the analogical theory.

This is, in my opinion, a sound objection—though I would add that it touches only the letter and not the spirit of the theory of analogical predication. I think that the intention of the many philosophers who have supported the theory of analogical predication can be preserved in a way that gets around this objection. This can be accomplished through what I shall call the theory of *symbolic* predication. It is a kind of analogical theory, but with sufficient differences from the traditional theory to warrant a special name.

Symbolic Predication

The real purpose of the analogical way was to emphasize that (as well as to show how) our language about God is qualitatively different from our language about finite objects. The theory of analogical predication fails not because it does not recognize this important insight, but because it tries to express it in an inadequate way—namely, at the level of discursive meaning. At that level, however, there are just three formal possibilities: (a) the meaning of a term in each of two instances is absolutely identical (univocal); (b) the meaning of a term in each of two instances is absolutely different (equivocal); (c) the meaning of a term in each of two instances is partly identical and partly different (analogical). To affirm that our talk about God is analogical, if this is what is meant by analogical, is not to escape the difficulties of "univocal" predication at all.

The kind of meaning that our language about God can have is, however, closely related to the kind of knowledge that we have of Him. If it were the case that we had some straightforwardly empirical knowledge of God, then there would be no problem at all in accounting for our language about God. This, however, is not the case. Our apprehension of God's reality and our knowledge of His nature do not occur at the discursive level. It is not "technical," or "scientific," reason that knows God but reason in its depth; hence, the language of scientific discourse (including the ordinary language of everyday experience) cannot adequately express this knowledge.

When we use language with reference to God, therefore, we are using it not in its ordinary literal meaning, but *symbolically*. When we say that God is good, wise, or merciful, we are not saying that He is these things in the same way that some men are good, wise, and merciful (only more so), nor are we saying that He is these things minus whatever elements of meaning connote finitude and imperfection. We are saying, rather, that God is *not* these things in the literal sense of "good," "wise," or "perfect," but that these terms point beyond themselves to realities in the ground of goodness, wisdom, and mercy—realities that cannot be grasped discursively but can only be acknowledged as dimensions of the reality of the divine mystery.

It is important to realize that in saying that our language about God is symbolic we are not saying that it is thereby inferior to literally descriptive language: on the contrary, we are saying that the mystery of the divine being so far surpasses our understanding that the descriptive language of everyday discourse is altogether inadequate to describe God. He knows God best who acknowledges that whatever he thinks and says falls short of what God really is. Our language cannot describe God, even imperfectly; it can only point to Him. And this function of "pointing to" is precisely the function of a symbol.

What governs our choice of symbols? Why do we say (symbolically) that God is "good" and "wise," but not that He is "material" or "numerous"—for surely He is the ground of matter and number as well as of goodness and wisdom? It is our apprehension of the divine reality itself that governs our choice. Just as discursive reason learns the art of choosing terms to describe the realities with which it is conversant, so reason in its depth learns the art of choosing symbols to indicate the divine reality. Talk about God is, in the last analysis, an attempt to *make language revelatory* of the divine nature. It is the language that is adjudged successful in this effort that is retained as the language of theology.

The question as to whether or not it is possible to speak meaningfully about God, and, if so, what sort of meaning theological talk must have, cannot be decided on the basis of purely logical considerations. We must first take a stand on some very important ontological and epistemological problems: Does "God" denote a reality? Do we have any knowledge of this reality? The theory of theological language here suggested presupposes an affirmative answer to both these questions. The view that theological language is meaningless—though it may claim to be nothing but the plain implication of a neutral principle of logic—just as evidently presupposes a negative answer to one or both of these questions. A theory of theological language that pretends to be neutral with respect to these questions only succeeds in confusing the issue.

This being the case, the recent uncertainty about the meaningfulness of theological language appears to be little more than a pale reflection of the waning awareness of the divine reality that is so frighteningly evident in the modern world. Men have always known that God is not a thing among things: hence, they have always known that there is something peculiar, something odd, something unique, about our language with respect to Him. But only men for whom God has altogether ceased to be—only men for whom, as Friedrich Nietzsche said, God is dead—could seriously hold that our language about God is altogether devoid of meaning. Let the awareness of the divine reality be reborn among us and our doubts about the meaningfulness of theological language will quickly disappear. Pending that, our talk about God must be empty, and our talk about that talk an exercise in futility.

STUDY QUESTIONS

1. Symbolist rejects the empiricist criterion as a general criterion of meaning. On what grounds? What more limited role does he assign to it? Do you agree with him on this?
2. Why according to Symbolist is the status of the empiricist criterion "a matter of considerable embarrassment to its supporters"? Can you think of any way by which an advocate of the criterion might get around this difficulty?
3. What is the "older and much more serious problem" to which Symbolist invites our attention? Is it in fact a different problem from the one discussed in the three preceding chapters?
4. What exactly is "analogical" predication? What does Symbolist have to say in support of this proposal? What objection does he raise against it? Is the objection, in your opinion, a sound one?
5. What is Symbolist's own proposal regarding the meaning of statements about God? Does it overcome the objection that he raised against the analogical theory?

FOR FURTHER READING

Aquinas, St. Thomas. *Summa Theologica*. Many editions. See Part I, Question 13.

Ayer, A. J. *Language, Truth and Logic*, 2nd ed. New York: Dover Publications, 1946 (paperbound).

Braithwaite, R. B. *An Empiricist's View of the Nature of Religious Belief*. Cambridge, Eng.: Cambridge University Press, 1955.

Carnap, Rudolf. "The Elimination of Metaphysics through Logical Analysis of Language," in A. J. Ayer (ed.). *Logical Positivism*. New York: Free Press, 1957.

Christian, William A. *Meaning and Truth in Religion*. Princeton: Princeton University Press, 1964.

Coburn, Robert C. "The Hiddenness of God," *The Journal of Philosophy*, 57 (1960), 689–712.

Ewing, A. C. "Religious Assertions in the Light of Contemporary Philosophy," *Philosophy*, 32 (1957), 206–218.

Ferré, F. *Language, Logic and God*. New York: Harper & Row, 1969.

Flew, A., and A. Macintyre. *New Essays in Philosophical Theology*. New York: Macmillan, 1964 (paperbound).

Hempel, C. G. "Problems and Changes in the Empiricist Criterion of Meaning," in A. J. Ayer (ed.). *Logical Positivism*. New York: Free Press, 1957.

Hick, John. *Faith and Knowledge*. Ithaca, N.Y.: Cornell University Press, 1957.

High, D. M. (ed.). *New Essays on Religious Language*. London: Oxford University Press, 1969.

Lazerowitz, M. *The Structure of Metaphysics*. New York: Humanities Press, 1955.

Macintyre, A. (ed.). *Metaphysical Beliefs*. London: SCM Press, 1957.

Marhenke, P. "The Criterion of Significance," in L. Linsky (ed.). *Semantics and the Philosophy of Language*. Urbana: University of Illinois Press, 1952.

Mascall, E. L. *Words and Images*. New York: Ronald Press, 1957.

Miles, T. R., *Religion and the Scientific Outlook*. New York: Humanities Press, 1959.

Mitchell, Basil (ed.). *Faith and Logic*. London: G. Allen & Unwin, 1957.

Munz, Peter. *Problems of Religious Knowledge*. London: SCM Press, 1959.

Ramsey, Ian T. *Christian Discourse*. London: Oxford University Press, 1965.

———. *Religious Language*. New York: Macmillan, 1963 (paperbound).

Tillich, Paul. *Systematic Theology*, vol. I. Chicago: University of Chicago Press, 1951, pp. 235–289.

Wieman, H. N. *Man's Ultimate Commitment*. Carbondale: Southern Illinois University Press, 1958, chaps. 1–7.

PART XII

WORLD-VIEWS

58

THE FUNDAMENTAL PROBLEM

Many chapters ago, when we first set out on this study of philosophy, we observed that the positive goal of the philosopher is to construct a picture of the whole of reality, a picture in which every element of man's knowledge and every aspect of man's experience might find its proper place. Philosophy, we said, is man's quest for the unity of knowledge: it consists in a perpetual struggle to create the concepts in which the universe can be conceived as a *uni*verse and not a *multi*-verse. The history of philosophy, then, is the history of man's search for an adequate world-view. The problems of philosophy are the problems that arise as we pursue this quest.

We can say, therefore, that the fundamental problem of all philosophy—the problem that underlies and in some sense ties together all of the other problems that we have been considering—is the problem of world-views. Which "total view" of reality is most adequate to the known facts? What are the foundational truths about reality in relation to which everything else that we can know needs to be understood?

The reader who has worked his way through any significant number of the problems dealt with in the preceding pages will surely have become aware of the fact that these problems are interrelated in a variety of ways. The relations that obtain among these various problems are, of course, *logical* relations: if we embrace a given position on one problem, we may be logically excluded from adopting certain positions or logically obliged to adopt a certain position on some other problem. Hopefully, the positions we hold on various problems are at least consistent with each other: that is a minimum requirement that all of us must seek to satisfy. If we look with some care at the various positions that we have taken on the problems considered, we should be able to discern the outlines of a world-view that might be called "our philosophy."

How Philosophical Problems Are Interrelated

Let us explore by means of a few examples some of the logical interrelationships between and among philosophical problems. Suppose, for example, that on the problem of freedom and authority (Chapters 6–10) I adopt the natural law theory. Then I cannot—if I am to be consistent—accept empiricism, for this would exclude the possibility of having any knowledge of natural law (in the sense intended by the defenders of the natural law theory). Hence I must be a rationalist. And if I am a rationalist, then certain options are open to me on other philosophical problems—intuitionism in metaethics (Chapter 18), the rationalist solution to the problem of induction (Chapter 39), a belief in the possibility of proving the existence of God (Chapters 48–50), etc.—that would not otherwise be open to me. If, on the other hand, I decide that on the rationalist-empiricist question I must take my stand on empiricism, then I must—for the sake of logical consistency—reject those views on other problems that presuppose a kind of knowledge that as an empiricist I cannot acknowledge to be possible.

No matter where we take our stand among the various philosophical views that we have discussed, certain implications will follow with respect to at least some of the others. Every position that we adopt on any particular question implies certain positions and excludes certain positions on countless other questions. This is what we meant when we spoke in Chapter 3 about the systematic character of all philosophical thinking and the multidimensional relevance of all philosophical questions.

To the extent that we engage seriously and honestly in the study of philosophy, we become involved in what might be called a systematic clarification of our world-view and in a systematic testing of this world-view by means of a rigorous evaluation of certain of its elements. There is more at stake in the answer that we give to this or that philosophical problem than the resolution of that particular problem. Indeed, as we remarked earlier, every philosophical problem is a kind of test case for an entire world-view. The serious study of philosophy requires great intellectual courage.

World-Views

At the center of every world-view is what might be called the "touchstone proposition" of that world-view: some proposition that the proponents of that world-view hold to be *the* fundamental truth about reality. From the point of view of someone who holds a given world-view, this touchstone proposition serves as a criterion to determine which other propositions may or may not count as candidates for belief. If a given proposition *p* is seen to be inconsistent with the touchstone proposition of a man's world-view, then—so long as he holds that world-view—he cannot but regard proposition *p* as false. Only if or insofar as a proposition appears to be consistent with his touchstone proposition can the holder of a given world-view admit it as a candidate for belief.

One important feature of a world-view, then, is that it serves as an intellectual framework in terms of which someone who holds that world-view will attempt to understand whatever he has occasion to try to understand. So long as his experience presents nothing that cannot be satisfactorily accounted for within his world-view, he will presumably continue to hold it without question. If, however, he is confronted with some phenomenon that cannot be assimilated within his world-view—if reality gives the lie to the world-view he has espoused—then, if he is honest, he has no choice but to modify his world-view in such a way as to allow for the troublesome new fact.

Suppose, now, that the holder of a certain world-view encounters some fact that he cannot incorporate into it, and suppose further that he is unable to think of any way in which he can modify his world-view to accomodate the new fact. What are his options? He may retain his world-view and acknowledge that he has an unresolved problem on his hands, or he may abandon his world-view altogether in favor of another that appears to him to be more adequate to the facts as he perceives them.

Alternative World-Views

There is, of course, no theoretical limit to the number of world-views that might be developed. The world as we experience it is a sufficiently complicated affair to support (with varying degrees of plausibility) a rather wide variety of world-views. Therefore, we cannot hope to be exhaustive in our classification of alternative world-views. At best, we can list those that are regarded as the major options by most educated and informed people at the present time.

Ethical theism is probably the most widely-held world-view in the Western world, though it has undoubtedly lost some ground in the modern era. The touchstone proposition of ethical theism might be stated thus: *God, who is infinitely good, wise, and powerful, is the creator and sustainer of everything that exists, and man is the crown of His creation.* One form of this world-view is presented in Chapter 59.

In contrast to ethical theism and in perpetual conflict with it stands *naturalism*. The touchstone proposition of naturalism might be stated as follows: *the primary constituents of reality are material entities whose internal structures and external relations determine absolutely everything that happens in the world.* This world-view is further elaborated and defended in Chapter 60.

Some philosophers who have wrestled with the problem of world-views have found themselves unable to accept either ethical theism or naturalism and have adopted instead a world-view called *transcendentalism.* The touchstone proposition of transcendentalism is difficult to state with precision, but a fair approximation would be: *there are dimensions of reality that are not a part of this spatiotemporal world that we perceive with our five senses* (dimensions of reality that "transcend" the natural world), *and these transcendent dimensions of reality impinge upon man and his world in a variety of ways.* A world-view of this type is advocated in Chapter 61.

The fourth and last type of world-view that we shall consider is called *humanism.* Humanism differs from the three world-views previously mentioned in that it is, so to speak, less global. The touchstone proposition of humanism might be stated thus: *whatever may be the whole truth about nature, man, and God (if He exists), man at least is unique and not merely a part of nature.* Humanism says, in effect, "Whatever view of the whole you choose to adopt, I insist that you take care to preserve the dignity of man." Such a view is further elaborated and defended in Chapter 62.

It is evident that these four world-views cannot be construed as straightforward alternative answers to a single substantive question, since as a matter of fact they are not even mutually exclusive. Humanism, for example, could ally itself with any of the other three world-views and has in fact done so in the thought of many philosophers. Blaise Pascal, for example, could be described as a theistic humanist, Jean-Paul Sartre as a naturalistic humanist, and Paul Tillich as a transcendentalistic humanist. World-views may be more or less comprehensive and may be worked out in greater or lesser detail: what they have in common is that they are organized around some truth-claim that the holders of the respective world-views take to be *the* fundamental truth about reality. A world-view is a basic intellectual stance, a way of trying to comprehend the totality of things.

Arguments About World-Views

How can anyone argue for or against—or even think intelligently about—a world-view? What sorts of arguments can reasonably be brought forward to support the claim that this world-view is right, or that one wrong? Actually, in discussing the preceding problems we have already been arguing for and against various world-views. Insofar as a given philosophical problem is logically related to the question of world-views, any argument that arises in the course of the discussion of that problem is thereby a discussion of world-views as well. Indeed, confrontations between the proponents of conflicting world-views most commonly occur not in the direct and overt way that we shall observe in the chapters that follow, but rather as disagreements over subordinate issues on which they find themselves obliged to differ by virtue of their basic philosophical commitments.

If, however, the world-views question is explicitly under discussion, several sorts of arguments are open to the disputants. First, the advocate of a given world-view may appeal to certain facts or alleged facts that in his opinion favor his view over those of his opponents. The range of facts to which appeal may be made in the discussion of this question is of course extremely broad. Second, a participant in this debate may "go on the attack" and attempt to show that the views of his opponents are inadequate in certain specified ways. A world-view may be attacked in either of two ways: it may be attacked on grounds of *internal inconsistency* or on grounds of *factual error*. And third, a holder of a particular world-view may present rebuttal arguments (after attack or in recognition of points vulnerable to attack) to show that his view is not internally inconsistent or not guilty of factual error in the ways alleged.

These are the principal ways in which arguments may be employed in discussions about world-views. Let us see what kind of case can be made for each of the principal world-views held today.

STUDY QUESTIONS

1. List the philosophical problems that you have studied thus far, and the positions that you have been inclined to take on each. Do you see any inconsistencies in the positions you have taken? Do you see any instances where your position on one problem logically compels you to adopt a certain position on some other problem?
2. List the positions that you have adopted on the problems studied thus far in order of decreasing certainty: At the top of your list will be the position about which you feel most certain, at the bottom the position about which you feel least certain. Assume that the position you have listed as "most certain" is correct. What implications does this have for the remaining positions on your list?
3. What exactly is a world-view? Does everybody have one?
4. How would you describe the world-view that you were given as a child? What, for example, would you say is the touchstone proposition of that world-view? How, if at all, has that world-view been modified to date?

59

ETHICAL THEISM

As most of my readers are no doubt aware, I speak as an advocate of one of the oldest and most widely-held world-views in the world. Indeed, ethical theism is more than a world-view: it is an attitude toward life, a sense of man's place in the scheme of things that is felt as well as thought. Many of the values that Western men prize most highly—the dignity of man, the sacredness of human life, the significance of the individual, the meaningfulness of history—derive from this world-view and may be incapable of surviving apart from it. The question as to whether this world-view is true is therefore of great importance.

The Fuller View

Let me begin by sketching in some of the details of this world-view. God exists. That is the fundamental truth from which all thought about reality should begin. I may or may not be able to prove God's existence—but God exists. My understanding of God's true nature may be ever so fragmentary—but God exists. I may be puzzled about the ontological status of the physical world, or about the nature of the self, or about many other things—but God exists. His existence is the elemental fact, the foundational truth from which thought begins and to which it must return whenever we are driven to inspect once again the foundations of the edifice of truth. God exists.

Everything else that exists—inanimate matter, life in all its forms, consciousness, intelligence, everything—has been created by God and is dependent on Him for its continued existence. I of course do not know the manner of God's creation. I do not know, for example, whether the "big bang" that apparently occurred some ten billion years ago should be understood as "the moment of creation," or whether it is even correct to think of the original creation as an event that occurred at some moment in time. My point is simply that everything that we now see existing has its ground and origin in God: if He did not exist, nothing would exist.

God, having created this world that we perceive and of which we are a part, continues to love it and to care for it. The process of evolution, for example, despite the appearance of randomness, is in reality one of the arenas in which the marvelous creative activity of God may be discerned. The course of human history, notwithstanding the suffering and tragedy that are so inextricably a part of it, is not merely the story of man's halting efforts to emerge from the jungle and the cave: it is the story of God gently luring His human children toward a future in which His creation will achieve a richness that we cannot yet imagine.

Man, moreover, is in some sense the most glorious product of God's creation. That there should be anything at all—that matter should exist—is truly marvelous. That there should be life, organisms capable of nourishing and reproducing themselves, is more marvelous still. And that there should evolve out of these materials organisms that not only are and live, but organisms that are conscious, organisms that are aware that they are, is a wonder almost beyond comprehension. But beyond this, consider that among these conscious creatures one has emerged with a capacity for rational thought, speech, science, an appreciation for beauty, and a sense of right and wrong. Whatever may be in store for God's creation beyond this point, surely it is clear that it is through man that it will be accomplished.

Philosophical Implications

My theistic commitment provides the basic context within which I approach all philosophical problems. It also gives me a certain bias with respect to at least some philosophical problems: certain philosophical positions are very attractive to me because they fit in so nicely with my theistic world-view. I make no apology for this, however, since those who hold other world-views are biased toward the philosophical opinions that favor their world-views. We cannot avoid looking at the world through world-view-colored glasses.

On the question of freedom and authority, for example, I am persuaded that some form of the Natural Law Theory is correct. To me it seems virtually self-evident that if man was to rise above the lex talionis—the law of the jungle—he had to grasp and cherish the concept of a human community ruled by just and humane laws. It seems altogether natural that God should desire the human species to achieve such a community and should have guided the evolution of man in such a way that man would at length begin to discern the outlines of a law (already conceptualized in the mind of God) by which community might be achieved. The question of freedom and authority must of course be decided on the merits of the arguments for the alternative answers that may be given. My point is merely that within the context of my world-view one of those answers is especially attractive, though I could adopt some other view without in any way violating my basic philosophical commitments.

Since space does not permit me to discuss in detail my positions on all of the problems raised in preceding sections, I shall have to be content merely to list my preferences:

Philosophical Problem	Preferences of an Ethical Theist
Freedom and Authority	Natural Law Theory
Man's Highest Good	Eternal Happiness
Language of Morals	Intuitionism
Freedom and Determinism	Soft Determinism
Mind and Body	Dualism
A Priori Knowledge	Rationalism
Induction	Rationalism
Ontological Status of the Physical World	Direct Realism
Existence of God	Endorse Cosmological Argument
Religious Language	Analogical Theory

Please note that my theistic world-view in no way obligates me to adopt these positions. Part of the attraction of theism is that it is an extremely "open" world-view: it is consistent with many philosophical opinions that other world-views must automatically exclude. A theist could, for example, be a hedonist in ethics, an empiricist in epistemology, and a skeptic with respect to the problem of induction—but a naturalist could not hold many of the views included in my list. Theism, far from shackling thought (as some people appear to think it does), actually enables consideration of alternatives that other world-views will not allow.

There is, in fact, not a single position among all of those surveyed in the preceding pages that I am *compelled* to adopt by virtue of the fact that I am a theist. Furthermore, the only position among all those discussed that I am *excluded* from adopting by virtue of the fact that I am a theist is the one presented in Chapter 51—and that for the obvious reason that it denies the existence of God.

Why I Am a Theist

That theism maximizes a person's philosophical options does not, of course, constitute any kind of a proof that theism is true. What, then, can be said in support of this world-view? Why am I a theist? In dealing with this question, I do not wish to reopen the discussion of proofs for the existence of God. The question before us now concerns not merely the grounds for believing that God exists, but rather the broader question of the reasons why we ought to adopt a theistic world-view.

I hold, of course, that theism is adequate as a world-view in the sense that there are no facts that contradict it, no facts that cannot be explained within the context of this world-view. In citing certain sorts of facts, therefore, I am merely intending to direct attention to those groups of facts that in my opinion uniquely favor the theistic view. I would urge my readers to look very carefully at the accounts that the representatives of other world-views are forced to give of these facts.

Theism provides the most plausible answer to the question, Why is there something and not nothing? That this particular object exists— a chair, let us say—is satisfactorily accounted for by the statement that it was made by a chair-maker. The existence of the wood out of which the chair was made is in turn explained by the laws governing the growth of trees, whereby nourishment is drawn from the soil via the root system, etc., until at length what began as a tiny acorn has developed into a mature oak. But the elements that were in the soil and that became a part of the oak (and eventually a part of the chair) —why should these exist? Or, given the fact that they exist in this moment, why do they not cease to exist in the next? Why does anything at all exist? According to theism, God created it and sustains it in being moment by moment. Only in the belief that God exists do I find an adequate answer to this inescapable question.

Consider next the place of man in the scheme of things. When I compare the endowments of man with those of any other creature I cannot avoid the conclusion that man is not merely a species of animal, not merely a part of nature: by virtue of his capacity for rational thought, for language, for morality, and for the appreciation of beauty, man rises above nature. Say, if you will, that man is merely the winner of the grand prize in the evolutionary sweepstakes: I say that this was no accident and that the aspirations that characterize the spiritual life of this most fortunate creature point toward a destiny that lies beyond the confines of this life. Theism enables us to believe that these hunches about the nature and destiny of man are true, for it depicts man as the favorite of God's creatures, the crown of His creation.

Our intuitive sense of the seriousness of good and evil lends further support to the theistic view. I cannot take absolutely seriously a moral law that is nothing more than an expression of my private tastes, or those of my social subgroup, or of my nation, or even of the majority of mankind. The moral imperative, the injunction to do good and shun evil, is an infinitely serious matter. The seriousness of the moral law is satisfactorily accounted for only on the hypothesis that it is ultimately grounded in the will of God.

Lastly, I am convinced that an acceptable philosophy of history cannot be developed apart from a theistic world-view. What is the meaning of the struggles, the suffering, the tragedy with which the pages of human history are so distressingly replete? Toward what eventual goal is the story of mankind tending? How can a man believe that his life, his tiny contribution to the common life, has any significance?

Within the context of some world-views, the answers to these questions are all too obvious: no meaning, no goal, no significance. Ethical theism, on the contrary, asserts that history is a meaningful process through which God is patiently and lovingly working out His purposes for His creation. Every moment of a man's life, every good or evil thought or word or deed, makes some contribution to the totality of events that constitute human history. Where this history is tending, or what will be the next significant milestone on the path toward that unknown goal, we do not know. But theists believe, nonetheless, that history is moving toward some *télos* and that its progress toward that goal is being guided by God, who will not abandon the creation that He loves.

There is in the heart of every man, as Alfred North Whitehead once observed, an "insistent craving that zest for existence be refreshed by the ever-present, unfading importance of our immediate actions." [1] In the views that it enables us to take of man, morality, and human history, theism answers to this craving in the heart of man. The facts that most strongly support the theistic world-view are the specifically "human" facts—the facts about man and his life by virtue of which he is able to aspire to a life and a destiny appropriate only for one who is a child of God. Man is most truly man when he understands himself in this way; apart from theism, man is swallowed up in the system of nature and becomes nothing more than the most fortunate of the beasts.

STUDY QUESTIONS

1. Summarize the basic tenets of ethical theism as expounded in this chapter.

---

[1] Alfred North Whitehead, *Process and Reality* (New York: Harper & Row, 1960), p. 533.

2. Can Ethical Theist consistently hold all of the positions he lists on page 446? Is he logically compelled to adopt any of these positions simply by virtue of being a theist?

3. Theist claims that the only position presented in the earlier portions of this book that he is excluded from adopting by virtue of being a theist is the "naturalistic rejoinder" of Chapter 51. Is he correct about this?

4. Summarize the arguments offered by Theist in support of his world-view. Which do you find most persuasive? Which least persuasive?

60

NATURALISM

A world-view, in order to be judged acceptable, must meet three conditions. First, it must be *logically coherent:* it must be free of internal logical inconsistencies. Second, it must be *relevant:* it must provide a plausible interpretive scheme in terms of which at least some facts that fall within the range of our experience can be understood. And third, it must be *adequate to the known facts:* there must be no single fact or realm of facts that cannot be accounted for within the context of the proposed view. Every time a world-view is put forward for consideration it is implicitly claimed that the proffered view meets these three conditions.

I admit that it is extraordinarily difficult to develop a view that simultaneously meets all three conditions. Theism, for example, despite its attractive (and, to man, highly flattering) account of morality and history, has always had to struggle—unsuccessfully, in my opinion—to maintain some semblance of logical coherence. The most dramatic illustration of this is theism's notorious failure to solve the problem of evil. Anyone who is not an apologist for theism can see without difficulty that at least one of the following propositions must be false:

1. God is perfectly good.
2. God's power is unlimited.
3. God is all-knowing.
4. God is the sole creator of everything that exists.
5. There is evil in the world.

Try as they will, the apologists for theism cannot make coherent logical sense out of this story. All of the theodicies that have been written, all of the arguments that have been so laboriously woven, have failed to meet the basic issue: if God is perfect in goodness, knowledge, and power, and is the sole creator of this world, then there cannot be evil in the world; if there is evil in the world (and who can deny it?), then this world is not the product of a God who is perfect in goodness, knowledge, and power. The problem of evil is a problem inherent in the theistic world-view. It is a weakness of that world-view because it exhibits a logical inconsistency within the view itself. And it can be solved only by abandoning at least one of the five propositions stated above.

It is not my intention, however, to develop a systematic critique of theism. I want instead to describe briefly an alternative world-view— naturalism—and to indicate what seem to be the most compelling reasons for adopting this view. It has been my observation that on the question of world-views men are seldom persuaded by arguments as such: rather they become bothered by the problem, wrestle with it for a while, perhaps leave it, and one day return to discover that some place along the way they have abandoned the view they once had for another that is more coherent, relevant, and adequate.

A Brief Description

Naturalism asserts, first of all, that the primary constituents of reality are material entities. By this I do not mean that only material entities exist; I do not wish to deny the reality—the real existence—of such things as hopes, plans, behavior, language, logical inferences, and so on. What I am asserting, however, is that anything that is real is in the last analysis explicable as a material entity or as a form or function or action, etc., of a material entity. Theism says, "In the beginning, God"; naturalism says, "In the beginning, matter." If the theoretical goal of science—an absolutely exhaustive knowledge of the natural world—were to be achieved, there would remain no reality of any other kind about which we might still be ignorant. The "ultimate realities," according to naturalism, are not the alleged objects of the inquiries of theologians: they are the entities that are the objects of investigation by chemists, physicists, and other scientists. To put the matter very simply: materialism is true.

Naturalism asserts, secondly, that what happens in the world is theoretically explicable without residue in terms of the internal structures and the external relations of these material entities. The world is—to use a very inadequate metaphor—like a gigantic machine whose parts are so numerous and whose processes are so complex that we have thus far been able to achieve only a very partial and fragmentary understanding of how it works. In principle, however, everything that occurs is ultimately explicable in terms of the properties and relations of the particles of which matter is composed. Once again the point may be stated simply: determinism is true.

It follows from what I have said that the categories of space and time are categories of great importance for naturalism—are, in fact, ontological categories. If you cannot locate something in space and time, or if you cannot understand it as a form or function of some entity or entities located in space and time, then you simply cannot say anything intelligible about it. *To be is to be some place, some time.*

Naturalism, therefore, denies the existence of any real entities corresponding to such concepts as God, angel, devil, spirit, or soul (as these concepts are usually understood). The reason for denying the existence of such entities is that they are asserted by those who affirm their existence to be nonmaterial entities that are nonetheless the subjects of activities of various kinds—they allegedly do such things as think, decide, regret, suffer, etc. But from the point of view of naturalism, any activity must ultimately be understood as an occurrence within space and time of processes involving material entities. Since the above concepts cannot be understood in this way, naturalism cannot but regard them as bogus concepts, concepts that claim to denote some real entities but in fact denote nothing at all.

Unacceptable Philosophical Theories

From the point of view of naturalism, several of the philosophical theories put forward in earlier sections of this book must be judged unacceptable. This does not mean, of course, that a naturalist simply "rules out" these theories in advance. It means, on the contrary, that he attends with special care to the arguments put forward in support of these theories, for he knows that his world-view is at stake in the argument. Naturalism is secure as a world hypothesis precisely because it has had to defend itself—and has done so successfully—on so many vital points.

Anyone who has grasped the "vision of the whole" that naturalism espouses will readily understand that a consistent naturalism must in the end reject the following philosophical positions:

Philosophical Problem	*Positions Unacceptable to Naturalism*
Freedom and Authority	Natural Law or Social Contract Theory
Man's Highest Good	Eternal Happiness Theory
Language of Morals	Intuitionism
Freedom and Determinism	Libertarianism
Mind and Body	Panpsychism or Dualism
A Priori Knowledge	Rationalism

Induction	Rationalism
Ontological Status of the Physical World	Direct Realism
	Any Position Implying Belief in God's Existence
Existence of God	
Religious Language	Analogical or Symbolic Theory

Anyone who wishes to hold the world-view that I represent must be prepared to refute the arguments put forward in support of these theories. As a naturalist I am of course convinced that every such argument can be convincingly refuted.

Why Naturalism

Naturalists cannot point to certain facts about the world and say, "these facts *uniquely* favor the naturalist world-view." Our claim is that *all* of the known facts support the naturalist account of the world and that no facts warrant our asserting more than this. The evidence warrants our asserting that material entities exist and are involved in numerous processes that together give us the world as we encounter it in ordinary perception and scientific inquiry. But the evidence does not warrant the assertion that any entities or processes exist other than material entities and the processes in which they participate. Naturalism is simply the modest claim that a generalized account of the world in terms of material entities and spatiotemporal processes is adequate to the known facts and will remain adequate to explain any facts still to be discovered in the future.

Let me illustrate my point with a single example. Consider the question, What causes the noise in the heavens that we call thunder? Any number of hypotheses can be constructed to account for the phenomenon of thunder. One hypothesis might be that the gods are angry and are having a fight. Another might be that God is scolding one of His angels. And yet another is that air is expanding rapidly as a result of being heated by a sudden discharge of electricity (lightning). The expansion-of-air hypothesis is, of course, a "naturalistic" explanation of the phenomenon that we call thunder. It is more modest than the other two in that it does not require us to posit unobserved entities (God, gods, angels). It is, therefore, the *kind* of explanation that naturalism claims is possible in principle for all phenomena. Naturalism is simply the generalization of this explanatory model. "What can be explained by the assumption of fewer things is vainly explained by the assumption of more things" (William of Ockham).

In order to support the naturalist position, then, it is not necessary to construct independent arguments that supposedly "prove" naturalism to be true: it is necessary only to show that the phenomena that lead some men to posit immaterial entities can be satisfactorily explained in a way that is consistent with naturalism. The only intelligent way to deal with people who make unwarranted assertions is to show that those assertions are indeed unwarranted. Let us look, then, at the considerations that have been advanced in support of a theistic world-view.

It is not true that theism has an answer to the question, Why is there something and not nothing? whereas naturalism does not. The truth is that *no* world-view is able to answer this question. All that theism does is to move the question back one stage: to the question, "Why does *God* exist?" it has no answer. When we are dealing with the question of ultimate origins we are forced to acknowledge that we have reached one of the boundaries of human knowledge. The only honest answer that we can give to the question, Why is there something and not nothing? is that we do not know. It adds nothing to our knowledge to pretend that by uttering the word "God" we have answered this unanswerable question.

Nor is it the case that naturalism is in any way demeaning to man, as our critics frequently suggest. I am sure that I am no less impressed than is Theist with the marvelous complexity of man and with the immeasurable richness of experience that is possible for man by virtue of his capacity for rational thought, language, morality, and the appreciation of beauty. How does asserting that man "rises above nature" add to this description? Why must I posit a divine "cheater" at the evolutionary gaming table in order to be properly appreciative of man's unique endowments? The evidence warrants the belief that life emerged from lifeless matter on this planet some millions of years ago and that the various forms of life we now observe have evolved from earlier forms by means of processes that we understand reasonably well. The hypothesis of "God's love" or "God's plan" adds no more to this account than the hypothesis of "God's anger" adds to the account of thunder.

All that the evidence warrants us in asserting about man's place in the scheme of things is that human life as we know it is "an episode between two oblivions." [1] Man emerged as one of the products of natural processes operating upon lifeless matter under conditions that made his emergence possible; there is every reason to believe that some day he will cease to exist when these conditions no longer obtain. In the meantime we have the task of making our life together on this planet as rich and meaningful as possible. Although naturalists can offer no divine forgiveness for the acts and omissions born of human frailty and no future paradise for either the few or the many, they are no less concerned than their nonnaturalist fellows with the quality of life here and now. Indeed, since we know of no paradise

---

[1] Ernest Nagel, *Logic Without Metaphysics* (New York: Free Press of Glencoe, 1956), p. 14.

apart from such approximations as we are able to achieve by our own efforts, we might even make some claim to being more deeply concerned about the human enterprise than some who do not share our views. The rejection of a divine plan for man, the refusal to acknowledge eternal values in the affairs of men, in no way prohibits a tender human concern for *human* plans, *human* values, and such *human* goods as we are able to achieve in a universe that wills us neither good nor ill.

Where, Theist asks, is history tending? The answer is that it is tending ultimately toward the extinction of all life on this planet—not necessarily because of what men may do, but because in the long-range evolution of the cosmos it appears inevitable that the conditions necessary for life on this planet will eventually cease to exist. For the next several millions of years, however, the history of the human race will be whatever we make it. We are the masters of our fate, the makers of our own history. The meaning of that history will be whatever meaning we give to it. Nothing is added to our understanding of history by positing a God-ordained *télos* in which all of the problems with which we must contend at present will finally be resolved.

Man is indeed, to use Theist's phrase, "the winner of the grand prize in the evolutionary sweepstakes." His unique endowments have enabled him in the space of just a few thousand years to emerge from a beast-like life into one that is infinitely rich both in its present qualities and in its potential for further improvement. If other men choose to turn their backs upon the challenges and the opportunities of this life in quest of an imaginary kingdom of God, that is their privilege. The available evidence warrants only a belief in the reality of this material world of which we are undeniably a part. The tasks that are set for us by our situation in the world are those inherent in the human enterprise. They are tasks of sufficient magnitude and sufficient difficulty to keep us all occupied for many generations to come, and with this we must be content.

STUDY QUESTIONS

1. Naturalist asserts that an acceptable world-view must meet three conditions. What are they? Do you agree that these are the criteria to be used in judging a world-view?
2. Is the problem of evil a serious problem for theists? How might a theist defend his position against Naturalist's charge that this problem represents an internal inconsistency that is fatal to theism?
3. Summarize the basic tenets of naturalism as they are presented in this chapter.
4. Naturalist presents a rather formidable list of philosophical positions that he says are inconsistent with naturalism. Identify the positions on his list with which you are acquainted, and explain in each case why that position is unacceptable to a naturalist.

5. "In order to support the naturalist position it is not necessary to construct independent arguments that supposedly 'prove' naturalism to be true: It is necessary only to show that the phenomena that lead some men to posit immaterial entities can be satisfactorily explained in a way that is consistent with naturalism." Is this correct? Could the holder of some other world-view reasonably make a parallel claim?

61

TRANSCENDENTALISM

Many readers of the preceding two chapters will, I suspect, find themselves in the following dilemma. On the one hand, they cannot honestly embrace the naïve supernaturalism offered by Theist as the key to an adequate world-view. On the other hand, they cannot escape the conviction that there is something more to human existence than Naturalist's account will allow. I propose to present an alternative view in which what is valid in both of these views can be retained.

Critique of Naturalism and Supernaturalism

Let us begin by taking a critical look at the two views just presented. Theist has presented a picture of a two-story universe, one part of which is perceivable by us and the other part of which is not. In the unseen part dwells God, who created the world at some moment in time and who continues to love and care for it. Indeed, He presumably interferes with its orderly operation from time to time (miracles), since He is said to have managed the evolutionary process in such a way that things turned out the way they did and since He is also said to be guiding history toward some *télos* known only to Him. It is also consistent with this world-view to hold (as does Theist) that this God has made provision for the eternal happiness of at least some of His human children.

It is apparent from the arguments that Theist uses to support this position that what he is chiefly concerned about is what might be called the dignity of man, or—better—the seriousness of human life. Theist cannot tolerate the view that man is merely "the most fortunate of the beasts," one species among many that have emerged in the evolutionary process. He seeks, therefore, to dignify man by making him the favorite child of a divine Creator and by placing him into a historical process that is being guided toward some good end by this same Creator.

The chief difficulty with this view, however, is that it is impossible for men who know as much about the world as we do to believe it. The evidence, as Naturalist would say, does not warrant these beliefs. Natural processes are not interrupted from time to time by divine tinkering, nor is it credible that some place out in space—perhaps beyond our solar system—God, like a rich uncle in Australia, is watching the affairs of men and doing what must be done to ensure that history moves in the desired direction. If we are required to choose between this view and naturalism, then intellectual honesty requires that we choose the naturalist view.

But naturalism is a bitter pill to swallow precisely because it does not take sufficiently seriously the hunger for meaning and the quest for human dignity that theism at least attempts to satisfy. Naturalism depicts man merely as an exceedingly complex physical organism, a unique animal whose artistic, technological, and cultural creations are as much the products of nature as beaver dams, ant hills, and the nests of birds. The world that Naturalist depicts for us is beautiful in its orderliness and in its potentially perfect intelligibility—but its orderliness and intelligibility are purchased at the high price of banishing from the world those dimensions of reality that give significance to human life. Faced with the human consequences of such a view, we withdraw in horror and consider the possibility that perhaps our rejection of theism has been a bit too hasty. Neither of these two views can satisfy the quest for a view of the world that is adequate to the full range of human experience.

No world-view could have won the large number of adherents that can be claimed for both theism and naturalism if there were not a very great quantity of truth in each of these views. Theism incorporates within itself some very important and profound insights, some genuine truths about man and his world: that is why, despite the onslaught to which it has been subjected in the modern world, it has been able to maintain itself. Naturalism also contains within itself some extremely important elements of truth: that is why, despite the opposition of a firmly entrenched theism (Medieval Europe), it was able to make such headway. The most important intellectual task of our times is the task of creating a new intellectual synthesis in which the truth that is implicit in theism and the truth that is implicit in naturalism can be comprehended in one all-embracing vision of the whole. Transcendentalism claims to be that synthesis.

The Transcendentalist Vision

The fundamental insight of naturalism, without which no world-view can ever be accounted adequate, is that in the attempt to know reality we must be completely honest in the face of the brute facts. The naturalist world-view was born in a kind of revolt against what was regarded by those who initiated the revolt as the "arid intellectualism" of the prevailing world-view (theism). Galileo's opponents could muster all kinds of reasons to show why the world ought to be the way they said it was: Galileo swept these reasons aside not by creating superior *arguments*, but by appealing to the *facts*. Respect for the facts has become a part of the mentality of modern man. Insofar as naturalism stands for humility before the facts it stands for truth.

Where, then, does naturalism go wrong? It goes wrong in assuming —indeed, in defiantly insisting—that these brute facts must be assimilated into a mechanistic, deterministic scheme in which there is no place for values, no place for purposes, and really no place for sentience and rationality. Naturalism appears to be haunted by the ghost of the Inquisition; it cannot forget that men who claimed to be God's representatives forced a man (Galileo) who was only trying to be honest before the facts to say that he had abandoned the beliefs that he was driven by the facts to adopt. But it is not only God and His angels that are banished from the naturalist universe: human consciousness as an agent in the world is banished as well. The scientist who is also a philosophical naturalist is in the position of claiming to know so much about the world that he knows that his very act of knowing is merely a complex physical process involving the material entities of which his brain happens to be composed—and nothing else.

Transcendentalism affirms, on the contrary, that there is a dimension of *depth* in everything that exists, that the complete reality of the world is not apparent on the surface of things. Consider yourself. You are, of course, a collocation of atoms and molecules—material entities—that are governed by certain laws. Like every physical object you have a certain weight, a certain size, a certain shape, a certain specific gravity, a certain temperature, and so on. You are also an animal organism: you are capable of nourishing yourself by assimilating nutrients from your environment, you are capable of locomotion, and so on. But you know that you are more than this: you are also a mind, a consciousness. Your being as a physical entity and as an organism is illuminated, so to speak, by the spirit that is within you, by the consciousness that you *are*. Deep within you, at a level of yourself that the objective observer cannot fathom, you are the bearer of hopes, fears, dreams, and aspirations that are as much a part of the reality that is you as your height, your weight, your blood pressure, and whatever other "surface facts" anyone may care to mention. It is not without reason that the technique by which modern physicians of the soul seek to penetrate this dimension of the self is called "depth psychology."

What is true of us individually is true also of our collective life as a human community. There are, to be sure, "surface" elements in the history of any era: there are natural occurrences, fortuitous events, influential personalities, and numerous other kinds of "historical facts" to which historians of any age can point with good empirical consciences. But there is also a depth to history, a dimension of meaning that lies beneath and behind the simple facts. It is not without reason that we commonly use metaphors of deep water when we speak of history: we speak of the "currents" of history and the "tides" of history; we know that what appears on the surface is but the troubled water reflecting the deep and lasting movement beneath the surface, in the depth of our common life.

Transcendentalism affirms that there is also a dimension of depth in things and asks us to consider things with regard to that dimension. Everything that exists is more than it appears to be, even as we ourselves and the historical events in which we participate are more than we and they appear to be. Every finite thing points beyond itself to that which is infinite, unconditioned, inexhaustible. That, in a word, is what transcendentalism means: that finite reality points beyond itself to that which is not finite, to that which is infinite.

The depth of our life and of our world is the source and ground of nearly everything that is most meaningful to us. If we believe, for example, in the true dignity and equality of men, if we believe that the struggle toward dignity and equality is one of the deep tides of the history of our times, then we are affirming convictions that have been nurtured not on the surface but in the depth of our souls and in the depth of the history of our times. And if we believe these things so passionately that we are willing to risk our own convenience and perhaps our own safety in order to further this goal, and if in the process we find that our lives are somehow enriched by those very experiences that externally considered must be described as instances of inconvenience or suffering, then we are demonstrating—at least to ourselves—that we are living in the strength of that depth whose very reality naturalism refuses to acknowledge.

The Truth in Theism

Theism knows that there is depth in life, in history, and in the world, but it attempts to give expression to this by means of a conceptual scheme that has become ludicrous to most of us. "God" is the religious name for the depth: that is what the word "God" really means. But since it is impossible to use this term without conjuring up the image of a celestial Superman who oversees the affairs of men in some mysterious way, perhaps it is best not to speak of God but to speak instead of the depth in our lives, in history, and in our world. For it is to this depth that theism, in its inner meaning, is attempting to point the way.

Theism knows, too, of that union of the self with the deeper self that we experience when we give ourselves unselfishly to a cause that transcends our own selfish interests—when we devote our efforts to the achievement of values that emerge from the depth of our selves and of our history. The religious term for this union of the self with the deeper self is "salvation." But since it is impossible to use this term without suggesting an imagined future blissful existence rather than a quality of life here and now, perhaps it is better that we also do not speak of salvation and speak instead about the recovery of meaning, the rediscovery of our depth, or the wholeness that we experience in the act of dedicating ourselves to a cause in which we deeply believe.

Some Philosophical Implications

If we take seriously the depth dimension in man's life and in the world, certain implications follow with respect to a wide variety of philosophical problems. In the realm of ethics, for example, a transcendentalist holds that moral imperatives emerge from the depths of our souls and of our common life—that they are, in fact, imperatives that stand over us as laws only because and insofar as we are estranged from our own depth. The natural law to which natural law theorists point and the intuited good to which intuitionists point are not strange entities floating aimlessly about in a kind of metaphysical nonspace, waiting to be "intuited" by the discerning mind: they are the voice of our own depth, the law of our own being, in obedience to which we find the wholeness that forever eludes us on the surface of our lives. There are, indeed, many intrinsic goods (see Chapter 14), but they are all grounded in that depth without which our lives would be pitifully shallow.

Space does not permit a detailed review of all the problems discussed in earlier sections or of my reasons for adopting certain positions on those problems. As a transcendentalist, however, I find myself attracted to the following positions: I am a libertarian with respect to the problem of freedom and determinism, a dualist with respect to the mind-body problem, a rationalist in my epistemology (and with respect to the problem of induction), a direct realist in my view of the ontological status of the physical world, a "sympathetic appraiser" (Chapter 52) in my view of the arguments for the existence of God, and a symbolist (Chapter 57) in my theory of religious language. I do not say that consistency *requires* me as a transcendentalist to hold these particular views on these problems. I do say, however, that on the basis of an independent consideration of the arguments I find these to be the most plausible positions to adopt with respect to these questions, and I say further that they are views that as a transcendentalist I find very attractive. Indeed, the chief considerations that may be offered in support of the transcendentalist world-view are precisely those considerations that tend to establish the views stated above.

Let me conclude by making a terminological proposal. "Transcendentalism" is a generic term: it denotes not only the world-view that I represent, but many others more or less similar to mine. In order to distinguish my view from others that might with equal appropriateness be called "transcendentalist," I propose calling the world-view I have presented *depth naturalism*. That name represents my position exactly; I want to take absolutely seriously the important truths for which naturalism stands, but I want also to go beyond this to a recovery of that infinite depth without which life becomes shallow and devoid of meaning.

STUDY QUESTIONS

1. What does Transcendentalist find unacceptable about theism? about naturalism? Do you agree with his objections? How might Theist or Naturalist defend their respective positions against these objections?
2. Transcendentalist presents (pp. 459–460) a theory of the self that is, he says, unacceptable to a naturalist. Is it? And is it, in your view, a plausible theory?
3. "But there is also a depth to history, a dimension of meaning that lies beneath and behind the simple facts." What does this mean? What do you think of this claim?
4. Transcendentalist lists a number of philosophical positions (libertarianism, rationalism, dualism, and so forth) which, he says, are especially attractive to him as a transcendentalist. What connections, if any, do you see between his commitment to transcendentalism and his espousal of each of these positions?
5. Transcendentalist proposes that his particular version of transcendentalism be called "depth naturalism." Does this seem to you to be an appropriate name for the world-view he has described? Defend your answer.

62

HUMANISM

A world-view is a way of trying to comprehend in one all-inclusive concept all that we know and believe about the universe and man's place in it. There is a wonderful grandeur in the very concept of a world-view. Every such view is a monument to man's hunger for knowledge and security. I agree with the sentiment expressed by W. P. Montague:

> The distinctive glory of the human mind is its power to detach itself, not only from the *here* and *now* but from the *there* and *then* of existence, and bathe its tired memories in ideal waters. So it is that the great visions of philosophy, even if considered merely as visions, are precious and imperishable possessions of our culture.[1]

Theism, naturalism, and transcendentalism are some of the intellectual homes that men have constructed for themselves, sanctuaries within which they can escape the madness of the endless pluralism that experience thrusts upon them. To some people they have not proved to be satisfactory. We who are in this situation and who also have certain positive beliefs in common call ourselves humanists. I shall try to present as accurate an account of humanism as I can.

The first thing to understand about humanists is that we are a miscellaneous lot. Some of us find our closest affinities with theists, others with naturalists, and yet others with transcendentalists. What we have in common is a vague dissatisfaction with all such world-views, including whichever one each of us individually may happen to favor, and a firm determination that human values and human potentialities shall not get swallowed up in a system that either takes no account of man or that makes of him something less than he truly is.

---

[1] William Pepperell Montague, *Great Visions of Philosophy* (La Salle, Ill.: Open Court, 1950), p. 16.

You may recall that Socrates protested when he was on trial for his life, "But the simple truth is, O Athenians, that I have nothing to do with physical speculations." [2] I think Socrates meant that he did not have time to speculate about the "big picture": he was completely absorbed in the effort to understand himself, to understand human existence. That task seemed so important to him that he had to devote his full attention to it.

Socrates' attitude describes rather precisely the situation in which humanists find themselves today. Humanism is not a fourth world-view to set alongside the other three: it is rather a group of insights that must be incorporated into *any* world-view if that world-view is to be regarded as adequate. We stand for the dignity, the rights, and the freedom of man, and we are willing to get along with no world-view at all rather than to allow man to be squeezed into the categories of a hypothesis that robs him of his humanity.

A Positive Description

Let me state somewhat more precisely the basic convictions upon which humanists are united in defense of human dignity. First, we believe that man is not completely subject to the physical laws that appear to govern the motions of all material particles. Therefore, we are libertarians on the problem of freedom and determinism, and we are firm and consistent in our opposition to determinism whether it be offered in a theistic form (as with Jonathan Edwards) or in a naturalistic form (as with most modern determinists). Man is free in a way that is not consistent with universal determinism.

It follows, therefore, that man is more than matter, more than a complex physical organism: mind, soul, and consciousness denote real entities that make a real difference in the world. Humanists, in spite of the well-known difficulties involved in the view, are for the most part dualists in their view of man (though some are panpsychists). The essential point is that man is not *merely* a material entity.

Man, moreover, is fittingly subject to no moral imperatives other than those he prescribes for himself. Man is answerable to man. Any law that man is counseled to obey that is not of his own making enslaves him and robs him of his dignity. For this reason we reject all versions of the natural law theory in favor of the concept of law advocated by social utilitarianism (Chapter 9).

It is important to the humanist view of man to assert that the future is to some extent open and undetermined, notwithstanding the

---

2 Plato, *Apology*, in *The Dialogues of Plato*, B. Jowett (tr.) (New York: Random House, 1937), Vol. I, p. 403.

extent to which the future is determined by natural and historical forces beyond man's control. Man is a maker of history, not merely its helpless victim. What man himself shall become in the future depends primarily on what man chooses to make of himself, not on what God or nature may have "programmed" him to become. William Ernest Henley (1849–1903) spoke for all men when he said, "I am the master of my fate, I am the captain of my soul." [3]

With these convictions clearly in mind, it should not be difficult to see why humanists are unable to fully embrace any of the world-views presented thus far. Let us review them briefly.

Theism

Consider, for example, the potentially dehumanizing aspects of theism. From the point of view of humanism, the chief danger of theism is its implicit authoritarianism. If man is a creature of God, as theism asserts, then presumably he is as totally subject to the will of the Creator as is a potter to the pot: he has no right to stand up to the Power that made him and can as easily destroy him. Surely this is the view of the God-man relationship that we find, for example, in the story of the flood:

> When the Lord saw that man had done much evil on earth and that his thoughts and inclinations were always evil, he was sorry that he had made man on earth, and he was grieved at heart. He said, "This race of men whom I have created, I will wipe them off the face of the earth . . . I am sorry that I ever made them." [4]

That there are humanistic elements in theism is, of course, true. Theism in its Judeo-Christian form, for example, speaks of God not only as a wrathful and jealous deity before whom man must cower in fear, but also as a loving Father who cares deeply for His children and as the Good Shepherd who seeks and rescues lost sheep. But these elements, sad to say, have always been subordinate to the authoritarian elements in the theistic view. Historically, the Good Shepherd has been no match for the Grand Inquisitor.

There can be no doubt that theistic authoritarianism is destructive of man's humanity. In the intellectual sphere, for example, it tends to intimidate him in such a way that he is no longer free to follow an argument wherever it may lead, to seek the truth wherever it may be found. In the moral sphere theism subjects man to an alien law: it requires ceremonies, rituals, and "good works" of various sorts that

---

[3] William Ernest Henley, "Invictus," in R. B. Inglis *et al.*, *Adventures in English Literature* (New York: Harcourt, Brace, 1945), p. 726.

[4] Genesis, 6:5–7.

may or may not commend themselves to him as morally worthwhile. He is counseled to think of himself as a creature of little worth, a worm, a nothing. John Calvin expresses this exactly:

> We cannot think of ourselves as we ought to think without utterly despising everything that may be supposed an excellence in us. This humility is unfeigned submission of a mind overwhelmed with a weighty sense of its own misery and poverty; for such is the uniform description of it in the word of God.[5]

In this view man is nothing, God is everything. Any good that he may hope to achieve man must beg from the Celestial Artisan, who in His sovereignty may or may not respond, as He sees fit. Humility, sin, rebellion, self-abasement—these are among the most prominent words in the vocabulary of theism. And it is these words that chiefly define how man is taught to think of himself in the theistic system.

Naturalism

Man fares little better in the naturalistic system, however, than in the theistic. As Bertrand Russell wrote in a famous essay: "Brief and powerless is man's life; on him and all his race the slow, sure doom falls pitiless and dark. Blind to good and evil, reckless of destruction, omnipotent matter rolls on its relentless way." [6] In such a world, as Transcendentalist has rightly discerned, it is impossible to find a place for all those things that are most precious to man. In a world where "omnipotent matter rolls on its relentless way" and where mind is at best an impotent epiphenomenon of material processes, the loftiest ideals and the noblest aspirations of the human spirit appear to dissolve into nothingness. What is the status of honor, courage, and the passion for truth in a world where nothing exists but the elemental particles of which matter is composed? How can man abide a world that makes a mockery of his conviction that he is before everything else a conscious agent in the world, a being capable of doing deeds of worth and nobility?

Nor is it only the materialism of the naturalistic view that is offensive to humanism: its determinism is equally unacceptable. Whatever difficulties there may be in understanding man's freedom in relation to the law-like regularity with which natural processes seem to occur, humanists will not acquiesce in the view that man is simply a part of

---

5 John Calvin, *Institutes of the Christian Religion* (Presbyterian Board of Christian Education, 1928), p. 681.

6 Bertrand Russell, "A Free Man's Worship," in *Mysticism and Logic* (New York: Norton, 1929), p. 58.

nature, his actions as much a product of her workings as the ocean tides and the revolutions of the heavenly bodies. Man is free. He can make a difference in the course of events—a difference that is not merely the inevitable product of the physical processes in which "his" atoms will inevitably participate. The future is to a certain extent open and, as yet, undetermined. Man has it within his power to put an end to all war—or to terminate all life by unleashing a holocaust that will engulf every living thing. Man has it in his power to end poverty —or to perpetuate conditions that make it inevitable that millions of fellow human beings will live their entire lives as victims of malnutrition and attendant miseries. Man has it in his power—*really in his power*—to change the course of history, to make a difference in the way the future unfolds. Naturalism, by virtue of its deterministic element, will not allow this.

Transcendentalism

A humanist's chief concern about transcendentalism is that it seems to be perpetually in danger of merely substituting the tyranny of the depth for the tyranny of God (theism) or the tyranny of physical laws (naturalism). For too long, man has been intimidated by laws that are not of his own making, laws that hold him in subjection, render him guilty, and stifle his humanity. Moral imperatives that arise "out of the depth," even if the depth is the depth of our own selves, are nonetheless "alien laws" with respect to the empirical self that is supposed to obey them. Man in his sovereign freedom has the right not to be subjected to imperatives other than those that he prescribes for himself. Only so can the full freedom and dignity of man be preserved and enhanced.

Conclusion

Where do these considerations leave us with respect to the quest for an adequate world-view? They leave us free to continue the search without the fear that we may be seduced into adopting a view that robs us of our human dignity. In the defiant demand that the "big picture" shall allow full place to those convictions about man that we hold dear we are, in effect, demanding that the whole truth, which at present we do not know, shall be consistent with the partial truth that even in our present state of knowledge we see clearly. The philosophical quest, whose ultimate goal is the achievement of a comprehensive view of things in which every element of truth and every aspect of experience shall find its proper place, is one of the most stupendous efforts of which man is capable. Humanism's contribution to this quest comes in the last analysis to just this: he who pursues this quest, being a man, should pursue it in such a way that he does not lose sight of man.

STUDY QUESTIONS

1. "Humanism is not a fourth world-view to be set alongside the other three." Do you agree? Explain.
2. List the propositions that are offered by Humanist as "the basic convictions upon which (all) humanists are united." Are there any with which you disagree? Would Theist disagree with any? Naturalist? Transcendentalist?
3. What does Humanist find objectionable in theism? in naturalism? in transcendentalism? With which of his criticisms do you agree, and with which do you disagree?
4. Does humanism seem to you to have anything to contribute to the quest for an adequate world-view? Explain.

Boyce Gibson, A. *Theism and Empiricism.* London: SCM Press, 1970.

Britton, Karl. *Philosophy and the Meaning of Life.* Cambridge, Eng.: Cambridge University Press, 1969.

Edman, Irwin. *Four Ways of Philosophy.* New York: Henry Holt, 1947.

Feigl, Herbert. "Logical Empiricism," in Dagobert D. Runes (ed.). *Twentieth Century Philosophy.* New York: The Philosophical Library, 1943. Reviews several philosophical problems from the point of view of a contemporary naturalist.

Flew, Antony. *God and Philosophy.* London: Hutchison, 1966. Detailed critique of arguments for theism.

Krikorian, Yervant H. (ed.). *Naturalism and the Human Spirit.* New York: Columbia University Press, 1944.

Lamprecht, S. P. *The Metaphysics of Naturalism.* New York: Appleton-Century-Crofts, 1967.

Maritain, Jacques. *Existence and the Existent,* tr. by Lewis Galantiere and Gerald B. Phelan. Garden City: Image Books, 1956 (paperbound). See Chapter 5, "Ecce in Pace." Representative of what might be called a "Christian humanist" point of view.

Montague, W. P. *The Chances of Surviving Death.* Cambridge, Mass.: Harvard University Press, 1934.

Nagel, Ernest. "Naturalism Reconsidered," in his *Logic Without Metaphysics.* New York: Free Press, 1956, chap. 1.

Niebuhr, Reinhold. *Beyond Tragedy.* New York: Scribner, 1937. A collection of essays by a modern theist.

Otto, M. C. *The Human Enterprise.* New York: Appleton-Century-Crofts, 1940.

Pepper, Stephen C. *World Hypotheses.* Berkeley and Los Angeles: University of California Press, 1942. For patient readers only!

Russell, Bertrand. "A Free Man's Worship," in his *Mysticism and Logic.* New York: Norton, 1929, pp. 46–58. A very famous delineation of the naturalist position.

Sartre, Jean-Paul. *Existentialism,* tr. by Bernhard Frechtman. New York: The Philosophical Library, 1947. Atheistic humanism as expounded by one of its best-known modern spokesmen.

Sorley, W. R. *Moral Values and the Idea of God,* 3rd ed. New York: Macmillan, 1924. See especially Chapters 18 and 19 for an interesting discussion of some of the problems implicit in the theistic view.

Stace, W. T. "Man Against Darkness." First published in *The Atlantic Monthly* in September 1948, and in several anthologies since. A rather despairing account of the naturalist position.

Tillich, Paul. "Realism and Faith," in his *The Protestant Era.* Chicago: University of Chicago Press, 1948, pp. 66–82. A very condensed statement of Tillich's form of transcendentalism.

Whitehead, Alfred North. *Process and Reality.* New York: Harper & Row, 1960 (originally published in 1929). See Part I, Chapter I, "Speculative Philosophy."

GLOSSARY OF
PHILOSOPHICAL TERMS

Controversial issues can be fruitfully discussed only insofar as a neutral language—that is, one acceptable to everyone discussing the controversy and understood in the same sense by all—is available for the discussion. Unfortunately, it is uncommonly difficult in philosophy to formulate neutral definitions of many key philosophical terms. The definitions that follow will indicate the usage observed throughout this book, and this in turn reflects the usage of a large number of English-speaking philosophers. The reader should be aware, however, that some philosophers have used and do use some of these terms in slightly different ways, and he should accordingly be prepared to modify his understanding of any term which he encounters being used in some other way.

Ambiguous: quality of a term that has different meanings when used in different contexts. (*Ex.:* "line" means one thing to a painter, another thing to a mathematician, and yet a third thing to a plumber.)

Analogical predication: a mode of speaking about God, first advocated by St. Thomas Aquinas (1225–1274), which is said to be a kind of mean between *univocal* and *equivocal* predication (see below). The idea is extremely complex, no less than three varieties of analogical predication having been distinguished by followers of St. Thomas.

Analytic: quality of a sentence, statement, or proposition which does not purport to say anything about reality, but simply explicates some part of the meaning of one or more of its terms. (*Ex.:* "All circles are round.") Contrasts with *synthetic* (see below).

Anarchism, militant: the view of one who is committed to the overthrow of existing government without regard to the practical consequences, and with no intention of supporting any new government that might be established in its place.

Anarchism, naïve: the view that government actually hinders rather than enhances the good of society, and that greater good would result if government simply ceased to exist.

Anarchism, theoretical: the view that the authority of government to restrict the freedom of individuals has no theoretical justification.

A posteriori: completely dependent on, and a product of, experience; mode of knowledge in which experience is the source as well as the occasion of knowledge. Contrasts with *a priori* (see below).

A priori: not completely dependent on experience; independent in the sense that experience, though it may be the occasion for one's coming to know, is not the source. Contrasts with *a posteriori* (see above).

Argument: (1) an attempt to show that certain considerations or alleged facts provide evidence in favor of the truth of some proposition. (2) A group of propositions about which it is claimed that the presumed truth of some (the premises) constitutes evidence for the truth of one (the conclusion).

Behaviorism: the view that man is constituted in such a way that every detail of his experience and behavior is the inevitable consequence of causes lying outside himself.

Circumstantial freedom of self-realization: the opportunity to do what one wants to do; a situation in which neither personal limitations nor external restraints prevent one from doing a given thing. (*Ex.:* religious freedom, that is, the opportunity to worship as one wishes.)

Cognition: (1) the act or process of knowing (cognizing). (2) That which is known (cognized).

Commonsense realism: the view that the world as it really is does not differ in any important respect from the world as it appears to us; direct realism.

Consciousness: a center of awareness, feeling, and perception; mind.

Constructive empiricism: the view, with respect to the problem of induction, that induction is a legitimate logical procedure, and that its legitimacy can be established in a way that is consistent with empiricism, that is, without invoking any *a priori* principles.

Contingent: (1) (in logic) quality of a proposition that is not necessarily true, that is, a proposition the denial of which does not involve a self-contradiction. (2) (in metaphysics) Quality of a being that does not have the cause of its existence within itself; ontologically dependent. Contrasts with *necessary* (see below).

Contra-causal: incompatible with determinism.

Cosmological argument: (1) an argument for the existence of God that takes as its first premise some empirical or quasi-empirical observation about the world. (2) Some particular formulation of such an argument.

Cosmology: (1) the study of the origin and general structure of the physical universe. (2) A theory or system regarding the same. Most of the inquiries that once belonged to cosmology have now been taken over by the physical sciences.

Critical realism: any view which affirms that the world as it really is is in some respects similar to, and in some respects different from, the world as it appears to us.

Deduction: the act of drawing a conclusion from a set of premises; the act of inferring. In the case of a correct deduction, the conclusion (inference) must be true if the premises are true. In this respect *deduction* differs from *induction* (see below). Also, that which one deduces from a set of premises.

Defining characteristic: a characteristic that a thing must have in order to be a member of the class of things being defined. (*Ex.:* being unmarried is a defining characteristic of bachelorhood; hence, any person who is to qualify as a bachelor must have the characteristic of being unmarried.)

Determinism: the theory that the universe is constituted in such a way that everything that occurs is the inevitable consequence of antecedent causes; universal determinism; strict determinism. Contrasts with *indeterminism* (see below).

Direct realism: the theory that the physical universe as it really is does not differ in any important respect from the world as it appears to us; commonsense realism.

Double-aspect theory: the theory, first advanced by the Dutch philosopher Benedict Spinoza (1632–1677), that mind and body are simply two different aspects of a single underlying reality.

Dualism, mind-body: the theory that body and mind are ontologically distinct, neither being reducible to the other.

Dualism, ontological: the theory that reality consists of two different kinds of being (for example, mind and matter) neither of which is reducible to the other.

Emotivism: a metaethical theory according to which moral utterances are held to be ejaculatory in nature, that is, expressions of the feelings (of approval or disapproval) of the speaker; a form of noncognitivism (see below).

Empirical: (1) derived from observation; *a posteriori.* (2) About the real world; capable of being exhibited in sense experience.

Empirical generalization: a general statement about a class of objects made on the basis of observation of some members of the class.

Empiricism: the epistemological theory that all knowledge of reality originates in, and is a product of, sense experience, that is, all knowledge of synthetic truths arises out of experience. Contrasts with rationalism (see below).

Epiphenomenalism: the theory that mind or consciousness is a mere by-product ("epiphenomenon") of physiological processes, and that it does not influence those processes in any way; the theory that mind is constituted by physiological processes, and is influenced causally by them, but that it has no causal influence on the body.

Epistemology: (1) a study of the nature and limits of human knowledge. (2) A theory concerning the same (for example, "the *epistemology* of Kant").

Equivocal: quality of a term having different meanings in each of two or more applications.

Ethical pluralism: the view that many things are intrinsically good, and that man's highest good consists in securing a maximum quantity of such goods.

Ethical theism: a world-view, the central claim of which is that everything that exists (except God Himself) is the creation of a good, wise, and powerful Creator.

Ethics: see *normative ethics* and *metaethics.*

Eudemonia: literally, "having a good spirit"; from the Greek word *eudaimonia,* usually translated "happiness."

Existential: of or pertaining to existence, particularly human existence.

Fallacy: an error in reasoning that makes it impossible to establish the conclusion in question on the given premises; a logical mistake. In the case of a deductive argument, the effect of a fallacy is to render the argument *invalid* (see below).

Formalist ethics: a type of ethical theory in which moral obligatoriness is held to be a characteristic of some acts quite apart from any tendency those acts (or acts of that type) may have or be presumed to have to produce a good result. Deontological ethics.

Freedom: (1) the opportunity to do what one wants to do. (2) The power to enact any of two or more genuinely open alternatives; free will. (3) The state in which "ideal manhood" is realized, in which one has become everything that man ought to be. (*Note:* This term is highly ambiguous. It is always important to try to determine the precise sense in which a given writer is using the term.) See also *moral freedom; natural freedom of self-determination; circumstantial freedom of self-realization; free will.*

Free will: power of the self to enact any of two or more genuinely open alternatives; contra-causal freedom; natural freedom of self-determination.

Hard determinism: the view that determinism is true, and that it is not compatible with moral freedom, and that man is therefore not morally responsible.

Hedonism: (1) (analytic form) the theory that "good" (in the moral sense) means "pleasurable." (2) (synthetic form) The theory that pleasure alone is intrinsically good.

Heuristic principle: a principle that is not judged as to its truth or falsity (it is neither affirmed nor denied), but which is assumed for the purposes of some particular inquiry because of its demonstrated usefulness in raising fruitful questions.

Humanism: the view that man, unlike all other creatures, is in some respects not merely a part of nature.

Hypercritical realism: the view that the world as it really is is highly dissimilar to the world as it appears to us; a radical form of *critical realism* (see above).

Immanent: within; near; not transcendent.

Imperativism: a metaethical theory according to which moral sentences are held to be a species of directive language, that is, implicit commands or recommendations to act in certain sorts of ways and not to act in other sorts of ways; a form of *noncognitivism* (see below).

Indeterminism: the theory that the universe is constituted in such a way that some events are not the inevitable consequences of antecedent causes.

Induction: the act of affirming a general statement about a class of things on the basis of observation of some members of the class; the act of making an empirical generalization. Also, an empirical generalization affirmed on the basis of observation of some members of the class.

Inductive skepticism: the view, associated with the Scottish philosopher David Hume (1711–1776), that induction is not a legitimate logical procedure, that is, it is a procedure that is not capable of rational justification.

Inference: (1) a proposition that follows as a logical consequence of certain other propositions; that which is inferred; an implication. (2) The act of inferring, that is, of deriving the actual or apparent logical consequences from a set of assumed premises.

Interactionism: the theory that body and mind are ontologically distinct, and that they influence each other causally.

Introspection: the act or process of observing or noting one's own feelings, thoughts, or mental states.

Intuition: the act whereby, according to rationalists, the mind discerns nonempirical qualities and grasps a priori truths.

Intuitionism: a metaethical theory according to which "good" (in the moral sense) is held to denote a simple, nonnatural quality; nonnaturalistic objectivism; nonnaturalism.

Invalid: quality of a deductive argument whose conclusion may be false even if all of its premises are true; not valid.

Legalism: an ethical theory according to which it is held that right and wrong are determined by one's adherence or nonadherence to a set of moral rules (laws) which are applicable at all times, in all places, and under any circumstances.

Libertarianism: the view that free will is a necessary condition of moral responsibility, and that man has this freedom, and, consequently, that determinism is not the case. Contrasts with *hard determinism* (see above) and *soft determinism* (see below).

Logic: (1) a study of the principles whereby one may distinguish correct from incorrect reasoning. (2) A system or theory regarding the same (*Ex.:* "The *logic* of John Stuart Mill").

Materialism: the metaphysical theory that the whole of reality consists of matter and its determinations; a form of *monism* (see below).

Metaethics: a study of the logical structure of ethical reasoning and the logical characteristics of ethical discourse. The main effort of metaethicists to date has been directed toward the elucidation of the precise meanings of the key terms of moral appraisal ("good," "bad," "right," "wrong," "duty," "ought," etc.).

Metalanguage: a language used for the purpose of talking about language, that is, a language whose terms denote features of language rather than features of nonverbal reality; a language about language. (The language of grammar, for example, constitutes a metalanguage.)

Metaphysics: (1) the study of the nature and structure of being (ontology) and of the origin and general structure of the universe (cosmology); first philosophy. (2) A theory or system concerning the same. (Some philosophers use this term simply as a synonym for ontology, excluding cosmology. Others use it pejoratively as a synonym for "nonsense.")

Monism: the view that the whole of reality consists of various determinations of some one ultimate substance, or kind of "stuff." The principal forms of monism are *materialism* (all is matter), *idealism* (all is mind), and *neutral monism* (all is some substance that is neither mind nor matter, but is the ground of both). Monism contrasts with *dualism* (see above) and *pluralism* (see below).

Moral freedom: the freedom (whatever be its nature) that is a necessary condition of moral responsibility; the freedom without which man is not, or would not be, morally responsible.

Morally responsible: answerable for one's behavior; a fitting subject of moral appraisal.

Multi-functionalism: a metaethical theory according to which moral sentences are held to serve a variety of functions, and are therefore not translatable without loss of meaning into sentences of any single logical type.

Naïve realism: see *Commonsense realism.*

Natural freedom of self-determination: the power of the self to enact any one of two or more genuinely open alternatives; contra-causal freedom;

free will. Libertarians affirm that man has such a power, determinists that he does not.

Naturalism: (1) any philosophical system which holds that the whole of reality consists of objects and events occurring in space and time. Contrasts with *transcendentalism* (see below). (2) (in metaethics) The view that "good" (in a moral sense) denotes some empirical quality or qualities; naturalistic objectivism.

Naturalistic fallacy: the mistake, according to the intuitionism of G. E. Moore (1873–1958), of attempting to define "good" (in a moral sense), particularly in terms of some natural (empirically discernible) quality or qualities.

Naturalistic objectivism: a metaethical theory according to which the key moral predicates are held to denote some empirically verifiable quality or qualities; ethical naturalism. A hedonist who affirms that "good" *means* "pleasurable," for example, would be affirming one very common version of this theory.

Natural law: a fundamental principle of right or justice which, according to some philosophers, human reason can discern merely by attending carefully to the proposition stating that principle.

Necessary: (1) (in logic) quality of a proposition the denial of which involves a self-contradiction. (2) (in metaphysics) Quality of a being which has the cause of its existence within itself; not ontologically dependent. Contrasts with *contingent* (see above).

Negative predication: see *Via negativa.*

Noncognitivism: any metaethical theory which holds that moral sentences are not informative, that is, they assert nothing, and therefore are incapable of being either true or false. *Emotivism* and *imperativism* are examples of theories of this type.

Nonnaturalistic objectivism: a metaethical theory according to which "good" (in the moral sense) is held to denote a simple, nonnatural quality, the presence of which in some things is what makes them good; intuitionism; nonnaturalism.

Non sequitur: an argument containing a fallacy; an argument in which the conclusion does not follow from the premises.

Normative ethics: the quest for general principles of right and wrong; the attempt to determine what things really are good or bad, right or wrong, and to identify the general principles by virtue of which they are so.

Occasionalism: the theory that mind and body are ontologically distinct (therefore a *dualistic* theory), and that each operates according to its own laws, but that they appear to interact because of the fact that God from time to time does whatever is required in order to keep them synchronized.

Ontological: of or pertaining to ontology; having to do with being.

Ontological argument: a famous argument for the existence of God, devised by St. Anselm of Canterbury (1033–1106), in which the attempt is made to show that the denial of the proposition "God exists" is self-contradictory.

Ontologically distinct: belonging to different ontological categories, neither of which is reducible to the other.

Ontological status: kind of being. To disclose the ontological status of something is to put it in some ontological category; it is to state in what precise sense it is true to say that that thing *is.*

Ontology: (1) the study of the nature or structure of being. (Some philosophers use this term as a synonym for *metaphysics;* others use it as the

name for one main branch of metaphysics, the other being *cosmology*.)
(2) A theory or system put forward as a result of such a study.

Panpsychism: the view that the whole of reality consists of minds ("psyches") of varying degrees of consciousness; one of the classical ways of attempting to overcome ontological dualism.

Paradox: an apparently self-contradictory assertion which is made nonetheless on the ground that to eliminate the apparent contradiction would allegedly involve denying some truth.

Parallelism: the view that mind and body are ontologically distinct (therefore a *dualistic* theory), and that each operates according to its own laws, the appearance of interaction between the two resulting from the fact that God has established a perfect harmony between them. This view was first advocated by the German philosopher Gottfried Wilhelm Leibnitz (1646–1716).

Percept: that which is "before the mind" in the act of perceiving; that which is immediately present to consciousness in perception; sense-datum.

Perception: the act or process of taking cognizance of the world by means of the senses.

Phenomenalism: the view that the reality of a material object consists in its being perceived by some perceiver, with the corollary that the physical world does not exist apart from the perceptions, actual or possible, of some perceiver; subjective idealism.

Pluralism: the view that reality is not reducible to one ultimate substance, or kind of "stuff," but that on the contrary there are several. Contrasts with *monism* and *dualism* (see above).

Premise: a proposition which, in conjunction with other propositions, is alleged to provide evidence for some proposition (the conclusion).

Primary quality: according to the critical realism of John Locke (1632–1704), a quality that belongs to an object in such a way that no particle of which the object is composed could be conceived to exist without it. Locke gives extension, shape, size, and mobility as examples of such qualities. Contrasts with *secondary quality* (see below).

Private subjectivism: a metaethical theory according to which moral utterances are held to be statements about the personal likes and dislikes of the person making the utterance.

Proposition: that which is affirmed or denied by a declarative sentence; the meaning of a sentence which affirms or denies that something is the case. Propositions (and the sentences in which they are expressed) have the property of being either true or false.

Rational eudemonism: the view that man's highest good consists in "activity according to reason" (Aristotle).

Rationalism: (1) the view that some truths about reality are knowable in a way that is in some degree independent of experience, that is, some synthetic truths may be known a priori. (2) A European philosophical movement the most prominent representatives of which were René Descartes (1596–1650), Benedict de Spinoza (1632–1677), Gottfried Wilhelm Leibnitz (1646–1716), Christian Wolff (1679–1754), and Immanuel Kant (1724–1804).

Reality: (1) the totality of the real, everything that is. (2) What truly or in actuality is the case, as over against what may appear to be the case. In this sense, reality is often contrasted with *appearance*.

Reason: (1) a proposition which, in conjunction with some other propositions, supports a conclusion not deducible from the other proposition(s) alone; a premise. (2) A statement which purportedly justifies a belief or act. (3) The faculty of knowledge. (4) The essential nature of the self.

Reasoning: the act or process of drawing conclusions from premises.

Res cogitans: literally, "thinking thing"; that which, according to René Descartes (1596–1650), man essentially is—in contrast to unthinking, extended being (that is, material objects).

Secondary quality: according to the critical realism of John Locke (1632–1704), the capacity of a material object to produce in a percipient an impression (of color, sound, taste, and so on) unlike anything in the object itself. Such a quality is thus said to be "mind-dependent." Contrasts with *primary quality* (see above).

Self: that which one designates by the pronoun "I"; consciousness; mind. (Its status has long been a matter of philosophical controversy.)

Self-evident: quality of a proposition that can be seen to be true merely by considering the proposition itself, and that therefore does not need to be proven either by deduction from other more evident propositions or by an appeal to factual evidence.

Sense-data: the immediate, uninterpreted objects of sense experience; the patches of color, geometrical shapes, and so forth, which one sees when looking at a material object, the vari-pitched noises which one sometimes hears (which may subsequently be interpreted as a melody on a violin), and so on.

Social contract: a voluntary agreement among a group of individuals whereby, according to some political theorists, the members of society acquire a set of mutual obligations legitimately enforceable by established authority.

Social utilitarianism: the view that the authority of government is justifiable in terms of its capacity to secure the greatest good for the greatest number of people.

Societal subjectivism: a metaethical theory according to which moral utterances are held to be statements about the approval- and disapproval-tendencies of some social group of which the person making the utterance is a part.

Soft determinism: the view that determinism is true, but that the conditions of moral responsibility are such that man is nonetheless morally responsible whenever he has the opportunity to do what he wants to do.

Solipsism: the theory that oneself is the only mind or consciousness which exists, and that everything else exists only as a perception of this self.

Sound: quality of an argument which is formally valid and contains only true premises.

Subjective idealism: the view, associated with George Berkeley (1685–1753), that the being of material objects consists in their being perceived by some perceiver (*esse est percipi*), that they have no "independent" existence; phenomenalism. Contrasts with all types of *critical, direct,* and *hypercritical realism* (see above).

Summum bonum: literally, "highest good"; that which is worthy of being sought for its own sake.

Synthetic: quality of a sentence, statement, or proposition which purports to say something about reality. (*Ex.:* "Some camels have two humps.") Contrasts with *analytic* (see above).

System: a comprehensive set of coherent and interdependent propositions in terms of which one attempts to understand and explain the phenomena within the range of its alleged relevance. An *ethical system,* for example, purports to provide a context for the understanding and explanation of all ethical phenomena. A *philosophical system* purports to provide a context for the understanding and explanation of all phenomena.

Teleological: of or pertaining to ends, goals, purposes (from the Greek *telos*, meaning "end" or "goal"). *Teleological* explanations (explanations in terms of ends), for example, are often contrasted with scientific explanations (explanations in terms of causes). The term is sometimes used to describe a kind of thinking, also to designate a very famous argument for the existence of God (see below).

Teleological argument: an argument for the existence of God made famous by William Paley (1743–1805). The argument begins with the allegedly empirical premise that there is order (means subservient to ends) in the universe, and by analogy with human contrivances asserts the necessity of positing a cosmic Intelligence to account for this order.

Teleological ethics: a type of ethical theory in which the moral value of any act is held to consist in the tendency of that act (or of acts of that type) to produce a good or bad result.

Touchstone proposition: central truth about reality as perceived in some particular world-view.

Transcendent: (1) (Kant's usage) beyond the categories of human experience. (2) (as commonly used in theology and philosophy of religion) Beyond the world of space and time; other. Contrasts with *immanent* (see above).

Transcendentalism: any philosophical system which holds that there are dimensions of reality in addition to objects and events occurring in space and time. Contrasts with *naturalism* (see above).

Univocal (applied to terms): having the same meaning in all instances in which it is used, or in all instances being considered. Contrasts with *equivocal* (see above).

Utilitarianism: (1) the theory that the goodness or badness of acts consists in their tendency to promote or hinder the realization of that which is intrinsically good. (2) The particular version of this theory advocated by the English philosophers Jeremy Bentham (1749–1832) and John Stuart Mill (1806–1873). This view is more properly called "hedonistic utilitarianism."

Vague (applied to terms): imprecise in ordinary usage in such a way that any attempt at precise definition would render the term more exact than ordinary usage will allow. (*Ex.:* "warm" is a vague term; it would be inconsistent with ordinary usage to define it precisely in terms of a definite temperature range.)

Verbal: of or pertaining to words. Often applied to a given philosophical controversy to indicate that there is no "real issue" dividing the parties to the dispute, but simply a confusion or disagreement over the meanings of certain terms.

Via negativa: literally, "negative way." A mode of speaking about God wherein one attempts to say not what God *is* but what He is *not*. Thus "simple" (= non-complex), "incorporeal" (= non-corporeal), and so on, are "negative predicates." Used by several medieval philosophers, including St. Thomas Aquinas.

Volition: (1) the act of exercising choice, of choosing among alternatives. (2) The power to exercise choice.

World-view: a comprehensive view of reality in terms of which one attempts to understand and "place" everything that comes before one's consciousness.

INDEX